Demand for Labor
The Neglected Side of the Market

IZA Prize in Labor Economics Series

Since 2002, the Institute for the Study of Labor (IZA) has awarded the annual IZA Prize in Labor Economics for outstanding contributions to policy-relevant labor market research and methodological progress in this sub-discipline of economic science. The IZA Prize is the only international science prize awarded exclusively to labor economists. This special focus acknowledges the global significance of high-quality basic research in labor economics and sound policy advice based on these research findings. As issues of employment and unemployment are among the most urgent challenges of our time, labor economists have an important task and responsibility. The IZA Prize in Labor Economics is today considered one of the most prestigious international awards in the field. It aims to stimulate further research on topics that have enormous implications for our future. All prize-winners contribute a volume to the IZA Prize in Labor Economics Series published by Oxford University Press, which has been established to provide an overview of the laureates' most significant findings.

The IZA Prize in Labor Economics has become an integral part of the institute's manifold activities to promote progress in labor market research. Based on nominations submitted by the IZA Research Fellows, a high-ranking IZA Prize Committee selects the prize-winner. In conjunction with the Award Ceremony the IZA Prize Conference brings together a number of renowned experts to discuss topical labor market issues.

It is not by coincidence that the IZA Prize in Labor Economics Series is published by Oxford University Press. This well-reputed publishing house has shown a great interest in the project from the very beginning as this exclusive series perfectly complements their range of publications. We gratefully acknowledge their excellent cooperation.

Winners of the IZA Prize in Labor Economics

2013	Daniel S. Hamermesh (University of Texas at Austin and Royal Holloway, University of London)
2012	Richard Blundell (University College London and IFS)
2011	George J. Borjas (Harvard University) Barry R. Chiswick (George Washington University)
2010	Francine D. Blau (Cornell University)
2009	Richard A. Easterlin (University of Southern California)
2008	Richard Layard (London School of Economics) Stephen J. Nickell (Nuffield College)
2007	Richard B. Freeman (Harvard University)
2006	David Card (University of California, Berkeley) Alan B. Krueger (Princeton University)
2005	Dale T. Mortensen (Northwestern University) Christopher A. Pissarides (London School of Economics)
2004	Edward P. Lazear (Stanford University)
2003	Orley C. Ashenfelter (Princeton University)
2002	Jacob Mincer (Columbia University)

Daniel S. Hamermesh
2013 IZA Prize Laureate

Demand for Labor

The Neglected Side of the Market

Daniel S. Hamermesh

Edited by
Corrado Giulietti
Klaus F. Zimmermann

OXFORD
UNIVERSITY PRESS

OXFORD
UNIVERSITY PRESS

Great Clarendon Street, Oxford, OX2 6DP,
United Kingdom

Oxford University Press is a department of the University of Oxford.
It furthers the University's objective of excellence in research, scholarship,
and education by publishing worldwide. Oxford is a registered trade mark of
Oxford University Press in the UK and certain other countries

First Edition published in 2017

Published in the United States of America by Oxford University Press
198 Madison Avenue, New York, NY 10016, United States of America

British Library Cataloguing in Publication Data
Data available

Library of Congress Control Number: 2016963304

ISBN 978–0–19–879137–9

Award Statement of the IZA Prize Committee

The 2013 IZA Prize in Labor Economics is awarded to Daniel S. Hamermesh (University of Texas at Austin; Royal Holloway, University of London) for his fundamental contributions to the analysis of labor demand. In his work, Hamermesh has demonstrated that many important topics in labor economics, such as the unemployment implications of minimum wages or job security programs, can only be understood within a framework that allows a thorough analysis of demand-side reactions in labor markets. Hamermesh's research is characterized by a focus on thought-provoking questions, a high level of creativity, and careful combination of theoretical and empirical methods. He has shaped the way other scholars, as well as policy makers, think about some of the key issues in labor economics.

The question how firms adjust employment in response to fluctuations in product demand and other exogenous shocks is of fundamental importance for assessing unemployment and labor market dynamics. Hamermesh was among the first scholars to point out the importance of detailed micro-level estimates of adjustment costs for understanding firms' demand for labor. In his article "Labor Demand and the Structure of Adjustment Costs" (American Economic Review, 1989), he used plant-level data to demonstrate that adjustment processes in individual firms occur in discrete jumps rather than continuously. A key reason for this effect is that firms face important fixed costs when adjusting their labor inputs. For instance, the costs of advertising vacancies and interviewing candidates do not depend – at least within certain ranges – on the number of workers that a firm seeks to hire. The presence of such fixed costs generates non-convex adjustment cost functions for firms, resulting in incentives to adjust their workforce in a "lumpy", non-continuous way. In contrast, most of the earlier labor demand models had neglected fixed costs in hiring and laying off workers, and instead assumed a convex variable cost structure, leading to smooth adjustments of factor inputs. Hamermesh's analysis also demonstrated that detailed establishment-level data is necessary to gain deeper empirical insights into the dynamic aspects of labor demand, and that the use of more aggregated data can be misleading. Hamermesh's findings led to a re-examination of the traditional labor demand model, and they have spurred the interest of many scholars in analyzing labor adjustments and their costs on a more fine-grained level.

Hamermesh also dealt with a variety of other fundamental issues in labor demand. For instance, he analyzed substitution patterns among workers of different demographic backgrounds; he studied the determinants of labor-demand adjustments at the extensive vs. intensive margin; and he contributed to a better understanding of how labor market institutions such as minimum wage laws affect labor demand. The increasing interest in labor-demand analysis spurred by his pioneering contributions, as well as subsequent work by others in the field, culminated in Hamermesh's book Labor Demand (1993). This book provides the most comprehensive overview on the theoretical contributions and key empirical findings on the topic to date.

Besides his long-standing interest in labor demand, Hamermesh pioneered the economic analysis of time-use data and contributed to a broad set of other topics in economics. He has a unique talent to use traditional economic rationales in novel and often surprising applications. Along the lines of his semi-popular book Economics Is Everywhere (2009), Hamermesh has analyzed, for instance, the economic determinants of suicide, the impact of beauty on individuals' labor market outcomes, and the question how umpires' ethnic preferences are expressed in their evaluation of Major League Baseball pitchers. In addition to his scientific achievements, Hamermesh is widely recognized as a mentor to many junior scholars. As the author of his own blog and a regular guest contributor to the popular Freakonomics blog, he has also helped communicate economic thinking to a wider audience.

Daniel S. Hamermesh is Sue Killam Professor in the Foundation of Economics at the University of Texas at Austin and Professor of Economics at Royal Holloway University of London. He earned his A.B. from the University of Chicago (1965) and his Ph.D. from Yale (1969). Before moving to Texas in 1993, he taught at Princeton and Michigan State. Hamermesh is a Research Fellow of the Institute for the Study of Labor (IZA), a Fellow of the Econometric Society and the Society of Labor Economists (SOLE), a Research Associate of the National Bureau of Economic Research (NBER), and Past President of SOLE and of the Midwest Economics Association. He received the Humboldt Foundation Research Prize in 2011 and the Mincer Award from the Society of Labor Economists in 2013.

George A. Akerlof, University of California, Berkeley; IZA

Corrado Giulietti, IZA

Richard Portes, London Business School; President CEPR

Jan Svejnar, University of Michigan, Ann Arbor; IZA

Klaus F. Zimmermann, IZA; University of Bonn

Contents

I Daniel S. Hamermesh: The Pioneer in Labor Demand Research

Corrado Giulietti and Klaus F. Zimmermann

The 2013 IZA Prize in Labor Economics was awarded to Daniel (Dan) S. Hamermesh (University of Texas at Austin and Royal Holloway) for his fundamental contributions to the analysis of labor demand. The IZA Prize has been conferred every year since 2002 to honor groundbreaking research in the field of labor economics. Past winners include Nobel Laureates like the late Dale T. Mortensen (Northwestern University) and Christopher A. Pissarides (London School of Economics). The 2013 Prize was presented to the Prize Winner during the award ceremony, which took place November 18, 2013 in Washington, DC. IZA Prize Laureate George J. Borjas of Harvard University gave the laudation speech, highlighting Hamermesh's notorious excellence and eclecticism as both a researcher and teacher. In Borjas' words: "Not only has Dan published a ton of papers, but the work shows an impressive depth and breadth. He has worked on: labor demand, time use, unemployment insurance, beauty, food stamps, the economics of sleeping, search theory, life expectancy, suicide, retirement, compensating differentials, academic labor markets, discrimination, the Phillips curve, unions, and much, much more. It is hard to think of any other labor economist who has tackled so many different topics so successfully."

The ceremony was followed by the IZA Prize Workshop on Frontiers in Labor Economics held in honor of Hamermesh and which featured presentations from distinguished scholars. Joseph G. Altonji (Yale University) presented a paper about the labor market outcomes of college graduates who entered the labor market during the last recession. George J. Borjas discussed the latest results from his analysis about the effects of winning prestigious prizes on future productivity of academics. Janet Currie (Princeton University) outlined her study about the impact of diagnostic and surgical skills on the rate of Caesarean sections performed in the United States. Gerard A. Pfann (Maastricht University) presented his research about the different procedures to dissolve permanent worker contracts in the Netherlands.

The work of Dan Hamermesh has substantially influenced the way labor economists think about labor demand[1], both under a theoretical and an empirical viewpoint. Until recently, economists have been more interested in the supply rather than the demand side of labor. As Hamermesh's famous labor demand textbook reports (Hamermesh, 1993 p. 7), the number of publications in top economics journals related to labor supply was much higher than the one related to labor demand. This was perhaps due to the larger availability of household surveys vis-à-vis the scarcity of firm data, as well as to the consequent greater effort that scholars would have to put forth to develop appropriate econometric techniques to analyze labor supply. To put it in Hamermesh's words, labor demand was for a long time the "neglected side of the market."

Against this background, Hamermesh tenaciously pursued the principle that learning how firms demand workers and hours is as important as understanding how individuals supply labor. His admirable research effort, marked by seminal scholarly contributions, culminated in his chapter "The Demand for Labor in the Long Run" included in the Handbook of Labor Economics edited by Orley Ashenfelter and Richard Layard (1986) and in the book "Labor Demand" (1993). Even today these two pieces constitute the most comprehensive and important references for labor demand research. One of the major elements emerging from Hamermesh's study of labor demand is that higher labor costs (such as higher wage rates induced by minimum wages or employee benefits) are beneficial for workers but could lead firms to reduce the number of jobs and shorten working hours. This argument is also effectively summarized in his contribution (Hamermesh, 2014) to the IZA World of Labor – a recently launched outlet summarizing the most important policy-relevant findings from research into an accessible format. The strong academic influence of Hamermesh is reflected by his remarkable citation record. As of the end of June 2015, the Handbook chapter obtained 503 Google citations, while the Labor Demand book attained as many as 2,226 (see Figure I.1 Panel A).

Hamermesh has been a pioneer of other areas besides labor demand. What best characterizes his approach is the choice of controversial and

[1] For an intuitive introduction into labor demand, see his recent IZA World of Labor piece (Hamermesh, 2014).

Figure I.1A
Google Citations of Book "Labor Demand" (Total 2226*)

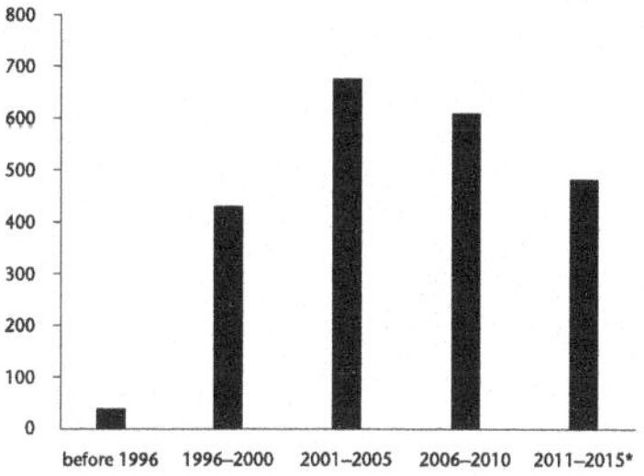

Figure I.1B
Google Citations of Articles Collected in Part III "Labor Demand" (Total 1081*)

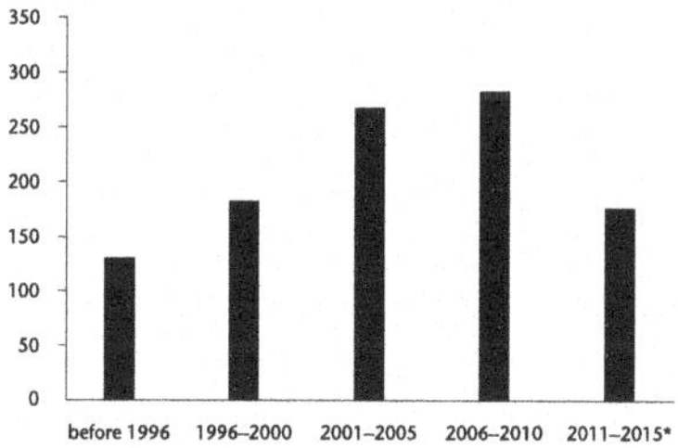

Figure I.1C
Google Citations of Articles Collected in Part IV "Policy on the Demand Side" (Total 277*)

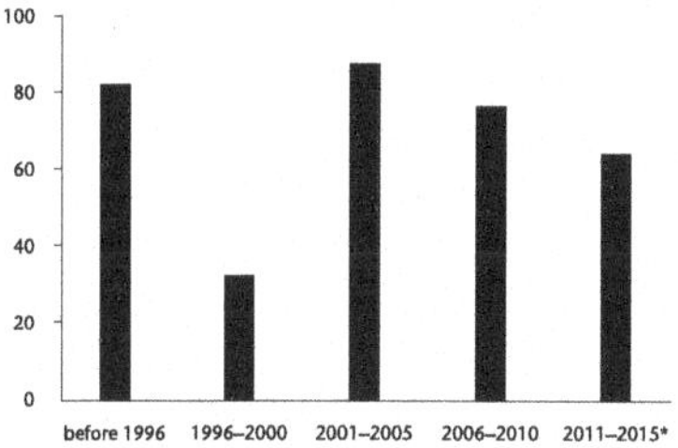

Figure I.1D
Google Citations of Articles Collected in Part V "Discrimination: Preferences for People" (Total 1595*)

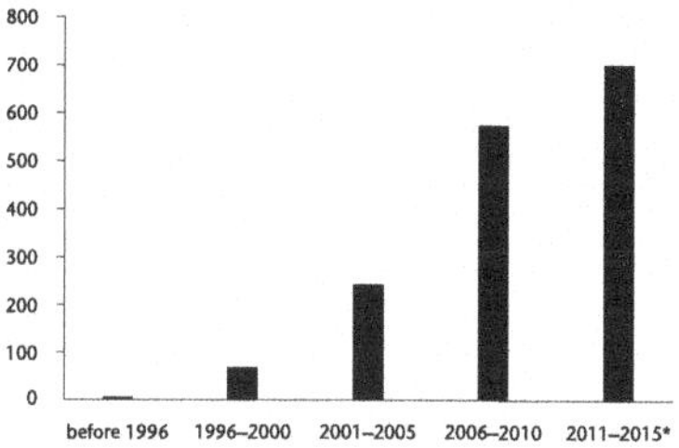

** until end of June 2015*

understudied areas that economists have yet to explore. Emblematic is the co-authored paper "An Economic Theory of Suicide" published in the Journal of Political Economy in 1974, in which suicidal behavior is cast into a utility maximizing framework and is empirically investigated. In this and many other areas (time use and beauty, to mention a few) Hamermesh has been a pathfinder for many economists, very much like the late Gary S. Becker of Chicago University. Hamermesh's work features rigorous (but simple) theoretical framework modeling and thorough data analysis. When the questions he poses cannot be investigated through existing surveys, Hamermesh searches, collects and assembles the data needed to test his hypotheses.

This Volume collects Hamermesh's key contributions on labor demand. Part II "Aspects of Labor Demand" follows this foreword and contains a brief overview by Hamermesh about labor demand research and its importance. The contributions are organized into three parts:

Part III "Labor Demand," Part IV "Policy on the Demand Side" and Part V "Discrimination: Preferences for People." Hamermesh's research covered in this Volume has had enormous impact in the academic community. As of the end of June 2015, the number of Google citations reached 1,081 (Part III), 334 (Part IV) and 1,595 (Part V), as seen in Figure I.1, panels B, C and D.

Hamermesh's early research provides empirical applications to the static theory of factor demand, which is represented by the first article collected in Part III "Labor Demand." Such microeconomic theory was the workhorse of labor demand for many years, but was lacking empirical evidence until Hamermesh and a few other scholars pioneered data analysis. Perhaps Hamermesh's finest intuition within this area has been that substitution in the demand of workers may occur not only between different occupation groups, but also between different demographic groups. To this aim, he and his coauthor exploit data from the sharp increase in the U.S. labor supply, which has been observed since the mid-1960s to estimate the elasticity of substitution between women and of young workers (Chapter 1).

Hamermesh's major interest, however, lies with the dynamics of labor demand, i.e., how firms adjust labor in response to large shocks. This was a question that was of interest to macroeconomists only – until scholars like Hamermesh demonstrated that labor economics could indeed provide important insights. The remainder of Part III contains his most important contributions in the theory and applications of labor demand dynamics. In one of his earliest works (Chapter 2) Hamermesh departs from the business cycle definition as classically defined by macroeconomists and argues that seasonal cycles can provide a greater deal of data to analyze. This allows him to investigate how fluctuations in hiring compare to those in layoffs.

Another challenge to traditional labor demand models comes from Hamermesh's analysis of employment adjustments. His pioneering contribution (Chapter 3) shows that firms do not respond to shocks by adjusting employment in a smooth way; they do so through discrete jumps due to the presence of fixed costs (e.g., for hiring). Hamermesh further delves into important aspects of adjustment costs. First (Chapter 4), he studies the nature of adjustment costs demonstrating the existence and importance of both gross costs (when hiring does not change the employment level) versus net costs (incurred when the scale of employment changes). Second (Chapter 5), he investigates whether the adjustment costs respond symmetrically to negative and positive shocks. In the study that concludes the Part "Labor demand" of this Volume (Chapter 6), Hamermesh and coauthor argue that it is important to keep the concept of job creation and destruction distinct from that of worker flow (i.e., hiring/firing). The distinction is critical since there can be hiring even when firms are not expanding employment; similarly, layoffs are not just a phenomenon of firms where employment is shirking.

Over the years, Hamermesh became interested in exploring how the study of labor demand could provide useful evaluations and predictions about the impact of labor policy. Many such policies – such as minimum wages and regulations on working hours – have a direct influence on labor demand. The contributions collected in Part III "Policy on the Demand Side" empirically investigate how labor policy affects wages and employment, as well as the substitution between different types of labor. The first study concerns the impact of a minimum wage (Chapter 7). Hamermesh's intuition is that minimum wage policies should be studied within a system of equations that include three factors: youth labor (the one most affected by the policy), adult labor and capital (for which the impact depends on the cross elasticity of demand). To date, his study remains one of the few that tackles the analysis of minimum wages within the rigorous framework of labor demand theory.

In a further study, Hamermesh and his coauthor exploit the introduction of an overtime wage premium for men in California to study how firms adjust employment (Chapter 8). By comparing the incidence of overtime work before and after the policy enactment, between men and women (for which the policy was already in force) and between California and other states (where the policy did not change for men), they provide estimates of the elasticity of demand in response to exogenous changes in wages. Starting from the observation that, besides working overtime, many people work outside regular working hours (e.g. weekends and/or nighttime), Hamermesh and coauthors explore the determinants of labor at different times (Chapter 9). The application to Portuguese data allows simulating what would be the effects of introducing U.S. regulations on working at unconventional times.

Hamermesh also embarked on studying the topic of job displacement (Chapter 10). His perspective, however, has been different from the mainstream labor literature, which was principally interested in understanding the consequences in terms of, e.g., re-employment wages. Instead Hamermesh poses the question about the necessity and efficacy of policy requiring employers to give notice of plant closure and mass layoffs. To this aim, he exploits longitudinal data from which he can infer whether workers expect plant closure (and thus pre-adjust their human capital investment). In the Part's last study (Chapter 11), Hamermesh and coauthor argue that a federally imposed tax ceiling increases the relative cost of low-skilled workers, making firms less likely to hire them. Hence, increasing the taxable amount per worker could alleviate such a distortion.

Part IV "Discrimination: Preferences for People" delves into the sources of discrimination. Hamermesh's key argument is that discrimination is attributable to employers' choices, and as such, is part of labor demand studies. Contrarily to mainstream literature interested in gauging discrimination, Hamermesh has been concerned with understanding its causes, mainly in relation to employers' preferences. Hamermesh's work into this area extends to postulating that beauty matters in the labor market since employers have preferences for it. The fascinating aspect is that he and his coauthor find empirical evidence that this is the case, even when using three separate datasets (Chapter 12). Similarly, and equally strikingly, Hamermesh and coauthor found that better-looking lawyers earn more than others (Chapter 14).

The study of another physical characteristic - height - lead Hamermesh to investigate whether employers discriminate more with respect to absolute or to relative differences in the characteristics they observe. In his study, he ingeniously exploits the fact that younger cohorts of Dutch men are much taller than older cohorts (Chapter 13). Hamermesh and coauthor explore gender discrimination in a thought-provoking study based on the American Economic Association's officer elections (Chapter 15). The book's concluding study (Chapter 16) investigates employee behavior when they expect that employers discriminate towards them. Hardly observable through standard employer-employee data, Hamermesh and coauthors creatively exploit baseball data where pitchers (read: employees) of certain minority groups behave differently when expecting that umpires (read: employers) will discriminate towards them.

Dan Hamermesh has been a devoted and energetic member of IZA and its network since the early days of the Institute. An IZA Research Fellow since 1998, Hamermesh was also Program Director of "The Future of Labor" area from 2001 to 2008, during which he contributed to shaping the vision. He served as IZA Director of Research from August 2008 until January 2009 and has been a Visiting Research Fellow on numerous occasions. Hamermesh has authored a plethora of important

IZA Discussion Papers (34 as of the end of June 2015), many of which are now published in major outlets such as the American Economic Review. Furthermore, he has been an Editor (from 2001 to 2004) and is still an Associate Editor of the Journal of Population Economics, which is edited at IZA. Together with Gerard A. Pfann he has implemented the IZA-SOLE Transatlantic Meeting of Labor Economists – 2015 marks the fourteenth edition – which provides a forum for distinguished labor economists worldwide. Over the years, Hamermesh has been an excellent mentor and a source of inspiration for IZA researchers in Bonn.

Hamermesh's work on labor demand intersects with essentially all of IZA's Research Areas, but perhaps most prominently with the "The Future of Labor," "Behavioral and Personnel Economics" and "Labor Markets and Institutions." Since its inception, IZA has been active in labor demand research on many fronts, covering this topic within its many workshops, conferences and projects. Modeling labor demand in simulations of labor market reform packages has proven to be essential in various policy studies, including Riphahn et al. (1999) and Schneider et al. (2002). Here the work of Hamermesh has been very influential. Such research has also generated research on the determinants of the demand for household work through subsidized household work agencies (Brück et al., 2006).

In 2010, IZA evaluated a field experiment in collaboration with the Federal Anti-Discrimination Agency in Germany to investigate the effectiveness of anonymous job applications as a tool for reducing hiring discrimination. One of the main findings of the IZA team is that through anonymous job applications, job seekers have equal chances to be interviewed. Thus, if discrimination about a certain characteristic exists, concealing such a characteristic in the job application may result in less discrimination (Krause et al., 2012).

Recently the Institute was part of NEUJOBS, a large collaborative research project financed by the European Union to analyze possible developments in the European labor market. Research from this project shows that labor demand analysis is crucial to our understanding of policy reform effects in the labor market (Peichl and Siegloch, 2012) and of the distributional consequences of economic crises (Bargain et al.,2012). The IZA World of Labor also includes many topics related to labor demand and to Hamermesh's work covered in this book, from the employment effects of minimum wages (Neumark, 2014), to the discrimination in hiring (Rinne, 2014) and the measurement of work hours (Steward, 2014).

The importance of labor demand at IZA is clear, as seen through the topic's extensive coverage throughout the IZA network's discussion papers. As of the end of 2014, nearly 400 out of about 9,000 IZA Discussion Papers investigated core labor demand issues (JEL code J23, see Figure I.2). These discussion papers alone generated over one million downloads through the IZA website.

Figure I.2
IZA Discussion Papers with JEL Code J23

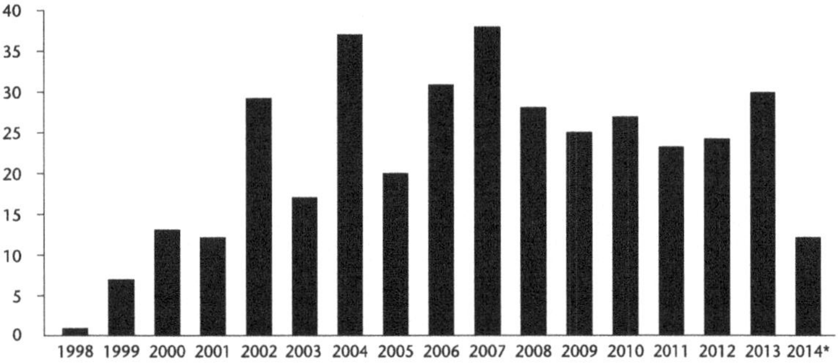

** until end of October 2014*

It is thanks to innovative and insightful scholars such as Dan Hamermesh – capable of blending theoretical insight with creative empirical analysis – that labor economics is nowadays a prominent field. The 2013 IZA Prize and this Volume cherish his pioneering contribution to the study of labor demand.

II Aspects of Labor Demand

The *apologia pro libra sua* here must lie in an answer to the question: Why another book on labor demand? The low-level answer is that there are in fact very few books on this subject. That in turn leads to the rejoinder: Perhaps there are few books on this topic just because it is not very important. The response to the rejoinder is that the topic is important, even central: A broad definition of labor demand is that it concerns any decision made by an employer regarding the company's workers - their employment, their compensation, and their training. This broadest definition of labor demand implicitly divides the study of labor economics into just two parts, labor supply and labor demand. While this decision may have made sense before 1960, before the burgeoning of empirical and theoretical work in labor economics, it is not very helpful now. There are too many variations that have themselves been so differentiated that they have now become major themes in their own right. Thus we need to dig deeper to justify this interest.

In Alfred Marshall's statement of neoclassical economics (Marshall, 1920) much of the focus in analyzing labor markets was on employers' decisions about how many workers to employ and how many hours each worker should work. The demand for labor was viewed as derived from consumers' demands for final goods and services, and as being concerned with the availability of employment. This view of labor demand is the one that I adopt here to delimit the study. The study of the demand for labor has, for historical reasons and because of the divergence of research on employers' behavior in a variety of contexts, become the study of the number of jobs offered, the hours that employees are required to work, and the responses of these quantities to external shocks.

Much of Marshall's discussion of labor demand was concerned with what, after Hicks's developments (1932), became the formal study of

Part of this Introduction is an edited version of part of Chapter 1 of Hamermesh (1993).

the structure of production and its implications for employment and hours. Indeed, this broad strand of research has become the core of the modern subfield of labor demand and is often viewed as synonymous with it. This core has been thoroughly studied. We know a lot about the nature of production, both conceptually and, as a result of the rapid growth of statistical work, empirically. For that reason only one of the essays in this volume deals with issues in this area.

There is more to the study of labor demand than the neoclassical theory of the comparative statics of employers' responses to marginal changes in product demand and factor prices. The study of the responses of employment and hours to non-marginal changes - large shocks that are not readily analyzed using the standard mathematical tools - surely belongs in the subfield of labor demand. So too, examining the time paths of adjustment of employment and hours to both marginal and non-marginal shocks - the comparative dynamics of employment and hours - deserves inclusion. Most of the rest of Section III in this volume treats topics in this area, which has more generally been of greater interest to researchers in the past 25 years than have the basic static models.

I have not thus far shown what, if anything, is unique about the study of labor demand. Why should labor demand be studied separately from the demand for other productive inputs? The same neoclassical theory of factor demand applies and has been applied to the study of the demand for investment goods, energy, materials and other inputs. Similarly, the same theory of the dynamics of employment demand has been used to study the dynamics of investment; and there has been the same growth of the analysis of non-marginal changes in investment as there has been in the study of employment (e.g., Thomas, 2002; Letterie et al, 2010).

Some of the characteristics of labor demand that seem so unusual are common to other productive inputs. While workers can be distinguished by age and skill (including education, training, and other forms of human capital), so too can investment goods. These latter differ in age and complexity, and studying firms' choices among heterogeneous investment goods is not very different from examining their decisions about employing workers with different characteristics. Admittedly, we are much more interested in the extent to which, for example, an influx of unskilled immigrants might affect the wages or employment opportunities of unskilled native workers than we are in whether introducing laser-guided lathes reduces the returns on conventional lathes. Qualitatively, however, these are very similar issues. The employment-hours distinction might seem unique; but it is not:

Machines can be worked at varying intensities, and among the firm's stock of machinery, only a varying fraction could be utilized.

One of the things that is special about labor among productive inputs is that its share of factor payments is by far the largest. Labor's share of national income grew rapidly during the Great Depression in the United States, so that in the late 1950s compensation of employees account for nearly 70 percent of national income in the United States. It has fluctuated somewhat since then, and has perhaps decreased a little, but labor's share is still the predominant flow of national income in most Western economies today.

Yet size alone does not make the subject interesting or, more important, any different analytically from the study of other inputs. It is true that we care more about people than we do about machinery; and much of government policy has to do with people, not with machinery. Yet the machinery does after all yield streams of income to the people with whom we are concerned. To the extent that our interest is in providing people with the income required to maintain consumption at least at some commonly agreed upon minimum level, income received from renting capital goods could be of as much concern as that received from selling labor services.

What is unique about labor is that it is the only productive input that requires, as Marshall (1920, Book. 6, Chapter 4) noted in his list of the peculiarities of labor, that the owner of the services, "present himself where they are delivered." The provision of labor services automatically engages workers' attention and affects not only their income, but also many non-pecuniary aspects of their existence. Time must be spent earning labor income, time that is thus unavailable for other purposes; the workplace can provide a focus for workers' socializing; and workers may expose themselves to dangers on the job.

Even this unique aspect relates more closely to the worker's use of time, and thus to supply decisions, than to labor demand. What then is unique about labor as an input into production? The best answer is that although none of these aspects of labor demand – labor's importance in production, and the requirement that workers be physically present on the job, or even our interest in policies that affect different types of workers – is sufficient to make the study of labor demand a subtopic in its own right, taken together they are.

Interestingly, the originators of neoclassical economics recognized that analyzing labor demand was not merely a matter of examining how employers responded to exogenous changes (though they were concerned about that too). Marshall (1920, Book 6, Chapters 2 and 13) expounds at length on the variability of workers' effort and its relation to productivity and hence to the demand for labor. This early recognition of the uniqueness of labor as a productive input returned to vogue among economists concerned with the microeconomic foundations of macroeconomic fluctuations (Shapiro and Stiglitz, 1984). While none of the essays here deals with fluctuations in effort, Section IV.9 is implicitly based on that variability, in that case in the unique context of hebdomadal variations in labor demand.

Having established that the study of labor demand is not merely a specific example of the general theory of production, the question remains: Why is it especially interesting to study labor demand? One obvious answer is that employers' demands for workers and hours determine to a large extent the well-being of workers and their families. At the most obvious level, without jobs most people's incomes would be greatly reduced; and knowing what determines whether people have jobs is thus crucial to understanding how their incomes are determined. At a slightly deeper level we know (Winkelmann and Winkelmann, 1998) that people's satisfaction/happiness when they are without work that they are seeking is greatly reduced. Thus the study of labor demand indirectly feeds into the analysis of workers' well-being at the basic level of their happiness (Easterlin, 2010, also in this series of volumes).

At another, broader level studying labor demand is important because so many government policies that affect workers and their families work on the demand side for labor. Section IV presents studies analyzing a few of these policies, but there are so many more that are not included in this sample. Perhaps most important, all of the research presented here deals with fairly high-income countries – there is little on the developing world. Yet if anything there is more scope for studying demand-side policies in the labor market in less developed countries, both because there may be less institutional rigidity – greater ease of altering policies – and because the evidence makes it clear that the changes that have been made to labor market policies in those countries have created a greater range of shocks to demand than typically occur in richer countries (Hamermesh, 2002; Heckman and Pages-Serra, 2004).

With the development of labor economics over the last fifty years the economics of discrimination has become a separate sub-field within this discipline (as suggested by its having its own second-level rubric in the Journal of Economic Literature classification scheme, and by its accounting for one of the earlier books in this series, Blau, 2012). But taking the older view that it should be possible to classify topics as supply, demand or the intersection of both, the discrimination is easily classifiable as more demand-based than anything else. The studies in Section V are motivated by this view and by the belief that, in the end, discriminatory outcomes do not just happen. Rather, as the original economic theory of discrimination (Becker, 1957) implied, they result from the application of the preferences of members of society; and in the context of labor market discrimination, they can be viewed as arising from employers' preferences – and thus fundamentally as an aspect of labor demand.

Mentioning "neglect" leads to the justification for the subtitle of this volume: Has labor demand really been neglected in the literature in labor economics? In Hamermesh (1993) I provided some evidence, mostly based on Stafford (1986), justifying this statement by showing that far more space had been devoted to labor supply in the leading academic journals than to labor demand up through 1990. A quick count of publications in these journals in recent years does nothing to alter this inference. This consideration suggests that, unless one views labor demand as being much the less important of the two areas, the marginal social product of additional work in this area is likely to have been higher than that of additional work on labor supply.

This volume is dedicated to my coauthors. "Only" thirteen of them are represented in the sixteen studies included here; but up through 2013 I had published papers with forty-five other economists in works not included in this volume. Truly, as Lennon and McCartney almost wrote, I've gotten by with a lot of help from my friends; and I thank all fifty-eight of them profusely.

III Labor Demand

The static theory of the factor demand for inputs has been well worked out for many years. Indeed, it seems fair to say that there have been no new central developments in this area for at least 30 years, and perhaps 50 years. The ideas are exposited and very slightly developed in Ferguson (1971), and I exposited them and linked them to empirical work in 1993 (Hamermesh, 1993, Chapter 2). In the 1960s, 1970s and 1980s a variety of econometric tools were provided that allowed economists to obtain explicit estimates of the theoretical parameters underlying factor demand. There was very little specific to labor in these tools and the estimates upon which they were based; but they did allow us to obtain information on the demand elasticity for labor in general and those for specific types of workers. Perhaps even more important, they provided measures of the extent of substitution among workers of different types, and of labor for physical and human capital. The first paper in this Section is part of this literature.

Economists, especially macroeconomists, had long realized that employment demand over the business cycle did not move proportionately with production, and thus that there were cyclical patterns of labor productivity (output/head). Walter Oi's fundamental work on quasi-fixed labor (Oi, 1962) provided a theoretical rationale for this realization (although it took some time for economists to recognize the link). Thus was born what is now referred to as the dynamic theory of factor demand. Here too there is nothing in the theory that is specific to labor – there are costs of adjusting capital and other inputs too. But because of the macroeconomic focus on labor productivity, and perhaps too because labor does account for well over half of national income in most countries, much of the theoretical and empirical work on factor dynamics has focused on labor.

While the theory is not specific to labor, there is one characteristic of labor, as opposed to other productive inputs, that makes analyzing the dynamics of demand for this particular factor especially interesting and complex: Unlike other inputs workers can choose to leave their employment. While physical capital does depreciate, we typically assume that it does so at a constant, or at least at known rates. Workers do not leave jobs at constant rates, and their voluntary departures are not exogenous with respect to employers' wage/benefit policies or the state of the labor market. Thinking about how this difficulty affects the dynamics of labor demand requires more complex modeling than is the case for analyzing investment (the dynamics of adjusting the capital stock).

The remaining four papers in this Section all deal with various aspects of the dynamics of labor demand. Much of the literature on this subject has been produced by macroeconomists, not surprising given the importance of aggregate labor productivity. In a sense that is unfortunate, because it has forced the analysis into a procrustean bed that was designed more for the analysis of investment demand. This is an area in which labor economists could still make substantial basic contributions.

As a final introductory note, as the publication dates of the studies included in this Section indicate, I have not worked on these topics recently (in nearly two decades). I am not alone among labor economists – there has been very little study of any of these issues in the sub-field of labor economics during that time. I attribute this neglect to the interaction of the profession's obsession with issues of exogeneity – can we be sure that X causes Y – and the difficulty of definitively arguing causation in this area of research. That is unfortunate, as the topics are important, both to understanding employers' behavior and to understanding the workings of the macroeconomy.

Does this neglect mean that the study of these issues belongs more rightly to the history of economic thought than to labor economics, and that this research has no bearing on how our understanding of current labor market developments? Obviously I think not; and my reason is that I have no doubt that some of the phenomena that motivated these studies, such as a sharp change in the demographic structure of the work force, and macro shocks that generate dynamic adjustments, persist today although in different forms. We tie our hands in understanding changes in today's labor market if we restrict ourselves to basing that understanding on studies that achieve a sufficient purity of method limited to causality. Most important issues cannot be studied, and little can be learned, if causal purity is the *sine qua non* of research.

The baby boom (best dated as consisting of cohorts of workers born 1946–1964) was one of the two most profound demographic changes affecting the American labor market in the second half of the twentieth century. Beginning in the mid-1960s it dumped a huge number of additional young workers onto the labor market, leading to changes in the wages of other young workers compared to previous years, and perhaps too to changes in wages of other groups of workers.

In Section III.1 I ask how this arguably exogenous shock to the relative size of the youth labor force altered young workers' relative wages and affected wages in other groups. Of particular interest were the wages of women, since the other central change in the labor market at that time was the growth in women's labor-force participation. How did women's wages change as a result of the increase in their participation? And how did the simultaneous increases in both female participation and the share of young workers in the labor market alter the relative wages of both? How did they affect the wages of adult male workers, and how did they alter the wages of minority workers? All of these outcomes depend on the substitution relations among the demands for workers in these different demographic groups; and the study aims at measuring these relations.

Because data on stocks of capital were also available, the study was able to provide information on the extent to which capital is complementary/substitutable for different types of labor (the so-called capital-skill complementarity hypothesis first posed by Griliches, 1969). This additional set of results is important, both narrowly, since the presence of capital may alter the substitution relationships between different types of labor that we are trying to infer (they may not be separable from capital) and more broadly for the study of capital-skill complementarity.

The essay began with James Grant's Ph.D. dissertation at Michigan State University (Grant, 1979). Jim had put together a data set linking 1970 Census data to measures of the capital stock and output in manufacturing, all assigned to SMSAs. Realizing that he had created a perfect tool for analyzing questions of substitution among types of labor; and with the econometric tools developed in the early 1970s to analyze factor substitution, Jim and I could answer the questions that had been thrown up by these demographic changes.

Macroeconomists and labor economists wishing to examine labor aspects of macro issues have a problem: There just are not that many business cycles over which to analyze behavior. Indeed, the problem has gotten worse (although better for society), since between 1980 and 2010 the time between recession troughs has been longer than in the previous thirty years. While not a perfect simulacrum for business cycles, labor market outcomes at seasonal cycles can provide some evidence on the determinants of labor demand over the business cycle.

Seasonal cycles have the virtue of being repeated every twelve months – there is one for each calendar year – allowing for many more true degrees of freedom than does the study of business cycles. It is true that seasonal cycles are expected – employers have a good understanding of patterns of output demand, and thus of the derived demand for labor that is altered by the seasonal cycle. But this greater certainty about patterns of demand actually makes it easier to identify the impacts of workers' and job characteristics on labor market outcomes, since employers are more likely to make fewer departures from an optimizing path due to mistaken expectations about the nature of shocks.

In Section III.2 I recognized this chance to exploit a different kind of shock to test Oi's theory of quasi-fixed labor. The test also allowed me to analyze labor turnover in a way that had not been done before and to go beyond simply charting demographic and inter-industry differences in quits and layoffs. The data used in this study came from an establishment survey that was conducted each month by the Bureau of Labor Statistics, beginning in 1958 and ending in 1981. The survey was resurrected in modified form (less information on the sources of labor turnover, but with information on vacancies) in 2000 as the Job Openings and Labor Turnover Survey (JOLTS).

The study uses a technique that grew out of electrical engineering, spectral analysis.* The technique, "... an algorithm that estimates the strength of different frequency components (the power spectrum) of a time-domain signal," (Wikipedia, http://en.wikipedia.org/wiki/Spectral_analysis, downloaded October 2, 2013), allows among other things the measurement of the extent of cycles in time series of data at various frequencies. It is thus perfect for analyzing the relative extent of seasonality in different economic time series, which is precisely what the hypotheses generated in the study dealt with. Today, as I have discovered by speaking with students at several universities, the technique is not even mentioned in graduate courses in econometrics, much less actually taught; and econometric hypotheses are only very rarely examined at seasonal cycles. Both changes are unfortunate, since we can learn a lot from looking at seasonal behavior, and spectral analysis is the perfect technique for such examinations (although it does require a substantial mathematical background).

This study began as a second-year paper in an advanced econometrics course taught by one of my thesis supervisors, Marc Nerlove. He

* See Granger and Hatanaka (1964) for the exposition of various aspects of this technique in the context of econometric analysis.

had done substantial research using spectral analysis, including even a paper (Nerlove, 1964) that focused on seasonal cycles; and I was fortunate to have him present the technique in that course. At the same time I discovered the data set on labor turnover, which was then available from 1958–66, and I realized that I had a great chance to test a new idea and as well as produce a paper for the course. Getting this published in a journal was my first real experience with the editorial process, so that the paper had the side benefit of acquainting me with the pleasures, and pains, of scholarly publishing.

Going back at least as far as large-scale models of the macroeconomy, employment adjustment had been assumed to proceed smoothly. That is, employers were assumed to alter their workforces continually in response to shocks. Indeed, for econometric convenience the adjustment was assumed to proceed as a distributed lag, in which some constant fraction of the gap between current and long-run desired employment was made up during each time period. This assumption allowed a very simple and estimable specification of dynamic equations describing the path of labor demand (and factor demand generally), although it did impose the econometric difficulties associated with the inclusion of a lagged dependent variable in regression equations.

This method was, however, based on very weak theoretical grounds. Indeed, Gould (1965) showed that smooth adjustment can only be justified theoretically under extremely restrictive assumptions about employers' expectations. Also, it makes the possibly restrictive assumption that the costs of adjustment are quadratic and only variable, so that the increase in the marginal cost of adjustment leads employers to spread changes in employment over multiple time periods. Indeed, the theoretical basis provided in the early literature, allusions to a discussion in Holt et al (1960) in fact show that those authors viewed smooth adjustment merely as an approximation to a structure that would generate a more complex adjustment path.

There is nothing sacred about the assumption about convexity in the structure of adjustment costs – it is one of many possible. Its universal acceptance in empirical research until the late 1980s was no doubt due mostly to the ease of estimating models based on it. The study in Section III.3 make an alternative assumption: That employers face only lumpy costs of adjustment – that the costs each period are the same whether the employer adds one worker or many. Given this structure of adjustment costs, it pays the firm to wait until the departure from long-run equilibrium will be large enough to justify incurring the one-time cost of making the leap from the old to the new equilibrium.

This study thus essentially ran a horse race between the standard assumption of convex (actually, quadratic) costs of adjustment and the particular alternative of lumpy costs. Since the hypotheses describe behavior at the micro level, the horse race required obtaining data on individual plants. I was fortunate enough to obtain those through a former classmate and colleague who worked as an economist for a large manufacturing firm. These data were especially apropos for testing the idea, as the company had sufficiently many similar plants that I could aggregate them and provide a similar test on more aggregated data. The results made clear that smooth adjustment did not characterize behavior at the very micro level, but that even at the level of aggregation of the set of (seven) plants it was difficult to distinguish between the two specifications of adjustment cost.

The study and the new hypothesis grew out of my then twenty-year-old interest in labor demand. The specific assumption of lumpy adjustment, however, was generated by my experience as chairman of an economics department. One of any department chairman's main tasks is hiring new faculty members; and in the large department that I headed we were hiring each year. It was clear to me that, what with advertising positions, going to the annual economists' meeting to interview job candidates, and other things, that the total cost of the process would have been less had we been able to bunch hiring rather than hire each year. Regrettably university approvals for positions made that impossible; but thinking about this in my administrative job provided the impetus for thinking about it more generally.

The research presented in Section III.3 looked only at the structure of the costs of adjusting employment levels – it focused only on net employment changes. But most firms do huge amounts of hiring even when they are not changing employment or changing it only a little, because they are faced with large flows of workers who quit the firm. (For example, in 2012 the flow of workers quitting their jobs in the U.S. nonfarm sector averaged 3.1 percent *per month*, far greater than the average monthly net growth or contraction in employment in this sector.) The question is whether the costs of changing employment that we observe arise from the costs of gross changes – adding new workers without changing employment – or from net changes – a changing employment level.

Even ignoring the structure of adjustment costs – whether they are quadratic, lumpy or some other shape – understanding their source imposes more stringent requirements on the data than would a study of their structure. One needs information for individual establishments on employment and at the least on flows of quits and hires. Moreover, given the magnitude of quits and hires, without monthly data one would fail to capture much of the dynamics that occur in the adjustment process.

The idea in Section III.4 was a logical outgrowth of the study in Section III.3 plus my long-standing interest in gross flows of labor (shown in the study in Section III.2 and the bulk of my Ph.D. dissertation, Hamermesh, 1969). Fortunately through various contacts, one with a former undergraduate student who was chief financial officer in a small manufacturing company, one with a contact of my wife who was a hospital administrator, I was able to obtain the requisite data. While the monthly data in each case covered only a few years, the time series are long enough to deduce the relative importance of these two sources of costs.

Both of these studies assumed that the costs of adjusting employment are symmetric – the same costs exist in response to positive and negative shocks to demand. A lot of evidence (e.g., Pfann and Palm, 1993) indicate that this assumption is incorrect, and, in particular, that at least in the aggregate the cost of upward exceed those of downward adjustments. Implicitly the costs of search and training, and perhaps to those of expanding employment, exceed those of firing workers and of temporarily functioning with fewer workers.

This discrepancy suggests estimating nonlinear models that allow for asymmetric adjustments in the path of labor demand in response to positive and negative shocks, and for distinguishing between costs due to gross changes in employment, both quits and layoffs, and net changes in employment, both positive and negative. Thus Section III.5 fills a gap that exists in both of the other studies, but at the cost, due to the complexity of specifying and estimating a complete model, of ignoring possible lumpiness in adjustment costs. Since, however, the data used in the study are highly aggregated, and since the results in Section III.3 showed that even a bit of aggregation makes adjustment costs look convex, as a broader description of the path of aggregate employment this simplification is not unreasonable.

Section III.5 grew out of my joint interest with Gerard Pfann in the dynamics of factor adjustment. Pfann had been studying asymmetry while a graduate student (e.g., Pfann and Verspagen, 1989), and we had met initially at a conference he organized in 1990. Out of that initial meeting and our similar interests, we realized that we could combine our expertise to answer a question that had been bothering both of us. This paper for me had the additional attraction that it required using the same data that underlay my Ph.D. dissertation (extended up to 1981, the end of the availability of the series). It also was the first paper that I wrote with Pfann, who is now my co-modal co-author.

While this Section covers many of the issues in labor demand, one small but growing area of inquiry has been ignored: The job-creation, job-destruction approach to the analysis of behavior at the level of establishments, pioneered by Dunne et al (1989) and Davis and Haltiwanger (1992). This approach has been especially important in macroeconomics, as it has underscored the fact that even during substantial recessions - times of substantial net decreases in employment - large numbers of new jobs are being generated. The distinction between expansions and recessions is that the balance between the huge numbers of jobs created and jobs destroyed turns negative during recessions.

That literature was novel and fundamental; but in its early stages it did not link flows of jobs to flows of workers - it did not inquire whether, for example, worker mobility, quits and layoffs were from jobs that were being destroyed or jobs that continued to exist; obversely, it did not inquire whether, for another example, new and re-hires were into newly created jobs or into continuing jobs. These are important distinctions, as they tie the micro-macro relationship between job creation and destruction to the nature of worker flows. And since we should care more about workers than about jobs *per se*, this expanded focus puts the question directly in the labor area - in the area of people and their work.

Today this kind of study is less difficult to do, since one could use the JOLTS data to examine hiring/firing and job creation/destruction at the micro and macro levels, as Lazear and Spletzer (2012) have done. Even the newly available data, however, do not allow one to get at what happens to job flows within an establishment. Thus, to take an academic example, my University would appear the same to an outside researcher if we unfortunately fired an economist and hired a sociologist as it would if we fired an economist and hired another one. Flows of labor in and out of the "firm" are identical in the two cases, and to the outsider there is no job creation or destruction. Yet these two cases clearly have different implications for what the "firm" is producing.

Even with the JOLTS there are interesting questions in labor mobility and job creation that cannot be answered, and the study in Section III.6 answers them. One of these is: How much of worker flows arises from flows of workers between jobs in the firm? How much arises from internal mobility to newly created jobs? How much is from jobs that have been destroyed? These are important questions, and gauging the magnitudes of these flows, as this study does, allows us to expand even the most recent work on worker and job flows in ways that have not been possible, or at least not considered, in any research available through 2013.

1

Labor Market Competition among Youths, White Women and Others

1.1. Introduction

The two most important phenomena in the labor market in the past fifteen years have been the influx of large numbers of young workers and the growth in participation of adult women. The former is the result of the baby boom of the 1950s; the latter stems from changes in attitudes, reductions in discrimination, and lowered prices of substitutes for women's time at home. Each phenomenon alone could have a substantial impact on the labor market. In conjunction, their effects are compounded, with each group possibly affecting the employment opportunities facing the other.

A number of observers have argued that the youth unemployment problem of the 1970s has been exacerbated by competition for jobs from the growing number of adult women workers. One has noted that "the job prospects of these youth are adversely affected, if indirectly, by the large supply of women still interested in joining the labor force. ..." Another has pointed out that even in the 1980s "competition for jobs will be intense and the three major groups of competitors will consist of young white males, young black males, and women of all working ages ..." Yet another has stated, "The growth in labor force participation by adult women probably diminished the recovery's impact on

The original version of this chapter was published as: Grant, James H./Hamermesh, Daniel S. (1981). Labor Market Competition among Youths, White Women and Others, in: The Review of Economics and Statistics, 63(3): 354–360. © 1981 by MIT Press.

the unemployment rates of all groups-especially those of teenagers and non-white women."[1] Implicit in all these remarks are two statements about how labor markets work: (1) Youth and adult women are close substitutes in production, so that an influx of the latter shifts the demand curve for youth sharply to the left; and (2) Wage rates of youth are downward rigid, so that this shift is reflected in increased unemployment rather than reduced wage rates. Because some research, e.g., Freeman and Medoff (1978), finds indirect evidence that contradicts this view, in this study we examine the direct evidence on the extent to which women and youth are in fact substitutes in production. The latter issue is ignored, though some recent evidence suggests it may not be so important a problem as many observers seem to think.[2]

While there have been numerous studies of substitution among workers of different groups, very few of these have considered substitution between age groups, and none has examined substitution among women and youth (see Hamermesh and Grant, 1979).[3] Only Freeman (1979) includes women workers as a separate category, and, because men ages 20 through 34 are aggregated, his estimates tell us little about the issue of substitution between women and youth.

To fill this gap in our knowledge and provide some substantive basis for accepting or rejecting the contentions cited above, we estimate substitution possibilities among a set of age-race-sex groups in the labor force. The estimates are based on cross-section data from SMSAs in 1969, and they allow us to consider how substitutable adult women are for young women or young men. The estimates are used, along with assumptions about the extent of wage rigidity and elasticities of labor supply, to simulate the direct and indirect effects of the growth of the female labor force on job opportunities for youth, assuming rigid wages for young workers, and on the wage rates of adult males, assuming these wages are flexible.

1.2. Estimating Equations, Methods and Data

Our estimates are based upon the translog approximation to a production surface (see Christensen et al., 1973). We estimate the production function using output shares, implicitly assuming that the production function is characterized by constant returns to scale, and firms are pricetakers in factor markets. The production function is used instead of the cost function because, at least for older workers, factor quantities are more properly viewed as exogenous than are factor prices. (See Hamermesh and

Grant, 1979, for a discussion of exogeneity assumptions appropriate for estimating production models defined over labor force subaggregates.)

Let the N-factor production function, $Q = F(X_1, ..., X_N)$, be approximated by the translog form:

$$\ln Q = \ln \alpha_0 + \Sigma_i \alpha_i \ln X_i + \frac{1}{2} \Sigma_i \Sigma_j \gamma_{ij} \ln X_i \ln X_j, \quad (1)$$

where the α_i and γ_{ij} are technology coefficients, Q is output and the X_i are inputs. With the assumption of competitive input markets, $\partial Q/\partial X_i = P_i$, the N-factor share equations for estimating the production technology are derived from the N output elasticity equations:

$$\partial \ln Q/\partial \ln X_i = P_i X_i/Q = S_i, \qquad i = 1, ..., N,$$

where P_i is the price and S_i is the output share of factor i. The factor share equations derived from (l) are

$$S_i = \alpha_i + \Sigma_j \gamma_{ij} X_j, \qquad i = 1, ..., N. \quad (2)$$

While most work analyzing production relations has focused on partial elasticities of substitution and price elasticities (see Allen, 1938), those concepts are inappropriate if we are interested in considering the effects of exogenous changes in factor quantities on factor prices. We therefore concentrate on the Hicks partial elasticities of complementarity, defined as $C_{ij} = FF_{ij}/F_iF_j$ where the F_i and F_{ij} are, respectively, first and second partial derivatives of the production function F.[4] For the translog share equations (2) these are calculated simply as

$$C_{ij} = (\gamma_{ij} + S_i S_j)/S_i S_j, \quad (3a)$$

and

$$C_{ii} = (\gamma_{ii} + S_i^2 - S_i)/S_i^2. \quad (3b)$$

They measure the ceteris paribus effect on relative factor prices of changes in relative factor quantities, holding output price and other input quantities fixed. Factors i and j are quantity complements (substitutes), so that increases in inputs of j increase (decrease) i's price, as $C_{ij} > 0$ (< 0). Associated with the C_{ij} are the factor price elasticities, $\theta_{ij} = S_j C_{ij}$, which show the change in the price of factor i given a 1% change in the quantity of factor j, holding output price constant.

In the production-function tableau of (2) one cannot derive unbiased estimates of the γ_{ij} parameters, and thus of the C_{ij}. unless one assumes input supply is exogenous. Obversely, in the more commonly used cost-function tableau, one must assume all input prices are exogenous. Since wage flexibility seems, as noted above, to be a pervasive characteristic of the U.S. labor market, and since the evidence suggests labor supply is quite inelastic for most groups of workers, we can be fairly confident that the use of the production function approach is more appropriate than would be the estimation of a cost function.[5] Nonetheless, in our study, as in *every* study that has estimated production technologies, a general equilibrium approach that specified supply relationships as part of the model would improve the results (at the cost of substantial complexity).

The data are constructed for 1969.[6] Employment data for manufacturing are taken from the one-in-a-thousand sample of the County Group *Public Use Samples of Basic Records from the 1970 Census*. Capital and output data are gathered from issues of the *Census of Manufactures* and the *Annual Survey of Manufactures*. The County Group *Public Use Samples* identify all SMSAs over 250,000 in population in 1970. The production model is estimated over the 67 SMSAs for which all the data could be constructed for the factor inputs youths 14–24 (*Y*); adult blacks (*OB*); white women (*OFW*); white men (*OMW*); and capital (*K*).[7]

The assumptions of symmetry, $\gamma_{ij} = \gamma_{ji}$, and homogeneity, $\Sigma\alpha_i = 1$, $\Sigma_i\gamma_{ij} = \Sigma_j\gamma_{ij} = \Sigma_i\Sigma_j\gamma_{ij} = 0$, are imposed upon the model in (2). The system of share equations (2) is then estimated using the iterativ Zellner method, a maximum-likelihood technique, over the cross-section data for manufacturing in 1969. In addition to being the first to examine substitution between youth and adult women, our estimates are among the few that use cross-section data to estimate parameters from flexible functional forms describing production relations.

Table 1.1

Tests for Weak Separability

Factor Inputs		χ^2	df
a.	(Y, OFW), OB, OMW, K	1. 29	3
b.	(Y, OB), OFW, OMW, K	35.16[a]	3
c.	(OB, OMW), Y, OFW, K	36.803[a]	3
d.	(Y, OB, OFW), OMW, K	20.03[a]	4
e.	(Y, OB, OMW), OFW, K	38.08[a]	4
f.	(Y, OB. OFW. OMW), K	28.90[a]	3

Note: Parentheses surround the inputs whose aggregation is tested.
[a] Denotes Significance at the 0.01 level.

1.3. Estimates of Elasticities of Complementarity and of Factor Prices

Before discussing the elasticity estimates based on the parameters estimated in the cross section for manufacturing in 1969, it is worthwhile considering whether the complete model in (2) is needed to describe production relations among the five factors, or whether instead some types of separability can be imposed. Most interesting would be if we found that the labor subgroups are jointly separable from capital. Though time-series studies using broad occupational categories (blue-collar and white-collar labor) do not find this (see Berndt and Christensen, 1974; and Denny and Fuss, 1977), it may be implied by cross-section data covering the small demographic subgroups used in this study that are of major interest for labor-market policy. If so, we can conclude that estimates of the potential impact of such policies can be simulated without using capital stock data that are often difficult to construct.

Table 1.2

Elasticities of Factor Complemenarity

	With Respect to Quantity of				
Price of	*Y*	*OB*	*OFW*	*OMW*	*K*
Y	-0.639	0.592	-2.35	0.128	0.236
	(12.37)	(0.46)	(4.78)	(2.89)	(3.09)
	(0.09)	(0.64)	(1.15)	(0.25)	(0.79)
OB		-11.2	0.312	-0.145	0.905
		(12.87)	(1.29)	(4.36)	(0. 39)
		(0.94)	(0.50)	(0.27)	(3.83)
OFW			-2.99	0.056	0.568
			(18.08)	(4.83)	(3.08)
			(1.76)	(0.15)	(3.99)
OMW				-0.349	0.261
				(9.51)	(5.80)
				(2.44)	(4.05)
K					-0.374
					(5.45)
					(2.88)

Note: The first number in parentheses below each elasticity here and in Table 1.3 is the absolute *t*-statistic on the γ_{ij} coefficient upon which the elasticity is based. The second is the absolute *t*-statistic computed using a Taylor-series approximation to the elasticity.

Unfortunately, the imposition of various restrictions implied by weak separability of various sets of inputs from the others is generally inconsistent with the data.[8] In Table 1.1 we present the χ^2 statistics testing for weak separability in six cases which implicitly test popular notions about the extent to which various groups are similar. The only pair of inputs for which the hypothesis of a consistent aggregate is not rejected is youths and adult white women. Youths and adult blacks cannot be treated as an aggregate, nor can adult blacks and adult white males. White adult males are also not separable from other demographic groups, nor are adult white women. Finally, and corroborating the results of the several time-series studies that have tested for separability of (blue- and white-collar) labor from capital, the hypothesis that they are separable is decisively rejected. This implies that studies that do not include measures of the capital stock are likely producing unreliable estimates of the parameters describing substitution between the labor subaggregates.[9]

Table 1.2 presents the estimated C_{ij}. It is difficult to decide what are the appropriate measures of variance to attach to these parameter estimates (and to the θ_{ij} in Table 1.3). Accordingly, the first number in parentheses is the *t*-statistic on the estimated γ_{ij} underlying the calculation of C_{ij} or C_{ii} in (3). The second is based on a Taylor-series approximation that implicitly treats the S_i and S_j in (3) as stochastic (see Anderson, 1979).

The most striking finding in Table 1.2 is clearly that youths and adult white women are strongly substitutable in manufacturing. The estimated γ_{ij} upon which the C_{ij} is based is highly significant; even if we assume that the shares are stochastic and approximate (3a) by a Taylor-series, we still find that the estimated C_{ij} exceeds its standard error. The casual empiricism cited in section 1 of this chapter appears to have at least some foundation on the demand side of the labor market. We also find that older blacks and adult white males are substitutes. This result follows unsurprisingly from the observation that older blacks in manufacturing are mainly adult men who are likely to be close substitutes for adult white men. All the other pairs of labor categories are seen to be complements, though in no case is the complementarity relationship very strong.

Table 1.3 shows the elasticities of factor prices computed from the average fitted factor shares and the partial elasticities of complementarity. It is worth noting that the largest cross elasticity between any labor pair is that between the substitutes *Y* and *OFW*. The own-quantity factor price elasticities are quite small. They suggest that relative increases in the supply of one type of labor can be absorbed with only a small decline in its relative wage (if wages are free to adjust). Though not strictly comparable to the factor demand elasticities discussed in Hamermesh Grant (1979), their implication is similar. Interestingly, too, the lowest own-quantity elasticity is for youths, implying that a market with flexible wages could very easily accommodate a large change in the relative size of the youth labor force.

As the results in Tables 1.2 and 1.3 show, each labor group is complementary with inputs of physical capital. This finding is inconsistent with Freeman's (1979) time-series results on adult women and adult men. It parallels, though, that for white-collar workers in the many time-series studies that use an occupational classification, but may be inconsistent with their results that blue-collar workers are substitutes for capital.[10] It suggests that, for purposes of evaluating labor market policies, most of which are directed at workers categorized by demographic group, we may infer that labor subaggregates and capital are complements. This implies generally that policies that increase employment in a particular labor subgroup will raise the rate of return to capital.[11]

Table 1.3
Elasticities of Factor Prices

	With Respect to Quantity of				
Price of	*Y*	*OB*	*OFW*	*OMW*	*K*
Y	-0.0300	0.0226	-0.1532	0.0476	0.1130
	(12.37)	(0.46)	(4.78)	(2.89)	(3.09)
	(0.9)	(0.28)	(1.34)	(0.24)	(0.84)
OB	0.0278	-0.4282	0.0203	-0.0536	0.4337
	(0.46)	(12.87)	(1.29)	(4.36)	(0.39)
	(0.30)	(0.92)	(0.50)	(0.29)	(3.93)
OFW	-0.1105	0.0119	-0.1943	0.0209	0.2721
	(4. 78)	(1.29)	(18.08)	(4.83)	(3.08)
	(1.62)	(0.45)	(1.39)	(0.16)	(5.26)
OMW	0.0060	-0.0055	0.0037	-0.1292	0.1250
	(2.89)	(4.36)	(4.83)	(9.51)	(5.80)
	(0.24)	(0.35)	(0.16)	(2.25)	(3.62)
K	0.0111	0.0346	0.0369	0.0966	-0.1792
	(3.09)	(0.39)	(3.08)	(5.80)	(5.45)
	(0.71)	(2.28)	(2.91)	(3.04)	(2.88)

1.4. The Effect of an Exogenous Increase in White Female Participation

In this section we examine the impact of a 10% increase in the number of white women in the labor force, using the five-factor production model involving youths, adult blacks, white women, white men and capital.[12] The simulation is designed to gauge the effects of the tremendous increase in female labor force participation that has occurred since the early 1960s. Whether employment displacement occurred, or whether the effect has been to reduce the relative wage rates of youth, depends on whether in fact relative wage rates of youth are rigid. In our simulation we calculate the impact of the increase in adult white female employment under the two extreme assumptions of completely flexible and completely rigid wages in the youth labor market.[13]

Let P_i be the price of factor i, $i = 1, \ldots, N$, and assume that all P_i are flexible except that of young workers, whose wage is fixed at P^*_1.[14] Firms determine their demands for factor inputs from the usual marginal productivity conditions:

$$(4) \qquad P^*_1 = F_1 (X_1, X^*_2, \ldots, X^*_N),$$

$$(5) \qquad P_i = F_i (X_1, X^*_2, \ldots, X^*_N), \qquad i = 2, \ldots, N,$$

where X^*_i is employment of the ith factor, which is exogenous to the economy under the assumption of inelastic labor supply, and F_i is the partial derivative of F.

Differentiating the N equations in (4) and (5), we have

$$-F_{11}dX_1 - \sum_{j=2}^{N} F_{1j}dX^*_j = 0;$$

$$dP_i - F_{i1}dX_1 - \sum_{j=2}^{N} F_{ij}dX^*_j = 0, \qquad i = 2, \ldots, N.$$

Solving this system yields

$$(6) \qquad dX_1/dX^*_j = -F_{1j}/F_{11}, \; j = 2, \ldots, N,$$

$$(7) \qquad dP_i/dX^*_j = (-F_{i1}F_{1j} + F_{ij}F_{11})/F_{11}; \qquad i, j = 2, \ldots, N.$$

Multiplying both sides of (6) by X_j/X_1; noting that $F_{ij} = P_iP_jC_{ij}/Q$ and that $X_i = QS_i/P_i$ under the assumption of constant returns to scale, we have

$$(8) \qquad d \ln X_1/d \ln X^*_j = -S_jC_{1j}/S_1C_{11}; \qquad j = 2, \ldots, N.$$

Similarly, multiplying both sides of (7) by X^*_j/P_i, and making the same substitutions for F_{ij} and X_i, we have

$$(9) \qquad d \ln P_i/d \ln X^*_j = S_j(-C_{i1}C_{1j} + C_{ij}C_{11})/C_{11}; \qquad i, j = 2, \ldots, N.$$

Equations (8) and (9) allow us to use the estimates in Table 1.2 to calculate the effect of an increase in adult white female employment on the employment of youths and on the wage rates of workers in other demographic groups, under the assumption that youths' wage rates are rigid. Equation (8) states simply that the effect on youth employment is larger and more negative the greater is the extent of *q*-substitutability of white women and youths, the larger is the share of white women in output, and the smaller is the share of youths. Equation (9) states that the effect on other factor prices depends both on their partial elasticities of complementarity with white women *and* on the degree to which they are *q*-complements or substitutes with youths and that youths are *q*-substitutes with white women. (The first term in parentheses enters because P^*_1 is assumed fixed.) If all wages are flexible, the calculations reduce to

(10) $$d \ln P_i / d \ln X^*_j = S_j C_{ij} = \theta_{ij}; \qquad i, j = 1, \ldots, N,$$

the factor price elasticities listed in Table 1.3.

The simulated effects of a 10% increase in the labor force of adult white women are shown in column (1) of Table 1.4, under the assumption that the wages of young workers are rigid. As they show, the ease with which our estimates in Table 1.2 imply employers can substitute white women for youths gives rise to an unbelievably large decrease in the employment of youths in this simulation. Moreover, even though white women and adult blacks, and white women and white men, are complements, the simulated effect of the increase in the white female labor force is to decrease the wage rates of adult blacks and white men. These effects occur because the first term in the numerator in (9) outweighs the second due to the relative ease with which employers can substitute white women for youths. The rise in adult white female employment induces a direct increase in the wage rates of its complements, adult blacks and white men, but this is more than offset by the induced decline in their wages as employers substitute white women for youths.

If one takes the view that wages of youth are not rigid in the long run, the appropriate estimates of the effect of the increased female participation are those shown in column (2) of the table. These are moderate decreases in the wage rates of white women and youths, and slight increases in the wage rates of the other inputs. These estimates are likely to be closer approximations to reality under the flexible-wage assumption than are those in column (1) under the fixed-wage assumption. This is because the translog estimates on which they are based are for a production function that implicitly assumes that factor quantities are all exogenous, and thus implicitly is based on a model of flexible wages.

Table 1.4
Simulation Results

Percentage Change in	(1)[a]	(2)[b]
Youth Employment	-51.1	
Wage Rate of		
Youths		-1.5
Adult White Women		-1.9
Adult Blacks	-1.2	0.2
Adult White Males	-0.3	0.04
Price of Capital	0.2	0.4

Note: (1) assumes rigid wages for youth; (2) assumes all wages are flexible.
[a] Based on equations (8) and (9).
[b] Based on equation (10).

Regardless of whether one believes that wages of young workers are rigid or flexible, we have shown that, because youths and white women are substitutes in production, the flow of white women into the labor market has caused some displacement in the earnings of young workers. Under the fixed-wage assumption this displacement would have taken the form of reduced employment; under the flexible-wage assumption, it would have manifested itself as a reduction in wage rates, and thus a steeper cross-section age-earnings profile than would have otherwise been observed. Part, perhaps 10%, of the sharp relative decline in earnings of young workers that occurred in the late 1960s and 1970s (see Freeman, 1979, and Welch, 1979) is thus attributable to the increase in the adult female labor force. The baby boom of the 1950s is not the only reason for the relative decline in earnings in the youth labor force.

1.5. Conclusions

Our estimates and those of Grant (1979) are the first that present tests for the separability of labor from capital using a disaggregation of the labor force based on a classification other than by occupation. The results are clear and somewhat depressing: Studies that seek to estimate the extent of substitution in production among demographic groups must include measures of the capital stock. Given the difficulties of constructing such measures even for the economy as a whole over time, and the near impossibility of building up a capital measure for nonmanufacturing industries in a cross section, our ability to derive accurate estimates of substitution parameters describing the demand for labor is limited. Indeed, because of the inappropriateness of assuming separability, even unbiased estimates of the own-price demand elasticity for small groups cannot be produced using data on the group alone.

Our most important finding is the extent to which white women and youths are substitutes in production. We have shown, at least in the cross-section data for 1969 that we have used, and assuming the production-function approach is the more appropriate one for this disaggregation of the work force, that market forces change the relative wages received by these two groups of workers in a direction opposite that of the change in their relative quantities. We have also demonstrated that each type of labor in our age-race-sex disaggregation is complementary with capital, a finding that is partly consistent with the time-series results for blue-collar and white-collar labor. It is inconsistent with past results that are based on the disaggregation of the labor force by age and that use the inappropriate (for this disaggregation) cost-function specification.

Our estimates of white female-youth substitution imply strongly that the growth of the white female labor force has hurt the earnings prospects of young workers. Whether this effect has worked through a decrease in employment or a reduction in wages cannot be determined here. However, that it has occurred is the logical conclusion from our finding that these two groups are easily substituted in production, and the observation that there has been a sharp increase in adult female labor force participation in the past fifteen years. Competition from adult women has very likely had a negative impact on the labor market for youths.

2

Spectral Analysis of the Relation between Gross Employment Changes and Output Changes, 1958–1966

This chapter has the dual purpose of presenting spectral analysis in a different, perhaps more appropriate application than that of past work and of analyzing differences among industries in the relation of gross changes in employment and changes in output. Spectral analysis has been applied to a problem in labor economics only once.[1] The cause of the dearth of studies using the technique is possibly the limited number of observations available on most variables relating to labor. Even if we had such information, there are relatively few problems for which spectral analysis might be expected to give interesting results. The technique does not seem to have produced much new evidence about the cyclical relationships to which it has been applied, perhaps because we have so few observations on complete cycles in economic activity, or perhaps because these low-frequency movements are of such irregular length as to be undetectable by spectral analysis.[2] Because of these problems the major use of this technique in labor economics must lie in the analysis of behavior reflected at higher frequencies, particularly to those we call "seasonal." It is only at those frequencies that we have enough information on behavior to make any inferences about it.

The original version of this chapter was published as: Hamermesh, Daniel S. (1969). Spectral Analysis of the Relation between Gross Employment Changes and Output Changes, 1958–1966, in: The Review of Economics and Statistics, 51(1): 62–69.
The research on which this chapter was performed under grant GS-818 from the National Science Foundation to Yale University. I am deeply grateful to Marc Nerlove for his helpful criticism of the paper, as well as to Mark Leiserson for numerous illuminating discussions.

2.1. Implications of Specific Training for Seasonal Changes in Employment

Interindustry differences in the relation between employment and output represent one area in which a theory can be developed and then tested by examining seasonal behavior using spectral analysis. Moreover, the theory cannot be adequately tested, at least as it applies to seasonal changes, by use of the familiar regression techniques of econometrics. Only spectral analysis, which transforms a time series from the time domain to the frequency domain, allows a complete examination of cycles in data.

Assume that some amount of specific training is required for jobs in an industry and assume further that firms have no control over the level of quits from the industry.[3] This implies that demands of firms for new hires and layoffs are residual demands from the level of quits. Given these assumptions, firms would, in order to avoid making unnecessary investments in the training of new workers, and to avoid losing the investments in workers they already employ, prefer to modify the size of their work forces by changing the level of new hires rather than that of layoffs. In particular, they should prefer to meet seasonal changes in output change by increasing or decreasing new hires and trying to avoid layoffs as much as possible. The present analysis abstracts from the presence of workers who are hired for a short period in full knowledge that they will be laid off at the end of that period (women in the canning industry are a standard example of such a phenomenon). Such hiring and laying off will of course give rise to seasonality in the layoffs series as well as in new hires. Nonetheless, the replacement of workers who quit will result in a seasonal component in new hires which is greater than that in layoffs, if output change itself has some seasonal variation. We should thus expect to find that in most industries the spectrum of new hires has more power at the seasonal frequencies than does that of layoffs.

If supply conditions are assumed to remain constant, firms in the industry in which training is essential for most workers will have an incentive to minimize changes in new hires and layoffs in response to seasonal variations in output changes. Such firms will try to avoid incurring training costs in workers who are only needed to help meet seasonal peaks in product demand. Industries in which little training is required to enable potential new hires to work efficiently, might be expected to expand and contract their work force to a greater extent as product demand changes seasonally.

In industries with high training costs we should expect relatively flat spectra for the series on new hires and layoffs, even when the series on output change shows decisive peaks at the seasonal frequencies. Industries with relatively unimportant specific training might be expected to have hires, layoffs and output changes series with spectra exhibiting marked seasonal peaks. A comparison of these spectra for a number of industries thus provides evidence as to whether the specific training hypothesis is a valid explanation for interindustry differences in the behavior of gross changes in employment.

The firm can also change its labor input in response to seasonal variations in output change by modifying the average workweek. Those industries in which much training is required would presumably show greater seasonal fluctuations in average hours worked, and this consideration should lead us to examine the spectra of such series. Data on average· hours *worked* unfortunately do not exist, and the series we do have, average hours paid for, will be poor substitutes because of the inclusion of *paid* vacations. Since these vary seasonally and are more important in precisely those industries in which training requirements are high, average hours paid for cannot be expected to reflect the seasonality in the average workweek.

These arguments have proceeded as if firms forecast perfectly the demand for their products and thus that adjustment costs alone determine desired labor input. In the seasonal context the regular annual variations in demand justify the assumption that firms forecast perfectly the seasonal component of that demand. In the cyclical context, however, we could not make this assumption, for expectations are rarely perfect over the business cycle. If we examined longer cycles we would have to modify the discussion to include some theory of firms' responses to deviations of actual from expected product demand.

It may be that a theory of union wage policy and of employer reaction to the policy can be constructed that would explain differences in the spectra of the employment changes series both within and among industries.[4] For example, if union work-spreading rules were prevalent throughout unionized industry we would observe little seasonal variation in layoffs there, and somewhat more in the layoffs series in non-unionized industries. It is more difficult to imagine union policy affecting the seasonality in new hires directly, since

Table 2.1 Analysis Based on Data for Twenty-Eight Industries

Industry and Group	SIC	Specific Training Required 1950 (years) (1)	Workers in Unionized Establishments, 1958 (per cent) (2)	Semiskilled and Unskilled Workers, 1960 (per cent) (3)	Payroll per Employee, 1963 (dollars) (4)
Group I:					
Cement, hydraulic	324	1.05	77.9	56.8	6522
Iron and steel foundries	332	1.15	88.6	50.6	6179
Aluminum rolling drawing and extruding	3352	1.24	88.6	49.5	6941
Nonferrous foundries	336	1.24	88.6	49.5	5950
Metal cans	341	1.26	70.6	43.4	7081
Heating equipment	3433	1.26	70.6	43.4	5803
Household refrigerators and freezers	3632	1.38	72.8	46.0	6501
Household laundry equipment	3633	1.38	72.8	46.0	6291
Radio and TV receiving sets	365	1.38	72.8	46.0	5053
Plastic materials and resins	2821	1.47	65.4	37.9	7130
Synthetic fibers	2823,4	1.17	65.4	53.1	6193

Column 1: Specific Vocational Preparation, in years, as estimated in (2, pp, 187–189). These figures and those in column 3 are based on the Census breakdown of industries, a division which is not as fine as three-digit SIC breakdown. Thus some of the industries in our sample fall into the same Census category and will have identical figures in columns 1 and 3, while in most cases the figures in these columns are based on other, closely allied industries, as well as on the industry for which we have listed them. While this is undoubtedly a problem, the estimates in this table are the finest breakdown available. Moreover, in view of the similarity of industries grouped together by the Census, the error should not, I believe, be overwhelming.

Column 2: Percentage of workers in the industry employed in establishments in which the majority of workers are unionized. H.M. Douty, "Collective Bargaining Coverage in Factory Employment," Monthly Labor Review (April, 1960), p, 347.

Column 3: Operatives + service workers + laborers as a per cent of total employment in the industry grouping, Census of Population, 1960, PC(2)-7C, Subject Report, Occupation by Industry, table 2.

Column 4: Total payroll divided by number of employees on the payroll in March, 1963, in operating establishments, Census of Manufactures, 1963, I, Summary Statistics "General Summary," table III, pp, 48–62.

Table 2.1 (Continued)

Industry and Group	SIC	Specific Training Required 1950 (years) (1)	Workers in Unionized Establishments, 1958 (per cent) (2)	Semiskilled and Unskilled Workers, 1960 (per cent) (3)	Payroll per Employee, 1963 (dollars) (4)
Group II:					
Sawmills and planning mills	242	.78	43.8	70.7	3856
Millwork	2431	.78	43.8	70.7	4914
Veneer and plywood	2432	.78	43.8	70.7	4909
Glass containers	3221	.88	77.9	61.9	5467
Brick and structural clay tile	3251	.79	77.9	67.9	4555
Confectionary and related products	207	.70	68.1	61.9	4490
Cigarettes	211	.63	62.6	67.5	5146
Cigars	212	.63	62.6	67.5	3285
Wool weaving and finishing	223	.98	30.1	72.9	4278
Men's and boys' suits and coats	231	.64	59.7	80.0	4029
Men's and boys' furnishings	232	.64	59.7	80.0	2943
Paperboard	263	.82	75.5	57.7	6767
Corrugated and solid fiber boxes	2653	.97	75.5	59.2	5834
Tires and inner tubes	301	.97	80.6	58.5	7292
Other rubber products	302,3,6	.97	80.6	58.5	5537
Leather tanning and finishing	311	.79	49.3	71.8	5198
Footwear, except rubber	314	.55	49.3	77.4	3541

most unions in manufacturing establishments concern themselves mainly with the job opportunities of current employees. In any case, it is true that the analysis of this chapter cannot discriminate between possible causes of the phenomena under consideration.

2.2. Data and Method

Data for twenty-eight industries form the basis for the analysis presented here. These industries comprise all three- and four-digit industries for which monthly production data are available and for which these data are based on physical or value measures rather than on man-hours worked. (Use of production data based on man-hours would have, of course, little value in a study relating employment change to output change.) The production data are computed by the Federal Reserve Board on the basis of trade association data and reports collected by the Bureau of Census (3). The series on new hires, quits and layoffs are published by the Bureau of Labor Statistics on the basis of a sample covering the majority of workers employed in manufacturing (1). These data are available from January 1958, and nine full years of data were used in the analysis.

The twenty-eight industries were divided into two groups according to the level of specific training required in each of them, as estimated by Eckaus (2) on the basis of the occupational mix in each industry and the estimates of the Employment Service of specific vocational training required for each occupation. (1.00 on Eckaus' index was used as an arbitrary dividing line.) Table 2.1 shows this breakdown and also gives measures of the extent of unionism, of the occupational structure in each industry, and of wages and salaries per worker in each industry. As can be seen from table 2.1, industries in group I are generally those which are more heavily unionized, which employ more highly-skilled workers and in which the wage level is relatively high. This points up the difficulty of identifying the causation of whatever results this study brings out.

The raw data on new hires, quits, layoffs and output changes were prewhitened using a stepwise autoregressive procedure (8) that selected from the detrended series $x(t) = X(t) - \bar{X}$ those lags which gave significant coefficients. The spectral density functions were then computed using the Parzen weighting scheme for the autocovariances, with weights defined as:

$$(1) \qquad W(j/M) = \begin{cases} 1 - 6j^2/M^2\,(1 - j/M) & 0 \leq j < M/2 \\ 2(1 - j/M)^3 & M/2 \leq j \leq M \end{cases}$$

where *M* is the truncation point in the summation of the series in

$$(2) \qquad f_{xx}(k) = 1/2\pi\,\{c_{xx}(0) + 2\sum_{j=1}^{j=M} c_{xx}(j)\cos \pi kj/MW \quad (j/M)\},$$

the equation for the spectrum of the process *x(t)*. In this study we restricted *M* to be 36 months, since our observations on the series were limited to 108 months. Finally, the raw spectra were "recolored" by dividing at each frequency by the transfer function of the fitted autoregression at that frequency.[5]

2.3. Comparisons of the Spectra

It is impossible to present graphically all 112 spectra which were computed in this analysis, so we show the results only for a typical industry in each of our two groups (Figures 2.1 and 2.2). Tables 2.2 and 2.3 present a coded summary of the spectral shapes of each of the 112 series. The degree of seasonal variation in a series cannot be represented by the spectral density at any single frequency. We have therefore superimposed a 90 per cent confidence interval around the density functions. If the function lies outside the confidence interval at any frequency band we conclude that there is a significant accumulation of power at that frequency. ((4, p. 63) for details on the construction of confidence intervals around power spectra.) With monthly data there are six seasonal harmonics, so that each density function may have as many as six significant seasonal peaks.

Remembering that our theoretical argument hinges on the presence of seasonal variation in the output changes series, we must first inquire whether this condition is satisfied. In all but four industries we find five or six significant peaks at the seasonal harmonics, and only one of those four fails to show any significant seasonal peaks. The requirement that there be significant seasonal movement in output thus seems well satisfied. The presence of greater power at the higher frequencies in these spectra is undoubtedly due to the use of percentage output change, a procedure which produces low-order negative autocorrelation if little positive autocorrelation exists in the original series.

We also argued that, if quit rates in the various industries have similar spectral shapes and layoffs and new hires have substantially different spectral shapes, we may conclude that quits are independent of conditions in the particular small industry grouping. This conclusion appears to be justified by the results of the analysis. The spectra of the new hires and layoffs series vary greatly in shape across industries. In sixteen industries, though, the spectrum of quits has significant peaks at all six seasonal harmonics, and in each industry there is a significant accumulation of power at one seasonal harmonic or more.

In short, both of our stipulations appear valid (or at least as valid as one may claim on the basis of empirical work) and we can proceed to examine whether one prediction based on the presence of specific training, namely the greater seasonality of new hires than of layoffs, is demonstrated empirically. A comparison of the spectra of these two series in each of the twenty-eight industries shows twenty for which the new hires series has more significant peaks than does the layoffs series. In three industries the strength of seasonal movements appears the same in the two series, while in five others the layoffs series has a stronger seasonal component than the new hires series. Thus in a substantial majority of industries the results can be explained by the effects of the specific training of workers on employer behavior.

Figures 2.1 and 2.2 illustrate these results for the nonferrous foundries industry, SIC 336, representing group I, and for the paperboard industry, SIC 263, representing group II. In both industries the spectra of output changes and quits have marked peaks at the seasonal harmonics, the spectral density at the harmonics being more than ten times greater than the density at the nearby troughs in most cases. The greater seasonality in new hires is especially apparent in the paperboard industry. The spectrum of the new hires series has seasonal peaks as strong as those in the output change series, while the spectrum of layoffs has only small blips at the seasonal harmonics.

The specific training hypothesis also predicts that industries in what we have designated group I will have spectra of new hires and layoffs which have relatively less power at the seasonal harmonics than those in the group II industries. In comparing the spectra of the new hires series we use a simple chi-square test on the two-by-two contingency table implicit in columns 1 and 3 of Table 2.4. This test yields $\chi^2(1) = 3.59$, significant at the sixth percentile of the chi-square distribution. The test is only as correct as our placing of the dividing line between the two groups of industries. Its results are corroborated, though, by the

Figure 2.1
SIC 336

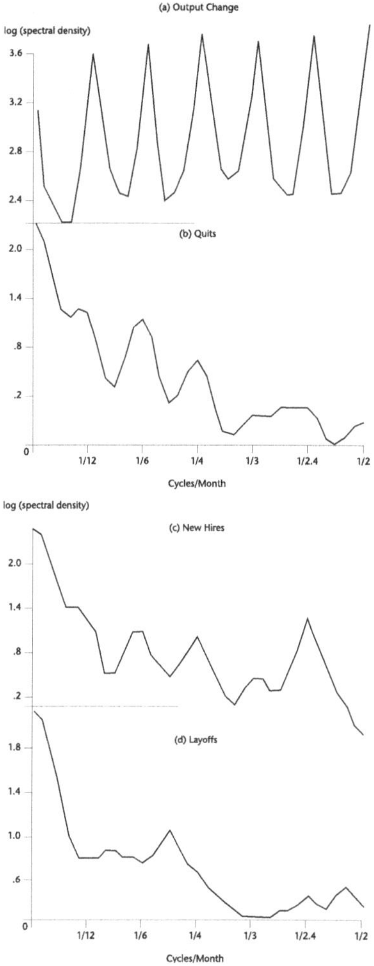

Figure 2.2
SIC 263

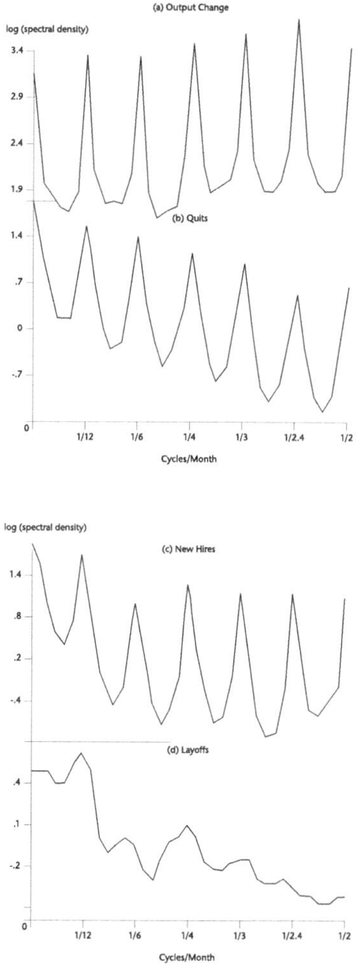

rank correlation of the number of seasonal peaks and the required level of training. The correlation coefficient is *-0.20*, negative and nearly significant, and it becomes significant (*-0.32*) when we delete SIC 2821 and 2823, the two nondurable goods industries in group I, from the sample. It appears that in those industries in which new workers must be better trained for their jobs the level of new hires fluctuates much less seasonally than it does in those industries which require less specific training.

There is some weak evidence that seasonal fluctuations in layoffs are

Table 2.2

Summary of the Shapes of the Spectra for the Time Series, Group I

SIC	Output Change	Quits	New Hires	Layoffs
324	5-F	6-D	6-D	2-D
332	5-F	2-D	1-D	0-D
3352	O-U-36	6-D	1-D	0-D
336	6-U	2-D	1-D	0-D
341	5-U	6-D	1-D	5-F
3433	6-U	6-D	2-D	O-D-36
3632	6-U	1-D	0-D	1-F
3633	6-U	3-D	0-D	0-F
365	6-U	6-D	2-D	1-D
2821	6-U	6-D	6-F	0-D
2823,4	2-F	6-D	6-D	0-D

U more power at the higher frequencies than the lower ones.
F spectrum is relatively flat, except for seasonal peaks.
D more power at the lower frequencies than the higher ones.
36 the power spectrum has an additional peak at the frequency band corresponding to a 36-month cycle.

Table 2.3

Summary of the Shapes of the Spectra for the Time Series, Group II

SIC	Output Change	Quits	New Hires	Layoffs
242	6-U	4-D	3-D	2-D
2431	6-F	6-D	3-D	1-D
2432	6-U	6-D	6-D	0-D
3221	6-U	6-D	1-D	1-D
3251	6-F	3-D	1-D	6-F
207	6-U	3-D	4-D	6-F
211	5-U	6-D	3-D	0-F
212	6-U	2-D	0-D	0-U
223	2-F	6-D	5-D	1-D
231	6-U	6-D	0-D	1-D
232	5-U	3-F	6-D	0-D
263	6-U	6-D	6-D	0-D
2653	6-U	6-D	6-D	0-D
301	3-U	6-D	1-D	0-D
302,3,6	6-U	2-D	1-D	0-D
311	6-U	3-D	4-D	1-D
314	6-U	4-D	5-D	2-D

Key: See Table 2.2

Table 2.4
Seasonal Components of the Spectra of New Hires and Layoffs

	Group I		Group II	
	New Hires (1)	Layoffs (2)	New Hires (3)	Layoffs (4)
Total seasonal harmonics with significant peaks	26	9	55	21
Total seasonal harmonics with no significant peaks	40	57	47	81
Total	66	66	102	102

Source: Tables 2.2 and 2.3.

more marked in those industries which require relatively little investment in specific training. A chi-square test on columns 2 and 4 of Table 2.4 yields $\chi^2(1) = 1.52$, which lies at the twenty-fourth percentile of the chi-square distribution. The rank correlation coefficient between the number of seasonal peaks and the level of training is negative (*-0.17*), but not significant.

Since the results for the spectra of the layoffs series do not provide satisfactory support of the specific training hypothesis, we proceeded to examine the spectra of quits in the group II industries. If those industries in which the spectrum of layoffs shows little seasonality are also those in which quits are strongly seasonal, it would indicate that seasonal fluctuations in quits enabled firms in these industries to avoid layoffs. There is some evidence in support of this latter hypothesis. SIC 242, 3251, 207 and 314, those four industries in which the spectrum of the layoffs series had at least two significant seasonal peaks, are among those for which the quits series show the fewest seasonal peaks. In addition, in all those industries in group II for which the spectrum of quits had six significant peaks the spectrum of layoffs had one or no seasonal peaks. Interindustry differences in the seasonality of layoffs are evident, but they are mitigated by the reliance of employers on seasonal variations in quits to avoid layoffs.

2.4. Conclusions

In this study spectral analysis was used to examine an economic problem manifesting itself in seasonal differences in behavior. The theoretical effects of required specific training of workers on hiring and laying off do appear to be substantiated by this interindustry comparison of seasonal behavior. We find that in most industries seasonal fluctuations in new hires are greater than those in layoffs, as expected if entrepreneurs minimize costs by avoiding layoffs of those workers in whom they have an investment in the form of specific training. It is clear that in industries in which specific training of workers is more important, the level of new hires fluctuates much less seasonally than it does in those industries in which less training is required. This difference is also reflected, though not very clearly, in seasonal movements in layoffs. These last two results may possibly be caused by differences among industries in the levels at which hiring and laying off take place. Without vastly more detailed data than are now available, though, we have no way of knowing if these differences exist.

The results of this analysis have an interesting implication for wage theory and perhaps for policy. Popular literature contains many discussions of the incentive effects of vested pension plans on worker mobility. Oi (6, p. 545) has analyzed empirically the effects of specific training on workers' desires to remain in their present jobs. Both of these considerations derive from the supply behavior of workers. The results of our analysis, in particular our finding of little seasonal variation in layoffs in most industries, indicate that investment in training affects the *demand* as well as the supply side to decrease the interfirm mobility of labor.

3

Labor Demand and the Structure of Adjustment Costs

Most models of factor adjustment assume smooth paths toward a final equilibrium when the fundamental determinants of factor demand are shocked. Most recent econometric work has even assumed that adjustment is characterized by a geometric lag structure. The purposes of this study are to reexamine the theory underlying these assumptions, to discover whether they make sense empirically, and to consider the implications of alternative estimates that allow one to infer the structure of adjustment costs.

This reexamination is necessary for several reasons. Without specifying and estimating equations properly, we cannot know if predictions of the paths of factor demand are affected by specifications that fail to embody the underlying structure of adjustment costs at the plant level. Second, in most European countries, and increasingly in the United States, too, a variety of labor market policies has been enacted in the past 15 years that could affect the adjustment of labor demand. (See John Gennard, 1985). Without knowing the structure of adjustment costs, we cannot link specific policies to the costs they might impose.

I begin by examining the conventional wisdom about factor adjustment, including issues of aggregation and discussing the nature of the costs associated with hiring and changing employment. I analyze the optimal path of employment under differing costs of adjustment and

---

The original version of this chapter was published as: Hamermesh, Daniel S. (1989). Labor Demand and the Structure of Adjustment Costs, in: The American Economic Review, 79(4): 674–689. I thank John Goddeeris, Steve Martin, Kevin M. Murphy. Sherwin Rosen, a referee, participants in seminars at the NBER and several universities in Australia and the United States, and especially the people who provided the data used in Section 3.3. The company in Section 3.3 must remain anonymous.

specify a set of estimating equations. These are studied using data on individual plants and then on longer timeseries on highly disaggregated industries. The analysis provides the first tests of competing hypotheses about the structure of the costs of adjusting labor demand, and it does so using the appropriate micro data.

3.1. The Conventional Wisdom and the Nature of Labor Costs

The standard model of dynamic factor demand specifies a system such as :

$$(1) \qquad X_{it} = F(X_{1,t-1}, \ldots, X_{i,t-m}, \ldots, X_{I,t-M}, Z_{1t}, \ldots, Z_{j,t-n}, \ldots, Z_{J,t-N}),$$
$$i = 1, \ldots, I;\ m = 1, \ldots, M;$$
$$j = 1, \ldots, J;\ n = 1, \ldots, N,$$

where t denotes time, the X_i are inputs, and the Z_j are exogenous variables. In early studies and in recent studies concentrating on how expectations affect the variables in Z, $I = M = 1$-a simple geometric lag structure is imposed and the adjustment of demand for the single input of interest is assumed to be independent of the adjustment of demand for other inputs. (Thus Sherwin Rosen, 1968, examines the employment hours ratio with $I = M = 1$). In the estimation of large macroeconomic models the assumption is that $M = 1$ has become standard (for example, Ray Fair, 1984).[1]

Convex adjustment costs underlie (1). Apparently this assumption originated in Charles Holt et al. (1960). Yet those authors noted, "Whether these costs (of changes of various sizes in employment) actually rise at an increasing or decreasing rate is difficult to determine" (p. 53). They justified convexity (a quadratic) as an approximation to a cost function with linear variable and no fixed costs. None of the subsequent early studies (Robert Eisner and Robert Strotz, 1963; John Gould, 1968) provided much more justification than did Holt et al. More recent work just imposes the assumption (for example, Thomas Sargent, 1978, p. 1016). There is nothing wrong a priori with this; but the exclusion of fixed costs and the insistence on increasing average variable adjustment costs are restrictive and not necessarily consonant with reality.

In the literature on labor demand only Stephen Nickell (1986, and some of his earlier work) recognizes that changes in employment may be characterized by average variable costs of adjustment that initially decrease but eventually increase. He derives the firm's dynamic demand for labor under both the standard assumption of increasing variable costs and the assumption of constant costs. No existing empirical work on labor demand goes beyond the conventional assumptions.[2]

P. K. Trivedi (1985) shows that there are severe difficulties in drawing inferences about microeconomic adjustment paths from aggregated data. This suggests that empirical work on the adjustment of labor demand should first examine microeconomic adjustment paths to infer the nature of those costs. It should then consider how these paths are aggregated to produce the more readily observable macro paths.[3]

As a first step in this direction, one should note that the cost of hiring facing the firm may be independent of the number of workers hired. Advertising, interviewing, and doing the paperwork to hire one assistant professor of economics is no more costly than that required to hire three. Taking experienced workers away from production to train one worker may be as costly as taking them away to train five workers. Some costs arise only if hiring is done and do not vary with its rate. Beyond the costs of gross employment changes, there are costs of making net changes. Does reducing employment by eliminating a shift reduce profits proportionately more or less than the layoff of a few workers? Do morale problems arise among remaining workers when staffing is cut regardless of the size of the reduction? The structure of the costs of adjusting employment levels need not be convex and may affect the path of employment just as much as the more visible costs of gross employment changes.

3.2. Estimating Adjustment Paths Under Alternative Cost Structure

A generalized adjustment cost function for a homogeneous labor input is:

$$C(\dot{L}) = b\dot{L}^2 + \left[\frac{k \text{ if } |\dot{L}| > 0}{0 \text{ if } \dot{L} = 0}\right.,$$

where the superior dot denotes the rate of change, and b and k are nonnegative parameters.[4] Implicitly this cost structure is on net changes in employment, an approach taken in some but not all of the literature. The firm is assumed to maximize the discounted stream of its concentrated profits $\pi(L)$, with $\pi'' < 0$:

(2) $$Z = \int_0^T [\pi(L) - b\dot{L}^2 - k]\, e^{-rt}dt + (\pi(L_T)e^{-rT})/r,$$

where $0 \le T \le \infty$ is the point when the firm stops adjusting labor demand in response to the shock that occurred at $t = 0$; the wage rate w is implicit in the function π; the product price is assumed to equal one, and L_T is the value of L that is chosen at the endogenous time T. I assume that $L \ge L_0$ (i.e., w has decreased, causing L to be at least equal to its initial level).[5]

In the standard case $b > 0$ and $k = 0$. The optimal adjustment path between $t = 0$ and T is described by the Euler equation:

(3) $$2b\ddot{L} - 2br\dot{L} + \pi'(L) = 0.$$

This is the standard solution, with $T \mapsto \infty$; the adjustment path is smooth, and equilibrium labor demand is approached asymptotically. As Gould (1968) has shown, it can yield a simple form of (1):

(4) $$L_t = [1 - \gamma]\, L^*_t + \gamma L_{t-1} + \mu_t,$$

where I have written L and L^* as logarithms of actual and long-run equilibrium labor demand. μ is a random error term appended for use in estimation.

In the case of only fixed adjustment costs, $k > 0$ and $b = 0$. The firm either maintains employment at L_0 forever or sets $T = 0$ and jumps immediately to L^*, the long-run equilibrium value of labor demand, depending on whether :

$$k \gtrless \frac{[\pi(L^*) - \pi(L_0)]}{r}.$$

The firm adjusts if L^* is sufficiently different from its most recent choice of L and if k is relatively small. We can describe its employment demand by:

(5a) $$L_t = L_{t-1} + \mu_{1t},\ |L_{t-1} - L^*_t| \le K,$$

and

(5b) $$L_t = L^*_t + \mu_{2t},\ |L_{t-1} - L^*_t| > K.$$

The parameter K is an increasing function of the fixed adjustment costs. It is the percentage deviation of last period's employment from desired employment that is necessary to overcome those fixed adjustment costs. μ_{1t} and μ_{2t} are disturbances, with $E(\mu_{1t}\,\mu_{2t}) = 0$.

To estimate (5), specify L^*_t as:

(6) $$L^*_t = aX_t + \varepsilon_t,$$

where a is a vector of parameters, X is a vector of variables that affect L^*_t, and ϵ_t is a disturbance term. Throughout the discussion I assume:

$$E(\mu_{1t}\,\varepsilon_t) = E(\mu_{2t}\,\varepsilon_t) = 0.$$

The firm operates on (5a) if:

$$\varepsilon_t \leq K + [L_{t-1} - aX_t]$$
$$\text{and } \epsilon_t \geq -K + [L_{t-1} - aX_t],$$

and on (5b) if:

$$\varepsilon_t > K + [L_{t-1} - aX_t]$$
$$\text{or } \varepsilon_t < -K + [L_{t-1} - aX_t].$$

It jumps to its new long-run equilibrium (moves along (5b)) if it is sufficiently shocked by changes in X or if forecasting errors overstate $|L_{t-1} - L^*_t|$.

We need to construct a method of estimating the parameters in (5) – the a parameters, K, and the variances $\sigma^2_{\mu 1}$, $\sigma^2_{\mu 2}$, and σ^2_ε, and to specify L^*. Equations (5a) and (5b) are essentially a switching regression (see Stephen Goldfeld and Richard Quandt, 1976), with the probability of being on (5a) equal to:

$$1 - p_t = \Phi\left[\frac{K + L_{t-1} - aX_t}{\sigma_\epsilon}\right] - \Phi\left[\frac{-K + L_{t-1} - aX_t}{\sigma_\epsilon}\right],$$

where Φ is the cumulative unit normal distribution function (and I have implicitly assumed that ϵ is normally distributed). p_t is then the probability that the firm jumps to L^*_t. The likelihood function for this model is:

(7) $$\mathcal{L} = \prod_{t=1}^{T} g(\mu_{1t})^{1-p_t} \cdot g(\mu_{2t} + \varepsilon_t)^{p_t},$$

where $g(\mu_{1t})$ is the density of μ_{1t} from (5a), and $g(\mu_{2t} + \varepsilon_t)$ is the density of the error term in (5b) after substituting for L^*_t. Both errors are assumed to be normally distributed. The logarithm of the likelihood function in (7) is maximized in the empirical work.

A huge literature has arisen on the appropriate specification of L^* (see Hamermesh, 1986). Since the available data limit the possibilities severely, I use two different approaches to represent L^*_t in (4) and (5). The first:

(8) $$L^*_t = a_0 + a_1 Y_t + a_3 t + \epsilon_t,$$

where the a_i are parameters to be estimated, can be viewed as perfect forecasting under rational expectations.[6] The second, based on a simplified version of Nickell's (1984) approach, estimates a transfer function for Y_t using all information available at time $t - 1$. This produces the predictions ${}_{t-1}Y_t^*$ and ${}_{t-1}Y_{t+i}^*$, $i = 1, 2, \ldots$. In this approach L_t^* is approximated as:

$$(9) \qquad L^*_t = a_0 + a_1\ {}_{t-1}Y^*_t + a_2\,\Delta Y^*_{t+i} + a_3 t + \epsilon_t,$$

where ΔY_{t+1}^* is the change in the forecasted value Y^* from time t to time $t + i$. This equation embodies labor-saving technical change and expectations about sales.

If behavior is described by (5), and firms' $|L_{t-1} - L_t^*|$ and K differ, at any time t some fraction γ_t of the firms in any aggregate will hold employment constant at L_{t-1} (will behave according to (5a)), while $1\text{-}\gamma_t$ will adjust according to (5b). If we observe only aggregate behavior, labor demand could be characterized by an equation that looks just like (4). If one ignores the time-varying nature of the p_t and the problems of aggregating firms' p_t to obtain $1\text{-}\gamma_t$, (4) may describe aggregate employment dynamics well even though the underlying behavior is characterized by (5).

The case of $b, k > 0$, is described in the Appendix. Essentially b and k jointly cause the long-run equilibrium value of employment to differ from the static profit-maximizing value. Higher fixed adjustment costs increase this difference but hasten the adjustment from L_0 to equilibrium; greater quadraticity of $C(\dot{L})$ also increases the difference, but it slows the rate of adjustment. Extensive empirical modeling of this general case is left for subsequent research and the collection of better data.

Figure 3.1
Plant 1

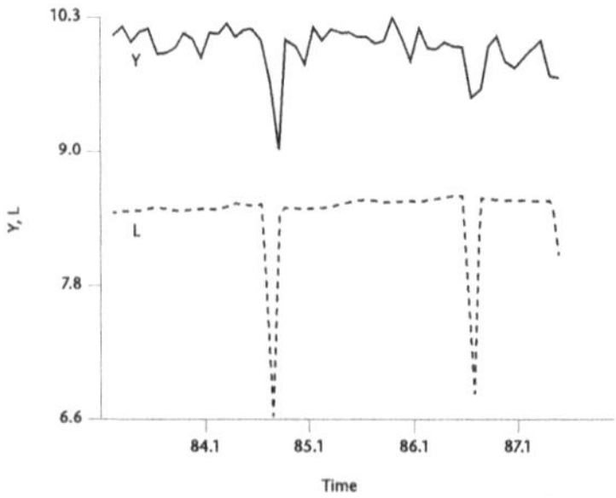

Figure 3.1
Plant 2

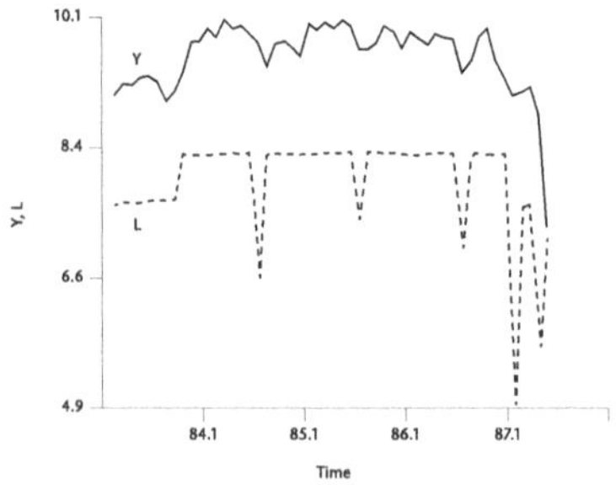

Figure 3.1

Plant 3

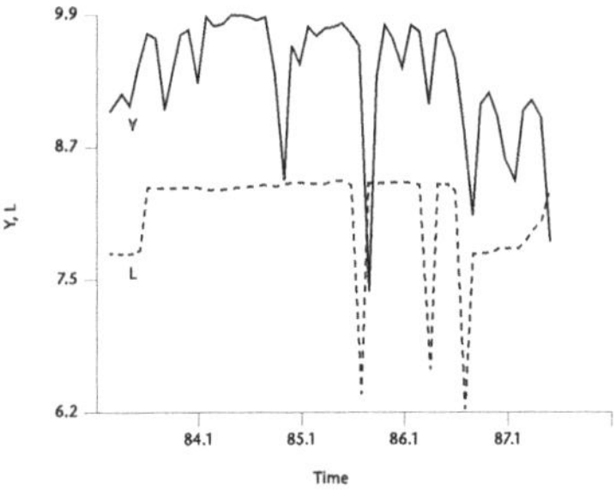

Figure 3.1

Plant 4

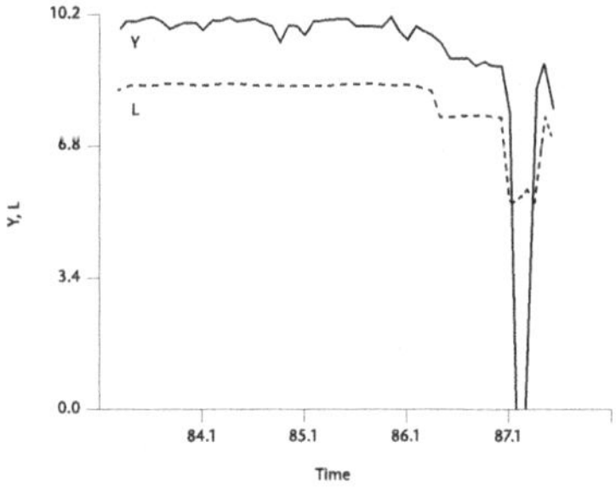

Figure 3.1

Plant 5

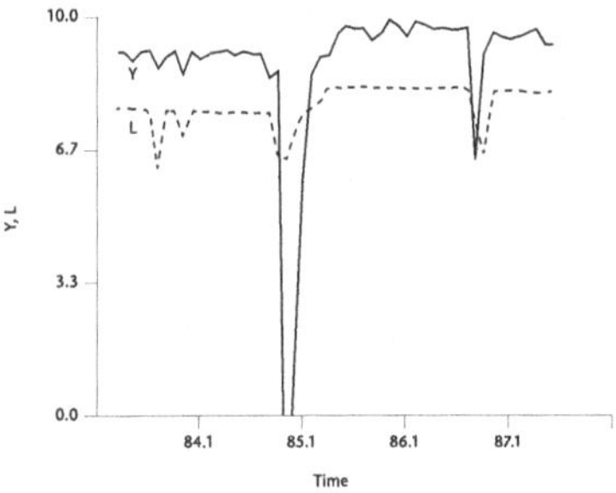

Figure 3.1

Plant 6

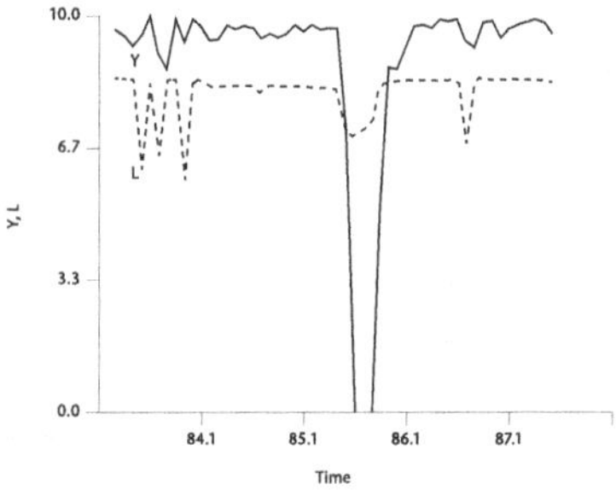

Figure 3.1

Plant 7

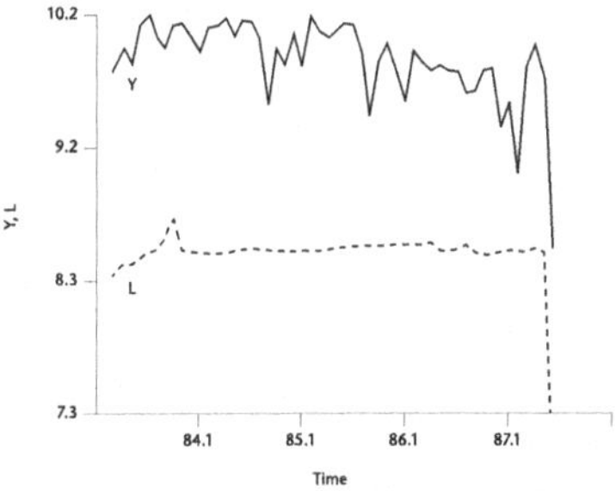

Figure 3.1

Seven Plants Aggregated

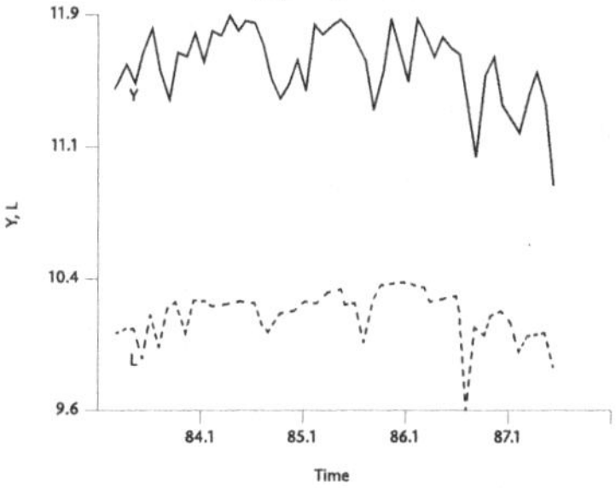

3.3. Estimates for Individual Plants

To examine the effects of differing structures of adjustment costs at the proper level of disaggregation I acquired data on seven manufacturing plants of a large U.S. durable-goods producer. Monthly data on output were obtained for December 1977 through May 1987, as were monthly employment levels from January 1983 through May 1987. The employment data are mid-month counts of production workers; the output data measure total units produced in the month.[7]

Before estimating (4) and (5), a detailed preview of the results can be obtained from plots of the logarithms of employment and output in each plant, and of the data aggregated over all seven plants. Each plot in Figure 3.1 shows the last 52 months of the sample; the origin on the horizontal axis represents the minimum value of logarithm (1 + employment). The first seven plots are striking. There are substantial fluctuations in output; but production-worker employment is essentially constant, except for large changes around the time of the larger changes in output. This is seen especially clearly in the data for Plants 1, 4, and 5, but appears to characterize the other plants too. This inference contrasts sharply with the appearance of the data aggregated over the seven plants, shown in the last plot. There are continuous fluctuations in employment, and these roughly coincide with the fluctuations in output. The first seven plots are inconsistent with smooth fluctuations in employment based on a model of convex variable adjustment costs; the last plot appears consistent with that model.

While these figures tell much of the story, they cannot tell us whether the underlying relationship between the logarithms of employment and output is consistent with the static theory of production; nor can they provide insights into the size of the shock, *K*, that is necessary to induce the firm to change employment in the plant. To make these inferences we must estimate (5) and the accompanying equation, alternatives (8) or (9). Throughout the analysis I use seasonally unadjusted data. Only in Plant 3 was there significant twelfth-order autocorrelation in *Y*.

To generate the sequences ${}_{t-1}Y_t^*$, I initially used a transfer function based on continuously updated regressions of *Y* on its 12 lagged values, a time trend, and the 12 lagged values of the company's retail sales. These regressions did fit better than those that excluded the firm's retail sales, but they did not predict *Y* so well. Accordingly, (4) and (5) are estimated using ARI (12) forecasts of *Y*. Each forecast is based on the most recent five years of output data.

A comparison of the estimates of (4) and (5) is essentially a test of how the standard model of convex variable costs of adjustment performs relative to a model in which there are fixed adjustment costs (and perhaps variable costs of degree one or less). Under alternative (8) the model in (4) has five parameters, the four regression parameters a_0, a_1, a_3, and γ, and σ_μ. Under the same alternative the switching model has seven parameters, the three a_i, K, σ_ε, $\sigma_{\mu 1}$, and $\sigma_{\mu 2}$.[8] To make estimation of the system somewhat easier, I assume that $\sigma_{\mu 1} = \sigma_{\mu 2}$. This means that I am restricting the variance of the error in (5a) to be less than that in (5b). This implicitly assumes that errors that occur when the firm seeks to hold employment constant are not so large as those produced when it tries to move from L_{t-1} to L_t^*. The basic switching model thus has six free parameters. We can discriminate between the models in (4) and (5), which are not tested, by examining the values of their likelihood functions.

I begin with a discussion of the estimates of an autoregression of L, and of (9) and two alternatives of (4), which are shown in Table 1.[9] The estimates for the individual plants are not too encouraging, as they contain some negative autoregressive terms in the AR(1) model and in (4), some positive time trends and even a negative coefficient on expected output for Plant 1. This instability across the plants is probably due to the use of microeconomic data and to the short time-series for each plant.

The estimation problems induced by this combination are overcome when either the pooled or the aggregated data underlie the estimation. The results for these two cuts of the data are shown in the first two tableaux of Table 3.1. In the aggregated data the coefficients on $_{t-1}$ Y^*_t are consistent with previous work using industry data; the time trends, particularly in the pooled data, imply that labor productivity grows at about 2 percent per year.[10] The coefficients on the autoregressive term in L, although somewhat lower than those found in most estimates based on monthly industry data, are not unreasonable in the pooled data. Moreover, while perfect forecasting (implicit in the fourth column in each tableau) gives a better fit, the forward-looking terms ΔY^*_{t+3} do add significantly to the equations.

Table 3.2 shows the maximum likelihood estimates of the switching model (5) for each of six plants, for the pooled data on seven plants, and for those data aggregated.[11] (That $\hat{\sigma}_\mu = 0$ in several plants is consistent with the observation that the firm can hold employment constant when that is optimal). While (4) is not tested in (5), and even standard tests of nontested hypotheses are not applicable with the highly nonlinear model (5), a comparison of log-likelihood values is striking. For all six plants

Table 3.1

Least-Squares Estimates, 1983:2–1987:5, Manufacturing Plants

N.	AR(1)	(9)	(4)		AR(1)	(9)		(4)
	Pooled (7 plants)				Aggregated (7 plants)			
Constant			4.479	4.532	6.502	5.874	5.036	5.319
			(11.90)	(12.44)	(4.66)	(4.81)	(3.44)	(4.11)
L_{-1}			0.312	0.269	0.361		0.164	0.014
			(5.94)	(5.10)	(2.64)		(1.03)	(0.09)
${}_{t-1}Y_t^*$			0.121			0.372	0.301	
			(5.03)			(3.54)	(2.39)	
ΔY^*_{t+3}			0.031			0.202	0.194	
			(3.76)			(1.53)	(1.46)	
Y_t				0.151				0.401
				(6.95)				(3.71)
Time		-0.0011	-0.0011	0.0004		-0.0010	-0.0010	0.0018
		(-0.62)	(-0.61)	(-0.25)		(-0.76)	(-0.81)	(1.42)
$\bar{R}^2$	0.220	0.219	0.287	0.310	0.104	0.149	0.168	0.278
log L			-262.62	257.11			34.76	37.93
	Plant 1				Plant 2			
Constant	8.966	8.445	8.759	-1.602	6.320	5.305	5.708	0.202
	(7.41)	(4.68)	(4.55)	(-0.73)	(5.67)	(3.05)	(3.18)	(0.12)
L_{-1}	-0.062		-0.077	-0.614	0.205		-0.136	-0.340
	(-0.43)		(-0.49)	(-3.98)	(1.47)		-0.94)	(-2.15)
${}_{t-1}Y_t^*$		-0.007	0.023			0.344	0.424	
		(-0.04)	(0.14)			(1.84)	(2.06)	
ΔY^*_{t+3}		-0.130	-0.144			0.593	0.616	
		(0.88)	(-0.95)			(1.98)	(2.05)	
Y_t				1.509				1.105
				(5.38)				(4.89)
Time		0.0027	0.0027	0.0069		-0.0236	-0.0267	-0.0048
		(0.57)	(0.56)	(2.25)		(-3.62)	(-3.64)	(-0.95)
$\bar{R}^2$	-0.016	-0.042	-0.059	0.339	0.022	0.273	0.271	0.336
log L			-20.60	13.04			-41.62	-39.72
	Plant 3				Plant 4			
Constant	6.870	7.187	6.823	6.524	1.355	6.537	4.187	3.556
	(6.10)	(6.13)	(4.69)	(4.86)	(2.04)	(13.85)	(3.67)	(4.07)
L_{-1}	0.150		0.065	-0.052	0.828		0.358	0.427
	(1.08)		(0.43)	(-0.30)	(10.01)		(2.24)	(3.27)
${}_{t-1}Y_t^*$		0.130	0.111			0.204	0.135	
		(1.01)	(0.81)			(4.57)	(2.54)	
ΔY^*_{t+3}		0.127	2.16			0.044	0.022	
		(0.90)	-0.88)			(3.12)	(1.32)	
Y_t				0.226				0.139
				(1.47)				(2.97)
Time		-0.0128	-0.0121	-0.0051		-0.0150	-0.0112	-0.0106
		(-2.03)	(-1.84)	(-1.06)		(-3.24)	(-2.35)	(-2.27)
$\bar{R}^2$	0.003	0.032	0.015	0.056	0.661	0.693	0.717	0.727
log L			-34.42	-33.82			-25.38	-24.95

N.	AR(1)	(9)	(4)		AR(1)	(9)		(4)
	Plant 5				Plant 6			
Constant	2.876	6.142	4.005	4.804	7.782	6.708	8.285	8.611
	(3.32)	(14.99)	(4.21)	(5.15)	(6.76)	(16.23)	(8.04)	(8.57)
L_{-1}	0.635		0.360	0.237	0.041		-0.241	-0.266
	(5.76)		(2.46)	(1.63)	(0.29)		(-1.67)	(-1.91)
${}_{t-1}Y_t^*$			0.076			0.115	0.149	
			(1.61)			(2.88)	(3.37)	
ΔY^*_{t+3}			(0.0061)			0.024	0.026	
			(0.29)			(1.67)	(1.82)	
Y_t				0.096				0.142
				(2.77)				(3.86)
Time		0.0196	0.0130	0.0128		0.0133	0.0164	0.0149
		(4.94)	(2.79)	(3.03)		(2.48)	(2.93)	(2.80)
$\overline{R}^2$	0.387	0.388	0.446	0.507	-0.018	0.174	0.203	0.250
log L			-23.79	-21.28			-41.87	-40.79

[a] Here and in Table 3.2 there are 52 observations in each case, except in the pooled equations, for which there are 364 observations. t-statistics in parentheses here and in Tables 3.2, 3.4, and 3.5 unless otherwise noted.

Table 3.2 Estimates of (5a)–(5b), 1983:2–1987:5, Manufacturing Plants

	$\hat{a}_0$	$\hat{a}_1$	$\hat{a}_2$	$\hat{a}_3$	$\hat{K}$	$\hat{\sigma}_\mu$	$\hat{\sigma}_\varepsilon$	$\log \mathcal{L}$	$\hat{p}_t$ (Mean, Standard Deviation) (Minimum, Maximum)
Pooled									
${}_{t-1}Y^*_t$, ΔY^*_{t+3}	6512	0.160	0.046	-0.0004	0.584	0.493	0.159	-230.77	(0.200 0.179)
	(40.80)	(9.24)	(4.00)	(-0.38)	(8.15)				(0.045 0. 999)
Y_t	5985	0.217		-0.001	0.573	0.494	0.621	-234.86	(0.465 0.089)
	(17.91)	(6.19)		(-0.34)	(3.52)				(0.399 0.894)
Aggregated									
${}_{t-1}Y^*_t$, ΔY^*_{t+3}	5.132	0.436	0.213	-0.001	0.019	0.128	0.020	38.75	(0.817 0.240)
	(3.42)	(3.34)	(1.71)	(-0.71)	(0.75)				(0.342 0. 999)
Y_t	5.488	0.399		0.002	0.031	0.119	0.039	44.09	(0.750 0.210)
	(4.56)	(3.84)		(2.09)	(0.89)				(0.438 0.999)
Plant 1									
${}_{t-1}Y^*_t$, ΔY^*_{t+3}	8.521	-0.075	-0.723	0.018	0.792	0.000	0.781	-17.85	(0.395 0.115)
	(2.35)	(-0.18)	(-1.92)	(0.96)	(1.80)				(0.311 0.814)
Y_t	-3.406	1.170		0.004	0.384	0	0.225	25.20	(0.236 0.232)
	(-17.19)	(57.13)		(2.33)	(2.09)				(0.104 0.999)
Plant 2									
${}_{t-1}Y^*_t$, ΔY^*_{t+3}	6.255	0.246	0.760	-0.027	0.355	0.512	0.412	-34.69	(0.577 0.186)
	(3.88)	(1.43)	(2.56)	(-5.24)	(2.57)				(0.405 0. 999)
Y_t	0.100	0.823		-0.001	0.086	0.555	0.107	-32.77	(0.696 0.221)
	(0.13)	(10.49)		(-0.34)	(2.67)				(0.423 0. 999)

	$\hat{a}_0$	$\hat{a}_1$	$\hat{a}_2$	$\hat{a}_3$	$\hat{K}$	$\hat{\sigma}_\mu$	$\hat{\sigma}_\varepsilon$	$\log \mathcal{L}$	$\hat{p}_t$ (Mean, Standard Deviation) (Minimum, Maximum)
Plant 3									
${}_{t-1}Y^*_t$, ΔY^*_{t+3}	7.673	0.086	0.139	-0.016	0.113	0.468	0.112	-26.47	(0. 739 0.248)
	(5.92)	(0.56)	(0.94)	(-2.21)	(0.85)				(0.311 0.999)
Y_t	6.482	0.188		-0.008	0.131	0.459	0.145	-25.69	(0. 724 0.227)
	(27.54)	(7.31)		(-2.20)	(2.34)				(0.377 0.999)
Plant 4									
${}_{t-1}Y^*_t$, ΔY^*_{t+3}	4.626	0.453	-0.069	-0.050	1.492	0.000	0.649	27.69	(0.154 0.177)
	(9.93)	(9.65)	(-8.32)	(-16.63)	(12.90)				(0.021 0. 995)
Y_t	5.005	0.378		-0.029	1.040	0.459	0.145	-25.69	(0.173 0.224)
	(14.70)	(11.83)		(-13.41)	(14.54)				(0.028 0. 968)
Plant 5									
${}_{t-1}Y^*_t$, ΔY^*_{t+3}	6.694	0.054	0.0179	0.025	0.957	0.063	0.968	-19.69	(0.363 0.080)
	(12.44)	(1.02)	(0.50)	(3.47)	(9.44)				(0.323 0.774)
Y_t	6.270	0.110		0.022	0.523	0	0.672	-16.51	(0.482 0.094)
	(19.01)	(3.25)		(5.66)	(2.10)				(0.436 0.954)
Plant 6									
${}_{t-1}Y^*_t$, ΔY^*_{t+3}	6.671	0.123	0.027	0.012	0.138	0.578	0.137	-35.44	(0.681 0.238)
	(39.21)	(7.57)	(2.91)	(3.54)	(2.15)				(0.314 0.999)
Y_t	6.651	0.127		0.014	0.131	0.579	0.128	-34.49	(0.591 0.272)
	(19.90)	(5.27)		(2.98)	(1.78)				(0.310 0.999)

the values of the log-likelihood of model (5) are higher by at least 2 than they are for the equivalent version of model (4) (which has one less estimated parameter).[12] The clearest comparisons are again on the pooled data. This confirms the impressionistic evidence in Figure 3.1 that the switching model describes these plant-level data far better than does a model of smooth adjustment.[13]

The estimates of K are quite large, implying that the firm varies employment only in response to very large shocks to expected output. In the pooled data $\hat{K} \approx 0.6$. Consider what an estimate this large means. Unless demand is very slack in these plants, increases in demand that do occur are met by combinations of greater effort and increased hours per worker. This inference is supported by the knowledge that there are large variations in overtime hours in the industry to which these plants belong. With very large changes in product demand, though, firms respond by non-marginal changes in employment. This is the same sequence of responses that is implicit in standard views of how firms adjust. Also as in standard models of adjustment, the estimated employment-output elasticity implies increasing returns to scale. This approach does not remove this well-known problem with partial adjustment models; however, the standard view that employment is adjusted marginally is inconsistent with these data.

The last column of Table 3.2 presents statistics associated with $\hat{p}_t$. There is substantial monthly variation in the probability that the firm switches to a new equilibrium. Moreover, for most plants, and in the pooled data, $\hat{p}_t$ ranges over most of the interval $(0, 1)$. This implies that the model can discriminate fairly well in separating observations onto (5a) and (5b). That the mean of $\hat{p}_t = 0.20$, though, shows that it is usually unlikely that the firm is choosing to change employment.

Recall that these estimates are based on employment levels, and thus, like the theory in Section 3.2, implicitly on costs of net adjustment. We do know, though, that voluntary turnover in the four-digit SIC industry to which these plants belong averaged 0.8 percent per month in the late 1970s.[14] If, as seems likely, this fairly large monthly outflow occurs repeatedly in the same jobs, we may conclude that either the variable hiring costs are not very important to this firm or, more likely, that they are not convex and that the fixed costs of hiring are small. The important non-convexity in adjustment costs in these plants is in the level of staffing itself rather than in the activities of the personnel office. The sizes of the estimated K indicate that the lumpiness results from economies of scale in maintaining intact an entire work shift.

I have treated each plant as the locus of decision making; yet the discrete adjustment that has been demonstrated could instead reflect the firm's response to *firmwide* demand shocks. Each plant could be treated as a unit, with the firm reducing output and employment in the least efficient plant when there are shocks to its total demand. This possibility can be examined in two ways. First, in the context of the standard model, add $\bar{Y}_t$ (alternatively, ${}_{t-1}\bar{Y}^*_t$ and $\Delta\bar{Y}^*_{t+3}$), where the superior (-) denotes output among all seven plants, to the versions of (4) estimated in Table 3.1 for each plant. Among the seven plants the *t*-statistic on the coefficient of $\bar{Y}_t$ was significant (at only the 90 percent level) in one plant (Plant 5), and the *F*-statistics on the vector (${}_{t-1}\bar{Y}^*_t$, $\Delta\bar{Y}^*_{t+3}$) were also significant only in Plant 5. Firmwide demand shocks add no information to the standard adjustment model at the plant level. Similarly, the contemporaneous correlations of the residuals from these models are low, suggesting there are no common unobserved factors affecting employment adjustment in these plants.

A second approach examines firmwide shocks in the context of the switching model. In particular, if the discrete adjustment is related among the plants, we should find that some plants lead in adjustment while others lag. To examine this, estimate all pairwise vector autoregressions among the $\hat{p}_{it}$, $i = 1, \dots 6$.[15] This yields 30 *F*-statistics testing the hypotheses that $\hat{p}_{jt}$ Granger causes $\hat{p}_{it}$. Of these 30 statistics, one was significantly different from zero at the 95 percent level, and three others were significantly different from zero at the 90 percent level. These results show little relation among the switching probabilities in the six plants. Along with the revised estimates of (4), they suggest that each plant is operated more or less independently of firmwide demand shocks.

It appears that much of the fluctuation in employment in Figure 3.1 represents temporary decreases that are soon restored to the initial employment level, though this is clearly not always true (for example, in Plants 2 through 5 at various points during the period). This suggests that, while smooth adjustment is not occurring, the discrete adjustment in these plants may reflect employment variation in the presence of contracting behavior. To test this hypothesis against the explanation based on fixed costs of adjustment, consider the model:

$$\text{(10a)} \quad L_t = L^{max} + v_{1t}, \qquad \text{if} \qquad L^{max} \leq a' + Y_t + v_{3t};$$

$$\text{(10b)} \quad L_t = a' + Y_t + v_{2t} + v_{3t}, \qquad \text{if} \qquad L^{max} > a' + Y_t + v_{3t},$$

where the v_{it} are random-error terms, a' is a parameter, and L^{max} is the highest value of L_t observed in the plant during the sample period.

This model captures the notions in the contracting literature that there is a pool of workers (L^{max}) attached to the plant and that workers in this pool are laid off in bad times in proportion to the size of the shock. (See Martin Feldstein, 1976). I estimate this model and a more general one that allows the firm to use overtime and other variations in hours as a buffer when demand shocks occur. (In the second model I assume the firm can change weekly hours by ±33 percent in response to demand shocks before laying off workers).

The mean-squared errors from these contracting models estimated on the data covering Plants 1–6 and on the pooled data are shown in columns (2) and (3) of Table 3.3. Column (1) shows the mean squared errors from the switching model, based on weighted averages of the residuals from the estimation of (5a) and (5b) with $1 - \hat{p}_t$ and $\hat{p}_t$ as weights. In Plants 1 and 2 the simple contracting model predicts as well as the switching model, while in Plant 3 the difference is not very large. In Plants 4, 5, and 6, however, the contracting model fails miserably. The reason is straightforward: In those plants output sometimes drops to zero, yet employment does not. The contracting model does not allow for the labor hoarding that takes place even in response to large demand shocks.

Table 3.3

Mean-Squared Errors, Switching Model and Contracting Models

	Switching	Contracting	
		No Hours Variation	± 33 Percent Hours Variation
Pooled (7 Plants)	1.262	3.293	3.271
Plant 1	0.340	0.372	0.330
Plant 2	0.545	0.556	0.542
Plant 3	0.458	0.669	0.661
Plant 4	0.492	1.435	1.427
Plant 5	0.358	1.733	1.729
Plant 6	0.550	2.119	2.193

No doubt an expanded contracting model that allowed for an employment-output elasticity less than one in the face of large demand shocks would describe the data as well as a model of fixed adjustment costs. Indeed, such contracting can be viewed as one underlying cause of the fixed adjustment costs that produce the behavior observed here. The data are not sufficiently rich to discriminate among alternative explanations for the existence of fixed adjustment costs.

They only show that smooth adjustment based on quadratic variable costs describes behavior poorly.

3.4. The Effects of Aggregation

The estimates on the data aggregated over the seven plants present an entirely different picture from those on the pooled data or on the individual plants. The $\widehat{K}$ for the aggregated data in Table 3.2 are insignificant and very small; and the average values of the $\widehat{p}_t$ are much higher than in the pooled data. While (5) describes the data better than does (4), the differences in the log-likelihood values are far below the differences in the pooled data, and below most of the differences in the estimates on the individual plants. Even at this very low level of aggregation much of the ability to discriminate between models of adjustment costs is lost.

To examine problems of model discrimination under further aggregation, I obtained monthly data on four 4-digit SIC U.S. manufacturing industries, ones that have had the same definition and have sufficiently long continuous time-series on output and total employment. These are: SIC 2821, plastics materials and resins; SIC 3221, glass containers; SIC 3632, household refrigerators and freezers; SIC 3633, household laundry equipment. Output is monthly also, with the seasonally unadjusted series used here.[16] For both series the data cover 1958–85, except in SIC 2821. Forecasts of Y are constructed exactly as in Section 3.3, and the same models are estimated here. With the loss of the observations needed to produce these forecasts and the desire to begin estimation with a full-year's data, the model is observed over the period 1965–85 (1973–85 for SIC 2821).

Table 3.4 presents estimates of the same models as did Table 3.1. In all industries except SIC 3221 the two versions of equation (4) add little explanatory power beyond that provided by a simple AR(1) model. This contrasts sharply with the results in Table 1, where a first-order autoregression generally explained little of the variation in employment. Moreover, except in SIC 3633 the term in ΔY^*_{t+3} is either insignificant or has an unexpected negative sign.

Estimates of (5) under both alternative assumptions about the formation of L^* are shown in Table 3.5. While the estimates $\widehat{a}_i$, make sense, unlike in the previous section the switching model does not uniformly dominate (4): In SIC 2821 the log-likelihood is higher in (4) in one case, and essentially the same in the other. The fluctuations

Table 3.4

Least-Squares Estimates, 1965:1–1985:12, Four Small Industries[a]

	AR(1)	(9)	(4)		AR(1)	(9)		(4)
	SIC 2821 (Plastics)				SIC 3221 (Glass Containers)			
Constant	0.035	3.382	0.328	0.255	0.794	-0.912	-0.490	-0.760
	(0.61)	(52.06)	(3.96)	(3.13)	(4.96)	(-4.98)	(-2.84)	(-6.57)
L_{-1}	0.992		0.895	0.906	0.812		0.375	0.288
	(76.40)		(44.22)	(46.78)	(21.38)		(7.89)	(9.96)
$_{t-1}Y_t^*$		0.135	0.032			1.215	0.742	
		(7.86)	(6.32)			(28.63)	(10.42)	
ΔY^*_{t+3}		0.010	0.017			-0.056	-0.165	
		(0.51)	(3.04)			(-2 34)	(-6 47)	
Y_t				0.038				0.892
				(7.44)				(25.16)
Time		-0.0018	-0.0003	-0.0003		-0.0028	-0.0017	-0.0020
		(-15.91)	(-6.74)	(-7.58)		(-31.20)	(-11.05)	(-23.71)
$\bar{R}^2$	0.974	0.742	0.981	0.981	0.645	0.828	0.867	0.902
log L			539.55	531.74			356.39	398.75
Constant	0.071	2.750	0.520	0.460	0.253	1.670	0.488	0.376
	(1.30)	(16.75)	(3.84)	(3.90)	(3.24)	(15.18)	(4.53)	(3.77)
L_{-1}	0.980		0.800	0.742	0.919		0.738	0.725
	(67.62)		(22.75)	(23.49)	(37.11)		(15.82)	(20.84)
$_{t-1}Y_t^*$		0.330	0.073			0.368	0.085	
		(9.01)	(3.10)			(14.81)	(2.72)	
ΔY^*_{t+3}		-0.019	-0.023			0.104	0.028	
		(-0.53)	(-1.14)			(5.67)	(2.06)	
Y_t				0.142				0.119
				(8.15)				(7.32)
Time		-0.0038	-0.0008	-0.0010		-0.0016	-0.0005	-0.0005
		(-38.56)	(-5.54)	(-8.05)		(-24.10)	(-4.54)	(-6.94)
$\bar{R}^2$	0.948	0.857	0.954	0.961	0.846	0.712	0.856	0.876
log L			336.88	359.26			399.15	417.71

[a] Except 1973:1–1985:12 for SIC 2821, here and Table 3.5.

Table 3.5 Estimates of (5a)–(5b), 1965:1–1985:12, Four Small Industries

	$\hat{a}_0$	$\hat{a}_1$	$\hat{a}_2$	$\hat{a}_3$	$\hat{K}$	$\hat{\sigma}_\mu$	$\hat{\sigma}_\varepsilon$	$\log \mathcal{L}$	$\hat{p}_t$
		(Mean, Standard Deviation) (Minimum, Maximum)							
SIC 2821									
${}_{t-1}Y^*_t$, ΔY^*_{t+3}	3.870	0.135	0.070	-0.002	0.104	0.008	0.037	535.65	(0.037 0.059)
	(39.59)	(5.94)	(3.01)	(-10.54)	(4.03)				(0.005 0.423)
Y_t	3.305	0.264		-0.002	0.167	0.008	0.069	532.05	(0.025 0.037)
	(10.08)	(3.48)		(-5.48)	(2.57)				(0.006 0.268)
SIC 3221									
${}_{t-1}Y^*_t$, ΔY^*_{t+3}	-3.483	1.795	-0.125	-0.004	0.375	0.017	0.164	613.02	(0.059 0.103)
	(-49.07)	(96.07)	(-2.24)	(-28.87)	(9.94)				(0.022 0.999)
Y_t	-1.593	1.383		-0.003	0.611	0.007	0.304	672.99	(0.059 0.083)
	(-2.02)	(7.56)		(-8.61)	(3.06)				(0.045 0.994)
SIC 3632									
${}_{t-1}Y^*_t$, ΔY^*_{t+3}	0.441	0.863	-0.669	-0.005	1.926	0.000	1.005	342.24	(0.065 0.013)
	(0.56)	(4.88)	(-2.45)	(-11.79)	(2.24)				(0.022 0.999)
Y_t	2.166	0.461		-0.004	0.376	0.050	0.228	370.93	(0.149 0.076)
	(3.87)	(3.49)		(-9.40)	(2.30)				(0.099 0.569)
SIC 3633									
${}_{t-1}Y^*_t$, ΔY^*_{t+3}	2.245	0.238	0.140	-0.001	0.297	0.000	0.224	412.55	(0.209 0.038)
	(8.68)	(4.03)	(3.20)	(-7.99)	(4.93)				(0.184 0.424)
Y_t	1.879	0.320		-0.001	0.237	0.000	0.182	435.93	(0.237 0.067)
	(225.96)	(57.98)		(-9.73)	(55.05)				(0.190 0.628)

in $|L_{t-1} - L^*_t|$ relative to the $\hat{K}$ are such that the average probabilities of switching to a new equilibrium are very low, and even the ranges are narrow. This too reflects the inability of the data to discriminate between a first-order autoregression and the switching model. At the level of four-digit SIC industries testing competing hypotheses about behavioral differences arising from alternative structures of adjustment costs is confounded by aggregation.

3.5. Conclusions and Implications

I have demonstrated *on data for a particular set of individual plants* that the standard model of convex variable adjustment costs for labor is inferior to a specification based on fixed costs of adjustment. For an aggregate of plants of one company, and for small U.S. manufacturing industries, one cannot discriminate between the two models. Lumpy employment adjustment in the plants studied here may be atypical of industry generally; but no one has demonstrated smooth adjustment is typical. Smoothness has heretofore only been assumed.

There are several reasons for believing that discrete adjustment of labor demand is important. The first relates to macroeconomic fluctuations in employment and productivity. There is a tradition (Fair, 1969; Robert Gordon, 1979) of including timing effects to capture the observation that productivity grows unusually slowly as the economy nears a cyclical peak. These are imposed in an *ad hoc* fashion; but they are consistent with structures characterized by fixed costs that make linear aggregation impossible. Abandoning the standard model requires expanding models of macroeconomic employment adjustment to include information about the sub-units (in the specification used here, the distribution across (5a) and (5b)).[17]

Slow adjustment has been linked to the imposition of policies that, for example, make it harder for firms to shed labor.[18] It is difficult to see how such policies impose an *increasing* variable cost of adjustment. Unemployment insurance benefits (that are not fully offset by a lower supply price of labor) impose a linear variable cost of adjustment on most employers. Mandatory advance notice of layoffs or plant closings imposes a lump-sum cost that is effective only if the drop in employment exceeds some minimum.[19] One must model the costs of these policies carefully and obtain microeconomic data to get satisfactory estimates of their effects.

These conclusions should give pause to researchers who worry about complex structures of error terms characterizing dynamic factor adjustment under the maintained assumption that adjustment is slow because of increasing variable costs. More attention needs to be paid to linking maximizing behavior to the underlying structure of adjustment costs. That linkage must be made at the micro level, with implications for macro behavior deduced by determining the correct mechanism for aggregation. The estimates here show that the most profitable approach to studying factor, and particularly employment adjustment requires microeconomic data to discover what firms actually do.

APPENDIX

The general solution to maximizing (2) is characterized by equation (3) and:

(A1) $$-2b\dot{L}_T + \frac{\pi'(L_T)}{r} = 0,$$

and

(A2) $$-b\dot{L}_T^2 + \frac{\pi'(L_T)\dot{L}_T}{r} - k = 0.$$

Equation (A2) is a quadratic in $\dot{L}_T$. It has real roots only if:

$$\left[\frac{\pi'(L_T)}{r}\right]^2 \geq 4bk.$$

Let $\tilde{L}$ be the static optimizing level of employment. Then $\pi'(\tilde{L}) = 0$, and $L_T < \tilde{L}$ (since we assumed w decreased). Rewriting and substituting in (Al):

(A1') $$\dot{L}_T \geq \left[\frac{k}{b}\right]^{0.5},$$

and

(A1) $$\pi'(L_T) \geq 2r\,[bk]^{0.5},$$

Equation (A1') shows that an increase in k raises the rate of adjustment at the terminal point; equation (A2') shows that as k increases the slope of the profit function at the terminal point increases. An increase in b also increases this slope, but it reduces the rate of adjustment at T.

4

Labor Demand and the Source of Adjustment Costs

A huge literature has studied the dynamics of labor (employment and workerhours) demand based on adjustment costs facing employers. The standard assumption underlying this research has been that these costs are convex, though recent investigations (e.g. Hamermesh, 1989; Holtz-Eakin and Rosen, 1991) suggest that nonconvex costs provide a better description of their structure. No standard assumption exists about their source. This study considers how alternative sources affect employment dynamics and provides the first measures of the relative importance of these alternatives.

Section 4.1 examines how this issue has been treated (more correctly, ignored) in the vast literature on dynamic factor demand. Since there are no publicly available data that allow the analysis of this issue, I collected two sets of data especially for use here. Section 4.2 describes them and discusses some descriptive statistics that shed light on adjustment in the firms under study. Section 4.3 proposes two (of the many possible) adjustment models, one based on the standard convex costs, the other based on lumpy costs, and offers ways of inferring the importance of the different sources of adjustment costs in each. Sections 4.4 and 4.5 use the microeconomic data to estimate these models.

The original version of this chapter was published as: Hamermesh, Daniel S. (1995). Labour Demand and the Source of Adjustment Costs, in: The Economic Journal, 105(430): 620–634. Support for this chapter was provided by the National Science Foundation under Grant SES-8821399. I thank the executives at the manufacturing firm and the hospital who allowed access to their data, and acknowledge Junsoo Lee's excellent research assistance. I am extremely grateful to the workers who assisted in gathering the information; to Steve Allen, François Legendre, Gerard Pfann, two referees, participants at seminars at several universities, and especially to Gerbert Hebbink for helpful comments.

4.1. History and Motivation

Adjustment costs are *gross* or *net*, depending on their source. Gross costs are incurred when a worker is laid off or hired and are independent of the impact of the change on the level of employment. They can be viewed as linked to the identity of the individual filling a job and thus arise from flows of workers. Net costs are incurred as the level of employment changes and arise from changes in the stock of employees. They reflect changes in the number of jobs rather than the incumbents' identities and are linked to changes in scale.

Early discussions of adjustment costs did not distinguish their sources. For example, Holt *et al.* (1960, p. 52) note that, 'The cost of laying off workers derives from terminal pay, reorganization, etc ...,' implicitly referring to both gross and net costs. Oi (1962, p. 539) observes that 'fixed employment costs can be separated into two categories ... hiring and training costs,' i.e. as gross costs. Nadiri and Rosen (1969, p. 659) mention 'search, hiring, training and layoff costs and associated morale problems among workers', which may mix gross and net costs.

Subsequent research has based the firm's dynamic profit-maximizing path of employment on one or the other of these concepts of adjustment costs, but never both. Sargent (1978) relied on net adjustment costs (in terms of changes in employment levels) , as did the previous work that assumed static expectations, and as has most subsequent research using his rational-expectations approach. Nickell (1986) and a few others modelled dynamics using costs of hiring and laying off - gross costs, paying little attention to the internal costs of adjustment that a net change in employment might engender.[1] Within both traditions nearly all the econometric work that is linked to formal models has examined the path of employment or worker-hours, levels rather than flows of workers. Nowhere has there been an empirical examination of the source of these costs.

Gross and net costs are distinct concepts; but if there are no voluntary separations from the firm, they cannot be distinguished without detailed costaccounting, for each net change in employment results from an equal-sized flow of hires or layoffs. Voluntary separations do occur, though, and constitute sizable fractions of the typical firm's workers each month.[2] The importance of voluntary turnover means that we should account for both sources of adjustment costs in modelling dynamic labor demand; and estimates tied to those formal models should generate estimates of the importance of the two types of cost.

Distinguishing between the two sources of adjustment costs would move us a step closer to being able to link policies that affect gross adjustment costs, e.g. restrictions on discharging workers, affirmative-action requirements, and others, to their impact on costs. On purely intellectual grounds it would demonstrate whether the focus on net changes in employment that pervades the empirical literature makes sense in terms of the nature of the underlying costs. Does slow employment adjustment result from disruptions in the workplace due to changes in staffing levels, or because new workers must be processed? Answers to this question may also underlie the problem of business-cycle asymmetry (see, e.g. Neftçi, 1984), though it is clearly quite a distance from inferring the sources of the firm's costs to understanding asymmetric cycles.

4.2. Some New Data and their Characteristics

Because lags in employment adjustment are fairly short and annual data produce biased estimates of them (Hamermesh, 1993, Chapter 7), we must observe the process generating the path of employment at least quarterly. Since it is impossible to draw correct inferences about lag structures from aggregated data unless adjustment costs are quadratic, we need microeconomic data. To be useful in estimating formal models of employers' decisions, any set of data must also contain information on some forcing variable(s), such as labor costs, expected sales, etc.

Because no publicly available data meet all these needs, it was necessary to obtain new data. These proprietary data meet all the criteria for analyzing the issues of the previous section, though the time series in each of the two data sets I collected are unfortunately quite short. Because they are short, though, and because they represent basically a first case study of this major issue, I spend this section describing them.

The first set of data covers a medium-size (250-bed) hospital for which employment, both a head-count and the number of full-time equivalent workers, was available from 1985:1 to 1990:1. The number of workers who quit each month was also available from 1987:12 to 1990:1. Since the hospital laid no one off during this period, we can use the data on L, employment, and Q, quits, to infer hires, H. Information is also available on real revenue (total in- and out-patient revenue deflated by the CPI component for hospital costs).[3]

The other set of proprietary data is a panel of three manufacturing plants operated by a small, technologically advanced firm that produces extrusions for use in downstream manufacturing. Data on employment and sales for these plants are available from 1985:1 to 1990:6, while data on hires are available from 1988:1 to 1990:6. According to company executives, no layoffs occurred in the plants during this 2½-year period.

Table 4.1 presents statistics describing patterns of percentage net changes in employment, $\Delta ln\ (L)$, and of hire rates, H/L. In two of the manufacturing plants the coefficient of variation of hire rates exceeds that of (the absolute value of) net employment changes, while in Plant 1 and for the two measures of employment in the hospital net employment changes are relatively more variable. An alternative view of the pattern of adjustment is obtained from the final two columns of the Table. They show that, except in Plants 2 and 3, the employers are changing employment levels and hiring new workers most of the time rather than bunching their expansions or hiring into a few periods.

Assuming that adjustment costs are convex, positive and roughly similar-sized coefficients of variation of $\Delta ln\ (L)$ and H/L suggest that both hiring and net employment costs are large enough to cause the firms to adjust each slowly. That Plants 2 and 3 are not hiring nearly half the time suggests that lumpy costs, especially those linked to hiring, may be important in some cases. Taken together, the results hint that both gross and net costs can be important, and that to measure their relative sizes we cannot restrict the analysis to the standard model with convex (quadratic) adjustment costs.

Table 4.1

Coefficients of Variation and Runs of Zero in Employment Changes and Hiring

	Coefficient of Variation		Fraction = 0	
	$\|\Delta \ln (L)\|$	H/L	$\|\Delta \ln (L)\|$	H/L
Manufacturing plants 1988.03–1990.06				
Plant 1	0.887	0.732	0.04	0
Plant 2	0.643	1.422	0.04	0.43
Plant 3	1.224	1.592	0.25	0.43
Hospital 1988.01–1990.01				
Employee count	0.763	0.388	0.04	0
FTE Count	0.756	0.665	0	0

4.3. Employment Adjustment with Gross and Net Costs

Table 4.1 cannot measure the relative importance of gross and net adjustment costs. To do this we must model these costs and attempt to infer them directly. A large variety of functional forms might be imposed and tested. I limit testing to two: (i) In Subsection 4.3.1, the standard convex (quadratic) adjustment costs that pervaded the literature in dynamic labor demand and macroeconomic employment adjustment until very recently; and (2) In Subsection 4.3.2, lumpy adjustment costs that describe some data on costs of net adjustment in employment better than do convex costs.

More general convex models, for example, those based on the possibility of asymmetric adjustment costs, have usefully described aggregated data (e.g. Burgess and Dolado, 1989; Pfann and Palm, 1993) and might dominate the two specifications used here. The difficulty with them is that they require using procedures, such as generalized method of moments or other nonlinear methods, that have very unsatisfactory properties when applied to short time series such as ours. Using other specifications of adjustment costs beyond the two estimated here awaits the collection of sufficiently high-frequency long micro time series on firms' employment, turnover and revenues/production to allow their identification.

I model labor as a one-dimensional stock of homogeneous workers. Implicitly this means that hours of work cannot vary, so that I derive the firm's demand for workers. Obtaining the simultaneous demand for workers and hours with both sources of adjustment costs greatly increases the complexity of the problem.[4] I assume the firm never lays off workers; negative net changes in employment occur through attrition. This assumption is obviously incorrect in general, but as noted in the previous section, it is correct in the micro data I have assembled.

4.3.1. *A Forward-Looking Model with Quadratic Costs*

The firm's adjustment costs are:

(1) $$C_{t+i} = C_{\Delta L_{t+i}} + C_{H_{t+i}} = b_1 \, (L_{t+i} - L_{t+i-1})^2 + b_2 \, H^2_{t+1},$$

where H_{t+i} denotes the number of hires during time period $t+i$, $i=0$, 1, ..., and b_1 and b_2 are parameters describing adjustment costs. The stocks and flows that contribute to these costs are linked by:

$$H_t \equiv L_t - L_{t-1} + Q_t, \tag{2}$$

where Q_t is the number of quits. The first term in Equation (1) reflects the cost of adjusting the level of employment (net costs), while the second measures the cost of hiring (gross costs). If $H_t = 0$, the only component of C_t is the net cost (of altering employment); if $H_t = Q_t$, C_t consists solely of the gross costs (of hiring).

Following Sargent (1978) the firm maximizes the stream of expected future profits:

$$\pi = E_t \sum_{i=0}^{\infty} R^i \left[(\overline{\alpha}_0 + \alpha_{0,\,t+i})L_{t+i} - 0.5\alpha_1 L_{t+1}^2 - w_{t+i} L_{t+i} - 0.5C_{t+i}\right], \tag{3}$$

where w is the wage rate, $R < 1$ is the discount factor, and the α are parameters of the production function, with $\alpha_{0,\,t+i}$ having a zero mean and positive variance. Equation (3) has become quite standard in the modern macroeconomics literature. It assumes that both the production function and adjustment costs are quadratic, and that the former is randomly shocked (by the random parameter $\alpha_{0,\,t+i}$). It ignores the simultaneous adjustment of capital and labor, consistent with the absence of data on capital on our establishments and with the substantial evidence (Hamermesh, 1993, Chapter 7) that estimates of employment dynamics are not biased if the adjustment of capital is ignored.

The novelty in this study is the inclusion of the two separate terms in adjustment costs in (1) with $b_1, b_2 > 0$. The model assumes implicitly that firms treat quits as exogenous. Firms probably can affect quits slightly; but overwhelming evidence suggests quits are mainly determined by job availability and the demographic structure of the work force, especially in the short run.[5]

The Euler equations describing the profit-maximizing path of L_t based on (3) are:

$$RE_{t+i} L_{t+i+1} - \left(\frac{\alpha_1}{b_1 + b_2} + R + 1\right) L_{t+i} + L_{t+i-1} \tag{4}$$

$$= (b_1 + b_2)^{-1}[w_{t+i} - \overline{\alpha}_0 - \alpha_{0,\,t+i} - b_2(RE_{t+i}Q_{t+i+1} - Q_{t+i})], \qquad i=0,1,\ldots$$

Note that if $b_2 = 0$ or $Q_{t+i} = 0$, (4) reduces to the standard rational-expectations model of dynamic factor demand in the presence of quadratic net costs of adjustment. The solutions to (4) are:

$$L_t = \lambda L_{t-1} - \lambda(b_1 + b_2)^{-1} E_t\left\{\sum_{j=0}^{\infty} \delta^{-j}[w_{t+j} - \overline{\alpha}_0 - \alpha_{0,\,t+j} - b_2(RQ_{t+j+1} - Q_{t+j})]\right\}, \tag{5}$$

where $0 < \lambda < 1$ and $\delta > R^{-1}$ describe the factorization of the quadratic equation implicit in the terms in L in the Euler equations. Equation (5) contains the usual results on dynamic labor demand, with the level of employment depending negatively on the wage rate and positively on productivity shocks. Also, however, the final term in (5) implies that a higher constant rate of voluntary turnover reduces labor demand by an amount that increases with the convexity of C_H in (1), reflecting the user cost of labor generated by quits.

Assume that the $\alpha_{0,t}$, w_t and Q_t are all described by first-order processes, with autocorrelation parameters ρ_α, ρ_w and ρ_Q. (The most important operational assumption, that Q_t is AR(1), is explicitly tested in the empirical work.) Then the path of labor demand can be described by:

(5')
$$L_t = \lambda L_{t-1} - \lambda (b_1 + b_2)^{-1} \left[w_t \left(1 - \frac{\rho_w}{\delta}\right)^{-1} - \bar{\alpha}_0 \left(1 - \frac{\text{(eq. 1)}}{\delta}\right)^{-1} - \alpha_{0,t} \left(\text{(eq. 1)} - \frac{\rho_\alpha}{\delta}\right)^{-1} - b_2 Q_t (R\rho_Q - \text{(eq. 1)}) \left(\text{(eq. 1)} - \frac{\rho_Q}{\delta}\right)^{-1} \right].$$

Equation (5') relates current-period employment to its lagged value, to the number of quits since the last observation on the process, and to a vector of forcing variables (wages and productivity shocks). The coefficient of interest, $ß_Q$, measures the impact of additional quits on labor demand:

(6)
$$ß_Q = \lambda \frac{b_2}{b_1 + b_2} (R\rho_Q - \text{(eq. 1)}) \left(\text{(eq. 1)} - \frac{\rho_Q}{\delta}\right)^{-1}.$$

The autoregressive parameter λ describing L can be inferred from (5'), while ρ_Q can be inferred from a first-order autoregression of Q. The solution (5) provides an inequality linking δ and R, so that (6) can be rearranged to yield:

(6')
$$1 \geq -\frac{ß_Q}{\lambda(\text{(eq. 1)} - R\rho_Q)} \geq \frac{b_2}{b_1 + b_2} \geq -\frac{ß_Q}{\lambda} \geq 0.$$

Using (6') , after some substitutions the ratio of gross to total adjustment costs in (1) becomes:

(7)
$$\frac{C_H}{C} > \frac{H^2}{-(\Delta L)^2 \left(\frac{\lambda}{ß_Q} + \text{(eq. 1)}\right) + H^2}.$$

The model does not allow us to infer the actual amount of adjustment costs or their size relative to wage costs. It does, though, enable us to bracket the fraction of the total cost of adjustment that stems from changing the identities of the employees as opposed to changing employment levels. In particular, the estimate of the right-hand side of (7) is based on the observed rates of hiring and net changes in employment, and on the estimates of the parameters $ß_Q$ and λ. It provides a lower bound on the fraction of the total cost of adjustment that is accounted for by gross costs.

The paucity of information in these new sets of data beyond that on employment and flows of workers severely limits our ability to represent the forcing variables in (5'). I use the only information available - on sales or revenue - to represent expected output, Y^*_t, as an autoregressive process with lags of one, two, three and twelve months.[6] Linear and quadratic time trends are also included in the vector of forcing variables in estimating both this model and that of the next subsection.

4.3.2. *A Model with Lumpy Costs*

An alternative approach to the standard assumption of convex adjustment costs assumes instead that lumpy costs arise whenever the firm hires and whenever it alters employment. In particular, let:

$$(8)\qquad C_t = \begin{cases} K_L, & \text{if } Q_t > 0, H_t = 0; \\ K_H, & \text{if } H_t > Q_t, \qquad H_t > 0; \\ K_L + K_H, & \text{if } H_t \neq Q_t, \qquad H_t > 0, \end{cases}$$

where the K_i are parameters measuring the size of the lumpy costs associated with gross and net employment changes respectively. The firm incurs adjustment cost K_L if workers quit and it does not hire (so that employment changes); it incurs adjustment cost K_H if it hires and replaces all quitters (thus holding employment constant); and it incurs both costs if it hires and also expands employment or lets it fall.

Assume that the firm forecasts demand conditions in period *t*, and let L^* be the level of employment that maximizes its expected profits in the absence of adjustment costs. Implicitly I am assuming employers have static expectations.[7] Under this assumption, assuming too that $Q_t > 0$, and given its endowment of workers, L_{t-1}, only three possible choices could maximize the firm's profits: (1) Hire no one, and incur adjustment costs K_L because employment has dropped; (2) Hire replacement workers, $H_t = Q_t$, and incur adjustment costs K_H; or (3) Hire sufficient workers to set $L_t = L^*$ and incur both types of cost. Letting π be the firm's profit function defined over employment, the conditions for making these choices are:

(9a) $H_t = 0,$

if $K_H + \pi(L^*) - \pi(L_{t-1}) > K_L + \pi(L^*) - \pi(L_{t-1} - Q_t),$

and $K_H + K_L > K_L + \pi(L^*) - \pi(L_{t-1} - Q_t);$

(9b) $H_t = Q_t,$

if $K_H + \pi(L^*) - \pi(L_{t-1}) < K_L + \pi(L^*) - \pi(L_{t-1} - Q_t),$

and $K_H + K_L > K_H + \pi(L^*) - \pi(L_{t-1});$

(9c) $H_t = L^* - (L_{t-1} - Q_t),$

if $K_H + K_L < K_L + \pi(L^*) - \pi(L_{t-1} - Q_t),$

and $K_H + K_L < K_H + \pi(L^*) - \pi(L_{t-1}).$

Figure 4.1

Lumpy Gross and Net Adjustment Costs and Hiring Decisions

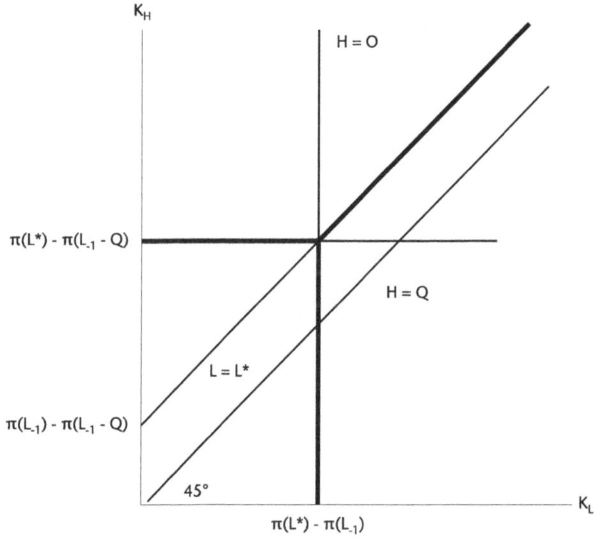

Rearranging the three separate inequality conditions in (9a)-(9c) yields a set of constraints that defines the optimal choice for the firm for all combinations of L^*, L_{t-1} and Q_t. These conditions divide the (K_H, K_L) space into three regions, as shown in Figure 4.1. When K_L is very large (relative to the departure of $\pi(L^*)$ from $\pi(L_{t-1})$), the best choice is to set $H_t = Q_t$, unless K_H is so large that failing to replace quitters dominates doing some hiring. If K_H and K_L are small relative to the loss in profits when no hiring or only replacement hiring is done, the profit-maximizing choice is to set $L_t = L^*$. The sizes of the regions in Figure 4.1 depend on the slope of π around L^*, with a greater slope increasing the firm's desire to set $L_t = L^*$ (enlarging the rectangle along the axes). Empirical work based on conditions (9) can generate direct estimates of the implied (lumpy) costs of hiring and of changing employment.

I follow my approach in Hamermesh (1989) and assume there are two sources of error in (9) . The first is a normally-distributed forecasting error ϵ stemming from:

$$L^*_t = \gamma X_t + \varepsilon_t,$$

where γ is a vector of parameters linking the forcing variables X to the desired stock of employment. The second is a normally-distributed error μ stemming from errors in hiring to meet the target, L^*. Line arising and rearranging (9) yields:

(9a') $H_t = 0,$
if $\varepsilon_t \leq K_H + L_{t-1} - Q_t - \gamma X_t.$
and $K_H - K_L \geq Q_t;$

(9b') $H_t = Q_t + \mu_t,$
if $\epsilon_t \leq K_L + L_{t-1} - yX_t,$
and $K_H - K_L < Q_t;$

(9c') $H_t = \gamma X_t - (L_{t-1} - Q_t) + \mu_t + \varepsilon_t,$

if neither (9a') nor (9b') holds.

The conditions (9a'-c') are defined by three inequalities. Let $\Delta = 1$ if the condition, $K_H - K_L \geq Q_t$, which is independent of the realizations of the disturbances, holds. The other two inequalities depend on the disturbances and require that this three-equation switching model be estimated in probabilistic terms. Thus extending Goldfeld and Quandt (1976), let:

(11a) $$D_1 = N[(K_H + L_{t-1} - Q_t - \gamma X_t)/\sigma_\varepsilon],$$

where N is the cumulative unit normal distribution, and:

(11b) $$D_2 = N[(K_L + L_{t-1} - \gamma X_t)/\sigma_\varepsilon].$$

Then the probability that (9a') holds is ΔD_1; the probability that (9b') occurs is $(1 - \Delta)D_2$; and the probability that the firm operates according to (9c') is $1 - \Delta D_1 - (1 - \Delta)D_2$. The likelihood function is defined over the three (probabilistic) events (9a'-c') and is maximized over the parameters γ, K_H, K_L, and the variances of μ_t and ε_t.

4.4. Estimates of the Quadratic-Cost Model

Estimates of (5') based on the microeconomic time series describing the manufacturing plants and the hospital are shown in Table 4.2. The equations are estimated in the logarithms of employment and output and using the quit rate.[8] The standard errors of the estimates of min (C_H/C) are computed from the variance-covariance matrix by assuming a Taylor series expansion around the ratio λ/β_Q. For the manufacturing plants I use an iterative seemingly unrelated method to account for the possibility that the error terms are correlated in these establishments that are subject to at least some central control.[9]

Figure 4.2

Estimates of the Quadratic Adjustment Model[a]

P_Q	λ	β_Q	$\min\{C_H/C\}$	ΣY	R^2	h
			Manufacturing Plants			
			Plant 1			
0.492	0.505	-0.353	0.910	0.148	0.633	-
(0.14)	(0.19)	(0.23)	(0.20)			
			Plant 2			
0.314	0.735	-0.228	0.499	-0.048	0.827	1.56
(0.18)	(0.12)	(0.29)	(0.44)			
			Plant 3			
0.073	0.544	-0.088	0.357	-0.050	0.948	2.29
(0.19)	(0.13)	(0.12)	(0.39)			
			Residual correlations:			
			$\rho 12 = 0.200$			
			$\rho 13 = 0.331$			
			$\rho 23 = 0.380$			
			Hospital Employee count			
-0.186	0.927	-0.734	0.929	0.104	0.974	-0.14
(0.21)	(0.12)	(0.19)	(0.09)			
			FTE count			
0.467	0.898	-0.602	0.871	0.067	0.862	-0.99
(0.19)	(0.14)	(0.18)	(0.12)			

[a] Standard errors in parentheses below the parameter estimates. All equations contain the additional forcing variables time and time squared. The separate equations for the manufacturing plants are estimated using an iterative seemingly unrelated estimator.

In no case is the first-order autoregressive parameter in the equation describing the quit rate, ρ_Q, significantly negative, and except in Plant 3 and for the employee count in the hospital it is significantly positive. Moreover, tests of higher-order autoregressive terms show they are not statistically important.[10] The results on ρ_Q suggest we are justified in using the estimate λ/β_Q to compute the lower bound to the ratio C_H/C.

While the estimates of (5'), which are autoregressions in L, fit the data fairly well, some problems exist. Durbin's h-statistic fails to reject the hypothesis of no serial correlation for Plant 2 in the manufacturing firm; but the hypothesis is barely rejected for Plant 3 and cannot be calculated for Plant 1 (because the term under the radical is negative). For both employment measures at the hospital the hypothesis cannot be rejected. These problems suggest that, while the firm may respond to shocks according to the model derived in Section 4.2, expected real revenue and the quadratic in time miss a substantial part of the determinants of L.

The main focus of this section is on the estimates of min (C_H/C), the lower bound on the fraction of quadratic adjustment costs arising from hiring as opposed to changing the level of employment. I calculate these using the estimates of β_Q and λ and the averages of H^2 and $(\Delta L)^2$ in each unit. In Plant 1 nearly all of the adjustment costs arise from costs of hiring, and the estimate is sufficiently precise that we can be quite sure that gross adjustment costs are very important. In the other two plants, while the point estimates imply that gross adjustment costs constitute over one-third of the total, the estimated min (C_H/C) is so imprecise that we cannot say much about this fraction. The entire cost of adjustment may stem from changing employment levels; or gross costs may account for most of the total. At the hospital the estimates of min (C_H/C) are essentially the same for both measures of employment, especially when we note that $\rho_Q < 0$ in the count of employees. Their size suggests that we can be quite sure that gross costs are important, and it may be that there are no net costs of adjustment.

The results strongly imply that gross costs (of hiring) are important. One could speculate why the point estimates are nearly one for Plant 1 and the hospital, but below one half for Plants 2 and 3. In all four units H^2 averages from two to four times $(\Delta L)^2$, so the estimates of min (C_H/C) do not differ because costs at Plants 2 and 3 are dominated by relatively large movements in employment levels. Rather, to the extent that the imprecise estimates for these two plants allow any conclusion, something inherent in their adjustment-cost technology may generate differences between them and the other units. With just four possibly independent units (the three manufacturing plants and the hospital) we cannot satisfactorily determine those cases where one type of cost or the other will be relatively greater. Suffice it to say that the evidence here corroborates the inference from the descriptive statistics in Table 4.1. that both types of cost may be important and especially suggests that we should pay closer attention to gross (hiring) costs in our models of labor demand.

4.5. Estimates of the Fixed-Cost Model

Attempts to estimate the three-regime switching model *(9*a'-c'*)* with the stochastic conditions (11a) and (11b) and freely-varying K_H, K_L and σ_ε using standard numerical methods for maximum-likelihood were unsuccessful. As a first step to overcome the problems of maximizing this function the parameters were restricted by imposing $K_H = \sigma_\varepsilon$. Even with this constraint the standard maximization algorithms failed to converge.[11] As a second step the likelihood function was concentrated on the parameters K_H, K_L and σ_ε, and the maxima of the partial-likelihood functions for each pair of a grid of values of $K_H (= \sigma_\varepsilon)$ and $K_H/(K_L + K_H)$ were found. The global likelihood function is maximized by the pair $[K_H, K_H/(K_L + K_H)]$ for which the maximum maximorum of these partial likelihoods is obtained.

This procedure was applied to the microeconomic time series. An examination of the partial likelihood functions shows that for all three plants in the manufacturing company, and for both the employee count and the count of full-time equivalents at the hospital, the global likelihoods have numerous local maxima. The failure to maximize these functions directly is thus hardly surprising. Although the global likelihood functions are quite flat along the vector $K_H(= \sigma_\varepsilon)$, they vary much along the vector $K_H/(K_L + K_H)$ so that, as in Section 4.4, we can reasonably interpret the findings here as showing the *relative* importance of gross and net (lumpy) costs of adjustment.

Table 4.3 presents estimates based on this search method. For the maximizing values of $K_H/(K_L + K_H)$ and K_H $(= \sigma_\varepsilon)$ I list the mean probabilities Δ, D_1 and D_2 describing the switching conditions and their standard deviations in the particular samples. Also shown are the mean probabilities that employment in the sample behaves according to each of (9a'-c').

The maximizing value of $K_H/(K_L + K_H)$ shows the relative importance of the two types of lumpy adjustment costs. It is analogous to the estimate of min (C_H/C) in the quadratic-costs model in Section 4.4. The difference is that there we were able to estimate the deterministic split between the two types of costs. It makes no sense to combine the ratio $K_H/(K_L + K_H)$ with indicator variables on whether the firm hires or changes employment, since in this model those decisions are explicitly probabilistic.

For the employee count in the hospital the likelihood function is maximized where gross (lumpy) costs are about the same as the net (lumpy) adjustment costs. In the other four sets of estimates we find that gross lumpy adjustment costs are larger than net costs. The results in Plants 2 and 3 show the interaction of gross costs with the shocks to labor demand. In those plants the probability that no hiring is done is quite high (as the count data in Table 4.1 implied). When hiring occurs, it is sufficient to keep employment at the long-run profit-maximizing level L^*, and this along with continued quitting means that $Pr\ (L_t = L_{t-1})$ is very small in these two plants.

Table 4.3

Maximizing Values of the Fixed-Cost Parameters and their Implications[a]

Unit $[K_H/(K_L+K_H), K_H = \sigma_\varepsilon]$	Δ	D_1	D_2	$Pr(L=L_{-1}-Q)$	$Pr(L=L_{-1})$	$Pr(L=L^*)$
Manufacturing						
Plant 1						
(0.67, 0.03)	0	0.491	0.731	0	0.731	0.269
	(0)	(0.41)	(0.35)			
Plant 2						
(0.67, 0.27)	0.931	0.788	0.726	0.733	0.050	0.217
	(0.25)	(0.17)	(0.19)			
Plant 3						
(1, 0.27)	0.966	0.834	0.712	0.805	0.0025	0.170
	(0.19)	(0.23)	(0.33)			
Hospital						
Employee count						
(0.50, 0.003)	0	0.420	0.597	0	0.597	0.403
	(0)	(0.48)	(0.48)			
FTE count						
(1, 0.001)	0.20	0.513	0.690	0.103	0.552	0.346
	(0.41)	(0.50)	(0.46)			

[a] Standard deviations in parentheses.

The estimates suggest the same conclusion for manufacturing Plant 1 and the hospital as the results in Section 4.4: Gross adjustment costs are at least as large as net costs. For Plants 2 and 3 the two sets of estimates suggest opposite conclusions, with gross convex costs being relatively unimportant, while gross lumpy costs seem large. Despite this apparent anomaly the two sets of results on these two plants are not necessarily inconsistent. The estimates for them in Table 4.2 were very imprecise and were in any case lower bounds. Also, in a complete model that allowed for gross and net convex and lumpy adjustment costs this apparent contradiction could arise.[12] Taken together they do, though, suggest the complexity of the problems of handling adjustment costs once we recognize that distinctions arise from both their structure and their sources.

4.6. Conclusions and Implications

The importance of the distinction between gross adjustment costs (of hiring) and net adjustment costs (of changing the level of employment) arises from the simple fact that rates of voluntary mobility are quite high. This first set of data that allows examining the issue demonstrates the new fact that both types of costs are empirically important. Within these microeconomic units, and given the particular, but standard specifications of adjustment costs used in this study, the preponderance of evidence suggests that gross costs account for the greater share of total adjustment costs. The results imply that recent research deriving models of employment demand based on gross adjustment costs represents a more profitable route than that based solely on net adjustment costs. That both *sources* of adjustment costs exist means that models must allow for how both affect the path of labor demand. We will not learn much about adjustment costs if we persist in estimating models without information on flows of labor such as hires and quits.

The dual nature of the cost of adjusting labor demand suggests that great care is in order in linking international or intertemporal differences in employment lags to imposed changes in the costs of hiring or firing.[13] Ignoring all the potential econometric problems and the possibility that varying supply constraints may affect lags in adjustment, differences in the lengths of lags by themselves tell us nothing about the effects of policies that alter hiring or firing costs. Lags in adjustment may lengthen, not because hiring/firing (gross) costs have increased, but because net costs of adjustment have risen, for example, due to a rise in the cost of changing the scale of operations to accommodate a new technology.

The presence of both types of adjustment costs in labor demand provides a basis for asymmetric business cycles. Voluntary turnover is strongly procyclical, much more so than employment. During booms quits rise rapidly, so that any expansion in employment generates net costs and substantial gross (replacement) costs. In a recession quits are very few, and the response to the drop in product demand represents nearly entirely the costs of changing employment levels. Even if net costs are symmetric, the procyclicality of quits and the presence of gross costs (whose importance I have demonstrated here) guarantee that we will observe asymmetry in the path of aggregate employment in response to output shocks.

The discussion was based on adjustment costs in labor demand. Yet the same distinction applies in the analysis of the demand for investment goods. Here too, some of the early theoretical literature was based on net costs (e.g. Lucas, 1967), while other studies assumed that adjustment costs arise from the cost of altering gross investment flows (e.g. Gould, 1968). Empirical research has not distinguished between these two types of costs – has not examined whether adjustment costs for replacing depreciated equipment differ from those generated by changes in the amount of capital in place. Examining the gross/net distinction in the market for capital goods should yield substantial advances.

Spoilage and scale changes both generate adjustment costs. Their simultaneous existence needs to be recognized in dynamic factor-demand models, and their relative importance in various markets needs to be examined empirically on broader and longer samples than were possible in this first, essentially case study approach. Such analyses will generate insights into factor market and macroeconomic dynamics that cannot be obtained by imposing the assumption that adjustment costs have only one source.

5

Turnover and the Dynamics of Labor Demand

5.1. Motivation

The burgeoning literature on the dynamic demand for labor is based in some cases on the costs of changing the level of employment, in others on the costs of hiring and firing (e.g. Nickell 1986). All the estimation, however, uses net changes in employment (variations in employment levels). A typical study of the aggregate demand for labor, of which Nickell (1984) provides one of the best examples, specifies net changes to be a function of expectations about future paths of wages and product demand (all based on their past realizations) and of lagged levels of employment.

In this study, we examine models of dynamic labor demand and account for variations in voluntary mobility (job-quitting) that are linked to net changes in employment, ΔL, by:

(1) $$\Delta L \equiv H - (F + Q),$$

where H, F, and Q are the numbers of workers per period who are hired, fired (laid off) and quit.

The original version of this chapter was published as: Hamermesh, Daniel S. (1996). Turnover and the Dynamics of Labour Demand, in: Economica, New Series, 63(251): 359–367. We are grateful to Francis Kramarz, Stephen Nickell, Franz Palm and seminar participants at the Universities of Bergamo, Chicago and Louvain-la-Neuve, and we acknowledge the support of the National Science Foundation under Grant SES-8821399 and of the KNAW.

Our purpose here is not to characterize or test microeconomic behavior, nor to attempt to aggregate that behavior up to the level of a major sector or the entire economy: instead, it is to test whether *at the aggregate level* a simple model of homogeneous labor in firms facing identical adjustment cost functions can add to our ability to track and understand the timing of aggregate employment fluctuations. This is, of course, identical to what has actually been done throughout the huge literature examining the dynamics of aggregate labor demand, though here we recognize explicitly that we may not be learning anything about behavior at the micro level.

Figure 5.1

Log (employment) and Quit Rate, US Manufacturing, 1960(1)-81(IV)

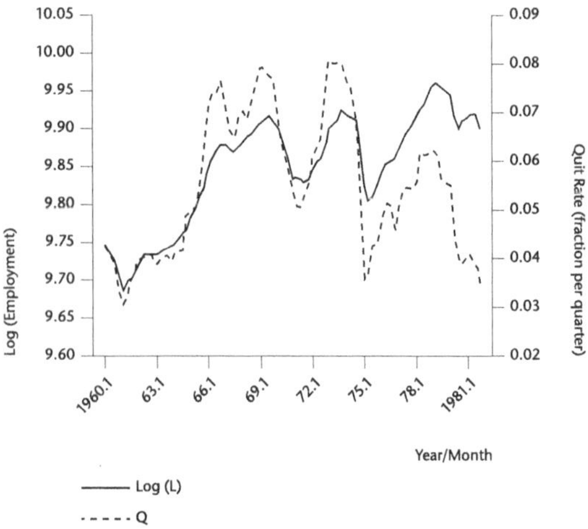

That this extension could be important is demonstrated by Figure 5.1, which illustrates, for US manufacturing for 1960–81, the cyclicality of the quit rate by presenting it along with the logarithm of the level of employment. The rate of quitting is substantial, and the quit rate is highly cyclical, tracking employment quite closely.

The causality in this relationship runs from quits to movements in employment, not the other way around, and reflects workers searching for alternative job opportunities that are more numerous during economic expansions. A formal test for the weak exogeneity of quits in an equation that also includes a linear time trend shows that we can reject the hypothesis that they do not Granger-cause movements in employment (χ^2 $(4) = 27 \cdot 44$ in a vector autoregression with four lagged terms). We cannot reject the hypothesis that movements in employment do not Granger-cause variations in quits (χ^2 (4) $= 3 \cdot 63$).[1] Given this evidence, we assume that employers choose the number of workers to hire or fire based upon the quit rate.[2]

Including quits in dynamic econometric models of aggregate labor demand may be important for two reasons. First, the theoretical models include the user cost of labor, which depends on the quit rate. Excluding quits from the estimation yields biased estimates of all the other parameters, especially given the size and variability of the quit rate. A few recent studies have been concerned about this (e.g. Burgess and Nickell 1990; Lockwood and Manning 1993), but none has had available a direct measure of the actual rate of quits.[3] Second, this absence has also prevented the growing literature on business cycle asymmetry based on differences in the costs of hiring and firing (Pfann and Palm 1993; Burgess 1993) from linking asymmetry to the underlying hiring/firing costs except under the demonstrably incorrect assumption that the quit rate is constant. The estimates here thus provide an application of asymmetric adjustment costs that recognizes the large role that flows of workers who quit might play in aggregate employment fluctuations.

5.2. Estimating Dynamic Labor Demand in the Presence of Quits

We assume that the representative firm faces a quadratic production function:

(2) $$Y_t = (\alpha + \varepsilon_t) X_t - 0.5 X'_t A X_t,$$

where $X_t = (L_t, K_t)$, and $\varepsilon_t = (\varepsilon_{1t}, \varepsilon_{2t})'$ is a vector of disturbances reflecting the impact of random shocks; α is a 2×1 vector of parameters, and $A = \{ \alpha_{ij} \}$ is a 2×2 positive-definite symmetric matrix of parameters. The static costs of labor are

$$VLC(L_t, W_t) = W_t L_t.$$

The finding of unidirectional causality from quits to employment implies that the cost of adjusting employment depends not only on net changes in employment, but also on the number of quits. The adjustment cost function then becomes

(3) $$AC = AC(\Delta L_t, Q_t, \theta),$$

where θ is a vector of parameters. The specification of (3) distinguishes among the models estimated here. However, because (3) includes Q_t, this general class of models differs from and expands on those estimated elsewhere.

All three models that we estimate specify versions of (3) allowing for quadratic adjustment costs in both the net change in employment and the difference between the endogenous hires and separations (contingent on the exogenous quits). Model I specifies AC as

$$\text{(4a)} \qquad AC(\Delta L_t, Q_t, \theta) = 0{\cdot}5\, \theta_2 (\Delta L_t)^2 + 0{\cdot}5\, \theta_3 (\Delta L_t + Q_t)^2,$$

with $\theta_2, \theta_3 \geq 0$. The terms in θ_2 and θ_3 embody the possibility that both net and gross changes in employment generate adjustment costs, as in Hamermesh (1995) in the micro context. In the context of the representative firm, the two terms can be interpreted as implying that there are increasing marginal costs of changing employment (hiring or laying off) and that these costs are greater when more workers have quit. For example, in such a firm adjustment costs would be generated by the disruptions to production engendered when employment changes. Also, even if employment were constant, adjustment costs would arise from the need to hire and train replacements for workers who have quit.

Model II allows for the additional possibility of asymmetric adjustment depending on whether ΔL_t is positive or negative:

$$\text{(4b)} \qquad AC(\Delta L_t, Q_t, \theta) = -1 - \theta_{11} \Delta L_t + exp(\theta_{11} \Delta L_t) + 0{\cdot}5\, \theta_2 (\Delta L_t)^2 + 0{\cdot}5\, \theta_3 (\Delta L_t + Q_t)^2.$$

This asymmetry is specified using the functional form proposed by Pfann and Palm (1993) that was very useful in describing British and Dutch time series on manufacturing employment.

A more general model allows for quadratic adjustment costs on both net changes in employment and on hires/layoffs, as in model I. It allows for asymmetric responses to positive and negative net changes in employment, as in model II; and it also specifies the possibility that there is asymmetric adjustment depending on whether $\Delta L_t + Q_t \equiv H_t - F_t$ is positive or negative. In this model (III), adjustment costs are

$$\text{(4c)} \qquad AC(\Delta L_t, Q_t, \theta) = -2 - \theta_{11}(\Delta L_t) + exp(\theta_{11} \Delta L_t) - \theta_{12}(\Delta L_t + Q_t) + exp(\theta_{12}(\Delta L_t + Q_t)) + 0{\cdot}5\, \theta_2 (\Delta L_t)^2 + 0{\cdot}5\, \theta_3 (\Delta L_t + Q_t)^2.$$

Even more general specifications could be written, e.g. allowing for interactions between ΔL_t and Q_t; but (4c) is the simplest general specification that allows for both gross and net adjustment costs and the possibility of asymmetric adjustment by a representative firm employing homogeneous labor.

We assume competition in the labor and product markets. The firm maximizes the expected present value of profits over an infinite horizon with respect to hiring and firing. It treats the processes of real wages and quits as parametric to its decisions about employment. We assume that in each period it chooses a contingency plan for L conditional on the predetermined capital stock, real wages and quits, and on currently available relevant information. It maximizes the objective function,

$$\underset{L_t}{\text{Max}}\left\{E_t\left[\sum_{i=0}^{\infty}\beta^i\,(Y_{t+i} - VLC_{t+i} - AC_{t+i})\right]\right\},$$

with respect to L_t, where E_t is the expectations operator conditional on the information available at time t, and $\beta < 1$ is the discount factor. We assume that decisions about L occur simultaneously with the exogenous flow of quits, Q. Assuming adjustment costs are described by (4c), for given values of K_t, Q_t and ε_t the representative firm operates each period according to the Euler equation:

$$\begin{aligned}(5)\qquad & \alpha_1 + \varepsilon_{1t} - \alpha_{11} L_t - \alpha_{12} K_t - W_t + \theta_{11} - \theta_{11} \exp(\theta_{11} \Delta L_t) \\ & + \theta_{12} - \theta_{12} \exp[\theta_{12}(\Delta L_t + Q_t)] - \theta_2 \Delta L_t - \theta_3(\Delta L_t + Q_t) \\ & + E_t\{\beta[-\theta_{11} + \theta_{11} \exp(\theta_{11}\Delta L_{t+1}) - \theta_{12} \\ & + \theta_{12}\, exp(\theta_{12}(\Delta L_{t+1} + Q_{t+1})) + \theta_2 \Delta L_{t+1} + \theta_3(\Delta L_{t+1} + Q_{t+1})]\} = 0.\end{aligned}$$

Let $\tilde{\theta}_2 = \theta_2 + \theta_3$, and $\tilde{\alpha}_1 = (\theta_{11} + \theta_{12})(\beta - 1) - \alpha_1$. The values of the variables realized during period $t + 1$ are substituted for the unobserved one-period-forward expectations of employment and quits, and a forecast error η_{t+1} is appended. Then (5) becomes

$$\begin{aligned}(6)\qquad \beta\Delta L_{t+1} - \Delta L_t = {} & \tilde{\alpha}_1 / \tilde{\theta}_2 + (\alpha_{11}/\tilde{\theta}_2)L_t + (\alpha_{12}/\tilde{\theta}_2)K_t + (1/\tilde{\theta}_2)W_t \\ & +(\theta_3/\tilde{\theta}_2)(-\beta Q_{t+1} + Q_t) + (1/\tilde{\theta}_2)\{\theta_{11}[-\beta \exp(\theta_{11}\Delta L_{t+1}) \\ & +\exp(\theta_{11}\Delta L_t)]+\theta_{12}[-\beta\exp(\theta_{12}(\Delta L_{t+1}+Q_{t+1})) \\ & + \exp(\theta_{12}(\Delta L_t+Q_t))]\} - \varepsilon_{1t}/\tilde{\theta}_2 + \tilde{\eta}_{t+1}.\end{aligned}$$

The estimating equation is

$$(7) \qquad L_{t+1} = \bar{\alpha}_1 + \bar{\alpha}_{11}L_t - \beta^{-1}L_{t-1} + \bar{\alpha}_{12}K_t + \bar{\theta}_2W_t + \bar{\theta}_3\bar{\Delta}Q_t$$
$$+ \bar{\theta}_2\{\theta_{11}[-\beta\exp(\theta_{11}\Delta L_{t+1}) + \exp(\theta_{11}\Delta L_t)]$$
$$+ \theta_{12}[-\beta\exp(\theta_{12}(\Delta L_{t+1} + Q_{t+1})) + \exp(\theta_{12}(\Delta L_t + Q_t))]\} + \tilde{\eta}_{t+1},$$

where $\bar{\alpha}_1 = \tilde{\alpha}_1(\beta\tilde{\theta}_2)^{-1}$; $\bar{\alpha}_{11} = [(1 + \beta)\ \tilde{\theta}_2 + \alpha_{11}](\beta\tilde{\theta}_2)^{-1}$; $\bar{\alpha}_{12} = \alpha_{12}(\beta\tilde{\theta}_2)^{-1}$; $\bar{\theta}_2 = (\beta\tilde{\theta}_2)^{-1}$; $\bar{\theta}_3 = \theta_3(\beta\tilde{\theta}_2)^{-1}$, and $\tilde{\eta}_{t+1} = \beta^{-1}\eta_{t+1} - (\beta\tilde{\theta}_2)^{-1}\varepsilon_{1t}$; $\bar{\Delta} = (1 - \beta F)$, where F is the forward-shift operator.

Model II is described by the same equations as model III, but with $\theta_{12} = 0$. These equations also encompass model I if $\theta_{11} = 0$.

5.3. Description of the Data

We estimate these models using the monthly establishment-based data on flows of workers collected in the United States until 1982. For each plant in the survey data were collected on accessions, divided into new hires, rehires and other accessions (mainly transfers between plants of the same firm, and returning military personnel), and on separations, consisting of layoffs, quits and other separations (mainly workers discharged for cause).[4] We stress that these are gross flows of *workers*, not jobs.

Rehires are well described as a constant fraction of recent layoffs, and other separations appear to be a small constant fraction of new hires (Hamermesh 1969). That being so, and ignoring the tiny flows of other accessions, we can estimate the models under the reasonable assumption that the identity in (1) is a good description of the link between net and gross changes in employment.

We estimate all the models for 1961(I)-81(IV), the last period with turnover data. The quit rate, and the number of workers implied by it, is the three month sum of the monthly flows of quits. Some of the other variables are quarterly averages of monthly series, while others, including several of the instruments, are based on series that are collected only quarterly. L is total manufacturing employment from the monthly establishment survey. The forcing variable W is represented by the quarterly series on real manufacturing compensation per hour paid for, an appropriately broader measure than hourly earnings. Non-stationarity in the employment data is accounted for by the inclusion of a linear trend.

Table 5.1

GMM Estimates of the Adjustment Cost Parameters[a]

	Model I		Model II		Model III
	$\{\theta_2\}$	$\{\theta_2, \theta_3\}$	$\{\theta_2, \theta_{11}\}$	$\{\theta_2, \theta_3, \theta_{11}\}$	$\{\theta_2, \theta_3, \theta_{11}, \theta_{12}\}$
θ_2	33.526 (2.171)	11.968 (2.159)	51.076 (2.718)	48.150 (2.703)	49.921 (2.705)
θ_3	0	0.430 (2.256)	0	-0.094 (-0.733)	0.748 (0.818)
θ_{11}			7.426 (5.293)	7.236 (5.329)	7.341 (5.368)
θ_{12}					0.888 1.949
			Goodness-of-fit indicators		
	0.97509	0.97596	0.99948	0.99950	0.99956
s.e.	0.01102	0.01003	0.00159	0.00155	0.00145
SB	2.214	2.076	2.567	2.602	2.552

[a] Asymptotic t-values in parentheses.

Table 5.1 presents GMM (generalized method of moments) estimates of the first-order necessary conditions based on a set of instrumental variables. To allow for autocorrelation of the disturbances in the form of a first-order moving average, the instruments must be lagged at least two periods. The instruments used are: two- and three-period lagged changes in *W* and *L*; three-period lagged changes in *Q*, the producer price index (PPI) and output; a three-period lagged term in manufacturing gross investment in structures and equipment; four-period lagged terms in *Q*, output, the civilian unemployment rate, the PPI and the rate of capacity utilization; a constant; and a time trend. Manufacturing output is measured by the series on manufacturing shipments minus the change in inventories of final goods. Capacity utilization is based on the index of industrial production for manufacturing and gross investment is from the national accounts.[5]

The lagged dependent variables are powerful instruments which by definition are included in the information set available at the moment of decisionmaking and are uncorrelated with the *MA(1)* error process $\tilde{\eta}_{t+1}$. This is also true for the lagged values of the forcing variables *W*, *Q* and gross investment in structures and equipment. The PPI is the only nominal instrument and is included to capture the effect of inflation. Output, the unemployment rate and the rate of capacity utilization are proxies for the state of the business cycle and thus for aggregate demand.

5.4. Results

Table 5.1 presents GMM estimates of the adjustment cost parameters for models I-III, as well as goodness-of-fit indicators such as the $\bar{R}^2$ and the standard deviation of the residuals (s.e.). Before discussing the economic meaning of the parameters, we first need to investigate the models' statistical properties. Necessary conditions for GMM to produce consistent parameter estimates are that $E_t\{\tilde{\eta}_{t+1}\} = 0$ and $\tilde{\eta}_{t+1}$ is stationary. The Sargan-Bhargava statistic (1983), which tests for the presence of a unit root in the residuals, indicates no significant non-stationarity in any of the residual series. The diagonal of Table 5.2 presents p-values of Hansen's (1982) J-statistic testing the over-identifying restrictions. None of these restrictions is rejected at the 1% level for any of the estimated equations, although the J-test of model I with $\theta_3 = 0$ does reject the orthogonality hypothesis at the 5% level, as is common in estimates of this simple, standard model.[6]

Table 5.2

Tests of Parameter and Over-Identifying Restrictions[a]

Model I		Model II	
$\{\theta_2\}$	$\{\theta_2, \theta_3\}$	$\{\theta_2, \theta_{11}\}$	$\{\theta_2, \theta_3, \theta_{11}\}$
$p = 0.027$ J1 11	$p = 0.024$ $H_0 : \theta_3 = 0$ 1	$p = 0.000$ $H_0 : \theta_{11} = 0$ 1	$p = 0.000$ $H_0 : \theta_3 = \theta_{11} = 0$ 2
	$p = 0.085$ J2 10		$p = 0.000$ $H_0 : \theta_{11} = 0$ 1
		$p = 0.322$ J3 10	$p = 0.597$ $H_0 : \theta_3 = 0$ 1
			$p = 0.234$ J4 9

a Each box lists the significance level, the hypothesis and the degrees of freedom.

The upper triangle of Table 5.2 presents Gallant's (1987) likelihood-ratio type statistic for testing nested restrictions. For example, to test whether quits matter in model I, we can look either at the asymptotic t-statistic on θ_3 of model I in Table 5.1 or, alternatively, at the p-value on $H_0 : \theta_3 = 0$, in the second row of Table 5.2. The estimates of θ_2 are significantly positive in all five equations. Positive estimates of θ_2 and θ_3 are sufficient – and in model I necessary – conditions for strictly convex adjustment costs and point at the usual quasifixity of labor.

The estimate of θ_3 is positive and significant in model I, but not significantly different from zero in models II and III.[7] These estimates, coupled with the joint test on the significance of θ_3 and θ_{12}, show that the costs of changing the net level of employment and the costs of replacing workers are both important in describing employment fluctuations in aggregate US manufacturing, but *only* if one assumes that adjustment is symmetric. Once one allows for asymmetry, the role of quits disappears.

The estimates of θ_{11} from models II and III are significantly positive. The intuition is that positive net changes in employment are more costly than negative net changes, so that employment drops faster than it rises. This result is consistent with earlier findings for manufacturing production workers (the bulk of manufacturing employees) in the Netherlands and the United Kingdom (Pfann and Palm 1993), and with findings for aggregate employment in the United States (Hussey 1992). It also reflects the more rapid job destruction that occurs early in American recessions that Davis and Haltiwanger (1992) demonstrated. Moreover, within the context of the representative firm, the observed asymmetry of the responses to $\Delta L_t + Q_t(\theta_{12} > 0)$ implies that it is less costly to lay off workers than it is to hire new workers. Even though quits vary procyclically, that variation is slow enough for its impact on hiring and firing to be overcome by the apparent substantial costs of hiring relative to those of firing.

5.5. Conclusions and Implications for Dynamic Labor Demand

We have developed and estimated a model of labor demand that accounts for dynamics arising from the costs of both net and gross changes in employment. The estimates suggest that observed lags in the demand for labor at the aggregate level arise from slow adjustment in both the level of employment and in replacing workers who quit. That inference is correct, however, only if one assumes that adjustment costs are symmetric. Once we recognize that they may be asymmetric, the impact of quits disappears. The large procyclical fluctuations in voluntary mobility are important in describing aggregate employment fluctuations only if one imposes symmetric adjustment. This underscores the importance of asymmetric costs, for it shows that the near-universal absence of aggregate data on flows of workers from jobs should not prevent us from tracking aggregate employment well, *provided* we expand standard models of adjustment properly.

People interested in estimating models of aggregate adjustment thus face two choices: either obtain new data on fluctuations in voluntary mobility, or broaden their assumptions about adjustment to allow for a generalized form of asymmetry. The estimates of the two forms of model I, which correspond to a slight expansion of widely estimated Koyck-type equations describing aggregate employment, show that much of the slow adjustment that is attributed to the costs of changing the level of employment in fact results from the cost of replacing workers who have quit. This means that the interpretation of lag parameters, including comparisons of employment lags across economies, must be made with great care.[8]

The assumption of convex adjustment costs is a convenience that may not be justified at the micro level. Similarly, problems of aggregation should give pause to any attempt to estimate a model of dynamic labor demand that proposes a micro-theoretic foundation. (See Hamermesh 1993, on both points.) None the less, economists will no doubt continue to use such models in their central task of describing aggregate employment fluctuations. To do this successfully, one must either find data on the highly cyclical variable, voluntary flows of workers, to add to one's models, or expand those models to allow for more complicated descriptions of the costs of factor adjustment. Without either of these extensions, simple models of symmetric convex adjustment costs are faulty even for the limited goal of prediction.

6

Job Turnover and Labor Turnover: A Taxonomy of Employment Dynamics

6.1. Introduction

Job creation, job destruction and worker turnover are a recent focus of both theoretical and empirical research. This study contributes to the empirical literature by presenting an organized set of stylized facts on the relations among flows of workers, changes in employment and changes in the number of jobs at the firm level. Various terms have been used to describe, summarize and analyze employment dynamics, including "job creation/destruction", "employment growth/decline", and "hiring/firing". Our purposes here are to sort out differences in these terms and examine how the concepts should be viewed from the perspective of the individual firm. The discussion alone should demonstrate that great care is required in using the various terms, as they mean very different things and have different implications for analyzing labor market adjustment and the impact of policies. We demonstrate some aspects of their importance using a data set that allows us to construct comprehensive measures of job creation and types of labor mobility. Our analysis confirms various results on employment dynamics and contributes important new facts.

The original version of this chapter was published as: Hamermesh, Daniel S./Hassink, Wolter H. J./van Ours, Jan C. (1996). Job Turnover and Labor Turnover: A Taxonomy of Employment Dynamics, in: Annales d'Économie et de Statistique, 41/42: 22–40. We thank Danny Blanchflower, Frank den Butter, Wim Groot, John Haltiwanger, Francis Kramarz and a referee for helpful comments, William Praat for computational assistance, and the Organization for Labor Market Research (OSA), The Hague, for the use of their data and for financial support.

6.2. Alternative Concepts of Employment and Job Dynamics

Underlying the entire discussion are two fundamental issues: 1) What patterns of changes in staffing at the firm level occur in the process of job and labor turnover? and 2) What microeconomic forces produce these patterns of changes? We do not consider the second issue. It has been analyzed from a variety of perspectives, including in the literature on adjustment costs (e.g., Hamermesh (1993), Sections 6.6 and 6.7) and job (stemming from the original work of Jovanovic (1979)). Our interest here is not in explanation but rather in illustrating and clarifying what occurs at the firm/establishment level. Are job creation hiring and employment growth interchangeable terms for the same phenomenon? Are job destruction, firing and employment decline interchangeable? What do we mean by job creation?

The terms job creation and destruction have been applied recently in the macroeconomic literature (e.g., Davis and Haltiwanger (1990)). Though it does not use the term, what this literature really discusses are simultaneous positive and negative *firm- (or plant-) level net employment changes*. Substantial empirical work (e.g., Leonard (1987); Dunne *et al.* (1989); and Davis and Haltiwanger (1992) demonstrates that employment falls (rises) in a large fraction of the micro units within a narrowly defined aggregate in which the net change in employment is positive (negative)[1]. That *interfirm (or interplant) reallocation* is important within an aggregate is useful for demonstrating the role and importance of the dispersion of shocks in determining macroeconomic adjustment (Caballero *et al.* (1995)).

Even assuming that workers are observationally homogeneous, concentration on net employment change ignores much of the potentially important adjustment costs that might be generated by shock to costs or technology. One can easily imagine a firm (a university) with no net change in employment over some period, but where, for example, all five assistant professors of economics quit and five new ones are hired to replace them. Net employment change is zero; the measured interfirm reallocation is zero; and no jobs are destroyed or created. Yet clearly the costs to the firm are nonzero and the costs to society are also much different from those that would have arisen if no quits had occurred. The net change in employment in an establishment can be decomposed in great detail as:

$$\Delta E = NH + R + TI - Q - F - D - TO, \qquad (1)$$

where *NH* are new hires; *R* are rehires; *TI* are transfers from other plants in the firm; *Q* are quits; *F* are fires (layoffs in American terminology); *D* are discharges for cause; and *TO* are transfers to other plants in the firm.[2]

Some attention has been given to (1). Burgess and Nickel (1990) examined aggregate of accessions (the first three terms) and separations (the last four terms); and Hamermesh (1995) considered the pattern of hires, quits and net employment change for several establishments. Leonard and Van Audenrode (1993) investigated hires and layoffs and demonstrated that Belgian manufacturing firms do both within the same year. We do not know, however, the extent to which establishments of firms can be classified using the identity (1) into those that are growing and hiring, and those that are declining and firing; or whether hiring and/or firing are activities that are only loosely related to net employment changes. That is, does growth in employment mean that the firm is in a "hiring regime" (Lockwood and Manning (1993))? Does a drop in employment imply a "firing regime"? We examine what net changes in employment in a firm or establishment imply about the type and extent of flow of workers into and out of it.

These distinctions are important because the assumptions underlying theories of the dynamics of labor demand equate expansion with hiring (and contraction with firing). The *locus classicus* in this area (Sargent (1978)) presents a rational-expectations approach to the firm's net change in employment. The vast subsequent literature in macroeconomics essentially ignores the possibility that negative net changes in employment may not only occur when firms fire workers, but may instead reflect substantial hiring. Much of the analysis of changes in employment in Europe (pioneered by Nickel, summarized by him, 1986, and which we call the "European approach") looks at the firm's decisions in terms of some of the gross flows in (1) that are the firm's proximate tools for altering its staffing. But this approach has had little impact on the discussion in macroeconomics, perhaps because data on these flows are very difficult to obtain.

With heterogeneous workers and jobs the distinction between job creation/destruction and hiring/firing/employment changes is essential. If, for example, the firm fires five assistant professors of sociology and replaces them with five assistant professors of economics, its costs differ from those in the example above, where economists who quit were replaced by others. If the firm abolishes one vice-presidential position and transfers the incumbent to a newly-created other such position, its costs will be greater than if no changes occurred. Most important, in both of these cases jobs are created (and an equal number are destroyed), even though there is no net employment change at the firm level.

Figure 6.1
Heterogeneous Jobs and Workers in the Firm

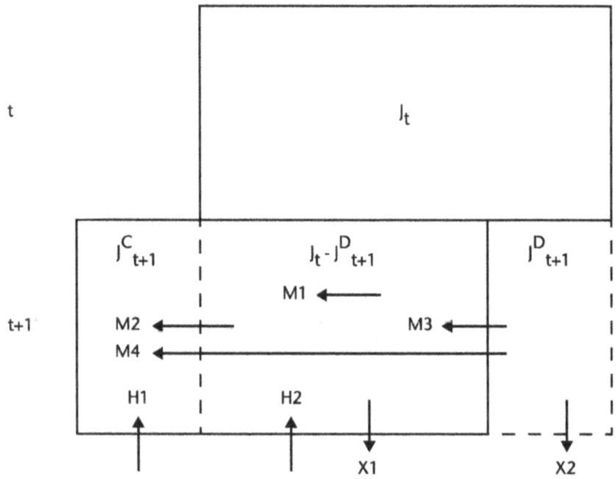

This view implies that some care is needed in defining what we mean by a job. For example, one could easily count any slight change in duties (e.g., switching from teaching two courses and doing research to one course and somewhat more research) as the creation and destruction of jobs. A variety of arbitrary definitions are possible. We take a purely empirical approach and define a job as a distinct set of duties and responsibilities that the employer recognizes as being attached to a position of employment. Obviously in any set of data different employers may have different notions about what constitutes a change in jobs within their firms. We rely on their identification of changes in jobs in a firm where the number of employees has not changed. This is exactly the same as our standard reliance in empirical research based on establishment or firm data on employers to identify who is an employee. While that issue seems straightforward, the existence of temporary workers on short-term contracts, of independent contractors, and of other peripheral work-performers should make it clear that, in the final analysis, notions of what constitutes an employee are fraught with the same ambiguities as attempts to define jobs.

Figure 6.1 offers a complete taxonomy of the dynamics of flows of workers and jobs in a single-plant firm.[3] Every worker in the firm fills a job. At time t there are J_t jobs. Between times t and $t + 1$ some jobs are destroyed, and some workers whose jobs were not destroyed either separate or *move internally* to existing or newly-created jobs (flows that we denote by M). Some of the separated workers were fired, either because of incompetence or because their jobs were destroyed. A flow of newly-hired workers takes the remaining newly-created jobs or fills the positions vacated by quitters.

The simplest concept illustrated in Figure 6.1 is the same net employment change, ΔE, as in (1), which by definition equals $J_{t+1} - J_t$. The second concept is the firm-level net employment change, $\Delta E^+ + \Delta E^-$; which measures the sum of all jobs created and destroyed (and ignores shifts of jobs within the firm). This is the now-standard calculation based on observations on plants or firms between two time periods. If the firm is expanding, its employment is part of the aggregate ΔE^+; if it is contracting its decline is part of the aggregate ΔE^-. The third measure, which we denote by $J^C + J^D$ (jobs created plus jobs destroyed) and call firm-level *job turnover*, adds gross shifts in jobs within the firm to the second measure. Thus just as $\Delta E^+ + \Delta E^-$ departs from ΔE by adding interfirm gross employment creation and destruction within an aggregate of firms, $J^C + J^D$ departs from $\Delta E^+ + \Delta E^-$ by adding intrafirm gross job creation and destruction in the aggregate of jobs within individual firms.

All three of these measures ignore workers' identities. All, including the third, which is novel here, are based on positions, not people. The fourth measure is labor turnover, based on total hires H and separations X. The relations among the four terms are:

$$\text{(2)} \qquad \Delta E \leq \Delta E^+ + \Delta E^- \leq J^C + J^D \leq H + X.^4$$

Net employment change within any aggregate is the same no matter on which concept it is based:

$$\text{(3)} \qquad \Delta E \equiv \Delta E^+ - \Delta E^- \equiv J^C + J^D \equiv H - X.$$

It is difficult to do justice to the complexity of Figure 6.1 in theoretical or empirical research. Even what we have called the European approach assumes that the firm never hires when it is firing, and vice-versa. That assumption is required by profit maximization in the presence of the homogeneous work force that the models always assume. That assumption is an expositional device, so that presumably no firm would hire and fire workers with the same sets of skills (though obviously it could profitably hire workers with one set of skills and fire those with another in response to relative demand or cost shocks). Simultaneous hiring and firing could, however, be rational as firms dissolve bad matches and replace workers with others who are observationally equivalent *ab initio.*

The possible coexistence of hiring and firing within a firm has implications for macroeconomic adjustment. The employment reallocation generated by macroeconomic shocks may greatly exceed the interfirm (or interplant) reallocation that has been the focus of so much recent research. The greater intrafirm and intraplant reallocation are, the greater are the implicit costs of changing output levels. The cost to the firm of a negative macroeconomic shock is indicated not by the loss in employment, but by the costs of hiring and firing that may accompany the shock. Because hiring and firing may occur simultaneously, these costs cannot be inferred simply by summing up hires in firms that are only hiring and fires in those that are only firing. The subtleties of analyzing employment fluctuations at the macro level are even greater than moving from aggregating firms' net employment changes to aggregating their gross changes would suggest.

6.3. Estimates of the Component Flows of Workers and Jobs

In this section we show that the distinctions between gross and net flows are important empirically and should condition how we discuss labor market dynamics. We make no attempt to model the determinants of these flows or their interrelationships. Rather, using a broad-based random sample that allows the simultaneous analysis of net employment changes, job changes and flows of workers at the firm level, we inquire about the definitional and conceptual issues raised in the previous section. These include examining the relationships between: 1) Flows of jobs within a firm and flows of workers to and from the firm; 2) Net employment changes within a firm and the firm's patterns of hiring and firing; and 3) Hiring and firing within a firm during the same time period.

This data set, whose inclusion of information on types of flows of workers and on internal mobility makes it unique for any industrialized economy, is based on two surveys by the Organization for Labor Market Research (OSA) of the Netherlands.[5] The surveys are of organizations, which we refer to as firms, and are representative of all industries (including government and education) in the Netherlands in 1988 and 1990. The samples are stratified according to the area of economic activity and the size of the firm (10–49, 50–99, and 100+ employees), with firms of fewer than 10 employees excluded.[6] While the data are representative only of one small economy, the Netherlands is highly advanced and typical in its mix of industries. Moreover, this data set, unlike many of those used to study employment dynamics that are restricted to the small and decreasingly important manufacturing sector, covers the entire economy.

Each survey uses two questionnaires. The first, which was administered by enumerators, concerned qualitative characteristics and financial data; the second concerned administrative information. The mail responses to this second questionnaire came some time after the first questionnaire was answered and had a nonresponse rate of 20–25 percent. The firms included in each survey contained roughly 3 percent of total employment in the Netherlands. The surveys were set up as a panel, but a large number of the 1988 firms did not cooperate in 1990, had a substantial change in activities or merged.

Tables 6.1 and 6.2 (illustrating Figure 6.1) are based on data for 1,158 firms from 1990. For each firm in that year, if there was any internal mobility, hiring or separation of workers, information on the most recent worker in these flows was registered. The respondent from the firm reported whether the worker came from a destroyed or existing job (in case of X and M), or whether the worker went to a (newly) created job or existing job (in case of H and M). Aggregation of the information on workers across all firms in the sample gives estimates of the relevant fractions. After multiplication by the average H, X or M we obtain the size of each of the subflows. The results in Tables 6.3, 6.5–6.8 and Figures 6.2 are based on the pooled sample of the 2,204 firms (with some firms appearing in both years) for which there are complete data on all the levels and flows. A panel of 558 firms with complete responses in both 1988 and 1990 forms the basis for Table 6.4. The data are weighted by sector and firm size to be representative of all Dutch firms having at least ten employees except in Tables 6.1 and 6.2 (because those data, unlike those that form the basis for the other tables, are from interviews with only one worker in each firm).[7]

In addition to the level of employment, which is calculated irrespective of the number of hours worked, we have information on the number of hires separations and internal mobility of workers. The cause of each worker's separation is also available. Generally there are two types of contractual forms of employment relationship in the Netherlands. First, workers may have a temporary contract for a period shorter than one year. In most cases such workers are hired from a specialized agency and are excluded from our measures of employment and worker flows. Second, workers may have a long-term employment relationship with a firm with a contract that is generally at least one year long. Their appointment is indefinite and begins with a probationary period during which either party may terminate the contract immediately. Workers with these contracts are included in the employment measure and the hiring and separation flows. Note that this second group also includes temporary workers who obtained a long-term contract at some point during their temporary relationship with the firm.

We define hire as employees who entered the organization during the year, including employees with a probationary period but excluding employees with a temporary contract shorter than one year. Outflows of workers are defined similarly using the number of separations. Internal mobility is defined as the number of workers who changed function and/or department within the organization during the year. We calculated the flows as annual percentages of employment at the start of the year. The Appendix presents definitions of the main variables.

One should note that the data are based on firms, not plants. This choice is dictated by the nature of the survey just as it has been in the literature on aggregating employment changes across units part of which uses firm data, part of which uses establishment data (Hemermesh (1993), Table 4). Firm data have the advantage that the firm is the main locus of decision-making about employment in its constituent units. They have the disadvantage of necessarily masking some worker mobility and some changes in employment to the extent that there are interplant transfers and that some of the firm's units expand while others contract. The former problem is likely to be unimportant, since old evidence from American establishment data suggests that interplant transfers are a minute fraction of all flows of workers. The importance of the latter difficulty is unclear; but since the results in this section differ little if the sample is restricted to firms employing fewer than 100 workers, it is unlikely that basing the study on establishment data would alter our conclusions qualitatively.

Table 6.1

Estimates of the Flows in Figure 6.1, Netherlands (1990)
(percent of employment)

Hires		Outflows		Internal Flows	
H1	3.2	*X1*	8.2	*M1*	1.8
H2	8.7	*X2*	1.9	*M2*	0.9
				M3	0.4
				M4	0.3
Total	11.9		10.1		3.4

6.3.1. *Job Flows and Flows of Workers*

Table 6.1 presents estimates of the flows in Figure 6.1 and demonstrates the well-known fact that there is substantial turnover of workers at the firm level. The distinction between existing and newly-created jobs in this taxonomy generates several interesting and novel observations however. Most important, the very large majority of mobility is to and from existing jobs: Nearly three-fourths of hires are in the category *H2*, hires to existing jobs, while an even greater fraction of separations are in *X1*, flows out of jobs that continue in existence. Over half of all internal flows are in the category *M1*, representing workers who move from one job that continues in existence to another that had been occupied previously. Most ouflows, inflows and internal flows represent reshuffling of people into and out of positions that had been filled and that continue to exist.

The most important use of the taxonomy in Figure 6.1 is its illustration of the inequalities in (2), which we present in Table 6.2. The standard proxy measure for job turnover that ignores internal mobility, absolute net employment change at the firm level, $\Delta E^{+} + \Delta E^{-}$; dwarfs average net employment change (6.2 versus 1.8 percent), as is usual in the burgeoning literature on this issue.

Table 6.2

Estimates of (2), 1990 (percent of employment)[a]

	Positive Part	Negative Part	Sum
ΔE			1.8
$\Delta E^{+} + \Delta E^{-}$	4.0	2.2	6.2
$J^{C} + J^{D}$	4.4	2.6	7.0
H + X	11.9	10.1	22.0

[a] E = employment; J^{C} = jobs created; J^{D} = jobs destroyed; H = hires; X = seperations.

Including intrafirm gross job creation and destruction to allow the calculation of $J^C + J^D$, which is novel in this study, raises the estimate of job turnover to 7.0 percent, roughly 15 percent above what the standard measure suggests. This is important; but it is obvious that the simultaneous creation and destruction of jobs within firms does not occur frequently, so that we should not greatly alter our views about the relative magnitudes of aggregate employment change and firm-level absolute net employment change.

Table 6.2 also demonstrates that job turnover is only one third of labor turnover.[8] The huge size of flows of workers compared to net changes in employment replicates results found for several American states by Anderson and Meyer (1994) and Burgess *et al.* (1994). Our results expand on those studies a bit, however, for they cover an entire economy and show how large these flows of workers are even compared to flows of jobs, not just to changes in employment. The sheer magnitude of worker flows shown here and in the two other studies suggests the value of paying more attention to the gross costs of adjusting employment rather than to the net employment changes that capture most of the attention of researchers studying the dynamics of labor demand.

6.3.2. Net Employment Changes and Flows of Workers

Table 6.3 presents summary statistics for the pooled sample. Because the data are weighted and cover both 1988 and 1990, the estimates are not identical to their counterparts in Table 6.1. The average annual hiring rate is 12.4 percent, while the separation rate is 11.8 percent, of which the firing rate is 1.5 percent, the quit rate 8 percent, and the rest miscellaneous separations. The average annual internal mobility rate is 3.3 percent.

Table 6.3

Means and Standard Deviations of Hires (*H*), Separations (*X*), Fires (*F*), Quits (*Q*) and Internal Mobility (*M*), 1988 and 1990 (annual percentages of employment at the start of the year)[a]

	H_t	X_t	F_t	Q_t	M_t	N
$\Delta E > 0$	20.3 (14.2)	9.8 (7.9)	1.1 (2.9)	7.0 (7.0)	4.2 (8.1)	890
$\Delta E = 0$	11 .3 (13.8)	11 .3 (13.8)	0.8 (3.0)	8.6 (12.1)	2.4 (6.4)	367
$\Delta E < 0$	5.9 (7.0)	13.9 (9.7)	2.3 (6.4)	8.4 (7.8)	3.0 (5.7)	947
Total	12.4 (13.4)	11.8 (10.0)	1.5 (4.7)	8.0 (8.4)	3.3 (7.0)	2204

[a] N = number of firms; ΔE = annual employment change.

Table 6.3 divides the pooled sample into firms with growing, stable or declining employment. Unsurprisingly, the hiring rate decreases as employment growth moves from positive to negative. Still, hiring rates in firms with declining employment average 5.9 percent. Most important, calculations based on the table show that only 58 percent of all hires occur in firms that are expanding. The firing rate where employment is declining is higher than where it is increasing or stable. Firms with expanding employment still fire 1.1 percent of their workers each year, though; and only 40 percent of all fires occur in firms that are contracting.

Table 6.4

Persistence in Employment Adjustment (percent of firms)

	1990					
1988	ΔE < 0, H = 0	ΔE < 0, H > 0	ΔE = 0, H = 0	ΔE = 0, H > 0	ΔE > 0, H > 0	Total
ΔE < 0, H = 0	1.3	1.8	0.0	2.3	2.3	7.7
ΔE < 0, H > 0	4.8	6.0	0.0	4.9	9.2	24.9
ΔE = 0, H = 0	0.6	0.0	0.0	5.7	3.5	9.8
ΔE = 0, H > 0	3.4	4.8	0.0	6.8	8.1	23.1
ΔE > 0, H > 0	3.6	8.0	0.0	8.6	14.3	34.5
Total	13.7	20.6	0.0	28.3	37.4	100.0

Table 6.4 examines the extent to which firms can be classified as remaining in the same regime over time (e.g., expanding and hiring, declining and hiring, etc.) by presenting data describing the panel of 558 firms. Roughly 14 percent of firms are declining in both years; and another 14 percent are growing in both years. A large majority, though, are growing in one year and stable or declining two years later. Probably most interesting is the relative lack of persistence in hiring. The probability that firms with stable employment in both years that are hiring in the first year are also hiring in the second year is only 0.54. Similarly, hiring behavior among firms that are declining in both years is quite variable over time. While there is some persistence in hiring among continuously growing and stable firms, even their hiring rates vary greatly. The implied on-off behavior may reflect the existence of nonconvex costs of hiring (Hamermesh (1989)), though with annual data we cannot explore this possibility in great detail.

Quit rates in firms with growing employment are somewhat below those in firms with decreasing or stable employment, but the differences in these averages are quite small. The quit rate seems relatively unaffected

Figure 6.2.1

Hiring Rate by Growth of Employment

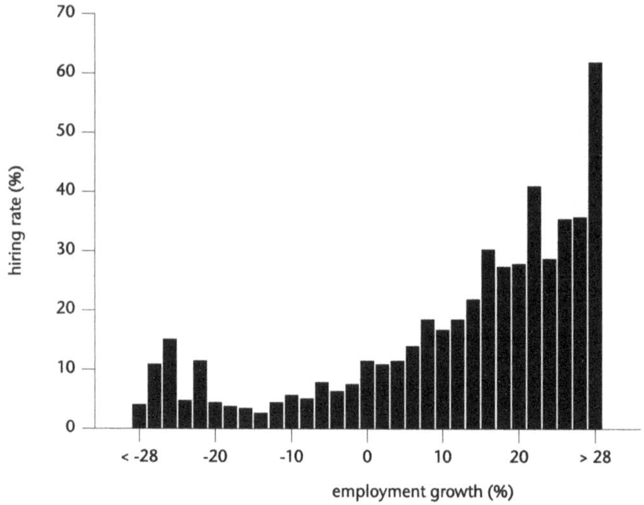

Figure 6.2.2

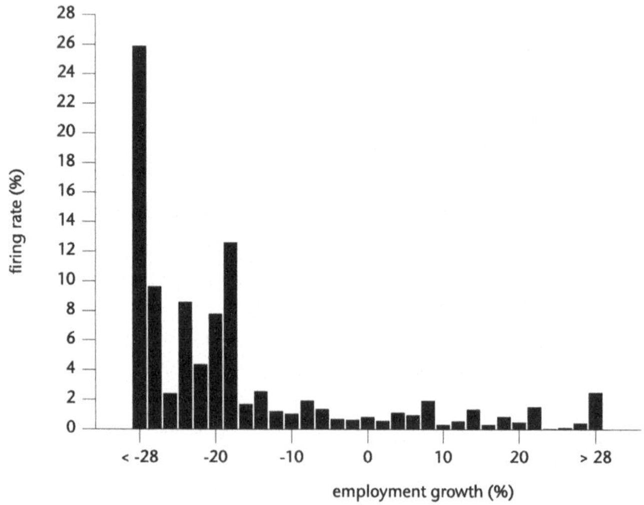

by conditions within the firm (presumably responding more to general labor market conditions). Internal mobility rates are highest among growing firms suggesting that the expansion of employment does lead to greater opportunities for incumbent employees.

The data on internal mobility are unique to this study and merit additional attention. Table 6.5 presents one novel, though perhaps unsurprising fact (demonstrated again by Hassink *et al.* (1994): Internal mobility is much more common within larger firms than in smaller ones. In nearly two-third of firms with fewer than 100 employees no internal mobility was reported, while three-fourths of larger firms reported some internal mobility. Greater opportunities for promotion have long been adduced as a reason for lower quit rates in larger firms. (Even in our data, which ignore firms with fewer than 10 employees and, most important, ignore workers on short-term contracts, we still find a slight difference of 0.3 percent per annum between firms with fewer and more than 100 employees). We believe this is the first demonstration that the opportunities for promotion are actually greater in larger firms. One should note, too, that chances for advancement are larger for white- than for blue-collar workers: Those firms where $M > 0$ have a higher proportion of white-collar workers in total employment (32 percent) than do firms where $M = 0$ (28 percent).

Figure 6.2 presents more detail about the relationships between rates of flows of workers and employment growth. Firms are classified into growth categories ranging in steps of two percentage points from -28 percent to +28 percent. The left- and right-most bars represent the average rates from the tails and contain 0.6 percent and 1.5 percent of the (employment-weighted) firms respectively. Figure 6.2.1 shows that hires occur even at large negative employment growth. The hiring rate is roughly stable between 5 and 8 percent where employment is declining, regardless of the size of the decline. Among expanding firms there is a clear positive correlation between employment growth and the hiring rate.

Figure 6.2.2 shows that the relationship between the firing rate and employment growth is the mirror image of Figure 6.2.1. The firing rate is quite stable at about 1 percent where employment is growing. Where employment is declining, the firing rate is greater the larger is the drop in employment.

Figure 6.2.3 graphs the quit rate by employment change. As was obvious in Table 6.3, there is no strong correlation between the two. Figure 6.2.4 shows that the average internal mobility rate also does not vary much with employment growth. If internal mobility were important in the reshuffling of employment, we would see a U-shaped

Figure 6.2.3
Quit Rate by Growth of Employment

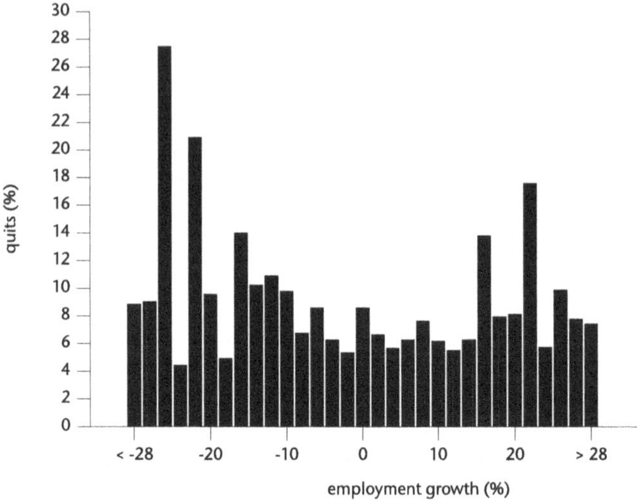

Figure 6.2.4
Internal Mobility Rate by Growth of Employment

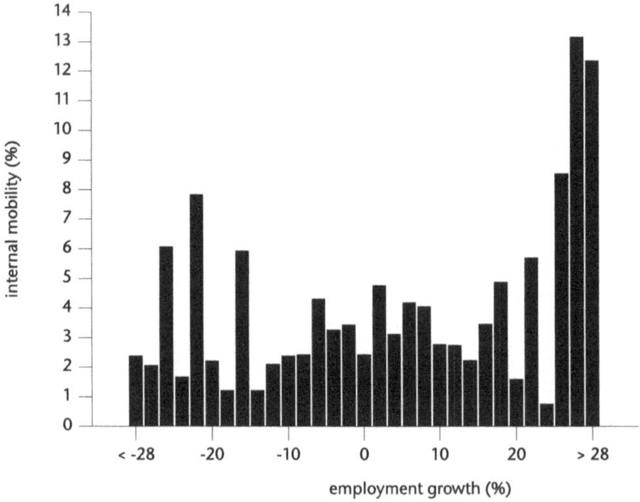

relationship between it and ernployment growth. Figure 6.2.4 gives at most only a very slight hint of this. Where employment is growing very rapidly, though, reshuffling is substantial: The internal mobility rate is highest among firms growing at least 24 percent per year.

Table 6.3-6.5 and Figure 6.2 produce several novel conclusions. Most important flows of workers are large even in firms where net employment changes are small. Hiring is not restricted to firms with expanding employment (mostly because of the very high rate of quitting). Firing is not restricted to firms with declining employment. Internal mobility is low, below the average hiring rate, even in firms with declining employment, though it is higher in larger firms. This fairly low rate suggests that most workers enter their jobs directly from outside the firm, while internal mobility chains, movements along Dunlop-type (1957) job ladders, are relatively few.

6.3.3. *Simultaneous Hiring and Firing*

Table 6.6 groups firms according to hiring and firing status and whether employment is growing, stable and declining. It shows that one quarter of the firms in our sample did not alter employment in a given year. The fractions of firms with decreasing or increasing employment are about the same. Most of the firms (83 percent) are hiring, either with (21.6 percent) or without (61.3 percent) firing. Together with the observation that only 2.6 percent of firms fire without hiring, this demonstrates that most firing is done by firms that are also hiring.

The remaining tables consider to what extent this apparent simultaneity of hiring and firing can be attributed to observable worker heterogeneity. One proxy for such heterogeneity is the size of the firm, since larger firms will generally employ workers in more skill groups. Table 6.7 relates the four possible combinations among hires and fires to firm size. 45 percent of the large firms (at least 100 employees) simultaneously fire and hire, substantially more than the 19 percent of small firms. The table demonstrates that with more heterogeneity of workers (greater firm size), there is also more simultaneous hiring and firing. This evidence suggests (albeit only indirectly) that some of the simultaneity arises from firms' altering the mix of workers of different observable types in response to various shocks.

Table 6.8 examines whether classification by one observable distinction - white-collar (WC) and blue-collar (BC) worker - can account for the apparent simultaneous hiring and firing. If, for example, employment declines among white-collar workers while quitters are blue-collar workers who must be replaced, we would observe both hiring and firing at the firm level. Among the 21.6 percent of firms that are hiring and firing, only 1.1 percent of all firms are firing only one type of worker and hiring only the other. By far the most common pattern among this 21.6 percent of firms is simultaneous hiring and firing of blue-collar workers (13.4 percent of firms). The table shows clearly that heterogeneity across broadly-defined occupational lines accounts for only a small part of the surprisingly common observation of firms that are hiring and firing in the same year. The apparent simultaneity even within a (broad) occupation suggests that much of what we observed are failed job matches that are replaced by new ones with a different worker in the same job.

Table 6.5

Internal Mobility by Firm Size, 1988 and 1990 (percent of firms)

	$E < 100$	$E \geq 100$	Total
$M = 0$	57.2	2.7	59.9
$M > 0$	32.4	7.7	40.1
Total	89.6	10.4	100.0

Table 6.6

Hires (H), Fires (F) and Annual Employment Change (ΔE), 1988 and 1990 (percent of firms)

	$\Delta E < 0$	$\Delta E = 0$	$\Delta E > 0$	Total
$H = 0, F = 0$	9.9	4.6	0.0	14.5
$H = 0, F > 0$	2.6	0.0	0.0	2.6
$H > 0, F = 0$	16.6	17.5	27.2	61.3
$H > 0, F > 0$	9.5	4.0	8.1	21.6
Total	38.6	26.1	35.3	100.0

Table 6.7

Hires and Fires by Firm Size, 1988 and 1990 (percent of firms)

	$E < 100$	$E \geq 100$	Total
$H = 0, F = 0$	14.2	0.3	14.5
$H = 0, F > 0$	2.3	0.2	2.6
$H > 0, F = 0$	56.1	5.2	61.3
$H > 0, F > 0$	17.0	4.7	21.6
Total	89.6	10.4	100.0

Another possibility is that the apparently simultaneous hiring and firing is an artifact of the temporal aggregation in our annual data. One might reasonably question whether such simultaneity is even possible: If we observed each firm every second we would never observe simultaneous hiring and firing. No doubt annual observations are not the most desirable for this purpose, any more than are observations every second (or even minute). Evidence from comparison of quarterly and annual data on firmlevel net employment change (e.g. Davis and Haltiwanger (1990)) shows, however, that the sum of these net changes in quarterly data is at least 50 percent of the sum when the calculation is based on annual data. With a finer temporal aggregation, perhaps to quarterly or even to monthly observations, we believe that simultaneous hiring and firing would still be observed fairly frequently. This analogy, though by no means resolving the issue, at least hints that this phenomenon is not purely an artifact of our data set.

How can we rationalize this subsection's finding that most of the firms that are firing are also hiring with the result of the first subsection that simultaneous destruction and creation of jobs within the firm is small? One compelling possibility consistent with the data is that, as we showed in Table 6.1, most jobs that are vacated by fired workers are filled by workers who are hired to replace them in jobs that continue. Apparently most mobility of workers is into and out of existing jobs rather than to newly created or from destroyed jobs. Labor turnover is to a large extent a self-driven process that is only loosely connected to job creation and job destruction.

6.4. Conclusions

We have investigated the phenomena of job creation and job destruction and of hiring and firing workers using a set of data on employment levels and types of flows of workers to, from and within firms. The terms job creation/destruction and hiring/firing are definitely not interchangeable. There is substantial hiring to existing jobs. Hiring is not restricted to firms with expanding employment; over 40 percent of hiring is done by firms that are not growing. Firing is not restricted to firms with declining employment; the majority of firing is done by firms that are not declining.

The huge difference between aggregate net employment change and firmlevel net employment change that has been noted frequently in

Table 6.8
Blue-collar (*BC*) and White-collar (*WC*) Hires and Fires, 1988 and 1990 (percent of firms)

Fires	Hires				
	BC = 0 WC = 0	BC > 0 WC = 0	BC = 0 WC > 0	BC > 0 WC > 0	Total
BC = 0 WC = 0	17.1	33.4	7.8	41.7	100.0
BC > 0 WC = 0	1.8	5.8	0.6	7.6	15.8
BC = 0 WC > 0	14.5	26.5	6.4	28.4	75.8
BC > 0 WC > 0	0.3	0.6	0.1	2.2	3.2
Total	0.5	0.5	0.7	3.5	5.2

the recent literature is enlarged only somewhat when simultaneous job creation and destruction within firms is accounted for. Using the job classfications that employers themselves use, our results suggest that ignoring the heterogeneity arising from job creation/destruction within firms does not detract greatly from our ability to analyze macroeconomic fluctuations that are related to interfirm heterogeneity.

The demonstration over the last decade that heterogeneity in employment growth among firms and establishments within narrowly-defined industries is immense has been a fundamental contribution to our understanding of the microeconomic bases of macroeconomic change. Here we have demonstrated that there is a concomitant heterogeneity in flows of workers into and out of the firm, and through and between jobs, among firms whose employment is changing at identical rates. Moreover, these flows are substantial. These facts suggest that further empirical work requires data on both job and labor turnover. Only then will we be able to understand and analyze the complexity of employment dynamics and labor mobility to the appropriate extent and be able to apply that analysis to enhance our understanding of change at the macro level.

APPENDIX
Definition of Variables

E: "How many workers were employed in your organization in December 1988 (1990) (no temporary workers)? This concerns the number of employees irrespective of the number of hours worked".
In the 1988 wave *E* is observed for 1988 and 1986. Employment for December 1987 and December 1989 are constructed by means of the hires (*H*) and the separation (*X*) of employees in the next year: $E_{t-1} = E_t - H_t + X_t$.

H: "How many employees entered your organization in 1988 (1990), including employees with a probationary period, excluding employees with a temporary contract shorter than one year?"

X: "How many employees left your organization in 1988 (1990), excluding employees with a temporary contract shorter than one year?" *X* is divided into the number of employees who left the organization for the following reasons: Pension, early retirement, death; outflow because of disability; firing; quit; end of temporary contract with a duration of more than one year.

M: "How many employees changed functions and/or changed department within the organization?"

IV Policy on the Demand Side

Perhaps the most important reason for studying the demand for labor is to understand how employers' behavior is affected by the policies that governments adopt to affect the labor market. Labor market policies differ from country to country, but it seems possible to classify them into several broad categories. That possibility means, even though there are cultural and other differences among labor markets, that analyzing the impacts of policies in one country has important implications more generally for policies elsewhere. Thus, even though all but one of the studies in this part examines policies in the United States, I believe they are much more broadly relevant than this one economy.

It should be stressed that, while the direct evaluation of policies is important (and is what the studies in this part do), at least as important in evaluating policies is the generalized knowledge about employers' behavior that stems from pure research of the kind in Part III of this volume. In many cases proposed policies are sufficiently novel - are not merely changes in the parameters of an existing policy - that the only way to gauge their likely impacts is to simulate them using the underlying behavioral parameters describing the behavior of the agents, including the employers, who are likely to be affected. *Ex ante* policy evaluation often requires pure research, and that is another reason why pure research, rather than the discovery of how X has affected Y, is so important.

One general type of labor market policy that is ubiquitous in both rich and poor economies is the regulation of wages and hours of work. This includes minimum wage policies, regulations on the length of the workweek and penalties for work beyond standard hours, mandatory weeks of holiday and legislated penalty rates on work outside normal hours. (It also includes maximum wage policies which, although absent from today's economies, have been imposed occasionally, particularly when, as after the Great Plague of the 14th century, shortages of workers were driving up equilibrium wages.) All of these policies represent attempts to keep wages or employment away from their free-market equilibrium values. Their general stated purpose has been to "protect" workers from exploitation – in the form of hourly pay below what society views as acceptable, of hours that are viewed as excessively long, or of requirements that work be performed at undesirable or even unhealthy times of day or days of the week. All of these policies fall under the general rubric of price floors or limits on quantities exchanged that are familiar to students of introductory economics.

Another type of policy protects workers from economic fluctuations, particularly those that cause them to lose their jobs. The general notion is that there is some living standard that workers who are viewed as out of work through no fault of their own should have. Nothing requires this form of income maintenance to operate through the labor market: A country could simply institute policies that guarantee every person, or at least every adult, some minimum standard of living independent of their current or prior attachment to the labor market. But most developed economies have chosen to link at least some income support to labor market behavior, so that policies providing unemployment insurance and/or severance pay are ubiquitous in the developed world and quite common in developing countries too.

This typology divides labor market policies into those that protect workers while they are at work and those that protect them when they are not at work. I have not included such policies as affirmative-action, which should be viewed as falling under the first rubric, since it imposes requirements on employers on the type of worker whom they employ. Requirements that employers provide certain non-wage monetary benefits are also easily classifiable as affecting the monetary conditions of work. Also so classifiable are requirements about safety in the workplace, since their economic effects are likely also to be on the monetary returns to work and on the amount of work offered by employers. In the end, of course, each policy is different, as are their effects. That is the motivation for the studies in this part: To provide answers to a few questions about some of the specific impacts of particular policies; but also to provide guidelines for answering some more general questions that in the end depend on our knowledge about labor demand.

In the United States minimum wages have been set nationally since 1938 by the Fair Labor Standards Act (FLSA) and in many states by state laws that in some cases have set higher minima. Relative to most countries the national minimum is quite low compared to the average wage, so that the laws affect the wages and employment of relatively few workers. Compared to their likely small impact on the labor market, minimum wages have attracted a remarkable amount of attention from labor economists. No doubt this interest has arisen because of the constant injection of highly partisan politics into the discussion of this policy.*

The evaluation questions about the minimum wage have revolved around its impacts on the employment of those workers most likely to have been affected, and on the indirect impacts on other workers' employment; on their wages and those of other workers; and, much less frequently, on how the distribution of incomes is affected by this policy, how prices are affected and how non-wage employee benefits are altered by changes in the minimum. The study in Chapter 7 falls under the first category – it analyzes impacts on employment of the low-skilled workers who are most likely to be affected by changes in the minimum wage, and on that of higher-skilled workers. It arose from two sources: 1) A substantial amount of research funded by the Minimum Wage Study Commission (MWSC, 1981), which was mandated by the 1977 amendments to the Fair Labor Standards Act. In addition to its reports Brown (1982) presented an excellent summary of our understanding of the employment impacts of the minimum wage up to that time; and 2) My recognition that the type of research included in Chapter 1 would be useful in expanding the analysis of the employment effects of changes in the minimum wage.

Obviously the study in Chapter 7 is old, based on a time series of aggregate data ending in the late 1970s. Nonetheless, while numerous more recent studies have examined the same issue – the extent to which minimum wages alter employment opportunities across demographic groups (see, e.g., Neumark and Wascher, 2008) – none appears to have done so in a formal way that is linked to the theory of labor demand. As such the study still seems highly relevant. Indeed, some evidence on that is that the estimates that I produced in that research are still quoted in the media every time a change in the minimum wage is proposed.

Overtime penalties on employers did probably arise initially to protect workers from exploitation. Even in the discussion surrounding the FLSA, and especially in discussions about proposed subsequent amendments, the focus has been more on applying overtime

* Perhaps the best example of the partisanship of this issue is the specific mention of Card and Krueger (1995) by President Clinton in a speech discussing minimum wages.

laws as a way of inducing employers to substitute workers for hours by raising the cost to employers of working existing employees more intensively. A substantial literature has demonstrated that this substitution does take place (Ehrenberg, 1972), although the market does to some extent mitigate this substitution by inducing changes in offered wage rates (Trejo, 1991).

Policy on overtime in the United States has been remarkably static since the enactment of the FLSA in 1938. While there have been proposals to reduce the length of the standard workweek and/or to raise the overtime penalty rate, these have been fixed at 40 hours and 50 percent for 75 years. The only variation has been in the types of workers and industries to which the law has been applied. This lack of variation has made it extremely difficult to obtain direct inferences about the likely impacts of proposals to alter the parameters of the legislation or to infer the effects of the FLSA as it stands.

One solution would be to compare outcomes across countries, since there is tremendous heterogeneity in laws on hours of work across developed economies; but that idea has not been pursued extensively, perhaps in fact because of the difficulty of making comparisons across the different countries' legislation. Absent that, we are thrown back either on historical changes, as in Costa's (2000) comparisons of hours of work in wholesale and retail trade, which became covered by the FLSA at different times; or we need to search for some other experiment that might allow us to infer how overtime laws affect hours of work and/or employment.

The state of California has long applied overtime penalties that go beyond the FLSA by imposing an overtime penalty on any hour of work beyond 8 hours on a given day. Its laws have long applied to work by women – indeed, they were designed to protect women from excessive work time. In the 1980s, as part of the push toward gender equality, the laws were extended to men's work. As such, they raised the cost to employers of using men more intensively on a given day, and thus raised it relative to the cost of an hour of work by women (and relative to the cost of men's workhours in other states). This experiment provided an excellent and rare opportunity to examine how employers' demand for hours is affected by changes in the price of an extra hour of work time, as the results in Chapter 8 show.

The study was engendered by an interview that Jonathan Marshall, then of the San Francisco Chronicle, conducted with me (I think in 1997) as part of a story about on-going policy discussions regarding the provisions of overtime laws in California. The discussion with him opened my eyes to the possibility of using the unique California experience to draw inferences about the impacts of overtime policy more generally. Fortunately I had known Steve Trejo since he was a graduate student in the mid-1980s, so I immediately telephoned him and asked him to collaborate with me on this research. His expertise on the overtime penalty and mine on labor demand combined and demonstrated more than in most cases the benefits from co-authorship.

Chapter 8 hints at an issue that has hardly been touched on by economists studying the regulation of hours: How is the timing of work, rather than the amount of work per week, affected by labor market policies? In the United States there is no national policy penalizing employers' demand for labor outside conventional work hours (typically viewed as weekdays and daytime). Yet in many countries such work is penalized, presumably with the aim of encouraging employers to reduce work hours at those unpleasant times. Such a policy is consistent with the goal of protecting especially those workers who are at the margins of the labor market, since there is now substantial evidence that work at unusual hours is performed disproportionately by minorities, quite young and quite old workers, and in general by workers in the lower parts of the distribution of wages (Hamermesh, 1996 and 1999).

In the United States a much greater proportion of all work performed occurs at unusual times of the day or the week (Burda et al, 2008). The question arises: To what extent could this work be shifted to more standard times if the U.S. adopted penalties on work performed at nonstandard times? More generally, how do penalties linked to *work-timing*, rather than to *work hours*, alter the time at which work is performed? To analyze this requires finding a country that has a widespread policy of government-imposed penalties on work at unusual times and that has information on the timing of companies' labor input on an hour-by-hour basis over an entire week.

These requirements are quite stringent, since many countries do not penalize work timing, and, more important, only one appears to have conducted a set of employer-based surveys that provide all the necessary data. This is Portugal, which in 2003 conducted a large-scale survey that had employers list the number of workers at each hour in the survey week. Longitudinal information on these employers makes it possible in Chapter 9 to apply the formal econometric models presented in Chapters 1 and 7 to estimate the technological parameters describing production generated by inputs defined as labor at different times (in this case, during weekday daytime hours, weekday nighttime hours, and weekends). The estimates of these parameters allow us to infer how altering the price of a nighttime or weekend hour creates incentives for employers to alter work timing. Applying them to the distribution of work we observe over the week in the U.S., we can then simulate how imposing the same policies as exist in Portugal would alter work timing in the U.S.

Along with labor demand much of my career has focused on how people use time outside the workplace and especially on the timing of work and non-work activities (e.g., Biddle and Hamermesh, 1990; Hamermesh, 1999). The research in Chapter 9, made possible by my two Portuguese coauthors, allowed me for the first time to combine the two major interests that have developed over my career. The question considered in this study is admittedly fairly narrow, but the general issue - putting time subscripts on labor and other inputs - seems quite general. Thus ignoring the potential implications that this study has for labor market policy, it also should be an indication of the kind of research that is necessary to move out along a hitherto unstudied dimension of labor demand.

During the severe recession of the 1980s in the United States attention began to be focused on job displacement, somewhat loosely defined but surely including workers who became unemployed through plant closings and probably too those becoming unemployed through mass layoffs. This concern eventually led to the enactment of the Worker Adjustment and Retraining Notification Act of 1988 (WARN), requiring many employers to give notice of plant closings and mass layoffs. Not surprisingly it also generated a flood of economic research, focusing disproportionately on the impacts of job displacement on subsequent wages and employment (e.g., Kletzer, 1989; Ruhm, 1991). Very little research examined whether in fact legislation like WARN was necessary, whether workers' expectations about subsequent job loss were built into their wages and working conditions.

Chapter 10 analyzes this question, using a trick that was being applied more generally in some contemporaneous research (Abraham and Farber, 1987): If we know the eventual cause of a job separation, for example, through a plant closing, we can see whether the implied paths of workers' and firms' investments indicate that they are aware of this eventuality. If they are, they will invest less in things specific to the plant, including the workers' skills, than at other plants where jobs will last longer. That being the case, the extent to which plant closings are expected can be inferred from the implied path of firm-specific investment in workers. This provides information on the extent to which plant closings are a surprise to workers. To the extent that they are surprises, that justifies legislation such as WARN and perhaps too mandated severance payments (which exist in many countries, although not in the United States).

This research, an increasingly rare sole-authored effort, was undertaken as part of my more general interest in the nature of worker-firm relationships. In some senses the motivation is the same as that underlying Chapter 2, since both studies deal with the determinants and effects of firm-specific human capital. Importantly, though, this research is an example of something that really could not have been done until the mid-1970s, as it explicitly depended on the availability of longitudinal data.

The American system of unemployment insurance is unique worldwide, in that it is truly federal and is financed by taxes on employers that are partly experience-rated – based to some extent on the amount of benefits paid recently to an employer's laid-off former employees. While the tax, mandated in the Social Security Act of 1935, initially applied to all of the earnings of each worker in a firm, a ceiling on the taxable amount per worker was quickly imposed; and today that ceiling means that well below half of the payroll is taxed. Some states, however, impose ceilings above the federal limit; the question is whether an increase in the federal limit alters total tax revenue in those states whose tax ceilings do, or do not, exceed the previous federal minimum. Answering this question in turn provides information on the impacts of the system on labor demand, since a higher tax ceiling means that the system biases employers' hiring decisions less against low-skilled workers, a greater fraction of whose earnings is covered compared to those of more-skilled workers.

Chapter 11 presents a theoretical model of the behavior of states' reactions to a federally imposed increase in the tax ceiling. The agents interact in a bargaining context, and the model predicts that a new policy equilibrium will be generated when the federal government raises the ceiling. Even in states where the ceiling had been binding, however, states' behavior, motivated by their employers' and workers' interests in the unemployment insurance system, leads to a less than one-for-one increase in tax revenues and in the amount of benefits paid out to laid-off employees. The theoretical model provides explicit predictions about the political reactions of lower-level government entities to impositions from a higher-level entity, and thus predictions about the process by which the higher-level entity can change the cost structure of firms, and thus their demand for labor.

Its unemployment insurance system is arguably the most complex labor-market program in the United States, due to its federal structure and the way it is financed. Understanding its arcane nature takes a substantial investment of intellectual energy. Having made that investment, which resulted in Hamermesh (1977), I have since then been alert for policy issues related to unemployment insurance that are linked to questions of labor demand. On the few occasions when the issue has come up in the political debate I have pushed for raising the tax ceiling, since it is clear that a tax on only a fixed amount of earnings raises the relative cost of employing low-skilled workers, and thus biases hiring against them. Chapter 11 provides a bit of input into that debate, since it shows that federally mandated increases in the tax ceiling are effective in expanding unemployment insurance, albeit far less than proportionately.

7

Minimum Wages and the Demand for Labor

7.1. Introduction*

Findings about the magnitude of the effect of higher wage minima on employment seem sensitive to minor changes in the data and specification.[1] A more careful specification of the underlying theoretical model may thus have a substantial payoff in terms of the confidence one can place in the estimates produced. In Section 7.2 I therefore estimate several models of demand for the labor of teen and adult workers that incorporate the effective minimum wage along with the wages of the two types of labor. Section 7.3 examines how changes in the effective minimum wage change the structure of firms' costs, using a translog approximation to a three-factor cost function involving youths, adults, and capital. In Section 7.4 I show how to calculate the net effects of higher minima and use the method to simulate the impact of the minimum wage on youth and adult employment and on factor shares.

The original version of this chapter was published as: Hamermesh, Daniel S. (1982). Minimum Wages and the Demand for Labor, in: Economic Inquiry, 20: 365–380. The results reported in this chapter are based on tax-supported research conducted under Contract Number J-9-M-0-0078 from the Minimum Wage Study Commission. Helpful comments and essential data were provided by Curtis Gilroy and Randy Norsworthy; useful criticisms were offered by Ronald Ehrenberg, Belton Fleisher, Robert Goldfarb, Jacob Mincer, Paul Osterman and participants in seminars at Harvard University, the London School of Economics and the NBER. Special thanks are due to Charles Brown for his insightful comments throughout the project.

7.2. The Demand for Teen and Adult Labor

Previous work (Welch, 1974) on the effect of higher wage minima on the demand for teen and adult labor estimates:

$$ER_t = \alpha_0 + \alpha_1 MINT_t + \alpha_2 U_t + \alpha_3 t + \alpha_4 DUMS_t + v_t, \tag{1}$$

where *ER* is the logarithm of relative teen/adult employment; *MINT* is the logarithm of the effective minimum wage; *U* is the logarithm of the adult unemployment rate; *t* denotes time; *DUMS* is a vector of three quarterly dummy variables, and *v* is a disturbance term. There are three problems with this equation: 1) It appears to be a relative demand equation, yet the relative price measure cannot be claimed to reflect the prices of the two types of employee. Implicitly the equation states that the price of adults (the denominator of the effective minimum) is average hourly earnings (or labor costs), while the coverage-weighted minimum (the numerator) is the price of teenagers; 2) If equation (1) is in part based on the theory of factor demand, it puts substantial restrictions upon the adjustment of the employment of youths and adults. Implicitly it states that employers are concerned only about the ratio of employment in these two groups, and that there are no separate disturbance terms that reflect random effects in the adjustment of employment in the two groups; 3) If the equations are intended to reflect the demand for labor, they should include a scale effect, measured by the demand for output. From this viewpoint the trend can be seen as reflecting changes in factor productivity, but the unemployment rate is difficult to rationalize as a good measure of shifts in demand.

As a first step toward grounding (1) in the theory of factor demand, I add the log of the relative price of teen and adult labor, *WR*. This is based on the relative earnings of full-time year-round workers by age group. *MINT* is the coverage-weighted minimum wage relative to the labor cost (including all fringes) of teen workers. (See (Hamermesh, 1981) for a description of the construction of these variables and a list of their values.) This revision gives us the estimating equation:

$$ER_t = \alpha'_0 + \alpha'_1 MINT_t + \alpha'_2 U_t + \alpha'_3 t + \alpha'_4 DUMS + \alpha'_5 WR_t + v'_t. \tag{1'}$$

I estimate this equation on quarterly data for 1954–1978, using the Cochrane-Orcutt iterative technique to account for serial correlation in the v'_t. The dependent variable is based on employment of 14–19 year-olds relative to persons 20 or over. Equation (1') is estimated for three large subsectors and for the private nonfarm economy.

(In the latter case the effective minimum is an employment-weighted average of effective minima in each subsector.)

Modifications that led to (1') force us to interpret the meaning of *MINT* in a way different from previous work. Increases in that term produced by legislated increases in *MIN*, the nominal minimum wage, imply the truncation of the distribution of the marginal productivity of teen labor. Essentially, *WR* is the ratio of the average prices of teen and adult labor, while the minimum wage variable shows how the distribution of productivity of teens is truncated from below by changes in the legislated minimum.[2] In terms of Figure 7.1, the relative price variable is based upon an average of the price of teen workers in the shaded area beyond MIN_0, while *MIN*, the numerator of *MINT*, reflects the truncation point. This suggests that the net effect of any increase in the minimum wage must be calculated very carefully. An increase in *MIN* from MIN_0 to MIN_1 will affect both *MINT* and observed relative prices (because the truncation point of the distribution of teen wages is changed). The cross-hatched area in Figure 7.1 will drop out of the observed distribution of wages.

The coefficient α'_1 in (1') can now be interpreted as showing the effect of a higher effective minimum on relative employment if *WR* is unchanged.

Figure 7.1

The Effective Minimum Wage and the Distribution of Teenagers by Productivity

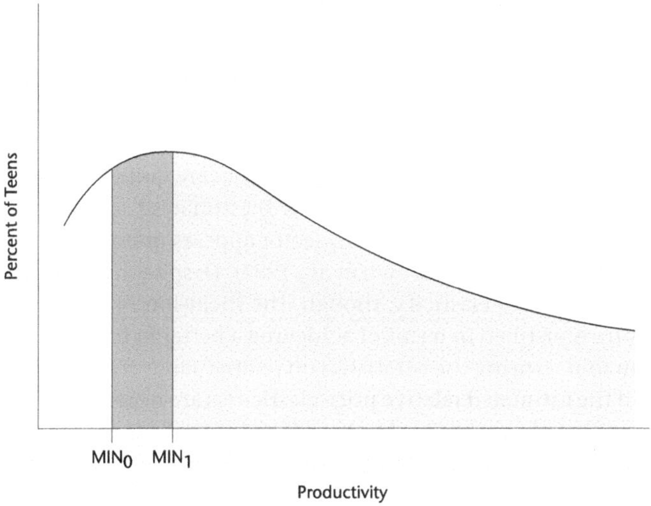

It shows the extra impact of a higher minimum once that effect has been compensated for by adjusting *WR* to account for the increased average wage of teenagers produced when the truncation point in Figure 7.1 moves rightward. The compensating change to hold *WR* constant must occur through a drop in wages of high-wage teens. That $\alpha'_1 < 0$ follows from the assumption, based on Hamermesh-Grant (1979), that the demand elasticity for low-wage workers exceeds that for high-wage workers; the net negative effect on teen employment of a higher *MIN*, *holding WR constant*, results from the partly offsetting positive and negative effects on high- and low-wage teens respectively. Thus the net effect of higher *MIN* must be calculated using both α'_1 and α'_5 (see section 7.4).

Table 7.1

Estimates of (1') for Relative Teen-Adult Employment, 1954:I – 1978:IV[a]

	Minimum Wage Elasticity	Relative Labor Cost Elasticity	$\hat{\sigma}_\varepsilon$
Private Nonfarm	-0.1131 (-2.40)	-0.3995 (-1.52)	0.0332
Services (Except private household)	-0.0383 (-0.64)	-1.96 (-3.07)	0.0691
Retail Trade	-0.0411 (-2.93)	-0.4601 (-1.42)	0.0370
Manufacturing	-0.4185 (-3.46)	-0.5652 (-0.99)	0.0575

[a] *t*-statistics in parentheses here and in Tables 7.2–7.5.

Table 7.1 presents estimates of (1').[3] Despite the drastic decline in the relative wages of youths since the 1960s, and the use of an effective minimum wage variable with the price of teen labor as the denominator, the addition of the relative labor cost variable has little impact: The estimated minimum wage elasticities are quite similar to Siskind's (1977) corrections of Welch's (1974) estimates.[4] The elasticity of about -.*1* in the private nonfarm sector appears quite robust to changes in specification (see Brown et al., 1981). Despite the stability of the minimum wage elasticity, though, the inclusion of a relative price measure is justified in terms of achieving a better fit to the data. Except in manufacturing the t-statistics on relative labor costs exceed one, and all the estimated relative price elasticities are negative.[5]

Equation (1') can be generalized by transforming it into the complete system of demand equations for the two factors of production, teen and adult labor:

(2a) $$ET_t = a_1 + \alpha_1 WT_t + \beta_1 WA_t + \gamma Q_t + \delta MINT_t + \kappa_1 X_t + \varepsilon_1,$$

(2b) $$EA_t = a_2 + \alpha_2 WT_t + \beta_2 WA_t + \gamma Q_t + \kappa_2 X_t + \varepsilon_2,$$

where *ET* and *EA* are logarithms of teen and adult employment respectively; *WT* and *WA* are logarithms of labor costs per hour; *Q* is the log of output; *X* is a vector including a time trend and quarterly dummy variables; and the ε are random disturbance terms.[6] It implicitly assumes, as did figure I, that an increase in the effective minimum wage facing employers of teenagers directly affects only their employment. Below I test whether *MINA*, the effective minimum wage facing employers of adult workers, belongs in (2b). This equation system accounts for the second and third problems with (1) that we noted earlier.

As it is written, system (2) imposes no restrictions on the effects of one wage rate on employment in the other group. This form allows us to test for the symmetry of cross-price effects, $\alpha_2 = R\beta_1$, where *R* is the ratio of factor shares; and to test for homogeneity in the responses of employment to changes in all prices, i.e., $\alpha_1 + \beta_1 = 0$ and $\alpha_2 + \beta_2 = 0$. We assume here and in Section 7.3 that the legislated minimum is included in the phrase "all prices." The model in (2) is estimated using the data for the private nonfarm sector underlying the estimates in Table 7.1. Separate first-order autoregressive processes are assumed for ε_1 and ε_2, and the parameters ρ describing these processes are estimated.

The restrictions of homogeneity and symmetry cannot be rejected at the 99 percent level of significance ($\chi^2(3) = 10.72$), though they can at 95 percent level. Since the restricted system is more consistent with economic theory, and the estimate of the coefficient on *MINT* from the unconstrained model differs only slightly from that from the model in which homogeneity and symmetry have been imposed, I present the restricted estimates in Table 7.2.[7] The equations were estimated by iterative least-squares, a procedure that is asymptotically equivalent to maximum likelihood.

As a result of the imposition of the constraints, there is only one independent coefficient on the labor cost terms, α_1. Though this coefficient is negative, its *t*-statistic is very low. Further, the elasticity is far below $\hat{\alpha}'_5$ found above, and far below values that seem reasonable in light of recent research (see Hamermesh-Grant, 1979). The output elasticity is also quite low in light of those found in previous work (Hamermesh, 1976). It is difficult to believe in the degree of increasing returns to labor implied by the estimate of γ. The trend coefficients are positive and always significant. This result too is disturbing in view of the usual interpretation of these coefficients as reflecting increases in productivity.

Table 7.2

Estimates of Parameters in the System of Labor Demand Equations, Private Non-farm Sector, 1954:1–1978:IV

Price Coefficients		Other Coefficients	
$\hat{\alpha}_1$	-0.118 (-0.42)	$\hat{\gamma}$ (Output)	0.269 (4.35)
$\hat{\beta}_1$	0.118 (0.42)	$\hat{\delta}$ (Minimum Wage)	-0.0834 (-1.62)
$\hat{\alpha}_2$	0.0067 (0.42)	$\hat{\kappa}_1$ (Trend)	0.0094 (8.09)
$\hat{\beta}_2$	-0.0067 (-0.42)	$\hat{\kappa}_2$ (Trend)	0.0033 (4.63)
		$\hat{\rho}_T$	0.804 (15.15)
		$\hat{\rho}_A$	0.935 (23.07)
		R_T^2	0.988
		R_A^2	0.998

The χ^2-test of the hypothesis that *MINA* belongs in (2b) is 1.50, not significantly different from zero.[8] We may conclude that the interpretation of the effective minimum wage variable here and above as a reflection of the truncation of the distribution of labor costs for *teenagers* is not inconsistent with the data. This finding allows us to interpret an increase in the effective minimum wage in the context of the models in (1') and (2) as directly affecting only the employment of teenagers. There is, though, an indirect effect on the employment of adults: With a rightward movement in the truncation point of the distribution of teenagers' labor costs, their average labor cost increases, and there is some substitution toward adult workers.

The elasticity of the effective minimum wage variable is negative and almost significantly different from zero, though its size is somewhat below that presented in Table 7.1. Even if we take the theory of factor demand seriously and modify it to include the effect of the minimum wage, we still find a negative employment effect on teenagers as the effective minimum rises. No matter what formulation used – from the hybrid nontheoretical model in Welch (1974) and Siskind (1977), to equation (1'), to system (2) – increased coverage and higher legislated minima are found to reduce the employment of teenagers.

7.3. The Minimum Wage and Factor Substitution

The models I have constructed must stem from some underlying production or cost function. Here I examine how the minimum wage affects the structure of firms' costs, using annual data on the employment of youths 14–24 and of adults, and on services of capital. The work in this section is based on the flexible translog form. (See Berndt-Christensen, 1974, for an early application). Since the labor supply of teenagers is likely to be elastic, and since our estimates must involve a price term in the form of the effective minimum wage, we use an approximation to a generalized cost function rather than to a production function.

The translog cost function for this study is:

$$(3) \quad \begin{aligned} C = {} & Q + \alpha_0 + \alpha_1\, WY + \alpha'_1\, [\, WY\, MINT\,] + \alpha_2\, WA + \alpha_3\, PK \\ & + \frac{\beta_{11}}{2}\, [\, WY\,]^2 + \frac{\beta'_{11}}{2}\, [\, WY\,]^2\, MINT + \frac{\beta_{22}}{2}\, [\, WA\,]^2 + \frac{\beta_{33}}{2}\, [\, PK\,]^2 \\ & + \beta_{12}\, WY\, WA + \beta'_{12}\, WY\, WA\, MINT + \beta_{13}\, WY\, PK \\ & + \beta'_{13}\, WY\, PK\, MINT + \beta_{23}\, WA\, PK, \end{aligned}$$

where *C* are the typical firm's costs, *Q* is output, *PK* is the user cost of capital, *WY* and *WA* are the labor costs of young and older workers, and the a_i, a'_i and β_{ij} and β'_{ij} are parameters describing the firm's costs. All variables are in logarithms.

Equation (3) is an approximation necessitated by the aggregation of all young workers, both those whose productivity far exceeds *MIN* and those likely to be affected by increases in *MIN*, into one employment category. If we could disaggregate youths into these two groups, we could estimate a cost function of the sort:

$$C = C\,(WY_L, WY_H, WA, PK\,),$$

where "L" denotes low-wage and "H" denotes other young workers. This simple four-factor cost function could be used to infer from the substitution elasticities involving type "L" young workers and the four factor , shares the effect of a higher minimum (mandated increase in type "L" wages) on total employment of youths, and on the inputs of adult labor and capital. No data on youth wages and employment are disaggregated this way; thus we must accommodate the available data and use (3). The interaction terms in (3) between *MINT* and *WY* and the three price variables reflect the assumptions that a higher effective minimum changes costs by affecting the mix of young workers, shifting it toward type "H" and away from type "L" workers. The mix of youth employed will then be weighted more heavily with type "H" workers, for whom demand is likely to be less elastic (see Hamermesh-Grant, 1979); thus η_{YY}, the own-price elasticity, will rise toward zero. Similarly, the substitutability of skilled and unskilled workers suggests that the observed substitution elasticity between youths and adults will fall toward zero when the least-skilled youth lose employment.

We can use (3) to derive equations describing the shares of total output accruing to each of the three inputs:

(4a) $S_Y = \alpha_1 + \alpha'_1 \text{ MINT} + \beta_{11} \text{ WY} + \beta'_{11} \text{ WY MINT} + \beta_{12} \text{ WA} + \beta'_{12} \text{ WA MINT} + \beta_{13} \text{ PK} + \beta'_{13} \text{ PK MINT};$

(4b) $S_A = \alpha_2 + \beta_{12} \text{ WY} + \beta'_{12} \text{ WY MINT} + \beta_{22} \text{ WA} + \beta_{23} \text{ PK};$ and

(4c) $S_K = \alpha_3 + \beta_{13} \text{ WY} + \beta'_{13} \text{ WY MINT} + \beta_{23} \text{ WA} + \beta_{33} \text{ PK};$

where S denotes the share of the particular factor. Implicit in this derivation are the standard assumptions of constant returns to scale and competitive factor markets.

The symmetry of cross-substitution effects has already been imposed in (4) by assumption in (3). However, homogeneity restrictions must also be imposed if the share equations are to make economic sense. These are:

(5a) $\beta_{11} + \beta'_{11} \overline{\text{MINT}} + \beta_{12} + \beta'_{12} \overline{\text{MINT}} + \beta_{13} + \beta'_{13} \overline{\text{MINT}} = 0;$

(5b) $\beta_{12} + \beta'_{12} \overline{\text{MINT}} + \beta_{22} + \beta_{23} = 0;$

(5c) $\beta_{13} + \beta'_{13} \overline{\text{MINT}} + \beta_{23} + \beta_{33} = 0;$ and

(5d) $\alpha_1 + \alpha_2 + \alpha_3 + \alpha'_1 \overline{\text{MINT}} = 1;$

These restrictions are quite standard in the empirical literature, though one should note that they are modified here by the inclusion of the effective minimum wage in (3).

One more homogeneity constraint is needed to complete the model. If the effective minimum increases, factor shares must still sum to one, so that:

(5e) $\alpha_1 + \beta'_{11} \overline{\text{WY}} + \beta'_{12} [\overline{\text{WY}} + \overline{\text{WA}}] + \beta'_{13} [\overline{\text{WY}} + \overline{\text{PK}}] = 0.$

Restrictions (5a) – (5e) cannot be valid for all values of the factor price variables and the effective minimum wage, so there is some problem in interpreting them. We assume that each constraint holds at the sample means of the factor prices (denoted by superior bars in (5e)) and the effective minimum wage, implying that the stochastic process generating (4) conforms with the restrictions imposed by theory only at the mean of the process. The presence of the constraints (5) means equations (4) contain eight independent parameters. This model too is estimated using iterative least squares.

Table 7.3

Estimates of Parameters for the Three-Factor Translog Cost Functions with Symmetry and Homogeneity Imposed, 1955–1975

Coefficients on Terms in:		Without Minimum Wage Terms	With Minimum Wage Terms
WY	α_1	-0.0778	-0.356
		(-0.67)	(-0.86)
	β_{11}	0.0368	0.0625
		(2.80)	(1.39)
	β_{12}	-0.0228	-0.0134
		(-1.23)	(-0.73)
	β_{13}	-0.0141	-0.0103
		(-1.38)	(-1.53)
MINT	α_1'		0.334
			(1.22)
	β_{11}'		0.0306
			(0.95)
	β_{12}'		-0.0090
			(-8.10)
	β_{13}'		0.0074
			(7.46)
WA	α_2	-2.00	-1.91
		(-3.53)	(-7.28)
	β_{22}	0.258	0.229
		(4.06)	(7.07)
	β_{23}	-0.235	-0.228
		(-4.66)	(-9.74)
PK	α_3	3.07	3.72
		(6.61)	(15.71)
	β_{33}	0.249	0.267
		(6.01)	(8.71)
ln L		142.64	157.14

The capital stock data cover both private and government capital, and are from Freeman (1979). The user cost of capital is computed accounting for changes in the tax treatment of capital, depreciation and capital gains. Data on the labor quantities and prices are based on the

Money Incomes of Families and Persons (CPR Series P-60). The estimates cover annual observations for 1955–1975. The input prices *WY* and *WA* are based on the annual incomes of full-time, year-round workers ages 14–24 and 25+ respectively; both were deflated to constant 1972 dollars using the deflator for the private business sector. Factor quantities were computed as fulltime equivalent employment by prorating the total number of persons in each age group who reported some earnings by the ratio of their earnings to those of year-round, full-time workers. Thus I implicitly assume that each person in the two labor subaggregates works the same number of hours.[9]

Table 7.3 shows the estimates of the parameters in (4). Those in the first column are based on a model in which all terms involving *MINT* have been deleted (in which α'_1 and the β'_{1j} have been set equal to zero); those in the second column are based on the complete model in (4). It is worth noting that the fit of the complete model is statistically better than that of the model from which the minimum wage terms have been excluded: The χ^2-statistic describing this test is 29.01, significantly different from zero at the 99 percent level. Most of the parameter estimates in the full model are quite significant, though $\hat{\beta}_{12}$ and some from the terms in *MINT* are not.[10] Given these findings, we should not expect high levels of significance for any of the estimated effects of the minimum wage of the substitution parameters that we calculate below.

The estimates in the second column of Table 7.3 enables us to calculate partial elasticities of substitution, own substitution elasticities, cross and-own-price elasticities. Partial elasticities of substitution are:

$$\text{(6a)} \qquad \sigma_{ij} = \frac{\beta_{ij} + \beta'_{ij}\,\text{MINT}}{S_i\,S_j}$$

Own-substitution elasticities are:

$$\text{(6b)} \qquad \sigma_{ii} = \frac{\beta_{ii} + \beta'_{ii}\,\text{MINT}}{S_i^2} + 1 - \frac{1}{S_i}.$$

Cross- and own-price elasticities are calculated from (6a) and (6b) respectively by multiplying by the share of the factor whose price is assumed to change.

Table 7.4 lists the values at the sample means of all the substitution and price elasticities involving youths.[11] The former are also presented as linear functions of the logarithm of the effective minimum wage. The estimated demand elasticity for young workers is quite low, -.59, though not nearly so low as that produced in the estimates of (2) (a system, though, that excluded capital). We find here that workers in the two groups are substitutes on average during the sample period. Young workers and capital are complements, though the cross-price elasticity is essentially zero, and its accompanying t-statistic is small.

Table 7.4

Substitution Parameters and Price Elasticities from the Translog Cost Model, 1955–75

Parameter		σ_{YY}		σ_{YA}		σ_{YK}
$\sigma = a + b\,MINT$	1.180 +	8.00 *MINT*	0.654	-0.233 *MINT*	0.465 +	0.383 *MINT*
	(1.39)	(1.22)	(0.73)	(-8.10)	(1.53)	*(7.46)*
$\bar{\sigma} = a + b\,\overline{MINT}$		-9.53		0.966		*-0.049*
		(-2.30)		(1.98)		*(-0.08)*
		η_{YY}		η_{YA}		η_{YK}
$\eta_{ij} = S_i\bar{\sigma}_{ij}$		-0.590		0.605		0.0156
		(-2.30)		(1.98)		(-0.08)

The most important finding of this section is implicit in the representation of the substitution elasticities as linear functions of *MINT* in the first row of Table 7.4. Increases in the effective minimum wage during the period 1955–1975 reduced the observed own-substitution elasticity of demand for young workers and decreased the extent to which employers were able to substitute older for young workers in response to an exogenous increase in the price of young workers. Based upon the value of *MINT* in 1955, σ_{YY} = -.718, and σ_{YA} = .643; for 1975 the comparable elasticities are -.233 and .500. We observe the same result for σ_{YK}, though the very low t-statistic attached to the estimate prevents us from drawing any useful inferences from it. These estimates support the rationale for including the minimum wage in the cost function (3). They imply that a higher effective minimum wage causes firms to decrease their inputs of unskilled young workers; thus an exogenous change in factor prices has less of an effect on the (relatively more skilled) group of young workers remaining.

7.4. The Net Employment Effect of the Minimum Wage and some Policy Simulations

In this section I use the results of Sections 7.2 and 7.3 to analyze the effects of changes in the minimum wage law. Separate data are not available on the price of the teen labor unaffected by these changes. As a result, equations (1') and (2) had to include both minimum wage and average wage terms, the latter of which is a function of the minimum. Effects of these changes cannot be computed on the basis of estimated minimum wage elasticities alone, for changes in the legislated minimum or its coverage will change the average labor cost observed and will, in turn, have an additional effect on teen employment through the variable *WT* included in (1') or in (2).

Assume that the distribution of the logarithms of teens' productivity is normal with mean μ and variance σ^2. Then following Johnson-Kotz (1970, p. 81), the observed mean of their wage rates *WT* (in logs) will be:

$$(7) \qquad E(WT) = \mu + \frac{\sigma f(MIN - \mu/\sigma)}{1 - F(MIN - \mu/\sigma)},$$

where *f* is the unit normal density function; *F* is the normal distribution function, and we assume all teens are paid their marginal products. From (7) the derivative of the observed mean of *WT* with respect to an increase in the effective minimum wage produced by an increase in *MIN* is:

$$(8) \qquad dWT/dMIN = f'/[1 - F] + [f/[1 - F]]^2,$$

where the arguments of *f* and *F* have been suppressed.

Use (2), and treat MINT as the log of the ratio of MIN to teen labor costs. (Similar manipulations would be done on (1') .) Then:

$$(9) \qquad dET/dMIN = \partial ET/\partial MINT\,[1 - dWT/dMIN]$$
$$+ [\partial ET/\partial WT][dWT/dMIN]$$
$$+ [\partial ET/\partial Q][dQ/dP][dP/dMIN],$$

where *P* is the log of the price of output. The first two terms on the right side of (9) represent the substitution effect against teen labor; the third represents the scale effect. For adults the employment effect is:

$$(10) \qquad dEA/dMIN = [\partial ET/\partial WT][dWT/dMIN]$$
$$+ [\partial EA/\partial Q][dQ/dP][dP/dMIN],$$

The first term is the substitution effect, and the second term is the scale effect.

The estimates of (2) can be used to represent the partial derivatives in the substitution effects in (9) and (10): δ estimates $\partial ET / \partial MINT$;

α_1 estimates $\partial ET \ / \ \partial WT$, and α_2 estimates $\partial EA \ / \ \partial WT$.[12] Alternatively $\partial ET \ / \ \partial WT$ and $\partial EA \ / \ \partial WT$ are also estimated by η_{YY} and η_{YA} respectively in Table 7.4.[13] To estimate $dWT \ / \ dMIN$ I make two alternative assumptions about how changes in the legislated minimum wage truncate the distribution of teen labor costs: (1) All unemployed teens owe that status to the effects of the minimum wage, but teens who are out of the labor force are unaffected. Based on averages from 1954 to 1978 this assumption implies the fraction truncated is .069. (2) The fraction truncated is equal to the highest fraction of teens (.115) inferred as being displaced from employment in the Meyer-Wise (1981) estimates of wage distributions of teens. To compute the scale effect I assume $dQ \ / \ dP = -1$, and $dP \ / \ dMIN = .0056$.[14] I assume alternatively that $\partial ET / \partial Q = \partial EA \ / \ \partial Q = .269$ ($\hat{\gamma}$ in (2)), or equal 1.

Table 7.5

Percentage Substitution Effects of a 75 Percent Youth Subminimum Wage[a]

	Teens		Adults	
	A	B	A	B
Assumption about Truncation (and Fraction Truncated)				
Unemployed Ratio (0.069)	2.63	3.92	-0.04	-0.21
	(1.20)	(2.70)	(-1.62)	(-1.98)
16–24 Year Olds	2.71	4.44	-0.06	-0.28
Disemployed (0.115)	(1.00)	(2.81)	(-1.62)	(-1.98)

[a] Simulation A uses substitution parameters from Table 7.2, simulation B uses those from Table 7.4.

Equations (9) and (10) and the parameter estimates can be used to gauge the impact on employment of a youth subminimum wage equal to 75 percent of the adult minimum. The two alternative assumptions about $\partial E \ / \ \partial Q$ yield scale effects of .044 and .164 percent respectively. The substitution effects under the pairs of assumptions about truncation and teen-adult substitution are presented in Table 7.5.[15] Adding the scale effect of .044 to the estimates under assumption A in Table 7.5, (so that all the parameters come from estimates of system (2)), the employment effects on teens are 2.67 and 2.75 percent under the two truncation assumptions; those for adults are +.004 and -.016 percent. Using Case B in Table 7.5 and the assumption of constant returns (a scale effect of .164 percent in response to the policy change) yields percentage employment effects for teens of 4.08 and 4.60, and for adults of -.05 and -.12. All these estimates clearly depend on the specific parameters assumed. Reduced employment of teens (lower employment loss of adults) would be generated by assuming that a smaller fraction of the distribution of teen productivity is truncated, by assuming still lower teen-adult substitution, or by accounting for increases in compliance with the law and reductions in the use of student exemptions that might occur.[16]

Based on 1979 employment of 9,356 thousand teenagers and 88,961 thousand adults, a 75 percent subminimum would create two hundred fifty thousand jobs for teens and *increase* adult employment by four thousand under the most conservative assumptions about truncation and substitution. Making the more liberal assumption in each case yields employment effects of 430 thousand teen jobs and minus one hundred seven thousand adult jobs. The major cause of the difference between these pairs of estimates is the difference in the extent of teen-adult substitution. Even under the more liberal assumption, many more teens are aided than adults are harmed.

7.5. Conclusions and Implications

This chapter provides several advances over the previous literature on employment demand and the minimum wage. Perhaps most important, it is the first that estimates the effects of higher minimum wages in equations that are derived from the theory of cost and production. These include relative employment demand equations; a complete system of demand equations for the factors teen and adult labor; and a translog cost tableau, in which the minimum wage affects measured substitution parameters between youths and others because it induces shifts in the skill mix of young workers.

The most striking finding is the remarkable robustness of the negative teen employment elasticity in response to higher minimum wages and expansions of the coverage of the minimum wage. Regardless of the choice of models, the elasticity for the private nonfarm sector is on the order of -.1. Though these minimum wage elasticities do not seem very large, they are estimated over a period that saw a tremendous increase in the effective minimum wage. Thus the implied effect of expansions of the minimum wage law on teen employment has been substantial. A youth subminimum wage would have offset some of these effects, with relatively little displacement of adult workers.

8

The Demand for Hours of Labor: Direct Evidence From California

8.1. Introduction

For many years, California required that most women receive an overtime premium of time-and-a-half for hours of work beyond eight in a given day. In 1980, this daily overtime penalty was extended to men as well. This situation provides a unique opportunity to estimate the impact of an exogenous increase in the relative price of overtime work. Using Current Population Survey (CPS) data from 1973, 1985, and 1991 that provide information on daily hours of work, we estimate the impact on work schedules of California extending its overtime law to cover men.

This analysis is important for at least two reasons. First, under conditions that are described below, statutory overtime penalties generate exogenous variation in the marginal cost of workhours that allow us to infer something about the elasticity of the demand for hours of labor. Indeed, our estimated effects of California's daily overtime law fit the profile of a labor demand response. A large body of research

---

The original version of this chapter was published as: Hamermesh, Daniel S./Trejo, Stephen J. (2000). The Demand for Hours of Labor: Direct Evidence from California, in: The Review of Economics and Statistics, 82(1): 38–47. Jonathan Marshall provided the impetus for this chapter. We thank George Borjas, Stephen Bronars, Ted Frech, Edward Funkhouser, Robert Hart, Jennifer Hunt, Jonathan Marshall, Cathy Weinberger, and two anonymous referees for helpful comments. Hamermesh is grateful to the National Science Foundation for research support under grant SBR-9422429.

attempts to estimate the parameters of various types of labor demand functions (Hamermesh, 1993), but this literature has been criticized for failing to address adequately the problem of endogeneity in the price of labor (Topel, 1998). The legislatively mandated wage increase that we study here is much less vulnerable to such criticism.

Second, by analyzing California's daily overtime penalty, we can gain a better understanding of the labor market effects of overtime pay regulation. Restrictions on overtime work are often proposed as a policy tool for creating jobs and reducing unemployment, yet there is relatively little direct evidence on the efficacy of this instrument.[1] Because of data limitations and the absence of suitable policy variation, most studies attempt to infer the effects of hours regulations from estimated demand functions for employment and hours, rather than by comparing outcomes before and after important policy changes.[2] We are in the fortunate position, however, of being able to track shifts in the work schedules of California men as they first became subject to that state's overtime law. Moreover, virtually all previous research on overtime pay regulation has focused on weekly hours standards, whereas the California setting allows us to study the impact of a daily overtime penalty.[3]

The study proceeds as follows. Section 8.2 describes relevant features of California's overtime law, and Section 8.3 discusses the implications of economic models of overtime pay regulation. Section 8.4 describes the data that we analyze, Section 8.5 lays out our empirical strategy for identifying the impact of California's daily overtime penalty, and Section 8.6 reports the basic results. In Section 8.7, we present estimates from alternative specifications that control in successively greater detail for observable variables. Section 8.8 discusses implications of our empirical findings, and Section 8.9 concludes with a brief summary.

8.2. California's Daily Overtime Law[4]

The overtime pay provisions of the federal Fair Labor Standards Act require that covered workers be paid time-and-a-half for hours of work beyond forty in a given week. California has been one of the few U.S. states to impose any additional restrictions on overtime pay.[5] Under California law, covered workers generally were entitled to receive time-and-a-half for hours worked beyond eight in a given day, even when weekly hours did not exceed forty. Amid considerable controversy, this requirement was recently repealed, so that, as of January 1, 1998, most California workers are covered only by the federal forty-hour weekly overtime standard.

California's daily overtime penalty was instituted well before federal overtime regulation began in 1938, but for a long time it applied only to women. In the wake of the Civil Rights Act of 1964, however, California's daily overtime standard was successfully challenged on the grounds that enforcing such a standard for women but not men is discriminatory. The ultimate response was to broaden California's overtime pay requirement so that it covered men as well. For our purposes, it is important to distinguish between three separate coverage regimes of overtime pay regulation in California: before 1974, only women were covered; beginning in 1980, both men and women were covered; and, during the intervening period, as a consequence of legal battles, to a large extent neither men nor women were covered. Because of the ambiguity and confusion about coverage status that existed during the 1974–1979 period, particularly for women, we avoid these years in our empirical analysis.

We exploit two useful features of these coverage changes. First, sometime between 1973 and 1985 - two years for which relevant data are available - California introduced a daily overtime pay requirement for men, whereas no such requirement existed at any time in most of the rest of the nation. Consequently, comparing male outcome changes in California over this period with those occurring elsewhere may tell us something about the impact of a daily overtime standard. Second, because California's overtime law applied to women in both 1973 and 1985, changes in outcomes for California women relative to other women do not represent the direct effects of overtime pay regulation but may instead reveal trends that are specific to California.

In California, state minimum wage and overtime pay standards are set through a series of fifteen "orders" issued by the Industrial Welfare Commission. Each order covers a different sector of California's workforce, with most of these sectors defined along industrial lines, but with a few defined according to occupation. In terms of required overtime pay, almost all of the orders specify time-and-a-half after eight hours of daily work; the orders for agricultural workers and live-in domestics are exceptions, in that they specify looser restrictions (for example, a ten-hour daily overtime standard for agricultural workers).[6] Certain groups, however, are exempt from state overtime pay regulation. Coverage exclusions for the self-employed, outside salespeople, and executive, administrative, and professional workers resemble the corresponding exclusions that appear in federal overtime law. Other groups exempt from California's daily overtime penalty are government workers, family workers, and workers involved in on-site activities such as construction, drilling, mining, milling, and logging.

8.3. Theoretical Background

Before turning to the empirical work, we briefly discuss what economic theory says should happen when California mandates a daily overtime penalty. Most analyses of overtime pay regulation have focused on labor demand, using models that distinguish between the number of workers hired and the hours that each worker puts in (Ehrenberg (1971), Hart (1987), Hamermesh (1993)). These models predict that California's overtime law will produce systematic effects on the distribution of daily hours of work. In particular, an overtime penalty after eight hours of daily work raises the marginal cost to employers of assigning overtime. Firms should respond by lowering the incidence of long workdays and shortening the workdays of workers who continue to put in more than eight hours per day. Moreover, the overtime penalty should increase the prevalence of eight-hour workdays, because some firms will find it optimal to avoid paying this penalty by limiting workdays to eight hours.[7] Indeed, the simplest labor demand models imply that the overtime penalty will not affect workdays under eight hours, so that the rise in the incidence of eight-hour workdays should be exactly the same magnitude as the decline in the incidence of overtime workdays (Trejo, 1998).

The analysis in the preceding paragraph ignores the fact that California's daily overtime law merely supplements the federal requirement for overtime pay after forty hours of weekly work. For workers already receiving time-and-a-half for weekly overtime because of the federal Fair Labor Standards Act, California's daily overtime penalty may not have any additional impact on the marginal wage. As a result, employers' responses to the California law may be muted by the overlap between state and federal overtime pay regulatlon. We will return to this issue in Section 8.8 when we discuss the implications of our empirical findings.

Labor supply behavior can also mute responses to overtime pay regulation. Often, analyses of hours policies stress only one side of the labor market, but hedonic models provide a simple way to equilibrate supply and demand in the market for work schedules. In these models, workhours are viewed as a job aspect over which both firms and workers have preferences, with compensating wage differentials arising in equilibrium for jobs with workdays of different lengths (Lewis (1969), Kinoshita (1987)). Under certain circumstances, straight-time hourly wages can adjust to mitigate or even completely neutralize the effects of a mandatory overtime penalty (Trejo, 1991). Consequently, if hourly wage rates are sufficiently flexible, California's overtime law does not necessarily restrict the ability of workers and firms to contract over packages of daily hours and earnings. Changes in the overtime premium or standard workday set by law could generate perfectly offsetting changes in straight-time hourly wages so as to leave daily hours and earnings unchanged.

Existing models of the effects of overtime pay regulation are thus consistent with a wide range of outcomes. California's daily overtime penalty could produce a substantial reduction in overtime work and a corresponding increase in the prevalence of eight-hour workdays, or it might have little or no effect on work schedules. This theoretical indeterminacy highlights the need for our empirical analysis.

8.4. Data

We analyze data from the May 1973, May 1985, and May 1991 Current Population Survey (CPS). In addition to the demographic and labor force information routinely collected in the CPS (including data on weekly hours of work), these particular surveys (as well as the May surveys from 1974–1978 and in 1997) provide information about daily work schedules that is not otherwise available in the CPS. All three surveys report the number of days per week usually worked by each individual, and the 1985 and 1991 surveys also ask about usual daily hours of work. Because direct information on daily work hours is absent in 1973, we impute this variable the same way in all three years by taking the ratio of usual weekly hours to usual days per week.[8]

Our sample includes individuals aged sixteen and older who held jobs during the CPS survey week and for whom data are available on daily workhours. As discussed in Section 8.2, some workers are either exempt from California's overtime law or are subject to a less restrictive standard than the eight-hour workday. To the extent possible, we exclude such workers from the analysis so as to sharpen our estimates of the law's impact. In particular, we use the CPS codes for industry, occupation, and class of worker to exclude the following groups: self-employed workers, government workers, managers and professionals, domestic workers, agricultural workers, and persons employed in on-site activities such as forestry, fishing, construction, and mining. One group of exempt workers that we cannot identify in CPS data is outside salespeople, but this group is relatively small and therefore its inclusion is unlikely to matter much.

As described in greater detail below, our estimation strategy involves comparing California with states that have not regulated daily overtime. For this reason, our "control group" excludes workers living in states (listed in footnote 5) that imposed any type of daily overtime pay requirement. As it turns out, these states are among those less-populated states not separately identified in the 1973 CPS data, but note that all are located in the West. Accordingly, in all years we define the control group to include only workers from the three non-Western regions of the United States (Northeast, North Central, and South). Our estimates therefore compare outcome changes in California with the corresponding changes that occurred outside the Western region.[9]

Table 8.1

Sample Sizes, May 1973, 1985 and 1991 CPS

	Men		Women	
Year	California	Non-West	California	Non-West
1973	1,409	12,896	1,107	9,993
1985	1,087	12,031	987	11,701
1991	1,218	11,000	1,014	11,254

Notes: The sample includes individuals aged sixteen and above who held jobs during the survey week and for whom data are available on usual daily hours of work. Excluded are self-employed workers, government workers, and other workers who are generally exempt from overtime pay regulation (managers and professionals, domestic workers, agricultural workers, and persons employed in on-site activities such as forestry, fishing, construction, and mining).

Table 8.1 displays the resulting sample sizes by year, sex, and region. In each year, we have samples of roughly 1,000 California women and somewhat more California men, and the corresponding cells for non-Western states contain 10,000 or more workers. The CPS sampling weights were used in all of the statistical calculations that we report here, but unweighted estimates are similar.

8.5. Estimation Approach

To estimate the effects of California extending its overtime law to male workers, our basic strategy is to track outcomes for California men before and after they were subject to a daily overtime penalty, and then compare these changes with the corresponding changes for men in non-Western states who were never subject to daily overtime pay regulation. This comparison generates the so-called "difference-in-difference" estimator (Card and Sullivan (1988):

$$\Delta^2_M = (Y^{85}_{CA,M} - Y^{73}_{CA,M}) - (Y^{85}_{NW,M} - Y^{73}_{NW,M}), \quad (1)$$

where the subscript M denotes men and $Y^t_{r,M}$ represents the outcome for men in region r (California or non-West) at time t (1973 or 1985). As described in Section 8.2, premium pay for daily overtime was mandatory for California men in 1985 but not in 1973, whereas in neither year did such a requirement apply to men in non-Western states.

The estimator in equation (1) assumes that, were it not for the expanded coverage of California's overtime law, outcome changes for men would have been similar across regions. Because the daily overtime penalty applied to California women throughout the period we study, it is natural to use outcome changes for female workers to control for idiosyncratic shocks that may have affected the California labor market. The resulting "difference-indifference-in-difference" estimator is

$$\Delta^3 = \Delta^2_M - \Delta^2_F, \quad (2)$$

where Δ^2_F is the female analog to equation (1).[10] In equation (2), changes for California women (relative to other women) are presumed to reflect region-specific period effects, and the impact of extending California's overtime law to men is estimated by the extent to which outcome changes for California men (relative to other men) differed from the relative changes experienced by California women. Other groups not directly affected by the extension of California's daily overtime penalty might be used in computing equation (2) (for example, exempt male workers), but, for this purpose, female workers have the unique virtues of being numerous and easy to identify.

For ease of exposition, we will refer to estimates based on equation (1) as *double-difference* estimates. Similarly, we will refer to estimates based on equation (2) as *triple-difference* estimates. It is convenient to compute the double and *triple-difference* estimators within a regression framework. For double differences, we pool the 1973 and 1985 CPS samples of male workers and estimate the following regression:

$$Y_i = \alpha + \gamma_1 T_i + \gamma_2 C_i + \gamma_3 T_i C_i + \varepsilon_i, \quad (3)$$

where Y_i is the outcome observed for individual i, T is an indicator variable marking observations from the 1985 survey, C is an indicator variable identifying people who live in California, and ε is a random error term. The coefficient γ_3 measures the double difference defined in equation (1). For triple differences, we add the data for women and estimate

$$Y_i = \alpha + \gamma_1 T_i + \gamma_2 C_i + \gamma_3 M_i + \gamma_4 T_i C_i + \gamma_5 T_i M_i + \gamma_6 C_i M_i + \gamma_7 T_i C_i M_i + \varepsilon_i, \quad (4)$$

where M is an indicator variable identifying male workers. The coefficient γ_7 represents the triple difference defined in equation (2).

As a check on our results, we also report analogous estimates for the period 1985–1991. Because this period witnessed no major changes in California's overtime law and the changes that did occur affected both men and women – our estimated effects for the 1973–1985 period are suspect if similar patterns emerge over 1985–1991. Finally, it is straightforward to add observable control variables to the regression specifications in equations (3) and (4), and we do this in Section 8.7 below.[11]

8.6. Basic Results

This section presents our basic empirical results. The outcome analyzed in Table 8.2 is the percentage of workers with workdays longer than eight hours. The top half of the table shows changes over the 1973–1985 period during which California's daily overtime penalty was extended to cover men, and the bottom half shows changes over the 1985–1991 period when no important changes occurred in California's overtime law. Standard errors of the estimated effects are displayed in parentheses.

The top half of Table 8.2 indicates that the extension of California's overtime law to male workers was accompanied by a substantial decline in the prevalence of daily overtime among California men as compared to men in non-Western states. In 1973, before California's daily overtime pay requirement applied to men, 18.5% of California men and 21.6% of men in the non-West worked more than eight hours per day. By 1985, after California extended overtime coverage to men, the incidence of daily overtime among male workers had fallen to 16.0% in California at the same time that it had risen to 23.6% in the non-West. The double-difference estimate, shown in row 4 of the table, implies that the daily overtime penalty reduced the incidence of long workdays among California men by 4.5 percentage points. This drop represents a 24% decline when measured against the proportion of California men working daily overtime in 1973.[12]

Table 8.2

Percentage of Workers with Workdays Longer than Eight Hours

	Men		Women	
	California	Non-West	California	Non-West
1973–1985 Change				
(1) 1973	18.5	21.6	4.6	6.7
(2) 1985	16.0	23.6	8.5	9.2
(3) Row (2) – Row (1)	-2.5	2.0	3.9	2.5
(4) Calif. (3) – Non-West (3)	(1.7)		1.4	
	-4.5		(1.2)	
(5) Men (4) – Women (4)		-5.9		
		(2.1)		
1985–1991 Change				
(6) 1991	20.0	24.6	11.1	10.9
(7) Row (6) – Row (2)	4.0	1.0	2.6	1.7
(8) Calif. (7) – Non-West (7)	3.0		0.9	
	(1.8)		(1.4)	
(9) Men (8) – Women (8)		2.0		
		(2.3)		

Note: Here and in the succeeding tables, standard errors are in parentheses, sampling weights are used in the calculations, and all numbers have been rounded independently.

Whereas for men the prevalence of daily overtime rose between 1973 and 1985 in the control states but not in California, a different pattern exists for women. Specifically, overtime incidence increased substantially (from 4.6% to 8.5%) for female workers in California but grew somewhat more modestly (from 6.7% to 9.2%) for women in non-Western states. Because California's overtime law applied to women in both 1973 and 1985, the triple-difference estimate, shown in row 5, assumes that this excess growth of 1.4 percentage points for California women measures the impact of California-specific shocks that had the same effect on the overtime hours of male workers. Accounting for these shocks yields an even larger estimate of the response to California's daily overtime pay requirement - namely, that extending overtime coverage to California men reduced their incidence of overtime workdays by 5.9 percentage points, or 32%.[13]

Row 3 of Table 8.2 tells the story quite clearly. Of the four sex/region groups, three show an increased prevalence of long workdays between 1973 and 1985. The one group that experienced a decline in the incidence of daily overtime - California men - is also the only group directly affected by the expansion of California's overtime law that took place during this period. In other words, the work schedules of California men moved opposite the direction observed for other workers over this period. We think it reasonable to attribute this divergent trend for California men to their becoming subject to that state's daily overtime penalty.

Between 1973 and 1985, the California economy improved relative to the rest of the nation.[14] Overtime is procyclical,which may explain why the incidence of daily overtime rose more over this period for California women than for other women. Thus, overtime work by California men fell in spite of business conditions favoring increased overtime. As a result, the estimated impact of California's daily hours standard is larger when we use the triple-difference approach that attempts to control for region-specific changes in business conditions than it is when we use the double-difference approach that does not control for such changes. The relative strength of California's economy over this period suggests that, in this particular case, the double-difference estimate will understate the true effect of the daily overtime penalty.

There is reason to suspect, however, that the triple-difference estimate may overstate the true effect of the daily overtime penalty. Suppose that overtime work by men and overtime work by women are substitute inputs. Because the daily overtime penalty already applied to California women, extending coverage to California men raised the marginal cost of male overtime relative to female overtime. California employers might respond by increasing female overtime to replace some of the reduction in male overtime. This substitution argument provides an alternative explanation for why the incidence of daily overtime rose more between 1973 and 1985 for California women than it did for women in other states. To the extent that the observed changes in female overtime are due to male-female hours substitution within California (rather than to the relative improvement of California's economy) the triple-difference estimate overstates the reduction in male overtime generated by the daily overtime penalty. Consequently, the discussion in this paragraph and the preceding paragraph indicates that the double- and triple-difference estimates may provide bounds on the true effect.

The bottom half of Table 8.2 presents analogous calculations for the 1985–1991 period when no major changes were made to California's overtime law. Consider the possibility that the double- and triple-difference estimates for the 1973–1985 period reflect ongoing trends that are unique to California men, rather than the effects of that state's daily overtime penalty being extended to male workers. We might then expect to find similar estimates for 1985–1991, and such a finding would raise concerns that the earlier estimates could be spurious. The data in the bottom half of Table 8.2 do not fit this scenario. The double and triple differences are positive for the 1985–1991 period, whereas these differences are negative for the 1973–1985 period. Although not statistically significant, the 1985–1991 differences suggest that the initially large impact that California's daily overtime penalty had on male workers may have been partially undone over time.[15] Nominal wage rigidities could explain this pattern, because, in that case, the wage adjustments predicted by hedonic models of overtime pay regulation would occur gradually as inflation facilitates reductions in the real straight-time hourly wage.

Table 8.3

Percentage of Workers with Workdays of Exactly Eight Hours

	Men		Women	
	California	Non-West	California	Non-West
1973–1985 Change				
(1) 1973	62.7	61.2	63.8	54.6
(2) 1985	64.0	57.1	58.1	50.5
(3) Row (2) – Row (1)	1.3	-4.1	-5.7	-4.1
(4) Calif. (3) – Non-West (3)	5.5 (2.1)		-1.5 (2.3)	
(5) Men (4) – Women (4)	7.0 (3.1)			
1985–1991 Change				
(6) 1991	60.1	54.9	56.9	49.9
(7) Row (6) – Row (2)	-3.9	-2.2	-1.2	-0.6
(8) Calif. (7) – Non-West (7)	-1.6 (2.2)		-0.7 (2.4)	
(9) Men (8) – Women (8)	-1.0 (3.3)			

Table 8.3 has the same format as Table 8.2, but the outcome examined in Table 8.3 is the percentage of workers who work exactly

eight hours per day. Once again, the 1973–1985 change for California men differs markedly from the corresponding change for every other group. Whereas eight-hour workdays became somewhat more widespread among California men over this period, California women and workers of either sex in non-Western states experienced a substantial reduction in the incidence of eight-hour days. The double-difference estimate in row 4 of Table 8.3 implies that California's daily overtime penalty increased the prevalence of eight-hour workdays among California men by 5.5 percentage points, and the triple-difference estimate in row 5 implies an even larger effect of 7.0 percentage points. The analogous estimates for 1985–1991 are relatively small and of the opposite sign as the 1973–1985 estimates, which provides some assurance that the estimates for the earlier period do not merely reflect spurious trends that are unique to California men.

The double- and triple-difference estimates compare the intertemporal changes experienced by different groups of workers, but the cross-section comparisons in Table 8.3 tell a similar story. In 1973, before the daily overtime penalty was mandatory for California men, eight-hour workdays were about equally prevalent among male workers in California and non-Western states. After California's overtime law was extended to men, however, the 1985 and 1991 data show that eight-hour days became noticeably more common for California men than for other men. California women, by contrast, were subject to the daily overtime penalty in all three years, and in all three years the incidence of eight-hour workdays is much higher for California women than for other women.

California's overtime law thus appears to have induced greater bunching at eight-hour workdays, just as labor demand theory predicts. Also in line with the theory is the fact that the double and triple differences for 1973–1985 reported in Table 8.3 imply effects that are opposite in sign and roughly similar in magnitude to the effects on the incidence of daily overtime reported in Table 8.2. Taken together, the results in Table 8.2 and 8.3 indicate that California's daily overtime penalty caused some long workdays to be shortened to eight hours, without much impact on workdays of less than eight hours.

In Table 8.4, the sample is limited to those who work more than eight hours per day, and the outcome studied is the average number of daily overtime hours worked by these overtime workers. In 1973, men working overtime averaged about an hour and three-quarters of overtime per day, regardless of whether they lived in California or elsewhere. By

1985, however, the conditional mean of male overtime hours was distinctly lower in California than it was elsewhere. The resulting double-difference estimate implies that California's overtime law reduced by one-quarter of an hour (14%) the amount of daily overtime worked by men who continued to put in overtime after they became subject to the law. This estimate just barely achieves statistical significance at the 10% level. Among female overtime workers, average daily overtime hours increased more in California than elsewhere between 1973 and 1985, and, as a result, the triple-difference estimate is larger (in absolute value) than the double-difference estimate. The triple difference is estimated imprecisely, however, because our sample includes relatively few California women who work overtime. Finally, the double and triple differences for 1985–1991 are small and swamped by their standard errors.

Table 8.4

Average Daily Overtime Hours Worked by Overtime Workers

	Men		Women	
	California	Non-West	California	Non-West
1973–1985 Change				
(1) 1973	1.76	1.70	1.61	1.58
(2) 1985	1.84	2.02	2.05	1.88
(3) Row (2) – Row (1)	0.08	0.32	0.44	0.30
(4) Calif. (3) – Non-West (3)	-0.25 (0.15)		0.15 (0.37)	
(5) Men (4) – Women (4)	-0.40 (0.40)			
1985–1991 Change				
(6) 1991	1.75	1.94	1.98	1.70
(7) Row (6) – Row (2)	-0.09	-0.08	-0.07	-0.18
(8) Calif. (7) – Non-West (7)	-0.01 (0.14)		0.11 (0.37)	
(9) Men (8) – Women (8)	-0.12 (0.39)			

The theory of labor demand suggests two avenues through which an overtime penalty may reduce overtime hours. First, to the extent that expanded use of other inputs can replace overtime hours and produce the same output at only slightly higher cost, firms will take advantage of these substitution possibilities. Second, when good substitutes for overtime hours are not available, marginal costs rise sharply, inducing firms to scale back production. In the first case, firms' costs and profits need not be greatly affected by overtime pay regulation, whereas, in the second case, firms will likely suffer declines in output and profits. Ultimately, the impact that California's overtime law had on businesses in the state depends on the relative importance of substitution effects versus scale effects in generating the large reduction in daily overtime that the law appears to have caused.

Increasing the number of days worked per week is one obvious way to compensate for shorter workdays. To investigate this possibility, we calculated double- and triple-difference estimates of the impact of California's overtime law on the number of days that employees usually work each week. These estimates (not reported here) give no indication that California men worked more days per week after they became subject to the daily overtime penalty. In a search for inputs that are close substitutes for daily hours, workdays would be high on the list of candidates. Consequently, the failure to find an effect on workdays may indicate that employers cannot easily avoid daily overtime by substituting other inputs. But there is little variation across years in the average number of days worked per week, which suggests that this input is not very sensitive to economic conditions and perhaps not a promising candidate for substitution, after all. (See also Hamermesh (1996, Chapter 5).)

In addition, we looked for evidence that California's daily overtime law caused firms to expand employment as a substitute for assigning long workdays. Double-difference estimates reveal that the employment rate of California men increased relative to the employment rate of men in non-Western states over the 1973–1985 period. California women experienced very similar gains in their relative employment rate, however, so triple-difference estimates show no impact on employment. Consequently, these data do not provide compelling evidence that the daily overtime penalty raised the employment rate of California men beyond what would have been expected from business-cycle movements.

8.7. Results with Control Variables

We next present double- and triple-difference estimates that control for observable variables available in the CPS. By adding controls, we hope to net out the influence of factors other than the daily overtime penalty that may have altered the work schedules of California men over the relevant period. For double differences (which include only men in the sample), equation (3) is extended as follows:

(5) $$Y_i = \alpha + X_i\,\beta_1 + X_i\,T_i\,\beta_2 + \gamma_1\,T_i + \gamma_2\,C_i + \gamma_3\,T_i\,C_i + \varepsilon_i,$$

where *X* is a vector of control variables. Notice that the coefficients on these control variables are allowed to differ across survey years. For triple differences, which add women to the sample, equation (4) is changed to

(6) $$Y_i = \alpha + X_i\,\beta_1 + X_i\,T_i\,\beta_2 + X_i\,M_i\,\beta_3 + X_i\,T_i\,M_i\,\beta_4 + \gamma_1\,T_i + \gamma_2\,C_i + \gamma_3\,M_i + \gamma_4\,T_i\,C_i + \gamma_5\,T_i\,M_i + \gamma_6\,C_i\,M_i + \gamma_7\,T_i\,C_i\,M_i + \varepsilon_i,$$

here, the coefficients on the control variables can vary by both survey year and sex.

We employ two different specifications of the control vector *X*. The first includes the following demographic characteristics of each worker:

Table 8.5

Impact of California's Overtime Law on Daily Work Schedules, Double and Triple Differences, with Successively More-Detailed Controls

	Double Differences			Triple Differences		
Dependent Variable / Time Period	(1)	(2)	(3)	(4)	(5)	(6)
Percent with workdays >8 Hours:						
1973–1985 change	-4.5	-3.3	-2.9	-5.9	-4.8	-4.5
	(1.7)	(1.7)	(1.7)	(2.1)	(2.1)	(2.1)
1985–1991 change	3.0	4.9	4.3	2.0	4.8	3.9
	(1.8)	(1.9)	(1.9)	(2.3)	(2.4)	(2.4)
Percent with workdays =8 hours:						
1973–1985 change	5.5	4.4	2.2	7.0	7.2	7.4
	(2.1)	(2.2)	(2.1)	(3.1)	(3.2)	(3.0)
1985–1991 change	-1.6	-2.1	-1.1	-1.0	-1.5	-0.1
	(2.2)	(2.3)	(2.3)	(3.3)	(3.4)	(3.3)
Average daily OT hours of OT workers:						
1973–1985 change	-0.25	-0.23	-0.13	-0.40	-0.33	-0.24
	(0.15)	(0.16)	(0.15)	(0.40)	(0.43)	(0.42)
1985–1991 change	-0.01	0.03	-0.05	-0.12	-0.07	-0.24
	(0.14)	(0.15)	(0.15)	(0.39)	(0.43)	(0.42)
Control Variables:						
Demographic characteristics	No	Yes	Yes	No	Yes	Yes
Major industry and occupation	No	No	Yes	No	No	Yes

Notes: Here and in Table 8.7 the demographic characteristics controlled for in specificstions (2) and (3) are age, education, marital status and race/ethnicity. The industry and occupation controls used in specification (3) identify ten industry categories and six occupation categories. For the double-difference estimates, the effects of the control variables are allowed to vary by survey year. For the triple-difference estimates, the effects of the control variables are allowed to vary by survey year and sex.

age, age squared, completed years of schooling, marital status (an indicator variable identifying those who are married with spouse present), and race/ethnicity (indicators identifying Hispanics, non-Hispanic blacks, and non-Hispanics whose race is neither white nor black).[16] In the second specification, we also include indicators that classify workers into ten industry categories and six occupation categories.[17]

Table 8.5 reports double- and triple-difference estimates from alternate specifications that successively add control variables. For comparison purposes, the columns labeled (1) reproduce the estimates from Tables 8.2 through 8.4 that do not control for demographic characteristics (other than region of residence and sex) or industry and occupation. Specification (2) adds the controls for demographic characteristics, and specification (3) includes controls for both demographic characteristics and major industry and occupation categories. The estimates for the 1973–1985 period measure the impact of extending California's overtime law to men and adding the control variables tends to shrink these estimates somewhat, particularly for the double differences. The triple differences are much more stable across specifications than are the double differences, which may indicate that the triple-difference approach does a good job of accounting for California-specific shocks that are correlated with changes in the demographic, industrial, and occupational composition of the work force. In any case, the overall pattern of the results reported in the previous section does not change dramatically when we add detailed controls for observable characteristics.

8.8. Implications

Our estimates of the impact of California's daily overtime penalty are consistent with labor demand models of overtime pay regulation. For illustrative purposes, we can compute rough measures of the price elasticity of demand for daily overtime hours implied by these estimates. Start with the identity

$$E(OT) = Pr\ (OT > 0)\ E(OT \mid OT > 0), \quad (7)$$

where *OT* represents daily overtime hours. Overtime hours per worker is the product of overtime incidence and the average amount of overtime worked by overtime workers. Note that the average E(*OT*) is taken over all workers, including those who work zero hours of overtime. To a first-order approximation, the percentage change in the average overtime hours of California men induced by that state's overtime law is

$$\%\Delta E\,(OT) = \%\Delta \Pr\,(OT > 0) + \%\Delta E\,(OT \mid OT > 0). \qquad (8)$$

The 1973–1985 double and triple differences in Table 8.5 provide estimates of the components of equation (8). For example, consider the double-difference estimates that do not control for demographic characteristics or industry/occupation. According to these estimates, extension of the daily overtime penalty to California men reduced their incidence of long workdays by 4.5 percentage points and lowered their conditional overtime hours by one-quarter of an hour. When compared to the initial levels observed for California men in 1973, the estimated effects represent a 24.3% decline in overtime incidence and a 14.2% fall in conditional overtime hours. Summing these percentage changes yields a 38.5% reduction in average daily overtime hours, which is the numerator of the labor demand elasticity that we seek. As for the denominator, assume for the moment that California's overtime law produced a 50% increase in the price of male overtime hours. Taking the ratio of these numbers yields an elasticity of demand for daily overtime of -0.77.

Table 8.6

Estimates of the Price Elasticity of Demand for Daily Overtime Hours

	(1)	(2)	(3)
Double-difference estimates	-0.77	-0.62	-0.46
	(0.25)	(0.26)	(0.25)
Triple-difference estimates	-1.09	-0.89	-0.76
	(0.51)	(0.54)	(0.53)
Control Variables:			
Demographic characteristics	No	Yes	Yes
Major industry and occupation	No	No	Yes

Table 8.6 shows what happens when we repeat this calculation for each of the various specifications in Table 8.5. All of the elasticities imply a sizeable demand response, although the estimated magnitude of this response shrinks somewhat as more-detailed controls for observables are included in the regressions. The elasticities range from -0.46 to -0.77 for the double-difference estimates and from -0.76 to -1.09 for the triple-difference estimates.

There are reasons to be skeptical, however, of these estimates of the price elasticity of demand for daily overtime hours. For one thing, although the daily overtime premium discourages firms from assigning overtime, it simultaneously makes overtime hours more attractive to workers. To the extent that the labor market changes generated by California's overtime law reflect both demand and supply responses, the observed reduction in overtime will be smaller than if offsetting supply effects were absent. Moreover, as noted in Section 8.2, standard characterizations of labor market equilibrium imply that compensating differentials in straight-time hourly wages can arise to mitigate the effects of a mandatory overtime penalty.

Even more problematic is our assumption that California's overtime law produced a 50% rise in the price of male overtime hours. For this to occur, it would have to be the case that no California men received an overtime premium before the law was imposed, and that afterward compliance was perfect. Because both of these conditions fail, the actual increase in the average overtime wage was less than 50%, and therefore the preceding calculations understate the implied demand elasticity (in absolute value).

What makes this issue particularly important is the considerable overlap between state and federal overtime pay regulation. In fact, the federal requirement for time-and-a half after forty hours of weekly work seems to render California's daily overtime standard redundant for most workers.[18] By this argument, the California law raises the marginal wage only for workers whose schedules satisfy the following two conditions: daily hours exceed eight *and* weekly hours are no greater than forty. The CPS data indicate that relatively few people work this combination of long daily hours but short weekly hours. In 1973, for example, only about 1% of male workers in California, or 6% of men with workdays longer than eight hours, were apparently in a position to gain overtime protection from state law that they did not already receive from federal law.[19]

Given the paucity of work schedules with long daily but not weekly hours, the effects that we attribute to California's overtime law must be driven by the responses of workers with workweeks exceeding forty hours. Table 8.7 provides direct confirmation of this point. It presents estimated effects of the California law on weekly work schedules that are analogous to the estimated effects on daily work schedules reported in Table 8.5.[20] The estimates in the two tables are similar. In other words, the impact of California's daily overtime penalty shows up even when overtime is defined on the weekly basis specified by the federal Fair Labor Standards Act, and the estimated effects of the California law on both daily and weekly work schedules seem to fit the predictions of labor demand theory.

Table 8.7

Impact of California's Overtime Law on Weekly Work Schedules, Double and Triple Differences, with Successively More-Detailed Controls

	Double Differences			Triple Differences		
Dependent Variable / Time Period	(1)	(2)	(3)	(4)	(5)	(6)
Percent with workweeks >40 hours:						
1973–1985 change	-3.3	-2.7	-2.3	-6.2	-4.9	-4.4
	(1.7)	(1.8)	(1.8)	(2.0)	(2.1)	(2.1)
1985–1991 change	2.5	3.9	3.4	1.5	3.9	3.2
	(1.7)	(1.9)	(1.9)	(2.1)	(2.3)	(2.3)
Percent with workweeks =40 hours:						
1973–1985 change	6.1	4.7	2.5	5.5	4.9	5.0
	(2.1)	(2.1)	(2.1)	(3.1)	(3.1)	(3.0)
1985–1991 change	-1.8	-1.8	-0.9	1.0	1.5	2.7
	(2.2)	(2.3)	(2.2)	(3.2)	(3.3)	(3.2)
Average weekly OT hours of OT workers:						
1973–1985 change	-2.40	-2.18	-1.61	-2.92	-3.18	-3.00
	(0.94)	(0.88)	(0.79)	(2.35)	(2.01)	(2.03)
1985–1991 change	1.73	1.67	1.13	1.48	1.25	0.55
	(0.75)	(0.77)	(0.77)	(1.98)	(2.20)	(2.17)
Control Variables:						
Demographic characteristics	No	Yes	Yes	No	Yes	Yes
Major industry and occupation	No	No	Yes	No	No	Yes

The results in Table 8.7 raise a puzzle: Why should California's daily overtime penalty affect employees who work more than forty hours per week and therefore presumably already receive overtime pay because of the Fair Labor Standards Act? We offer two possible explanations. First, when hours of work vary from day to day within a week, the California law can increase required overtime payments even to workers whose long workweeks make them subject to the federal overtime premium. For example, consider someone who works three ten-hour days and two six-hour days each week. According to the federal forty-hour weekly standard, this worker is due two hours of overtime pay, whereas under California's eight-hour daily standard the worker should receive six hours of overtime pay. Unfortunately, we do not know of any data that allow us to measure the intraweek variability of daily workhours.

A second possibility is that California's daily overtime law increased compliance with the overtime pay provisions of the Fair Labor Standards Act.[21] When the daily overtime penalty was first extended to California men, the state mounted a publicity campaign to inform employers of the change, and additional inspectors were hired to search for violations among newly covered workers. In California, then, overtime laws were policed by both state and federal regulators. A related point is that California's eight-hour workday may be more visible and easier for firms to monitor than the federal forty-hour workweek. Typically, a supervisor can observe with little effort whether the workers on his shift put in daily overtime, whereas detecting weekly overtime may require coordination between two or more supervisors (for example, a weekday supervisor and a weekend supervisor).

Setting aside the difficulties just discussed, the elasticities reported in Table 8.6 measure the price responsiveness of the demand for daily overtime hours. If we accept the evidence that increases in the overtime penalty induce little substitution toward additional days per week, then these elasticities also indicate how the demand for weekly hours responds to a change in the marginal wage. As the literature on substitution between workers and hours makes clear, however, demand elasticities for employment and hours will generally differ (Hamermesh (1993, chapter 3)). Because our estimates provide no information about the price elasticity of demand for employment, they cannot be used to infer the demand elasticity for "total" hours of work (that is, the product of employment and hours per worker). Instead, our estimates pertain only to the daily and (possibly) weekly hours dimensions of labor demand, but our evidence on these dimensions of labor demand is unique in that it originates from an exogenous shift in the marginal wage.

8.9. Conclusions

We find strong evidence that the distribution of daily workhours responded to the California overtime law exactly as the theory of labor demand predicts. After California's daily overtime penalty was extended to men, overtime hours and the incidence of overtime workdays declined substantially for male workers in California relative to men in other states, and the prevalence of eight-hour workdays rose by roughly the same amount that overtime incidence fell. The implied price elasticity of demand for daily overtime hours is at least -0.5. Unlike most prior studies of labor demand, our estimates represent the response to an exogenous price change. Regarding substitution possibilities, the data give no indication that, after becoming subject to the daily overtime penalty, California men worked more days per week to compensate for their shorter workdays. These results persist when we use analogous comparisons for women to account for idiosyncratic shocks that may have affected the California labor market.

Surprisingly, California's daily overtime law altered in important ways the work schedules of employees with workweeks exceeding forty hours, despite the fact that such workers were already entitled to overtime pay under the federal Fair Labor Standards Act. To the extent that workhours vary from day to day within a week, however, a daily overtime penalty can increase required overtime payments even to workers whose long workweeks make them subject to a weekly overtime penalty. In addition, California's efforts to publicize and enforce its overtime law may have improved compliance with the federal overtime law.

9

The Timing of Labor Demand

9.1. Introduction

The effect of labor costs on the number of workers firms seek to employ and the intensity with which those workers are employed is one of the most-studied subjects in labor economics. The theory has proceeded from analyzing production to examining profit-maximizing behavior in the face of per-hour and per-worker costs that are assumed to be exogenous to the firm. Implicit in the entire literature are "t" subscripts – labor demand functions and production functions are defined over particular intervals of time during which the factor inputs are assumed to be productive.

Hours of the day are not, however, the same to workers. In a relatively unregulated labor market like that in the United States, we observe, as one would expect from the hedonic model (Rosen (1974)), that those individuals performing work at unusual times (nights and weekends) tend to have relatively little human capital, and are workers for whom the attraction of a market-generated compensating wage differential makes work at these times relatively attractive (Hamermesh (1999a)). We may infer from the wage premium and the characteristics of workers observed on the job at different times that the timing of work matters to workers.

The original version of this chapter was published as: Cardoso, Ana R./Hamermesh, Daniel S./Varejão, José (2012). The Timing of Labor Demand, in: Annals of Economics and Statistics, 105/106: 15–34. © 2012 by GENES. We thank Thomas Bauer, Raja Junankar, Rachel Ngai, Luca Nunziata, Stepan Jurajda, participants at seminars at several universities and IZA, and two referees for helpful comments, and the Barcelona GSE Research Network, the Government of Catalonia, the IZA, the University of Texas at Austin and the Fundação para a Ciência e a Tecnologia for financial support. CEFUP is funded by FCT.

Economists know this, but few studies of labor demand have failed to treat time units as if they are all identical - one hour, or one week of labor input is the same regardless of the time of day or week when it occurs. Those exceptions have either derived general models of production with time subscripts (Winston (1982)), discussed shift work theoretically (Stafford (1980)), analyzed the extent of shift work using household data (Mayshar and Solon (1993), Hamermesh (1996)), or examined how firms add shifts as demand grows (Bresnahan and Ramey (1994)).

Many countries impose wage penalties in the form of mandatory premium pay on workhours that are utilized outside of what are deemed to be standard hours. These are quite different from the overtime penalties that many countries also assess on total hours (usual weekly) that an employee works beyond a standard amount. Yet, no study has examined the role of differences in the relative price of a unit of effective labor at different times of the day or week; and therefore none has been able to examine the impact of these penalties on the timing of work.

A possible reason why there have, to our knowledge, been literally no formal analyses of the general question and of labor market policies affecting high-frequency temporal differences in work timing has been the complete absence of employer-based data that would allow examining these issues. Fortunately, several Portuguese firm-level surveys can be combined to provide a cross-section examination of the issue, with the crucial data set showing the number of workers on the job at each hour of the week.

In what follows we therefore first outline the nature of legislative mandates on work timing in a number of countries and in Portugal. We then describe the Portuguese data, discuss how we select the samples to use in the estimation and describe some broad patterns of time use across the week. In Section 9.4 we discuss and estimate production tableaux describing the timing of work hours. Section 9.5 presents a policy simulation using the estimates of the determinants of work timing.

9.2. The Regulation of Work Timing

Work outside daytime weekday hours, especially night work, has long attracted regulatory attention. The International Labor Organization (ILO) alone has devoted eight conventions to night work, especially that performed by women and younger workers. The regulation of night work is typically justified by concerns about workers' health, although their ability to meet family and social responsibilities is also mentioned. Accordingly, most rules addressing the issue are targeted at night workers' health conditions and at the specification of workers' rights to being transferred to a similar daytime job for reasons of health. Existing rules also often call for compensation for night work, either in the form of a compensatory rest period or additional pay. ILO Convention No. 171, for example, calls for various benefits that recognize the "nature of night work." Many European nations and Japan (as well as many less developed countries) have followed this and similar recommendations and passed legislation that sets specific rules about the compensation of night workers.

Table 9.1 describes rules on night and weekend work in a number of countries and makes the point that wage penalties mandated on employers of night workers are of interest to many nations. In many more countries than Table 9.1 suggests, especially in Europe, night work is addressed by collective agreements rather than legislatively. For example, a survey of collective bargaining covering Spanish firms shows that 49 percent of collective agreements establish a specific pay rate for night work that is on average 23 percent above the pay rate for similar daytime work.[1]

Portuguese legislation, while allowing employers to organize working time as they see fit, sets a number of rules that may condition the timing of economic activity and whose impact is the focus of this study.[2] The duration of work is set by collective agreement, but the law stipulates the maximum length of both the workday (8 hours) and the workweek (40 hours), with these limits extendable up to 10 hours per day and 50 hours per week. Overtime work is permitted in cases of an exceptional workload or if there is the risk of an imminent economic loss by the firm, but even then it is limited to a maximum of 200 hours per year.[3] An overtime pay premium is payable, varying from 50 to 100 percent of the straight-time wage rate depending on the number of consecutive overtime hours.

All night work (defined in 2003 as work performed between 8PM and 7AM) carries a wage penalty of 25 percent (DL 409/71, art. 30). A number of health and safety regulations, including mandatory regular medical check-ups especially designed for night workers, are also in place. Regular night work may or may not be integrated into a shift-work system. That is likely to be the usual case, as the law

Table 9.1. Provisions Regarding Irreguar Hours in Selected Countries

	Criteria for Nightwork	Limits	Rest periods	Compensation	Health & Safety	Transfers	Rights to Equal Treatment	Prohibitions	Special Categories
Austria						×			
Belgium	×								
Czech Republic					×	×		×	
Denmark					×	×			
Finland	×	×							
France				×	×	×			×
Germany				×	×	×	×		
Greece	×			×					
Ireland						×			
Italy				×		×			
Latvia						×			
Luxembourg		×		×					
Netherlands		×	×			×			
Portugal				×	×	×			
Romania				×	×	×			
Slovakia				×					
Spain						×			
UK					×	×	×		
Japan				×					

Source: ILO-Database of work and employment. The U.S. is excluded from this table because no category would be checked off there.

Note: × indicates that the country has an entry on the ILO database for the corresponding column heading.

also establishes that a shift system has to be organized whenever the length of the operating period exceeds the normal period of work. Work on weekends is also subject to a number of rules, as Saturday and Sunday are the default mandatory weekly rest days. The corresponding wage penalty is not set by law, but collective bargaining can and usually does stipulate one.[4]

It is possible to consider four pay regimes corresponding to work done at different times: Regular hours, 7AM-8PM Monday-Friday, with no wage penalty; night weekday hours, 8PM–7AM Monday-Friday, penalized 25 percent; daytime hours on weekends, 7AM-8PM Saturday and Sunday, penalized varying from 0 to 100 percent; and night weekend hours, 8PM-7AM Saturday and Sunday, penalized varying from 25 to 150 percent.[5]

9.3. Data, Concepts and Descriptive Statistics

9.3.1. Creating the Data Set

Most of the data used in this study come from two sources: *Quadros de Pessoal* (henceforth *QP*) (Personnel Records) and an Annex to the Portuguese contribution to the *European Union Company Survey of Operating Hours and Working Times and Employment (EUCOWE).*[6] The *QP* is an administrative matched employer-employee data set collected by the Portuguese Ministry of Employment. Reporting is mandatory for all employers with at least one wage-earner, excluding public administration and domestic work. It is basically a census of the private sector. The data refer to one reference week in October of the given year and include the worker's wage (split into several components), age, gender, schooling, occupation, tenure, skill level, normal hours, overtime hours, the industry and location of both the firm and the establishment, and firm sales.

The Portuguese contribution to the EUCOWE survey was carried out in June 2003 by the Ministry of Employment, with questions referring to the week of May 5–11, 2003, during which there were no public holidays and when no major peaks or troughs occurred in sectors widely recognized to be subject to seasonal fluctuations, such as retail trade or tourism.[7] The choice of any single week cannot obviate concerns about seasonal variations, but this particular choice clearly should minimize those concerns. The survey was addressed to establishments in all industries (except agriculture and public administration) and all size classes. Beyond extensive information on the length and organization of working hours and hours of operation, respondents were asked to report the number of employees working at the establishment during each hour of the survey week. Only outside contractors, temporary agency workers and unpaid workers were excluded from this head-count. The questionnaire was administered to a sample that was stratified by size-class and industry and drawn from the universe of firms responding to the QP.[8] The initial sample included 6,002 establishments, 3,127 of which returned responses. Of these, 2,818 plants provided data that were internally consistent.

Given our focus on productivity, it is crucial that our proxy for production (total sales) be measured at the same level as employment. Sales in the QP are, however, recorded only at the firm level. Since only a very few multi-plant firms have all plants included in the EUCOWE, we can only link a firm's sales to the timing of its employment for single-plant firms. We thus restrict the data set to single-establishment firms (1,949 firms, approximately 70 percent of the sample with internally consistent data). Since annual sales for 2003 are reported in the 2004 wave of the QP, we use both the 2003 (for workforce characteristics in the plant) and the 2004 (for sales) waves of the QP in our basic estimates. The requirement that the firm be present in both waves eliminated another 371 establishments, generating a sample of 1,578 establishments. This set of constraints thus led to dropping 44 percent of the plants in the original dataset and a slightly larger share of workers (53).We have furthermore dropped one-worker firms (60) and those that, although they responded, did not complete the table on the timing of work (554), resulting in a final sample of 964 firms.

A major concern is whether these data constraints lead to biases in our analysis. There are nearly 200,000 single-plant firms in the population covered by the QP, making this sample potentially highly selected out of the population. A probit relating inclusion in our final data set to all the control variables used in the analysis suggests that, other than unexplained differences by industry, only firm size (sales) has an important impact, with doubling a firm's size increasing its chance of inclusion in our sample from 0.005 to 0.01. The fact that we explicitly dropped firms with only one wage-earner contributes to this outcome. Given that the original EUCOWE sample was representative of the population, these probits suggest that non-response to the EUCOWE and our further restrictions have not altered the representativeness of the data set along most dimensions.

We have also compared the diagrams that we present below for firms in our data set to analogous diagrams based on all firms that provided valid answers in the EUCOWE. The figures describing our sample and those from the complete sample are essentially indistinguishable, which also points to the absence of selection biases in our sample.[9]

Figure 9.1

Tempogram of Total Employment in Portuguese Establishments (Calculated from EUCOWE (2003))

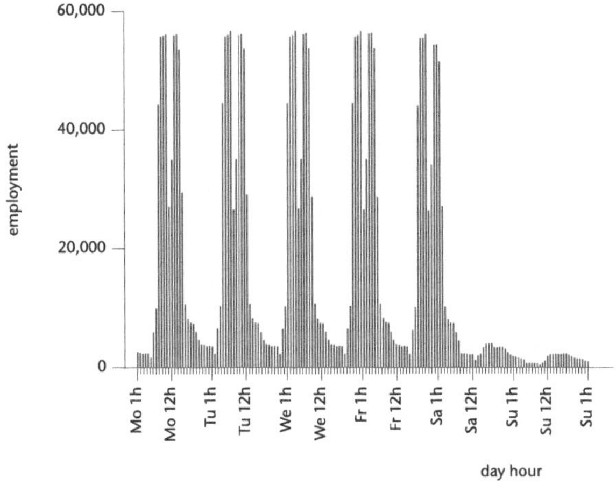

9.3.2. *Basic Facts about the Timing of Work*

Dividing the week into 168 one-hour intervals, Figure 9.1 is an establishment-based tempogram that presents the total number of workers present at work at each hour of the survey week.[10] The figure describes the rhythmic nature of the demand for labor services within a single week. It shows that the number of individuals working at nights is only a small fraction of the total present at work in the daytime and that the same pattern is repeated from Monday to Friday. It also shows that daytime workers do not all arrive at work at the same time, but rather that they spread their starting hours from 7AM to 10AM, at which time the majority of all daytime workers are simultaneously present in the workplace. The same is true for the transition between daytime and nighttime, as workers start to leave at around 5PM, although the minimum level of employment is not reached before 10-11PM.

Figure 9.2 Tempogram of Total Employment by Industry (Calculated from EUCOWE (2003))

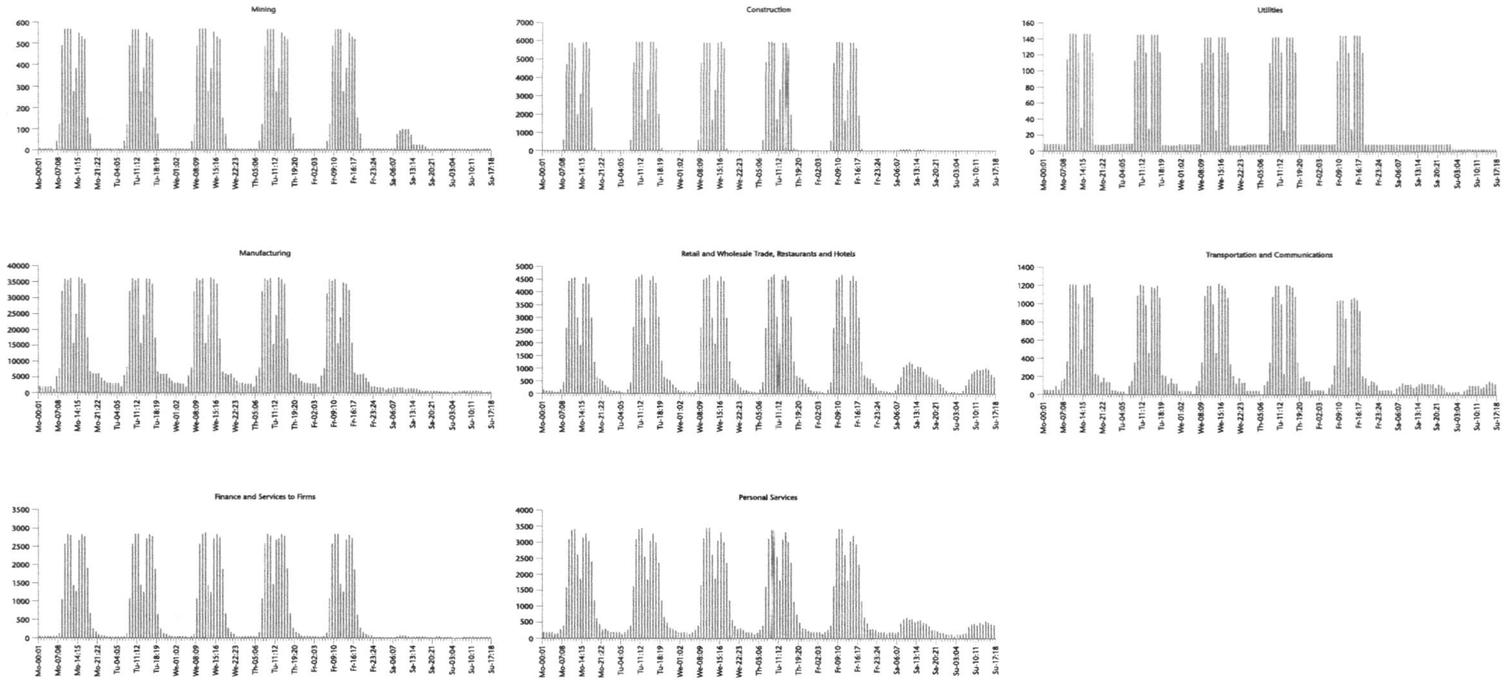

Figure 9.3

Tempogram of Work Timing Calculated from the American Time Use Survey, 2006–2007 (Fraction of Maximum at Work)

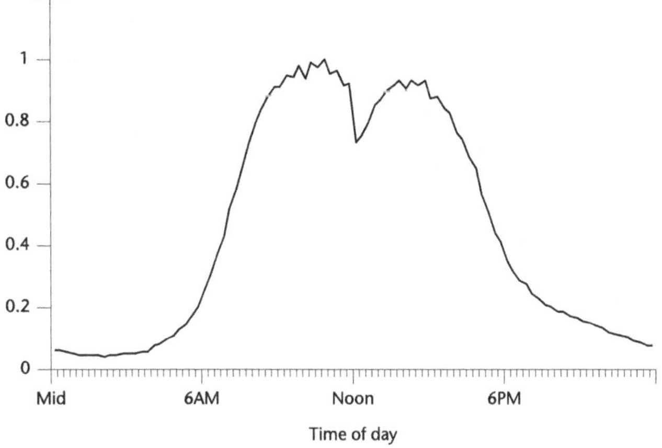

Another distinctive characteristic of intra-day employment variation is the abrupt reduction in the number of individuals working between Noon and 2PM, no doubt due to lunch breaks. The number working on weekends is also very small compared to the corresponding count on weekdays. The difference, however, is much more pronounced when we compare daytime hours than when we examine night hours. From Saturday to Sunday there is a slight reduction in the number of people working, independent of the hour of the day that we consider. Also on weekends, but especially on Sundays, there is a much smaller drop-off in the number of employees at work at lunchtime.

Because there may be both technical and economic reasons behind the choice of the timing of the economic activity, it is worth looking at how changes in the number of workers at work over the week vary from industry to industry, as different industries face quite diverse technical and demand constraints. Figure 9.2 shows that two sectors - construction, and finance and services to firms - stand out by their absence of weekend operations. To some extent this is also true for mining industries, except for a small amount of daytime Saturday work. The public utilities sector - typically associated with continuous operations - exhibits a very repetitive pattern over the week, high and above a constant baseline that corresponds to the level of employment necessary to guarantee emergency services/continuous production. This is also the case in the transportation and communications sector, although its employment level on weekends is significantly higher than during weekday nights. Manufacturing is the only sector (followed at a distance by personal services sector) to maintain a relatively high level of night work.

Some of the characteristics depicted in Figures 9.1 and 9.2 may appear unusual, especially to readers unfamiliar with the Portuguese economy. In comparison to the U.S. economy, for which a tempogram of work time based on time-use diaries from the American Time Use Surveys of 2006–07 is shown in Figure 9.3, Portugal does look unusual: Of particular note is the relatively sharp drop-off in employees at work over the weekday lunch-hour and, as compared to the U.S., the relatively low intensity of work at night. Had we compared Portugal to other European countries, however, it is the U.S. that would be the outlier (Burda et al. (2008)).

Figure 9.4

Tempogram of Work Timing from the EUCOWE and the 1999 TUS

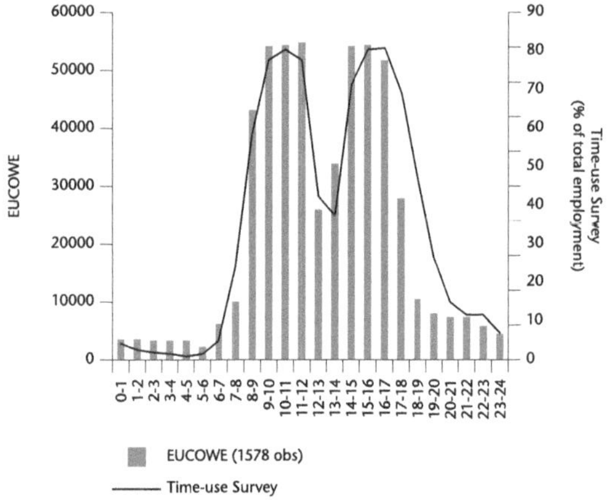

As a check Figure 9.4 plots jointly the tempogram from the EUCOWE along with that from the 1999 Portuguese Time Use Survey (TUS) (INE (2001)), which was based on individual time diaries. This tempogram makes it clear that, if anything, the Portuguese firm-based data give lower estimates of the decline in work intensity over weekday lunch hours than do household data, and they clearly do not overstate the rarity of night work compared to those data. The late evening interval seems to suggest that firms may be slightly more prone to report the contractual end of the workday (i.e. 5–6PM), whereas workers may report (or over-report) slightly later end times.[11] The similarity of the two tempograms depicted in Figure 9.4 is reassuring and should enhance confidence in our estimation of production functions that account for work timing.

We can summarize the information on work timing and workers' characteristics contained in the 2003 QP, which forms the framework for the data set used here. We present the averages for the entire sample and for two sub-aggregates that we use later in the study. As Table 9.2 shows, the overwhelming majority of hours are worked at standard times - weekday, daytime. Nonetheless, daytimes on weekends account for over 10 percent of total hours, with a scattering of hours at night-times. The paucity of hours in the last two categories underscores the need to focus on the simple distinction between standard hours and all non-standard hours in our estimation.

Table 9.2

Descriptive Statistics from Plant-Level Time-Use Data

	All plants		Manufacturing, Mining, Construction and Utilities		Services, Trade and Transport	
Variable	Mean	St. Dev.	Mean	St. Dev.	Mean	St. Dev.
Standard hours	2,149	3,662	2,599	4,069	1,221	2,377
Non-standard hours	275	1,210	338	1,424	145	528
Hours daytime weekend	42	246	34	263	60	206
Hours nighttime weekend	22	142	23	162	18	88
Hours nighttime week	211	1,002	281	1,199	67	288
Sales (1,000 Euro)	5,417	17,700	5,878	18,900	4,465	15,100

Note: Unweighted averages computed over plants from EUCOWE.

Table 9.3

Composition of the Workforce, 2004, by Timing of Work (Percent Distributions)

Characteristic:	Night	Saturday	Sunday	All hours
Gender (percent male)	67.0	59.7	57.2	54.4
Age (average years)	39.9	42.5	42.3	41.3
Education (percent):				
<9 years of school	28.6	42.2	38.6	36.4
9–11 years of school	39.1	38.0	35.8	36.6
12 years	16.4	11.3	13.9	13.0
>12 years	15.8	8.5	11.7	14–0

Note: Averages over Individuals, Computed from LFS.

9.3.3. *The Composition of the Workforce by the Timing of Work*

The Portuguese *Labor Force Survey (LFS)* is a quarterly household survey standardized across European countries that collects detailed information on individuals' demographic characteristics and labor market status. From this sample we obtain individuals' self-reported work schedules (daytime weekday, night, Saturday and Sunday), and their gender, age, and educational attainment to trace the demographic profile of the workforce, as shown in Table 9.3.[12] While we do not use this information in our estimation, it is interesting in its own right as a rare glimpse on the demographics of temporal variations in work timing, something that cannot be done with the EUCOWE data.

The table shows that male workers are dominant in all three irregular periods of work and that women are under-represented among night workers. Night workers are also younger than weekend and other workers. The most remarkable statistic is the relatively high educational attainment of those working at irregular times, with night-time work performed disproportionately least by workers in the lowest education group. This is strikingly different from what has been observed for the U.S. (Hamermesh (1999a)) and may be the result of the high penalties imposed on hours employed at irregular times in Portugal.

9.3.4. *Summary and Uses of the Individual Data Sets*

To clarify the large variety of data sets incorporated here and their uses, Table 9.4 summarizes them and indicates how we have and will use them. Given the required need to integrate the various sources of information, this table demonstrates how we have accomplished this task and allows the reader to follow the flow of discussion of our estimation.

9.4. Specification and Estimation of the Production Models

9.4.1. *Basic Estimates*

We want to identify the substitution effects that combine technology with the relative prices of hours facing firms at various times of the day/week. If we had a panel, or even cross-sections of establishments before

Table 9.4
Sources and Uses of Data Sets

Data Set	Unit	Year	Use
Quadros de Pessoal (QP)	Population of firms, plants, and wage-earners	1986 to 2002 (except 1990 and 2001)	Retrieve firm fixed-effects from production functions
QP		2003	Estimate production functions with time-use information
QP		2004	Estimate production functions with time-use information
European Union Company Survey of Operating Hours and Working Times and Employment (EUCOWE)	Sample of firms, stratified by size-class and industry	2003	Estimate production functions with time-use information
Time Use Survey (TUS)	Individuals, sample of households	1999	Check on EUCOWE time-use
Labor Force Survey (LFS)	Individuals, sample of households	2004: Q2	Characteristics of workers at different day/hour times, for descriptive statistics

and after some shock to those prices, we would measure its impact. No such data exist in Portugal or anywhere else. Instead, our identification strategy relies on combining the cross-section data on time use (the EU-COWE) with panel data on the sales, employment and other attributes of firms included in the EUCOWE and the QP.

Table 9.5

Estimated Production Function Using Longitudinal Data (Dep. Var. ln(Sales))

ln(Employment)	0.9998 (0.0179)
Share Age 35–49	1.1152 (0.0571)
Share Age 50 and Older	1.6090 (0.0826)
Share 9 Years Education	0.6003 (0.0701)
Share High School	1.1767 (0.0816)
Share University	0.8937 (0.1368)
Share Female	0.3830 (0.0845)
Adjusted R2	0.880
N =	8,887

Note: Also included in the Equations is a set of 964 firm indicators.

We specify a Cobb-Douglas technology and divide time into D (65 hours per week), 7AM–8PM, Monday through Friday, and the rest N (103 hours per week). Implicitly we assume for simplicity's sake that all irregular work time is linearly aggregable. The Cobb-Douglas specification assumes the usual unitary elasticity of substitution between worker-hours employed at these two times of the day/week. As is standard in the literature on production functions, in order to obtain estimates of the demand elasticities on which a policy that might affect the timing of work could be based, we relax the Cobb-Douglas assumption and specify the following translog approximation to a general function:

$$(1) \quad \ln(Y_k) = a_0 + a_D \ln(D_k) + a_N \ln(N_k) + .5\{a_{DD} [\ln(D_k)]^2 + a_{NN} [\ln(N_k)]^2 + 2a_{DN} \ln(D_k) \cdot \ln(N_k)\} + \xi_k,$$

where *k* denotes the firm, *D* is 1 plus the number of worker-hours employed during normal hours, and *N* is 1 plus the number employed during irregular hours. Testing the overall significance of the vector

$a_{ij}, i, j = D, N$, allows us to test the validity of imposing the Cobb-Douglas technology. With the translog approximation, and assuming constant returns to scale, the parameter estimates can be readily transformed (Hamermesh (1993)) and combined with estimates of the shares of D and N in total labor costs to obtain estimates of elasticities of demand for labor at the two times. In every case, we include variables designed to account for differences in the efficiency units of labor of various types. Thus we include indicators accounting for three age groups (under 35, 35–49 and 50 plus), four levels of education (< 9, 9–11, 12, and > 12 years), and gender.

None of our data sets allows for the construction of the capital stock at the plant level or for indicators of the use of materials. We know (Hamermesh (1993)) that capital and skill are complementary, so that this absence could bias the estimated parameters. The inclusion of plant-level fixed effects would be among the most rigorous ways of controlling for this problem. That procedure is precluded by the fact that we only have cross-section data on work timing, but we can solve the problem by exploiting the richness of the QP dataset and its longitudinal nature covering the population of firms. First, we estimate production functions using QP data for all years before the 2003 EUCOWE cross-section, which contains both the plants included in the estimation of (1) and many other plants.[13] In this first stage we use as regressors total employment in the firm and all the controls previously listed (employment shares of three age groups, four levels of education, and gender). Crucially, we further control for unobservable firm effects in this panel estimation.

Table 9.5 reports the estimates of this first stage. The first point to note here is that the output/labor ratio here is implicitly almost constant, once we adjust for differences in demographics across plants. Using these estimates, we retrieve the estimated firm fixed effects and use these as indicators of time-invariant differences across firms, which should capture interfirm differences in technology, amount of capital, use of materials, quality of the management, and other unobservables.[14] We then proceed, in a second stage, to use OLS to estimate the cross-section Cobb-Douglas and translog production functions augmented by the inclusion of the fixed effects (as a continuous regressor) from the first stage, which arguably measure unobservable inputs. These are aimed at removing potential spurious correlations between the time allocation of workers and production. This procedure works so long as firms' choice of work timing is separable from the amounts of its labor input (which we measure directly) and its other inputs (embodied in the fixed-effect variable). In this second stage we use the EUCOWE data and include as regressors the logarithms of total employment at regular (*D*) and irregular (*N*) hours in addition to the above-mentioned firm specific effects.

We estimate the models on the economy as a whole and separately for two groups of industries. The reason for defining the two groups relies on the different possibilities for substitution of labor across the week. We consider differences between two types of industry: Those where products may be inventoriable, in which the price incentives for production at different times may be less inhibited by the need for contemporaneous availability of workers and customers, and those in which products/services must be delivered at certain times to satisfy consumer demand. The possibilities for substitution may be greater in the former industries – but this is a matter for empirical investigation.

Table 9.6

Estimates of Production Functions with Work Timing (Dep. Var. ln(Sales))*

	All Industries		Manufacturing, Mining, Construction and Utilities		Services, Trade and Transport	
	Cobb-Douglas	Translog	Cobb-Douglas	Translog	Cobb-Douglas	Translog
ln(D)	0.9360 (0.0182)	0.3728 (0.1507)	0.9339 (0.0206)	0.3692 (0.1606)	0.9587 (0.0431)	0.4374 (0.3381)
ln(N)	0.0813 (0.0091)	0.2024 (0.0442)	0.0902 (0.0095)	0.2728 (0.0477)	0.0393 (0.0221)	0.0931 (0.1038)
$[\ln(D)^2]$		0.0458 (0.0111)		0.0462 (0.0116)		0.0430 (0.0254)
$[\ln(N)]^2$		0.0248 (0.0064)		0.0245 (0.0067)		0.0236 (0.0135)
ln(D) · ln(N)		-0.0389 (0.0076)		-0.0460 (0.0077)		-0.0290 (0.0184)
Adjusted R2						
N=p-value	0.841	0.848	0.882	0.891	0.763	0.766
on translog	964	964	650	650	314	314
terms		<.001		<.001		0.07

Notes: The equations all include a continuous variable measuring each firm's average departure from the overall production function, based on the estimates of Table 9.3. Also included are vectors of indicators for the age distributions of workers and the distributions of education in each plant, and a continuous measure of the share of workers who are women.

We have included four of the eight sets of industries depicted in Figure 9.2 in the group where substitution may be easier: Manufacturing, mining, construction, and utilities, in none of which does the timing of production seem to depend on immediate delivery of goods or services to customers. Production in the other four groups of industries: Services, to firms and persons, and finance; trade etc., transportation, and communications, may require simultaneous activity by customers and workers, so that incentives for firms to substitute intertemporally may be more muted or, in some instances, perhaps even absent.

Table 9.6 presents estimates of the expanded production functions, for the economy and the two groups of industries. There is some evidence of the short-run increasing returns to labor pointed out in the estimation of standard production frameworks by, among others, Morrison and Berndt (1981). It is also noteworthy that tests of the Cobb-Douglas restrictions are soundly rejected: In the entire sample and the manufacturing, etc., sub-sample the three higher-order terms are jointly statistically significantly different from zero at conventional levels, although they are not quite significantly different from zero in the service, etc., sub-sample.

Table 9.7

Estimates of Elasticities of Factor Price, ε_{ij}

Hours:	7AM-8PM M-F	Other
	All Industries	
7AM-8PM M-F	0.049	0.065
Other	0.349	-1.157
	Manufacturing, Mining, Construction and Utilities	
7AM-8PM M-F	-0.045	0.046
Other	0.251	-0.529
	Service, Trade and Transport	
7AM-8PM M-F	-0.066	0.100
Other	0.488	-0.552

Note: Computed from input shares and the estimated coefficients in Table 9.6.

As noted above, the translog tableau describes the data better than the restrictive Cobb- Douglas form, so we concentrate on it in discussing the structural parameters. The parameter estimates can be transformed into elasticities of complementarity and, multiplying by the shares of earnings at the two sets of times, we can then obtain the elasticities of factor price, ε_{ij}.[15] These are shown in Table 9.7. The calculations yield estimated structural parameters that have the expected signs. The own-quantity elasticities are all negative, and the cross-quantity elasticities are all positive, none of which was imposed on the estimation.[16] Moreover, there is little difference in the extent of substitution of weekday-time for other labor across the two groups of industries.

With the assumption of constant returns to scale, the elasticities of complementarity are transformable into the more familiar elasticities of substitution and then into the cross-price elasticities of demand, η_{ij}. In the entire sample the estimated $\eta_{ND} = 2.38$, and $\eta_{DN} = 0.38$; in the sub-samples of manufacturing, etc., and services, etc., respectively the estimated $\eta_{ND} = 2.85$ and 1.41 and $\eta_{DN} = 0.29$ and 0.52. All of the estimates suggest reasonable responses to changes in the relative price of operating at different times of the day/week and that qualitatively the responses do not differ greatly across sectors. The lack of inter-sectoral differences may be somewhat surprising in light of possible differences in daily set-up costs.

These estimates of the extent of substitution may be too small, because of the limitations imposed by the absence of plant-level sales data that have restricted the analyses to single-plant firms. These firms are inherently incapable of taking advantage of yet another margin of substitution as the relative price of hours at different times of the week changes. Multi-plant firms may be able to substitute production among plants that differ temporally in the technology of production. Regrettably, because most of the few firms with multiple plants included in the EUCOWE are absent from the QP in 2004, and thus do not have 2003 sales, we cannot analyze this possibility empirically.

9.4.2. A Few Checks on the Estimation

One might be concerned that many (nearly 2/3) of the observations show no hours worked outside weekdays between 7AM and 8PM. To deal with this problem we adopted the "fix" of adding 1 to each firm's labor input at standard and non-standard times before taking logarithms. This fix is arbitrary. To examine its validity we first simply estimated equations that include actual sales, number of hours of each type, and an interaction of the actual number of hours of the two types (times) of labor (without taking logarithms of any of these variables). After performing the required calculations, the implied production parameters (cross-price elasticities) are very similar to those presented above.

Another approach to this potential difficulty is to re-estimate the equations including only those plants with positive employment at both standard and non-standard times of the week. The results do not change qualitatively: In the aggregate, and in both sectors, the translog model again clearly dominates the Cobb-Douglas. The cross-quantity elasticities of factor price for weekday-time work in manufacturing, etc., are 0.062 and 0.175 - not qualitatively greatly different from those in Table 9.7, and with a similar lack of difference in the other results.

While we have accounted for unobservable differences in non-labor inputs and technology by including a continuous measure of the residuals from estimation over the panel, perhaps there are industry-specific effects, beyond those obtainable by dividing the sample into two broad sectors, that might be generating spurious results. To examine this possibility we re-estimated the equations adding indicators for each of the 41 two-digit industries to which the firms in the sample belong. The estimates remain almost unchanged; for example, the cross-quantity elasticities in manufacturing, etc., become 0.050 and 0.279, and the others also change only minutely.

9.5. A Policy Simulation

The estimates developed here are the first that allow the evaluation of the potential impacts of policies that might shift the timing of work. The application in this Section is fairly mechanical, but it is worth illustrating given the potential importance of such policies and of international differences in work timing of the kind shown by the comparisons between Figures 9.3 and 9.4. Applying the estimates directly to Portugal, we can ask what would happen to the distribution of work hours between daytime weekdays and irregular hours if the existing penalties on the latter were abolished. The starting point is the sample average penalty rate on irregular hours that we observe in the data, $\Theta = 0{:}44$.[17]

Clearly, working irregular hours is a disamenity, and one doubts that employers could avoid some penalty rate absent a legislative mandate. What would Θ be absent the mandate? There is little doubt that in a free labor market in industrialized societies Θ would be positive: If nothing else, people, and women especially, shy away from night work because it may be more dangerous because of the risks of crime (Hamermesh (1999b)). A variety of estimates of this parameter have been produced for the (along this dimension) unregulated U.S. labor market, including by Kostiuk (1990), Shapiro (1995) and Hamermesh (1999a). Estimates have ranged from 0 (or even negative) to above 0.2, but a fair reading of the literature suggests using $\Theta = 0.1$ is a reasonable estimate. Taking this penalty as the benchmark for what an unregulated Portuguese market would generate, the change in the wage differential between irregular and daytime weekday hours would be 31 percent. Applying the cross-price elasticity, η_{ND} = 2.38, that we estimated using the translog approximation suggests that deregulation of work timing might lead to an increase of perhaps 77 percent in the total number of worker-hours observed outside daytime/weekday slots.

This size increase in the amount of night work might seem fairly large, but one should remember that in Portugal only a very small fraction of workers are on the job outside daytime weekday hours. Even this large a percentage increase in work performed at night and weekends would leave the fraction of work performed outside weekday hours somewhat below that in the U.S.

The Portuguese labor law that became effective in 2004 changed the default starting boundary of night work from 8PM to 10PM. This effectively reduced the average penalty rate on irregular hours by some unknown amount from the 0.44 observed in our sample. In particular, 10 of the previously 55 nighttime weekday hours were converted to daytime weekday hours, clearly abolishing the legislated 25 percent penalty on nearly 20 percent of irregular weekday hours. Our results imply that this change would have caused a spreading out of the workday – a substitution of hours between 8PM and 10PM for hours between 7AM and 8PM.

While the estimates for Portugal obviously cannot be applied perfectly to evaluate policy changes in the U. S. or elsewhere, one might use our estimates as a first approximation to how work hours might be reallocated if the U.S. legislated a penalty on night/weekend work. The results here suggest that much of the reason for the unusually large fraction of hours performed outside of daytime/weekday hours in the U.S. may be the absence of government policy on this subject, the small extent of trade-union regulation of work hours, and the absence of any extension of trade-union policies on work hours beyond the unionized sector. General calls for policies to reduce and reallocate hours have been made (Burda et al. (2008), Nickell (2008)). The Portuguese results suggest that such policies might have fairly substantial effects on the temporal distribution of U.S. work time, especially since the U.S. labor market is viewed as being among the most flexible in the industrialized world.

9.6. Conclusions

We have examined the facts about and determinants of employers' demand for labor at different times of the day and week. We stress that the question of the timing of work is logically independent of the question of the amount of work – hours per time period – that employees are on the job. While substantial research has been conducted on the latter, no empirical research had previously been offered on variations in work timing across the 168-hour week based on evidence from employers. Our study has taken advantage of a new data set that, in conjunction with other data sets, allows us to illustrate hourly/daily fluctuations in the number of employees at work and to examine the role of pay penalties for work at irregular times of the day and week in affecting these fluctuations.

Although the timing of work is jointly determined in the labor and product markets, our results suggest that employers are able to substitute work at one time of the day/week for work at another time – the t-subscripts on the arguments of production functions need to be taken seriously. Both legislated and collectively-bargained penalties on work at different times of the day/week alter work timing. Such penalties can thus be a tool for social policy on work time, which may be especially important given our evidence on differences in the demographic characteristics of the distribution of work at irregular times in a regulated labor market (Portugal).

Obviously this study is only a first step. Our conclusions have been based on some reasonable assumptions about the impacts of prices of labor on employers' behavior. With existing data this work might inspire others to take advantage of the recent creation of employer-based surveys of work timing in other countries that could be expanded and then matched with other employer-employee data sets to shed light on other aspects of decisions about timing. Indeed, since our discussion has recognized the role of workers' and consumers' preferences in affecting firms' decisions about the timing of operating hours, one could well hope for the creation of a data set matching firms' opening times with their workers' time diaries that might permit the development of a complete structural model of the timing of work. It may be possible to combine some of these surveys with detailed information on collectively-bargained penalties on work timing, or with the differing application of statutory penalties across firms, to infer directly the impact of penalties on timing. Finally, one might also hope that data on work timing before and after exogenous changes in the price of labor at different times of the day/week might become available to allow a direct evaluation of their impacts.

10

The Costs of Worker Displacement

10.1. Introduction

One of the liveliest recent discussions of labor market policy has been about workers attached to declining industries. Calls for an inchoate "industrial policy"; proposals to aid "displaced workers"; and attempts to prevent future losses, are all responses to this perceived problem.[1] In this study I present an evaluation of the magnitude of part of the costs of displacement borne by workers. In essence, the study examines and measures the transaction costs of adjusting to shifts in production that are incurred by society both during and after the adjustment. These differ from the private costs incurred by those making the decision to displace workers. While these private costs are outweighed by the long-run private benefits of the changes, it is not clear that the benefits exceed the sum of the two sets of costs.

I concentrate on losses of the firm-specific human capital in which the worker and the firm have invested. To examine these, I develop a bargaining model that analyzes how the amount and burden of investment in firm-specific training is affected by changes in workers' and

The original version of this chapter was published as: Hamermesh, Daniel S. (1987). The Costs of Worker Displacement, in: The Quarterly Journal of Economics, 102(1): 51–76. © 1987 by Oxford University Press. Carl Davidson, David Card, Harry Holzer and a referee, and participants at seminars at the National Bureau of Economic Research and a number of universities provided useful comments on earlier versions of this chapter. The research was supported by National Science Foundation Grant No. SES-8404206 and by a contract to the Institute for Research on Poverty of the University of Wisconsin from the U.S. Department of Health and Human Services. The views expressed in this chapter are those of the author and do not necessarily reflect the views of the National Science Foundation, the DHHS, or the Institute for Research on Poverty.

firms' information about the payout period. The outcome is a framework for evaluating whether there is a social loss on prior investments in firm-specific human capital when workers lose their jobs, or whether the loss is solely a reduction in the returns to characteristics (such as sex, race, union status, etc.) that accrued to workers on their previous jobs, but that do not necessarily enhance productivity. As such, it provides a way of evaluating the social costs of worker displacement that is more closely grounded in economic theory than is the existing literature (summarized in Baldwin (1984)).

10.2. The Nature of Losses

The displacement of workers – due to exogenous changes in product demand, to technical change, or to government-imposed restrictions – may generate social costs that must be weighed against the social gains that result when the labor market adjusts to these shocks. These social costs include all the resources that are lost during the adjustment process. To measure the costs, one must obtain estimates of the difference between the value of the resource before and after the labor market has adjusted to the shock that changes its value. Also, the value of the resources lost during the adjustment process must be included in the calculation of the cost of switching to a new labor market equilibrium after the shock.

The large literature on displacement in the labor market has evaluated the losses incurred by displaced workers using two approaches (often together), neither of which captures the social cost of adjusting to the shock. The first considers the value of the time the displaced worker spends unemployed (Bale, 1976); the second compares workers' wages or earnings on the job that was lost with those on the job eventually obtained (Jacobson, 1978; Neumann, 1978; Jenkins-Montmarquette, 1979; Kiefer-Neumann, 1979; Sandell-Shapiro, 1985; Glenday-Jenkins, 1984). The first approach clearly includes only costs incurred while the adjustment is taking place, and only costs associated with workers who are unemployed during the adjustment; the second attempts to measure the gross social cost of switching to the new equilibrium as the present value of the wage losses of the displaced workers. This latter method measures the labor market costs of the shock correctly only if the following: (1) workers realize that some characteristics that produced high wages on the previous job have no effect on the wage-offer distribution they must search over; and (2) in calculating the lost earnings, one adjusts the earnings obtained on the previous job to exclude those components that did not reflect higher productivity.

To see the first point, assume that the wage on the previous job was

$$W_b = G\,(M, N_b), \tag{1}$$

where *b* denotes the previous job, *M* is a vector of characteristics of the worker that yield the same return on the previous job and in the market generally, and *N* is a vector of characteristics that do not yield equal expected returns on subsequent jobs. Thus, for example, the union status of the previous job (see Wachter (1984)); returns to racial or ethnic favoritism that exceed market premiums for these characteristics, or accumulated firm-specific human capital are included in *N*. Let the worker's reservation wage after displacement be characterized as

$$W^r = H\,(\mu^*, \sigma^*), \tag{2}$$

where the starred variables in $H(\cdot)$ are the mean and standard deviation of the lognormal density function of wages that the worker *perceives* at the time of displacement.

Assume that the displaced worker searches a density function of wages that is in fact described by $f(W)$, $0 < W < \infty$. Let $F(W^*)$ be the distribution function of f from 0 to W^*. Assuming for simplicity that the worker samples one offer each time period, the average duration of unemployment *D* will be $1/[\,1 - F(W^r)]$, and the expected wage rate on the worker's new job will be

$$W_a = \int_{W^r}^{\infty} \frac{WF(W)}{1 - F(W^r)}\, dW. \tag{3}$$

W^r is affected by N_b; i.e., as long as the mean and variance of the ex ante perceived distribution of offered wages are affected by characteristics specific to the previous job, the duration of unemployment and the subsequent wage will be affected by those characteristics. The duration of unemployment will be longer and the subsequent wage will be higher than otherwise. (That the previous wage, not merely the components of the vector *M*, affects the reservation wage is suggested by the evidence of Kiefer-Neumann (1979) and Sandell (1980).) These biases arise because, as the evidence suggests, workers leave their jobs with inflated expectations of how the market will reward them for some of the characteristics that raised their wages there.

The second problem is that one must (see Sandell-Shapiro (1985)) adjust wages (not wage functions) on the previous job for differences in the components of *N* between jobs. The difficulty with even this partial solution to the errors implicit in before-after wage comparisons is that not all of what is lost when the values of the components of *N* change represents a loss to society (though it does represent a loss to the particular worker). For example, quasi rents may have accrued because some factor that protected the worker from competition may be lost if a new job is not similarly protected. The best example is that of a worker displaced from a unionized job whose subsequent job is nonunion. This worker suffers a loss in wages, ceteris paribus. However, the loss will not affect the ability of employers in the union sector to fill jobs in the future; it is also unlikely that the union relative productivity effect is as large as the union relative wage effect.[2] For this reason, too, before-after wage comparisons cannot give a satisfactory estimate of the losses society incurs when workers are displaced.

An alternative approach to calculating the social costs of making the adjustment to the new labor market equilibrium is to focus on losses incurred on investments whose value abruptly falls to zero when the relationship between the firm and the worker is terminated. Here the distinction between general and specific training is crucial. General training is included in *M*; by definition it is as applicable in any subsequent job as in the job that disappeared. Firm-specific human capital, however, is included in N_b and is lost when the worker leaves the firm. This investment may have been made with the expectation of a longer payout period than in fact occurred. Both the firm and the worker may suffer a capital loss because of the separation, with the size of each party's loss dependent upon the length of the payout period that was expected, the amount invested, and the share of the investment costs borne by each party.[3]

These considerations suggest that calculations of the social costs of labor market adjustment include at least the lost firm specific human capital, and that these losses must be measured using information uncontaminated by the biases induced by the effect of N_b on subsequent wages.[4] Firm-specific human capital is the only component of N_b that clearly has no productivity on any subsequent job and that represents an investment on which the return may be below-market. Displaced workers may reap below-market returns on their investment in occupation- or industry-specific skills; but unless the entire occupation or industry disappears at once, the magnitude of this loss is also affected by the worker's search behavior in the face of a (possibly changing) distribution of returns to industry- or occupation-specific skills. Similarly, there is a social loss arising from the social value of the time the worker spends unemployed; but as we have seen, the components of that loss are also affected by their search behavior, and thus possibly by characteristics of their previous jobs. For these reasons, the remainder of this study examines lost firm-specific investment, recognizing that society may also lose both the worker's labor services during the time between jobs and part of a stream of expected returns on investment in skills specific to an occupation or industry.[5]

10.3. Interferring the Effects of Impending Displacement

Measuring lost firm-specific human capital is not an easy task, insofar as the stock must be inferred from wages, and the costs of investment in firm-specific human capital are shared by workers and firms. Nonetheless, one can use data on wage-tenure profiles along with some consideration about the efficient split of investment costs between workers and firms to discover whether there is any loss; i.e., whether investments are being made that have a payout period that extends beyond the date of displacement.

Consider the following technology for producing firm-specific training:

$$B = B(t), \tag{4}$$

where t is the fraction of the initial period of employment that is spent in training. (All firm-specific training is assumed to take place during this first period.) B is the amount that training adds to the worker's productivity each period; it is assumed constant over the entire life of the investment. I assume that production of specific training is characterized by diminishing returns, i.e., $B' > 0, B'' < 0$, and that $B(0) = 0$. The costs of producing training are also a function of t, with $C(t)$ described by $C', C'' > 0$, and $C(0) = 0$. There is little evidence either way on the assumptions describing the shapes of B and C; I have merely made standard assumptions about technologies.[6] In making them, I also ignore for simplicity any costs of training other than the value of trainees' time.

Assume that the worker and the firm have identical utility functions U, with $U' > 0, U'' < 0$, defined over the benefits and costs of firm-specific training.[7] Their discount rates are assumed to be the same.[8] Let T_i be each party's horizon, the length of time it expects to reap returns on the investment in specific training, where i refers to the firm (F) or the worker (W). This assumption implies point expectations about the duration of the job. It too is simplifying; but the results carry through with the more realistic assumption that both workers and firms maintain subjective probability distributions describing their beliefs about the job's duration.

The worker bears some fraction *s* of the cost of the investment and reaps that same fraction of the expected returns. The firm, in order to maintain its reputation in the labor market and to avoid quits, is assumed not to renege on implicit contracts defining the sharing of *B(t)*. The worker's expected utility stream is thus defined as

(5a) $$Z_W = U(sB(t))\, R(T_W) + U(-sC(t)),$$

where $R(T_W)$ is $\Sigma_0^{T_W} [1 + r]^{-k}$. The firm's expected utility stream is

(5b) $$Z_F = U([1 - s]\, B(t))\, R\,(T_F) + U\,(-[1 - s]\, C(t)).$$

Because this is a shared investment, in which each side has monopoly power, the outcomes, t^*, the optimal fraction of the initial period spent investing, and s^*, the optimal fraction of the benefits and costs accruing to the worker, are subject to bargaining between the firm and the worker. The Nash equilibrium solution to this bargaining problem is the pair $\{t^*, s^*\}$ that maximizes

(6) $$Z = Z_F\, Z_W.$$

Assuming $T_F = T_W$, the Nash result is $s^* = s^e = 0.5$, and some $t^*>0$ if $Z_i(t^* > O|\, T_i) > Z_i\,(t^*=0|T_i\,), i = W$ or F.

The burden of whatever costs displacement imposes is based in the parties' expectations about the nature of the shortened horizon over which the shared returns to the investment in firm-specific training will be reaped. Thus, the nature of the information available to both sides about the continued existence of the job in which the investment has been made determines t^* and s^*. I examine cases in which the information available to each party is identical (symmetric), and in which the firm has better information about the job's impending demise (asymmetric). Asymmetry in the opposite direction, with the worker better able to foresee the job's disappearance, seems unlikely given the firm's control over decisions about operating its plant.

10.3.1. Case I.A. Symmetric Lack of Information

In this case neither party is aware that the job will disappear until the day the firm discovers that its profit-maximizing conditions dictate that the worker be laid off permanently (or the plant closed). Thus, at all times up to the date of separation the horizon seen by workers and the firm is unchanged at $T_F = T_W$, both greater than the ex post payout period of the returns to the investment. Since in this case the information is identical to what it is in the absence of any information about the job's disappearance, the outcome of the bargaining problem that determines t* and s* is unchanged. Both parties will experience a capital loss when the displacement occurs.

10.3.2. Case I.B. Symmetric Information About Impending Displacement

Assume in this case that the worker and the firm realize that the worker's expected tenure in the firm has dropped to $T'_W < T_W$. Because information is symmetric, $T'_F = T'_W$. This change reduces both parties' perceived utility from investing in specific training. If training is still profitable at some $t^* > 0$, it will be undertaken. Given the assumptions about the shapes of B and C, though, $t^{*\prime} < t^*$: With a shorter horizon over which to reap the returns to firm-specific training, a smaller investment in such training will be made. The size of the profit over which the parties bargain will be smaller. For some $T'_W = T^*$ the investment will no longer be profitable, and t^* will be zero. With identical utility functions we can also be sure that s^* is unchanged.

10.3.3. Case II.A. Asymmetric Information with Worker Ignorance

Asymmetric information about an impending job loss presumably means that both the worker and the employer realize the horizon has shortened, but the firm acquires this information first. As a polar case, though, we can analyze the nature of the problem by assuming that the worker has no knowledge that the layoff is imminent until it actually occurs, while the firm knows that the horizon has shortened. Thus, $T'_W = T_W > T'_F$. This means that the stream of returns seen by the firm is lower for every t at s^e than that perceived (incorrectly) by the worker.

Unfortunately, the game theory literature has not produced an explicit solution to the game implicit in this particular type of asymmetry. Let us therefore merely consider two possible situations under this assumption. If T_F is sufficiently short, the firm will realize that it cannot make any profit if $s^* < 1$. (Clearly, if $T_F < 1$, the firm will lose money if it bears any part of the cost of training.) The solution is no longer bargained: the amount invested is determined solely by the worker maximizing Z_W with $s^* = 1$, with t^* smaller than before because $U'' < 0$. If T_F is not so short that $s^* = 1$, the parties will engage in bargaining. While nothing can be derived about the outcome, one might assume that continuity applies. If so, if T'_F falls from T_F to just above the point where the firm is indifferent about taking part in bargaining over s and t, s^* will be close to one. That being the case, t^* will also be lower than it was before the firm acquired information that led it to revise its horizon.

10.3.4. Case II.B. Asymmetric Information with Worker Knowledge

The general case of asymmetric information is a combination of Cases I.B and II.A:

$$T'_F < T'_W < T_W = T_F.$$

The equilibrium amount of training, t^*, will clearly decrease in this case. s^* will rise above 0.5 under our assumptions. More generally, s^* must increase if there is a sufficiently low value of T'_F.

One might ask why workers do not recognize that an increase in s^* signals that T_F has decreased to T'_F and reduce T_W to T'_F also. This question is equivalent to viewing the bargaining process over s and t as a supergame, in which each party learns from the outcome of a particular solution $\{ t^*, s^* \}$ something about the other party's horizon and modifies its own behavior accordingly on the next round. Indeed, if there were sufficient rounds in such a supergame, and if the firm knew with certainty the date of closing, there would be no loss from displacement: workers and firms would repeatedly modify the amount and sharing of investment based on the firm's horizon, as revealed by the outcomes of the previous stage. Investment would occur along a path such that the value of firm-specific human capital was zero at the date of displacement. What the empirical work in this study does is test whether, in fact, information is sufficient and the parties are clever enough bargainers to avoid investments that will not pay off.[9]

The likely outcomes on s^* and t^*, both the Nash solutions when $T_F = T_W$ and the results when information is asymmetric, are shown in Figure 10.1 as functions of T_F and T_W. The greater the divergence between the parties' horizons, the more the split in the burden of the benefits and costs of the investment differs from s^e. The shorter the horizons become, the smaller the investment will be.

Figure 10.1

Equilibrium Sharing of Firm-Specific Training

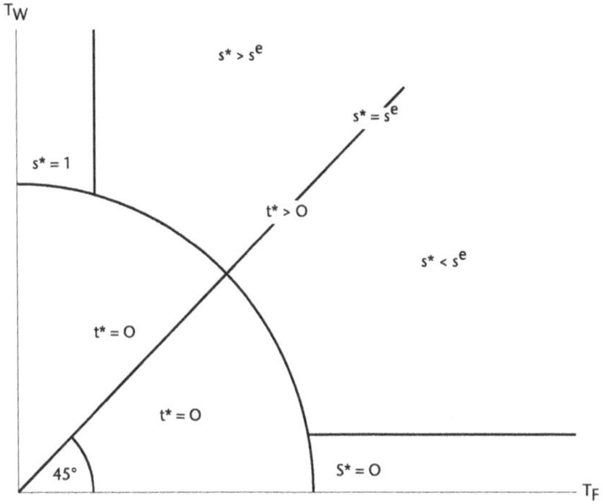

In this simple model the wage differential between workers undergoing training (with tenure of less than one period) and experienced workers (with tenure of at least one period) is

$$s^* [\, B(t^*) + C(t^*) \,]. \tag{7}$$

Indeed, with training concentrated during the initial period, (7) is also the slope of the wage-tenure profile as tenure increases from zero to one period of experience with the firm. The effect of changes in T_W and T_F on this slope is

$$s^* [\, B'(t^*) + C'(t^*) \,] dt^* + [\, B(t^*) + C(t^*) \,] ds^*. \tag{8}$$

Equation (8), the change in the slope of the wage-tenure profile, can be used to infer the extent of the information about T_i acquired by firms and workers. (1) If the profile does not change as workers near displacement, either Case I.A is correct, and $dt^* = ds^* = 0$; or Case II.B is valid, but the negative effect on t^* of workers' shorter horizons just offsets the increase in s^* induced because $T'_F < T'_W$. (2) If the profile becomes flatter as the date of displacement draws nearer, Case I.B describes the parties' information, so that t^* decreases and s^* changes little. Firms and workers have the same, fairly good, information that T has decreased. Alternatively, the asymmetric Case II.B is correct, but the worker's knowledge that $T'_W < T_W$ is sufficient to reduce t^* by more than enough to offset the effect of the increase in s^*.[10] (3) If the profile becomes steeper as the date of displacement approaches, we may infer that Case II is correct and that the effect of the decrease in t^* is less than that of the increase in s^*.[11]

10.4. Measurement and Estimation

The basic equation to be estimated is of the form,

$$\ln w = \beta X + \gamma X', \tag{9}$$

where w is the wage on the worker's main job, X is a vector of control variables, and X' is a vector containing measures of total experience and tenure. This equation allows us to examine whether the wage-tenure profile flattens as the date of separation approaches and thus to infer how good the information is that the workers and firm possess.[12] The data used are from the Panel Study of Income Dynamics. The data set is unique in that it allows one to distinguish between workers who left their jobs because of permanent layoffs, and those whose jobs disappeared because the place of business closed. In what follows, I classify the former group as laid-off workers, the latter group as displaced. Since some discussions of worker displacement lump both groups together, the empirical work analyzes the wage-tenure profiles of both groups together as well as each separately.[13]

The PSID has the virtue of providing a long, continuous panel, but it has one severe drawback for our purpose: tenure with the employer, a measure of the time available for investment in firm-specific training, is reported only in the interviews of 1976 and 1977.[14] Since the main purpose here is to observe the wage-tenure relationship among workers who are later separated, this lack greatly restricts the number of observations from the PSID that can be used. (Because no information on the tenure of people who report themselves displaced in 1976 or earlier is available, only people displaced between 1977 and 1981 have the required information.) The paucity of data on tenure with the employer combines with workers' mobility to limit the sample still further: many of the workers involuntarily separated in, e.g., 1981 had changed jobs several times since 1977, when their tenure was last reported.[15]

The panel nature of the data is exploited by using knowledge of the date of displacement or permanent layoff to estimate equation (9) over observations for years $T - 1, T - 2, T - 3$, and $T - 4$, where T is the date of involuntary separation.[16] Starting with 1,421 household heads who left their jobs because of a permanent layoff or a plant closing in 1977–1981, the exclusions reduce the sample sizes in the estimates of (9) in years $T - i, i = 1, \ldots, 4$, *to 362, 305, 246* and *200* observations, respectively. Of these people, 36 percent of those included in the samples for $T - 2$, $T - 3$, and $T - 4$ were displaced workers, while 33 percent of the sample for $T - 1$ were.

The variables included in X are standard in equations like (9). Among them are years of formal education, or a vector of dummy variables for completion of college, some college, or completion of high school; whether the worker is a union member, white, married, or male; whether the worker resides in the South or in an SMSA in which the largest city has a population above 500,000; the worker's occupation in the job that disappeared (professional or manager, craft, or operative or laborer); and the industry of that job (manufacturing, wholesale and retail trade, or finance and services). The means of these variables in the four samples suggest these involuntarily separated workers are not typical of the U.S. labor force: there are fewer whites, more Southerners and more manufacturing workers. These differences are consistent with the PSID's oversampling of low-income households and with the greater propensity of manufacturing employers to lay off workers.

The variables included in X' are tenure with the employer, *TN*, and years of actual full-time labor market experience since age 18, *EXP*. A quadratic term in experience is also included in the equations, as is a quadratic term in tenure in some of the estimates. The average tenure prior to involuntary separation is around five years. A large fraction of the separated workers have not been on the job very long. Nonetheless, between 33 and 37 percent of the workers in the four samples had more than five years' tenure with their employer, and between 17 and 20 percent had at least ten years of tenure. The average total experience in the samples implies a mean age in the middle thirties.

10.5. Estimates of Wage Profiles Among Displaced and Laid-off Workers

The estimates of β in (9) for the variables in X for years $T - 1$ through $T - 4$ are quite standard among estimates of wage equations using micro data and merit little comment here.[17] Suffice it to note that their very routineness suggests that, along most dimensions that produce wage differentials, the particular samples selected from the PSID are not unusual.

Table 10.1

Tenure and Experience Variables, Wage Regressions[a]

	Years before displacement			
	1	2	3	4
EXP	0.0119 (2.36)	0.0209 (3.55)	0.0181 (2.60)	0.0167 (2.75)
EXP^2	-0.00026 (-2.48)	-0.00037 (-3.09)	-0.00045 (-2.83)	-0.00042 (-3.38)
TN	0.00896 (2.40)	0.00619 (1.59)	0.01049 (2.42)	0.01070 (2.62)
$\bar{R}^2$	0.54	0.50	0.45	0.59

[a] t-statistics are in parentheses here and in Tables 11.2 and 11.3. The estimates in all three tables are from equations in which the full vector of variables X is included.

Table 10.1 presents the estimates of the parameters on the experience and tenure variables from (9), including only a linear term in tenure. The wage-experience profiles have shapes that have generally been found in research in this area (e.g., Mincer-Jovanovic (1981)). However, a comparison of the results in Table 10.1 to results that include a quadratic term in tenure shows only slight evidence of the usual concavity in the wage-tenure profile.[18] This may result from the peculiar nature of the sample, from the use of tenure with the employer instead of the less appropriate tenure in the job that has been used in many studies, or from the relatively small samples that the focus on involuntary separations produces.

The major issue of interest in this study is the pattern of effects of tenure with the firm. As a comparison of the coefficients in Table 10.1 on this variable makes clear, there may be some flattening of the wage-tenure profile, but it is not very pronounced. A test of the equality of the *TN* coefficients across the four time periods yielded $F(3, 1.041) = 0.27$, insignificantly different from zero at all conventional levels.[19]

It is quite clear that the wage-tenure profile is still far from flat even in the year immediately preceding displacement. It may of course be that the profiles for all four years are much flatter than those for years $T - 5$ and earlier, and flatter than those for workers who are not separated involuntarily. However, the slopes in Table 10.1 are remarkably close to those produced by Altonji-Shakotko (1985) using similarly specified equations covering employed white males in the PSID.

Table 10.2

Tenure and Experience Variables, Including Interactions with Union Status

	Years before displacement			
	1	2	3	4
EXP	0.0096 (1.75)	0.0175 (2.70)	0.0186 (2.38)	0.0144 (2.08)
EXP^2	-0.00024 (-2.08)	-0.00033 (-2.55)	-0.00046 (-2.61)	-0.00037 (-2.72)
$EXP \cdot UN$	0.0040 (0.26)	0.0070 (0.02)	-0.0002 (-0.01)	0.0173 (1.08)
$EXP^2 \cdot UN$	0.00008 (0.21)	0.00004 (0. 1 1)	0.00003 (0.08)	-0.00047 (-1.12)
TN	0.00873 (1.81)	0.00821 (1.62)	0.00223 (0.35)	0.00916 (1.64)
$TN \cdot UN$	-0.00304 (-0.40)	-0.00822 (-1.04)	0.01322 (1.49)	0.00416 (0.47)

Consider how the wage-tenure profiles vary with the worker's union status. Trade union wage-setting differs from that in nonunion plants in the effects of experience on wage rates (Johnson-Youmans, 1971) and in how workers process information about the workplace (Freeman, 1980). It may be that unionized workers, merely because the union provides a means of gathering information about the employer's plans, avoid investments in specific human capital that will not pay off, an avoidance that would be reflected in flatter wage-tenure profiles.

The results of estimating (9) including interaction terms of experience and tenure with union membership are shown in Table 10.2. While the vector of interaction terms is not jointly significantly different from zero in any of the four years, the results are nonetheless suggestive. The use of a quadratic in X makes it difficult to infer the effect of unionism on changes in the wage-experience profile simply by inspection, and I defer the discussion of that issue. However, inspection of the interaction terms with tenure suggests a striking pattern: the wage-tenure profiles for union workers are much steeper in the third and fourth years before displacement than they are in the first and second years: Among union workers the slopes are 0.013 and 0.015 in years $T - 4$ and $T - 3$, and 0 and 0.006

in years $T - 2$ and $T - 1$. While we cannot reject the hypothesis that the wage-tenure profile is constant for union workers across the four periods ($F(3, 1.029) = 0.95$), the changes do go in the direction of a flatter profile. Among nonunion workers there is essentially no change in the steepness of the wage-tenure profile as displacement nears. This difference is consistent with the interpretation of the role of unions in providing information that protects workers from management discretion, in this case, information about impending involuntary separation.

Table 10.3

Tenure and Experience Variables, Including Interactions with Cause of Displacement

	Years before displacement			
	1	2	3	4
EXP	0.0134 (1.74)	0.0264 (3.02)	0.0159 (1.48)	0.0197 (2.08)
EXP^2	-0.00032 (-2.24)	-0.00048 (-3.05)	-0.00043 (-1.94)	-0.00048 (-2.83)
$EXP \cdot LAIDOFF$	-0.0045 (-0.43)	-0.0143 (-1.14)	-0.0014 (-0.10)	-0.00169 (-0.13)
$EXP^2 \cdot LAIDOFF$	0.00015 (0.68)	0.00031 (1.10)	0.00006 (0.17)	-0.00006 (-0.22)
TN	0.01019 (2.07)	0.00406 (0.83)	0.00658 (1.20)	0.00124 (0.24)
$TN \cdot LAIDOFF$	-0.00473 (-0.63)	0.00343 (0.43)	0.00851 (0.96)	0.02010 (2.41)

Another possible difference in behavior may arise in those plants that experience closings. In such cases the employer may make more of an effort to hide information than in cases when an isolated worker, or group of workers, is to be laid off. To examine this possibility, equations (9) were reestimated including interaction terms of the tenure and experience variables with the reason for involuntary separation. The results are shown in Table 10.3. The vector of interaction terms is jointly significant in the equations for year $T - 4$, though not in the other equations. Most interesting, the implied slopes of the wage-tenure profiles decline steadily from 0.0213 to 0.0055 as the date of layoff approaches (though the decline is not significant, $F(3, 1.025) = 0.61$). Apparently, workers facing layoff obtain enough information about it to reduce their firm-specific investment. This is not true among the one-third of the sample who lose their jobs because of plant closings: the coefficients on *TN* alone in Table

10.3 show that the slope of the wage-tenure profile *increases* steadily as the date of closing nears (though also not significantly, $F(3,\ 1.025) = 0.52$).[20]

The constancy of the slope of the wage-tenure profile with impending displacement suggests in the context of the model developed in Section 10.3 either that s^* and t^* do not change, or that their changes are offsetting. Since we assumed that $T'_F \leq T'_W$, this observation implies either that workers have less information than their employers about the timing of the displacement, or that the displacement is an equal surprise to both parties.[21] In either case, the invariance of the wage-tenure profiles with time remaining until separation suggests that there is a high degree of ignorance on the part of the workers. If workers' knowledge of the impending displacement were less than employers', but still substantial, t^* would drop enough to offset the effect of the workers' increased share of the investment.[22]

Table 10.4

Wage Rates by Experience and Time Remaining until Displacement

	Years of experience				
Years before displacement	5	10	15	20	25
		All workers			
1	$5.36	$5.58	$5.73	$5.81	$5.82
2	5.33	5.76	6.10	6.34	6.47
3	5.40	5.71	5.91	5.98	5.91
4	5.65	5.95	6.14	6.20	6.13
		Displaced			
1	5.63	5.88	6.04	6.11	6.08
2	5.43	5.97	6.42	6.73	6.89
3	5.83	6.11	6.27	6.30	6.19
4	6.29	6.70	6.96	7.07	7.01
		Laid-off			
1	5.24	5.41	5.54	5.62	5.66
2	5.35	5.60	5.83	6.00	6.13
3	5.34	5.58	5.73	5.77	5.71
4	5.57	5.86	5.99	5.97	5.79
		Nonunion			
1	5.03	5.19	5.29	5.33	5.32
2	5.09	5.41	5.67	5.84	5.92
3	4.99	5.29	5.49	5.56	5.50
4	5.08	5.31	5.45	5.48	5.42
		Union			
1	6.30	6.66	7.00	7.30	7.55
2	5.86	6.48	7.07	7.59	8.04
3	5.90	6.27	6.52	6.64	6.62
4	6.74	7.42	7.83	7.92	7.68

For each year before separation Table 10.4 shows the average wage in the samples as a function of experience, evaluated at the means of the other variables. The clearest result is the lack of change in the wage-experience profile as separation approaches. Even among union workers, whose wage-tenure profiles indicated that they acquired fairly good information, the wage-experience profile changes little. Only when the profiles are calculated for laid-off workers separately is there a noticeable steepening of the profile, while among workers involved in plant closings the profile flattens out.

At first consideration the results for the subgroups, and for the entire sample, are surprising. If workers were fully rational, had perfect information, and did not face any liquidity constraints, they would invest more in firm-general training, the nearer the time when they would need such training to obtain a job in another firm. I have shown, though, that workers do not have good information about the approaching separation. The results for the entire sample can be rationalized by noting that workers who face liquidity constraints must trade off investment in general training for investment in firm-specific training. Since they do not change the pattern of investment in specific training, they are unable to change that in general training. Undoubtedly other explanations can be offered, but this one is at least consistent with utility-maximizing behavior, the inferences I have made about investment in firm-specific training, and the evidence for the entire sample. This view also explains the differences in the changing wage-experience profiles between laid-off and displaced workers: the former exhibit a steepening wage-experience profile along with a flattening wage-tenure profile, while the opposite pattern exists for workers who face plant closings.

The theoretical derivation and the empirical results have been couched in terms of the theory of investment in human capital, and institutional factors have been ignored. For example, rigid wage structures induced by custom or by collective bargaining may remain unchanged even in the face of complete knowledge of impending layoff. One cannot easily distinguish this possibility from the explanation presented here, except to note that the rigidity must imply fairly substantial transactions costs of changing wage structures, since we do examine wages for four years before the involuntary separation. One can also point to the (fairly weak) result that there is more evidence of a flattening profile among union than nonunion workers, which does not seem consistent with an explanation based on the transactions costs of changing wage structures.

10.6. Workers' Losses and Their Implications

The value of the worker's share of lost firm-specific investment can be estimated using the results from Section 10.5 along with assumptions about quit behavior. I calculate only that part of the social cost stemming from the worker's lost specific human capital. The firm's share of the forgone stream of returns on prior investments in specific training cannot be calculated without extraneous information on changes in s^* as the date of displacement approaches. In any case, its share of the lost returns is presumably taken into account in the calculations that led to its decision to close the plant or shut down part of it.

The present value of the loss for the typical worker with *TN* years of tenure in the firm is

$$L = H\,[\,w^*(TN) - w(0)\,]\sum_{t=0}^{68-A} \frac{P(TN+t)}{[(1+r)(1+\delta)]^t}, \tag{10}$$

where *L* is the loss; *P* is the probability the worker would otherwise have been employed in the firm *t* years after displacement; *A* is the worker's age; H is hours worked per year; *w*(TN)* is the wage rate gross of the cost of investment in specific training for a worker with *TN* years of tenure, and *w(0)* is the wage rate the same person would get with tenure of zero years; *r* is the discount rate; and δ is the rate of depreciation of firm-specific investment. Throughout I assume that $H = 2{,}000$; *L* is calculated over the range of values of *r* and δ on the intervals [0, 0.10] and [0.05, 0.15], respectively.[23]

The wage loss is estimated using a quadratic wage-tenure profile for $T - 1$; the effect of tenure on the worker's net wage is calculated using the coefficients on *TN* and TN^2 from that regression (see footnote 18). The gross wage loss, however, is the appropriate measure to use in estimating the value of lost firm-specific investment, since it measures the current return on the stock of past firm-specific investment without subtracting any current investment. It is calculated using the coefficients from this same regression under the assumptions that the rates of return to education and firm-specific training are equal, and that the ratio of investment in firm-specific training declines linearly with years of tenure (Mincer, 1974). Implicitly, equation (10) calculates what the wage at the time of displacement would be if the worker were not investing in training at that time. This wage is thus gross of the costs of additional investment and of depreciation. Comparing this wage with the wage of a worker with $TN = 0$ who is also assumed not to be investing in firm-specific human capital yields an estimate of the return to the worker's prior investment. Future returns are lower than the return at the time of displacement because the stock of firm-specific capital invested in up to the date of displacement would depreciate naturally thereafter.

I assume that workers would have remained in the firm unless they quit voluntarily. Thus, P is calculated as

$$P(TN+t) = \prod_{k=0}^{t} [1 - q_{TN}(k)],$$

where q_{TN} is the voluntary quit rate of a worker with TN years of tenure. Obviously, q cannot be calculated for the workers on whom the estimates in Section 10.5 are based. Instead, I use estimates of quit rates as functions of workers' characteristics based on micro data sets with broad coverage. Three of the available studies - Freeman (1980); Mincer-Jovanovic (1981); and Viscusi (1980) - are based on the Panel Study of Income Dynamics.[24] The other, Mitchell (1982), uses the Quality of Employment Surveys for 1973 and 1977.

Table 10.5

Average Present Value of Lost Specific Training (in Thousands)

	(r, δ)				
	(0, 0.05)	(0, 0.10)	(0.05, 0.10)	(0.10, 0.10)	(0.10, 0.15)
Quit function					
Freeman [1980] *PSID* 1968–1974, logit, all workers	$11.5	$8.3	$6.5	$5.4	$4.7
Mincer-Jovanovic [1981] *PSID* 1975–1976, OLS, men	10.6	7.9	6.2	5.2	4.6
Mitchell [1982] *QES* 1973, 1977, probit, men and women separately	15.7	10.5	7.8	6.2	5.3
Viscusi [1980] *PSID* 1975–1976, logit, men and women separately	12.1	8.8	6.8	5.7	4.9

The loss in (10) is calculated for each of the 362 displaced workers included in the sample over whom equation (9) was estimated for the year before displacement. The average loss in the sample is presented in Table 10.5 for each of the four quit functions and for various pairs of r and δ. The estimated losses (in 1980 dollars) are quite large, even when high values of the discount and depreciation rates are assumed.[25] The failure of workers who are later displaced to adjust the path of investment in firm-specific training generates large losses in their share of the value of the remaining specific human capital when the involuntary separation occurs.[26]

One should remember that I have not included the value of workers' losses of occupation- or industry-specific training. Since the results suggest that workers do not expect displacement, it is likely that they made ex post unprofitable investments in these types of training too. Also, I have not made the conventional calculation of the value of the time the workers spent unemployed. Viewed in this way, the costs borne by displaced workers seem quite large compared with the measures of workers' losses that have been produced in the literature. Thus, for example, Glenday-Jenkins (1984) estimate losses of less than $1,000 for male workers, and between $2,000 and $7,000 (Canadian dollars) among women; Neumann (1978) estimates an upper bound on private losses at between $3,300 and $12,000, with the latter estimate assuming the short-term wage loss is permanent.

One cannot know whether employers' decisions to close plants would be reversed if the losses that I have demonstrated are borne by workers were internalized in those decisions. All I have done is to show that such losses do exist, that they are probably quite large, and to provide a measure of the size of one of their components. Since our results indicate that they are unexpected, it is clear that the particular workers affected suffer losses. Whether the market makes up for this by paying compensating wage differentials commensurate with the risk of displacement cannot be inferred from this study (or from the available literature).

Assuming that the market does not compensate workers (and penalize high-risk employers), there is a justification on efficiency grounds for government policy to induce firms to internalize the large costs of displacement that we have shown their workers bear. Policy responses to this assumption fall into two categories: (1) the provision of information to the workers involved about impending plant closings; and (2) compensation to workers whose plants close.

Policies in the first category include various bills in Congress, laws in Maine and Wisconsin, and a host of requirements for advance notification of plant closings in other OECD countries (see Gennard (1985)).[27] However, unless notification is given much further in advance of the closing than the 30 or 60 days required by the state laws in the United States, the reduction in the amount of specific investment that is rendered worthless by subsequent plant closings will not be very great. Firm-specific investment occurs during most of a worker's tenure; and with average tenure in our samples at roughly seven years, unless depreciation rates are very high, only a small part of the eventual loss of specific human capital would be obviated. Whether employers can even be cognizant of impending closings sufficiently far in advance to allow for provision of that information to reduce the costs of adjustment is itself not clear.

Policies in the second category include retraining and unemployment allowances such as those in the Trade Act of 1974. While these do compensate the losers from labor market readjustment *if they are targeted effectively*, they help internalize the social costs of the adjustment only if the affected employer bears the cost of the transfer. This was not the case under federally funded Trade Adjustment Assistance. It is even less likely to be possible under a program aimed at workers whose plants close. Where employers become bankrupt, requiring that they also finance compensation for their ex-employees obviously cannot produce the correct incentives; and where employers suffer losses that lead them to reduce employment, adding the burden of a tax to finance compensation merely makes bankruptcy or the eventual closing of the entire plant more likely.

Even ignoring any detrimental impacts on static efficiency that policies to make firms internalize the social costs of labor market adjustment might produce, this discussion suggests it is not clear that one can construct policies that would provide much incentive for internalization. Barring outright bans on plant closings, the results leave the painful recognition that, if appropriate compensating wage differentials do not exist, there is a divergence between social and private costs of change. The discrepancy may be quite large, but it cannot easily be removed without severe negative impacts. Perhaps the best that can be done is to use the results here to justify compensation to losers from labor market readjustment and to recognize that more readjustment through plant closings may be occurring than would be justified if firms had incentives to account for the apparently substantial externalities they impose when they close plants.

10.7. Conclusions

This study points out that the costs of adjusting to labor market changes are largely the costs of the resources specific to the abandoned activity. I have shown how differences in firms' and workers' beliefs about the returns on one specific resource, the shared investment in firm-specific training, affect the amount and burden of that investment. The predictions of that demonstration were used to analyze how wage-tenure profiles change in a particular sample of workers as they approach the date of their displacement. The estimates indicate that involuntarily separated workers incur a loss in the form of a depreciation of the firm-specific human capital in which they had mistakenly invested. This loss is one component of the social cost of labor market adjustment. Other components – including the value of the time displaced workers spend unemployed, and the value of lost occupation- and industry-specific training – must be added to obtain an estimate of the total social cost of labor market adjustment.

The evidence in this study merely documents the existence of losses of firm-specific human capital due to worker displacement. To the extent that information about the ex ante risk of incurring such losses is sufficient to engender compensating wage differentials, the market will be providing insurance for the risk of displacement. If the information is not sufficient, though, policies that compensate for the loss might be desirable, if they can be instituted with minimal disincentive effects. Still better would be policies that also provided firms with incentives to account fully for the social costs of decisions to close plants. Unfortunately, the nature of the costs not now borne by firms makes it very difficult to construct policies that produce the correct incentives.

11

Policy Equilibria in a Federal System: The Effects of Higher Tax Ceilings for Unemployment Insurance

11.1. Introduction

Research on endogenous policy formation often yields positive implications (e.g. Becker, 1983; Grossman and Helpman, 1994), but rarely does it contain explicit links between these theoretical notions and any tests or measurements. Here we consider how to model the endogeneity of a particular policy and use the predictions as guidelines for testing. The discussion may illustrate more general issues in which some superior agency imposes constraints on the policies set by lower-level agencies. Such structures are federal systems, for example, states within the United States, or Canadian provinces; counties or localities within an American state; and (increasingly) member countries within the European Union. In all of these examples the superior agency mandates some aspect of the inferior agency's policy and may both shift the particular constrained policy and, most important, indirectly alter outcomes of related policies that were determined at the lower level by bargaining among affected interest groups.

The original version of this chapter was published as: Hamermesh, Daniel S./Scoones, W. D. (1999). Policy Equilibria in a Federal System: The Effects of Higher Tax Ceilings for Unemployment Insurance, in: The Journal of Public Economics, 74: 191–213. © 1999 by Elsevier Science S.A. Helfpul comments were received from Don Fullerton, Derek Neal, Donald Parsons, the editor and two referees, and participants at several seminars. We thank John Benedetto for excellent research assistance, and the Employment Policies Institute for early financial support.

The specific example that we use asks how changes in federal maxima on the amount of a worker's earnings on which employers in American states are taxed to finance unemployment insurance (UI) benefits alter other aspects of those state systems. This issue has a number of elements in common with the so-called 'flypaper effect,' the evidence that funds transferred directly from central to local governments have a greater impact on local spending than does an equivalent transfer to the median voter, who is presumed by simple theory to determine local expenditure policies (for a recent survey, see Bailey and Connolly, 1998). In each case, the question is why, since tax levels could in principle totally offset the transfer, there should be any difference at all. Section 11.2 presents a brief institutional history and description needed for understanding the issues. Section 11.3 constructs the specific bargaining-theoretic model that encompasses the minimally necessary apparatus to allow analyzing the possible effects of federal imposition of a higher tax ceiling. Section 11.4 offers a suggestive empirical exploration of the impact on states' behavior of a changing federal constraint on their unemployment insurance systems.

11.2. Institutions and Policy Issues

Unemployment insurance benefits, which totalled $22 billion and accounted for 0.4 percent of total personal income in 1995 in the United States, are financed by a payroll tax that is partly related to the amount of benefits paid to a firm's laid-off workers (partly experience rated). While states determine the parameters of their own tax systems, their choices are directly affected by the stipulations of the federal government. Under the Federal Unemployment Tax Act (FUTA) each state effectively must choose a set of ranges of tax rates, with a maximum rate of at least 5.4 percent (2.7 percent before 1985) in each set, to finance regular state UI benefits.[1] Those taxes must balance total benefit payments in the state over time, so that each system is ultimately self-financing out of its payroll tax revenues. The FUTA currently requires that states tax at least the first $7,000 of a worker's annual wages on each job, an amount that states can exceed if they wish. The history of this federally imposed ceiling since 1946 is shown by the solid line in Figure 11.1. It was raised three times from the $3,000 at which it settled shortly after the program's inception, to $4,200 in 1972, to $6,000 in 1978, and to its current value in 1983.

Figure 11.1. UI Ceilings and Taxable/Total Payrolls (Weighted)

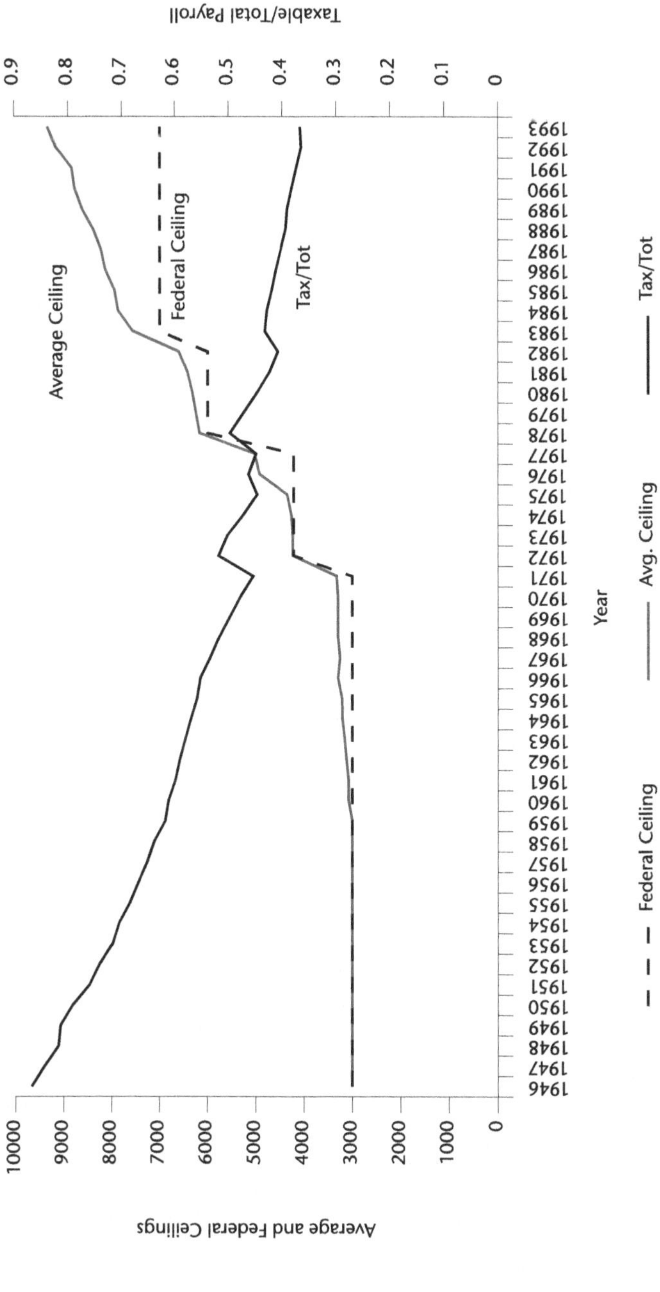

The dashed line in Figure 11.1 shows the employment-weighted average of the tax ceilings that states have chosen. While not all states treat the federal ceiling as a maximum as well as a minimum, some do, for the weighted average of states' ceilings rises sharply at those points when the federal ceiling is raised. The dotted line in Figure 11.1 shows the employment-weighted ratio of taxable to total payroll, where the numerator is earnings below each state's ceiling and thus subject to the state's UI tax on employers. While states are free to raise their ceilings above the federal ceiling, and many have done so (in 1995, 40 out of 51 jurisdictions), they have not raised them sufficiently rapidly to prevent the tax from becoming essentially a lump-sum tax on payrolls. (Appendix B lists the jurisdictions' UI tax ceilings in 1995.) Thus by 1995 the ratio of taxable to total payroll was barely 37 percent.

Despite the slow but extremely pronounced change in the nature of taxation to finance this program there has been very little study of the tax ceiling. Brechling (1977) focused on the nature of the ceiling in relation to voluntary turnover. Hamermesh (1990) examined the time-series relationships between taxes and UI benefits, but did so using national totals, thus preventing any study of the political economy of states' setting their taxable ceilings. While there may be enough interstate variation to examine this issue, with only three distinct events when the federally-imposed minimum ceiling was raised we cannot treat the increases themselves as endogenous. Because the federal government uses the revenues that it receives from the FUTA to finance administrative costs and provide loans to state UI systems, one might infer that the major impetus for the 1978 and 1983 increases was to replenish federal trust funds that had been depleted by earlier recessions (Advisory Council on Unemployment Compensation, 1996, pp. 76–83).[2]

The policy question that we focus on is the effect of raising the federal minimum ceiling.[3] Since state UI systems are essentially self-financing, and since a higher federal minimum ceiling implies more earnings are taxable by states, one would immediately think that net revenues would be unchanged, with tax rates falling commensurately with the rise in earnings below the tax ceiling. We show, however, that this need not be the case. Federal mandates on the tax ceiling lead states to restructure the parameters determining benefits and taxes in such a way as to alter total spending and total taxes under their UI programs. While several studies (e.g. Inman, 1989; Courant and Gramlich, 1990; Poterba, 1994) have examined the impact of federal tax changes on state revenues, none has done so for a specific program (and none has derived predictions about the impact from a behavioral model).[4] The specific model that we develop provides testable insights about where we should expect to observe greater departures from what would appear initially to be a simple shift between ways of raising earmarked revenue.

11.3. Interest Bargaining Under a Superior Mandate – The UI Tax Ceiling

There are a number of ways to model state policy formation. For example, we might assume that a benevolent social planner acts to maximize some index of residents' aggregated preferences. This approach requires both specifying what those preferences are and determining how they should be aggregated. We choose instead to model state policy formation as bargaining between interest groups. In essence, we make a strong assumption on aggregation, and focus our attention on the specification of residents' preferences. We assume that each state legislature comprises two political interest groups, which for convenience we call parties, each of which represents a relatively homogenous economic interest group. We assume that majority rule is used to aggregate individual interests within parties and that the final policy is selected by bargaining between parties. By confining attention to this special but not unrealistic framework, the model can generate testable predictions about the effect of changes in the federal tax ceiling from primitive assumptions on interest groups' preferences.

To test the model's bargaining equilibrium prediction directly the threat points of the parties must be specified. That is a daunting task in the legislative context: even if one assumes that one party can hold up passage of all bills, it is difficult to gauge the value of such an action without considering the entire legislative agenda. The traditional recourse is to comparative-static analysis, but this too is not without difficulties: One must consider the interaction between levels in the federation as well as between states. Furthermore, in most cases the overall political context will still be relevant, since states with heterogeneous policy considerations will choose different policy vectors, and so will be affected differently by changes in policy elsewhere in the federation.

We believe that in the present case this problem can be overcome. First, since the federal government sets a minimum tax ceiling that is uniform across states, it is reasonable to assume that the state governments disregard the impact that their policy adjustments have on federal policy-makers. Put differently, the federal government can be assumed to be the 'policy leader' on this issue, and can account for the responses of states to its policy adjustments. Provided there are sufficiently many states, each can ignore the possibility that the federal government will make another round of policy adjustments in response to a particular state's actions.[5] Second, since the tax ceiling takes the form of a simple constraint on the policy adopted by states, heterogeneity across states is much easier to control for in estimation. State-level heterogeneity leads some states to exceed the federal mandates. The states that are unconstrained by the federal policy are only going to respond to changes because of interaction with the responses of other states which are constrained. By examining differences-in-differences in the responses of constrained and unconstrained states to the imposition of the superior policy mandate, we can test the model's predictions while accounting for these difficulties.

There are two principal questions. First, is there any interaction at all? That is, do states change their own policies in response to changes in federal policy? Second, if states do respond, are they able to adjust their own behavior sufficiently to offset the mandate from the federal government? The second question is the central issue and requires diligence not to exclude relevant state policy instruments.

11.3.1. The Unemployment Insurance System

We stylize each state's UI system by four parameters: the weekly benefit, b_j; the tax rate, t_j; the (admittedly simplified) constant fraction of b_j that is charged to the firm generating the insured unemployment (the level of experience-rating), e_j; and the tax ceiling, C_j. Individual states can set all these parameters, subject to the uniform federal constraint that at least the first C dollars of earnings are taxed. In some states the federal ceiling binds, in others it does not, and it is this difference that we exploit in the empirical work below. To make the model tractable we focus on policy-setting in a representative constrained state and ignore interactions between states that may cause these responses to spill over into unconstrained states. This is somewhat unrealistic, but to the extent that interstate competition produces spillovers, the unconstrained jurisdictions will in part mimic the behavior of their constrained neighbors. Such mimicry will make it more difficult to discern empirically the behavior we are studying, making any evidence supporting the theory stronger than it would otherwise appear to be.

State-level parameters are chosen subject to the balanced-budget constraint within each state:

$$b_j U - t_j Y + e_j b_j U = T$$

where U is the total number of weeks of insured unemployment, Y is taxable wages and T are total UI taxes.[6] Implicit in this set of accounting identities is the notion that a higher taxable maximum effectively increases the experience-rated nature of the system if nothing else changes (FitzRoy and Hart, 1985). We assume that the state sets the tax rate t to ensure fund balance:

(1) $$t_j = [\, 1 - e_j \,]\, b_j U \,/\, Y$$

This leaves (b_j, e_j) to be set by bargaining between the two representative j's parties within a constrained state j's political process. The rest of this section analyzes this process. Since we focus on a representative state, for ease of notation the subscript j is suppressed. First, we set out the preferences of the parties in the negotiation and characterize an equilibrium in which a modified version of the median-voter theorem is shown to hold. We then examine the comparative-static predictions of the state's response to a change in the federally mandated tax ceiling. Finally, in section 11.3.6 we discuss an alternative approach to modeling the state's political process as well as some of the stronger assumptions that we employ in our preferred approach.

11.3.2. The Firms' Party

One of the parties engaged in policymaking represents the political interests of employers in the state. The preferences of firms are aggregated into the firms' party platform by majority voting. We model every state in the federation as containing a continuum of profit-maximizing firms, each of which employs a single worker with a fixed-length workweek. Since the policy platform of the firms' party is selected by one-firm one-vote, this assumption means that majority rule is based on the size of the workforce rather than the number of firms, so in effect we assume that larger firms have more political power. Firms have two defining characteristics, the wage they pay and the proportion of time their employee is not employed. Each firm's profit maximization can be separated into two components.

The first comprises day-to-day operational decisions, such as product pricing and staffing, which are made conditional on the parameters of the UI system. Over the longer term, firms are also involved in the political process that sets the UI parameters. Our primary interest lies in these latter activities.

Firms face stochastic prices: With probability p firm i's product price is p_i, and with probability $[1 - p]$ it is q_i, where $p_i > q_i$. In all periods when it employs a worker the firm must pay the payroll tax to finance UI. During periods when its price is high each firm produces one unit of output by employing one worker, for whom it must pay the going wage w_i, which in general depends on the type of activity engaged in by the firm. During periods when its price is low each firm that currently has an employee must decide whether or not to retain the worker. If it retains the worker, it must again pay both the wage and the payroll tax. If it lets the worker go, it may do so in one of two ways. A layoff allows the worker to qualify for UI and permits the firm to avoid the wage and the payroll tax, but results in a liability to the UI system equaling the experience-rated share of one period's benefit, *eb*. Alternatively, the firm can 'fire' the worker, preventing him or her from qualifying for unemployment insurance. Firing avoids wages, taxes and UI liabilities but entails a range of other costs, which we denote by k, such as dissipation of goodwill with future workers and perhaps the anticipated costs of retraining new workers. We assume that these costs are random across episodes of employment and vary according to the distribution $F(k)$ on the interval $[0, K]$. Finally, during periods of low prices when a firm does not currently have an employee, we assume that it remains committed to whichever decision it made in the first period of reduced prices. For simplicity, we assume that k recurs in each period of unemployment. The firm's decision about whether to contest its workers' claim to UI depends on the comparison between *eb* and k: the higher is *eb*, the more likely is the firm to fire the worker.[7]

Since policy determines profits, firms engage in the political process to maximize their long-run average per-period profit. This assumption implies that firm i's political preferences are independent of both its current UI account balance and its current state of employment. Long-run average profits for firm i are:

(2) $$\Pi(t, e, b, C) = \rho[P_i - w_i - t\min\{w_i, C\}] + [1 - \rho][-E\min\{eb, k\}]$$

Implicit in (2) is the assumption that firms never retain a worker when prices are low, i.e. $eb < w_i - q_i$, (on the other hand, since it may well be that

$k > w$, in the absence of UI firms may choose to hoard labor). Denote as $u^i = [1 - \rho] / \rho$ the i proportion of time firm i's worker is not employed. For convenience u^i is referred to as firm i's rate of unemployment.

Because of the ceiling C, total wages do not equal taxable wages. To simplify the calculation of taxable wages we assume that the wage a firm pays is a monotonically decreasing function of its unemployment level, $w(u^i)$, $w' < 0$. At first glance, this appears to be inconsistent with compensating differentials for the risk of unemployment arising in a competitive labor market. However, because employers compete for workers within labor submarkets differentiated by skill level, any positive wage differential that compensates for a higher chance of unemployment across jobs at a given skill level can be outweighed in the aggregate by the negative intergroup differential. Our assumption accords with the empirical fact that low-wage workers experience more unemployment than high-wage workers. Taxable wages are:

$$Y = \int_0^{\hat{u}} CN(\mu)\, d\mu + \int_{\hat{u}}^{\infty} w(\mu)\, N(\mu)\, d\mu$$

where $\hat{u}$ is defined implicitly by $w(\hat{u}) = C$ and denotes the proportion of time the worker earns exactly C experiences insurable unemployment, and $N(\mu)$ is the measure of firms with unemployment rate μ. We call firms paying wages above C high-wage firms, those paying less, low-wage firms.

This simple model determines the representative firm's preferences over two dimensions of the UI policy, b and e. However, since at any level of experience all firms prefer lower benefits, the platform of the firms' party is determined on this single issue. For a given level of benefits firms do not agree on the optimal amount of experience rating. This is clearly a strong simplification: it is easy to think of reasons why some firms that receive subsidies through UI might prefer higher benefits, and we discuss this simplification in section 11.3.6.

To see the trade-off between experience rating and benefits, consider a representative firm's isoprofit line in (b, e) policy space, $e^i(b)$. With the tax rate equilibrium condition and the definition of taxable income substituted into (2), the firm's objective function, an isoprofit line relating different combinations of b and e that yield the same profit, is defined implicitly. Applying the implicit function theorem demonstrates the slope of this line to be:

$e^i_b(b) = [[1 - e^i(b)]\,U\min\{C, w^i\} + e^i(b)\,u^i Y\pi]/b\,[U\min\{C, w^i\} - u^i Y\pi]$,

with $e^i_{bb} \leq 0$, and where $\pi(eb) = 1 - F(eb)$ is the probability that the firm lays off *bb* rather than fires the worker and is a function of the degree of experience rating and the benefit level.

The sign of the slope of firm *i*'s isoprofit line depends on the balance between its relative insured unemployment level and its relative share of taxable wages. If its share of insured unemployment is exactly the same as its share of taxable wages, an increase in *e* simply shifts the form in which it pays its share of the cost of UI but does not affect its profits, and the isoprofit line is vertical. Unless benefits rise as well, firms with relatively low levels of unemployment earn higher profits if experience rating is increased. The converse is true for firms with *m* relatively high levels of unemployment. One isoprofit curve, e^m, for one firm is shown in Figure 11.2. In all cases the isoprofit curve is convex, and profits increase as isoprofit curves shift leftward.

Figure 11.2

The UI Political Equilibrium

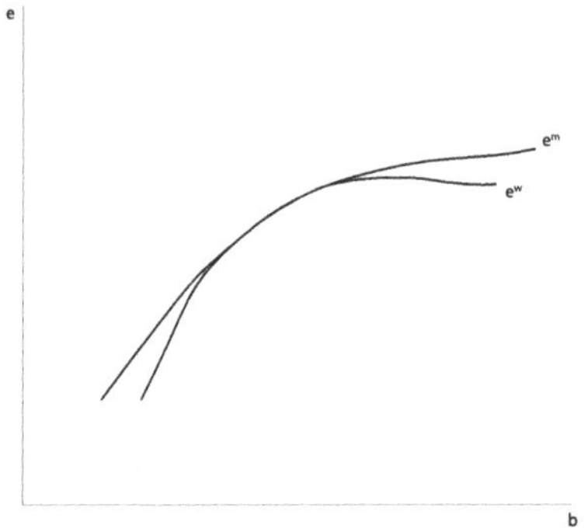

11.3.3. The Workers' Party

We assume that the other party represents the political interests of the workers in the state. UI benefits provide workers with income only if they are laid off. Workers value only income and engage in the political process to maximize their long-run expected utility. We assume that every worker anticipates the same long-run prospects of employment at each firm in the economy. Each seeks to maximize:

$$V = \rho EU(w) + (1 - \rho)\,[\pi(eb)\,v(b) + [1 - \pi(eb)]\,v(\overline{w})],$$

where v is the worker's von Neumann–Morgenstern utility function, π is the proportion of time a worker expects to be employed, and $EU(w)$ is the long-run average expected utility of wages, which depends on the probability of employment across firms. We assume that all workers receive the same wage $\overline{w}$ if they are fired, which for convenience we normalize to zero. Since all workers face the same long run prospects, the policy choice is unanimous among workers.

We have implicitly assumed that wages are set exogenously to the political process determining the UI parameters. Thus, the model is really in partial equilibrium, and its analysis is dependable only if the feedback through wage setting is sufficiently muted. Ultimately, whether this assumption proves useful depends on the empirical results, but we believe that the fact of a 'political process' effected through surrogates separated from face-to-face wage negotiation is enough to warrant exploration of this partial-equilibrium model. The alternative approach includes endogenous wages and is discussed in section 11.3.6.

Assuming that wages do not adjust, workers' indifference curves in policy space are defined implicitly by $V(e^{w}(b),b) = \overline{V}$. An increase in experience rating always reduces the expected utility of workers, since it raises the probability of firing.[8] An increase in benefits may increase or decrease utility depending on whether the higher payment in the event of a layoff outweighs the attendant increase in the probability of firing. Assuming, as seems reasonable, that the first effect dominates the second, workers' indifference curves are upward-sloping:

$$e^{w}_{b}(b) = [\, \pi v'(b) - ev(b)\, f(eb)\,)] \,/\, bv(b)\, f(eb) > 0.$$

A typical worker's indifference curve, e^{w}, is shown in Figure 10.2.

11.3.4. *Equilibrium*

The policy is determined by bargaining between the parties in the legislature. If the firms' party had sufficient political power to impose UI parameters unilaterally, benefits would be driven to zero. On the other hand, if the workers' party alone could set the system's parameters, experience rating would be eliminated, and, since we have ignored the implicit non-negativity constraint on profits, benefits would be raised without limit. Because neither of these is consistent with the facts, we focus instead on the more interesting and plausible class of equilibria that require cooperation between the two parties to determine b and e.[9] These cooperative equilibria are characterized by the following proposition:

Proposition 1. *If neither Party alone can impose a policy, then the equilibrium policy will lie in the set of efficient agreements between a representative worker and the median firm.*

The reason that firms can be divided so that the decisive vote in the Firm's Party lies with the median firm is that firms' ranking of any two policy pairs is monotonic in firm type, as is demonstrated by the following lemma (proven in Appendix A):

Lemma 1: Monotonicity. *Let i, j, and n be any three firms such that* $u^i < u^j < u^n$. *If the outcome* (b'', e'') *is preferred to* (b', e') *by both firms i and n, then it must also be preferred by firm j.*

Lemma 1 shows that low- and high-unemployment firms will never be able to form a coalition to support a policy alternative that is not also preferred by all firms with intermediate unemployment rates. If a policy is neither at a boundary nor a point of tangency between the isoprofit line of the median firm, $e^m(b)$, and the indifference curve of workers, $e^W(b)$, then the median firm can propose a new policy that reduces its costs, preserves (or increases) the utility of workers, and attracts the support of enough additional firms to win against all possible alternative policies. Specifically, if the proposed policy requires increasing experience rating, all firms with lower unemployment rates will prefer it to the status quo, while firms with higher unemployment rates will prefer the status quo. To block the proposed policy these high-unemployment firms need the support of some additional firms. If the median firm preferred the counterproposal, it would have made it itself. Monotonicity of preferences guarantees that if the high-unemployment firm's counterproposal lacks the median firm's support, it is also less preferred by all firms with lower unemployment. Thus as proposition 1 asserts, the equilibrium agreement will lie in the set of efficient agreements between the workers and the median firm.

The contract curve can be found by maximizing the median firm's profit, subject to the provision of a fixed level of utility to a representative worker. At an interior solution this requires tangency between the isoprofit and indifference curves: $e^w_b\ (b) = e^m_b\ (b)$, or:

$$(3) \qquad \frac{[\pi v' - evf(eb)]}{bvf(eb)} = \frac{[[1-e]U\min\{C, w^m\} + eu^m Y\pi]}{b[U\min\{C, w^m\} - u^m Y\pi]}$$

For an interior solution the median firm must have positively-sloped iso-profit lines, as in Figure 11.2. If the median firm preferred less experience rating, the equilibrium policy would involve no experience rating.[10] An equilibrium is depicted as the tangency in Figure 11.2.

11.3.5. Comparative Statics

We now can examine how the total cost of the UI system changes when the federally mandated ceiling C is increased exogenously. In the absence of changes to (b,e) workers are unaffected by an increase in C, so it is natural to think of the changes as resulting from new policy proposals by the high-wage firms. Which firm proposes the change is not important: The equilibrium must be efficient with respect to workers and the median firm, so we can imagine that the policy revision is selected by the latter.

The change in C creates a surplus for the workers and the median firm that can be exploited by revising (b,e). We shall assume that the median firm proposes a new policy that leaves the workers with the same level of utility as the status quo. (Hamermesh and Scoones (1996) consider the more general case in which workers might gain surplus in the renegotiation). Note that this does not mean the median firm is better off with the higher C, but simply that the increase in cost is the minimum compatible with securing the workers' agreement with the policy change. Consider the effect of workers and the median firm sharing the surplus from renegotiation.

Proposition 2. *If the median firm is high-wage ($w^m > C$), the level of benefits is m non-decreasing in C. If the median firm is not high-wage ($w^m < C$), the level of benefits is non-increasing in C.*

Proof. Differentiating (3) with respect to C at an interior solution yields:

$$(4) \qquad \frac{\partial b}{\partial C} = \frac{bUu^m\pi[Y_C \min\{C,w^m\} - Y\chi[w^m > C]]}{[[bU\min\{C,w^m\} - u^m Y\pi]]^2[e^w_{bb} - e^m_{bb}]}$$

where $Y_C = \partial Y / \partial C > 0$, and χ is the indicator function, taking the value one if $w^m > C$, and zero otherwise. The denominator is negative by the second-order conditions (see Footnote 10). If $w^m < C$, the bracketed term in the numerator is m positive. If $w^m > C$, it is:

$$CY_C - Y = -\int_{\hat{u}}^{\infty} w(\mu)\, N(\mu)\, d\mu < 0.$$

On the boundaries either e is unaffected by C or e moves to the interior. Since in fact the large majority of payroll is currently above C in the United States, it is likely that the median firm is a high-wage firm. This restriction is even more sensible if political power in the firms' party increases with payroll rather than simply with employment. Nevertheless, the model predicts that, if C were to become high enough, further increases would lead to a drop in benefits. Proposition 2 focuses on benefits, but an increase in C also affects taxes and experience rating. Since in the long run total taxes equal total benefits, $sgn\{\partial T/\partial C\} = sgn\{\partial b/\partial C\}$. Also, assuming that workers are held to their initial level of utility, higher benefits directly imply higher experience rating along the indifference curve: $sgn\{\partial e/\partial C\} = sgn\{\partial b/\partial C\}$.

11.3.6. Discussion

This section briefly describes an alternative approach to modeling the state policy process and explains our rationale for some of the stronger assumptions that we make. Perhaps the most important question is why choose a bargaining framework at all? In particular, why separate firms' from their employees' interests? For example, the model could be closed by including an equilibrium condition on wages, and then a single median worker/firm could select the best policy. This could be achieved with either a constraint that holds workers to a reservation level of utility, or a zero-profit constraint on firms. In either case the rent-maximizing policy choices of b and e are equivalent. This approach has the added benefit of permitting consideration of the optimal choice of C (subject to the constraint imposed by the federal government), as well as b and e.

We have explored the model incorporating a zero-profit constraint in an unpublished appendix and find two principal results. First, depending on the responsiveness of taxation to increases in the ceiling, it may be that the decisive worker will choose a finite, but positive level of C. However, if the optimal level of C is larger than the worker's wage, that worker will choose to raise it without limit, since it has no effect on payments except through a lower tax rate. Taken perhaps too seriously, this suggests that there may be an instability in some states' responses to an increase in C: if the constraint pushed the ceiling above the decisive firm's wage level, that firm would then choose to raise it still further.

The second result is that all comparative-static predictions depend on the shapes of distributions in the model, so very little can be said without assuming functional forms, and even then the limits of tractability are severe. Recall that the full model requires distributions of firing costs and of firms, each of which is characterized by a distribution of prices. The interaction of curvature properties of these distributions leads to few general conclusions.

Though it accounts for feedbacks from wages to the policy process, an alternative formulation begs the question of which worker is decisive. With more than one dimension of policy parameters, majority rule no longer provides a median-voter result. On the surface this may seem a small cost relative to the model above. Since the weighting we choose is somewhat arbitrary and ignores costs or benefits from the UI program, the notion that the 'median' firm is the policy dictator in the firms' party may seem quite contrived. Undoubtedly this is so; however, the assumptions that we make are much stronger than necessary, as proposition 2 demonstrates. What we need is that the 'wage' of the dominant coalition of firms, however composed, is larger than C. As long as the decisive firm pays wages above the ceiling, it will prefer a new agreement with workers that has higher experience rating and higher benefits. This latitude in identifying the decisive firm is the main reason that we believe we can ignore the fact that firms with subsidized workforces may prefer more benefits to fewer. Assuming that these firms capture some of the surplus from higher benefits (in particular, that higher benefits are not used by workers as an outside alternative to bargain for higher wages) we need only assume that they are unable to dominate the firm coalition. Finally, note that unlike 'tests' of the median-voter theorem, none of the empirical work stemming from our model depends on a correct identification of the decisive firm.[11]

11.4. Direct Tests of the Effects of Higher Tax Ceilings

Our analysis of the nature of the process determining the structure of each state's UI system and how it changes in response to an imposed increase in the taxable ceiling offers explicit testable predictions about the impact of the increase on states. Most important, it suggests that a federally-imposed increase in the ceiling will cause UI systems to expand in those states where the increase is binding. We can tie the model directly to the evidence and focus on the impact of changes in the federal ceiling by examining the three occasions when the federal government mandated a higher ceiling for state UI taxes. One might view these changes as 'natural experiments,' but they are neither. We assume that the agents were not completely surprised by them; and, since other causes will not produce identical changes in behavior in unconstrained and constrained jurisdictions, we also model the determinants of interstate differences in the time paths of total taxes.[12]

The basic data used throughout this section are from *UI Financial Handbook, 1994*. The data set includes information for each jurisdiction for the relevant years on the taxable ceiling, total taxes, taxable and total payroll and the state's insured unemployment rate. The sample consists of the 50 states and the District of Columbia. Let T denote a year when a federally-imposed higher tax ceiling became effective, so that $T = 1972, 1978$ or 1983. (In each instance the increase in the ceiling became effective on January 1). We divide jurisdictions at each time T into two groups, those where the state's ceiling at $T - 1$ was below the new federally mandated C^* that became effective at time T and those that already had a ceiling of at least C^*.

Table 11.1

Jurisdictions with $C_{T-1} > C^*$

Frequency	Jurisdiction
All 3 years	Alaska, Hawaii, Minnesota, Utah, Washington
1978 and 1983 only	Connecticut, Iowa, Idaho, Nevada, Oregon
1978 only	Arizona, California, Georgia, Vermont, Wisconsin
1983 only	District of Columbia, Illinois, Kentucky, Montana, North Dakota, New Jersey, New Mexico, Rhode Island, West Virginia

Table 11.1 lists the states according to whether or not their tax ceiling at $T - 1$ was *ABOVE* the new ceiling C^* for each year T. States not listed had $C_{T-1} < C^*$ in all three years. For 1972, table 11.1 shows that there is substantial scope for comparing behavior in those states where the federal law might have disturbed a political equilibrium to those where it could not have done so (since the law did not constrain behavior). At the time of the increase in 1972, 46 of the 51 jurisdictions had ceilings below the newly imposed ceiling; 36 had low ceilings at the time of the 1978 increase, and 32 did before the 1983 increase.[13]

We focus on differences in the time paths of taxes at and after time *T* in states classified BELOW and ABOVE. The estimating model that allows testing the theory of section 11.3 is:

$$\text{(5)} \qquad TAXES_{T+t,j} = \alpha_0 + \Sigma\alpha_{1i}TAXES_{T-i,j} + \Sigma\alpha_{2i}UR_{T+t-i,j} + \alpha_3 BELOW_{T,j}, \quad i = 1, \ldots, 4, t = 0, \ldots, 4$$

where *j* is a jurisdiction, *UR* is its insured unemployment rate, and TAXES measures total state UI tax payments under the state's program of regular benefits. The estimated α_3 directly measure the $\partial T/\partial C$ in our theory. Including *UR* accounts for interstate differences in the single biggest determinant of time-series variation in UI taxes (through its effect on benefits). The coefficients α_3 are thus not simply measures of 'differences-in-differences' before and after *T* between constrained and unconstrained states, but instead reflect an attempt to account for factors that might have changed interstate differences in taxes around time *T*.

Table 11.2

Estimates of α_3 based on seemingly unrelated estimates of (5), using the indicator variable BELOW[a]

	Year					
T	*T*	*T+1*	*T+2*	*T+3*	*T+4*	*p*-value on α_3
1972	-1432	-917	-536	-44	899	0.99
	(11.418)	(4093)	(12.496)	(11.662)	(21.667)	
1978	5529	2735	11675	19216	28244	0.85
	(9793)	(12.364)	(20.352)	(17.064)	(22.433)	
1983	18.778	64.801	59.298	39.295	31.862	0.38
	(22.719)	(20.266)	(25.265)	(41.614)	(67.732)	
Pooled[b]	27.188	44.547	40.514	44.118	41.903	0.03
	(7965)	(15.906)	(17.926)	(19.371)	(22.894)	

[a] Standard errors in parentheses below the estimated α_3 here and in table 11.3.
[b] Also includes indicator variables for each year.

The parameter estimates are from seemingly unrelated (SUR) estimation of the five equations implicit in (5). The estimated α_3 are presented in the first three rows of table 11.2. The parameter estimates are in thousands of dollars; e.g. for Year $T + 1$ for $T = 1978$, the table shows that total taxes in the typical constrained jurisdiction were (a statistically insignificant) \$2.7 million above where they would have been without the federal mandate. In none of the separate estimates for the three events can we even come near to rejecting the hypothesis that there is no difference in taxes at any time $T + t$ between states where $C_{T-1} < C^*$ and those where $C_{T-1} \geq C^*$. Moreover, the vectors of α_3 are also not significantly nonzero.

The results change when we pool the three cases and thus include a larger number of ABOVE jurisdictions, 39, in one set of equations. The estimates of (5) for all three years T pooled (including time indicator variables) are shown in the final row of table 11.2. All of the estimated individual α_3 are positive and larger than their standard errors; all are significantly greater than zero; and the vector of α_3 is itself significantly nonzero. Most interestingly, and quite consistent with expectations, the difference between the constrained and unconstrained jurisdictions rises initially and then begins leveling off several years after the mandated increase becomes effective. With the larger sample of 'controls' our stringent test provides some suggestion that total taxes are eventually increased in jurisdictions that were constrained.[14]

Table 11.3

Estimates of α_3 based on seemingly unrelated estimates of (5), using the AMOUNT BELOW

	Year					
T	*T*	*T+1*	*T+2*	*T+3*	*T+4*	*p*-value on α_3
1972	0.974	0.831	-1.113	-1.353	22.621	0.76
	(9.958)	(11.331)	(10.457)	(9.973)	(16.788)	
1978	6.477	4.570	16.381	17.743	23.178	0.45
	(5.697)	(7.187)	(11.607)	(9.480)	(12.506)	
1983	18.272	65.513	59.562	42.713	37.865	0.54
	(11.419)	(37.012)	(43.196)	(45.482)	(46.107)	
Pooled[a]	16.682	27.370	29.647	33.437	31.974	0.12
	(5.942)	(11.709)	(13.157)	(14.133)	(16.693)	

[a] Also includes indicator variables for each year.

Table 11.3 presents estimates of sets of equations like (5), but with a variable AMTBELOW $= \max\{0, C^* - C_{T-1}\}$. The estimates in table 11.3 are qualitatively quite similar to those in table 11.2. While none of the estimated α_3 is significantly positive in any of the three individual sets of estimates, and in two cases not even positive, they are positive (some significantly so) in the pooled estimates that offer more degrees of freedom. Given the difference in the results when we pool the three episodes, one might be concerned that the estimates here and in table 11.2 are due to unobservable state-specific effects. They are not: when the equations are reestimated with state fixed effects the results are qualitatively unchanged: The vector of coefficients on AMTBELOW (and BELOW) is significant or nearly so, and the individual coefficients are increasing from T to $T + 2$ and essentially unchanged thereafter.

In table 11.2 the estimated long-run rise in total taxes in the constrained jurisdictions, roughly $40 million, represents an increase of 18.5 percent over the average level of taxes in those states. Despite the absence of any legislation that compels a state to set higher taxes in the long run when it is forced to raise its tax base, total tax payments do rise. At the same time the imposed increase in C raised the taxable base by 27.2 percent in those states, so that the average tax rate t (taxes as a percent of earnings below the ceiling) drops as a result of the mandated increase, from 2.10 percent to 1.96 percent. These results are consistent with the model of section 11.3 that suggested that opening up the opportunity for new legislation on this issue results in interested parties restriking the bargains that determined other parameters of the UI system.

We have estimated a model describing the time path of TAXES. Because state UI systems must balance in the long run, however, we could just as well have estimated (5) replacing TAXES by benefits. Indeed, estimates of a version of (5) that uses total benefit costs differ very little from the results in tables 11.2 and 11.3; but because of potential problems of reverse causation from UR to benefits, the estimates based on TAXES are preferred.[15]

The model of section 11.3 offers implications about the interrelation of the tax ceiling and the extent of experience rating, with exogenous differences in the latter leading to different equilibrium responses of total TAXES to shocks to C. Data on the extent of experience rating in state UI systems are regrettably sparse, with the best information (Topel, 1984) covering only 19 states from 1973–1976. No panels of e are available, so we cannot estimate the effect of increases in C on e. We can, however, add the cross-section measure of e and an interaction of it with AMTBELOW to the equations described in table 11.3 (but estimated only over these 19 states). The great reduction in sample size makes the statistical significance of the effects quite low; but we do find that total taxes in states that have more experience rating are less affected by federally-imposed binding increases in the tax ceiling (see Hamermesh and Scoones, 1996; table 3), which is consistent with the spirit of our theoretical model.

11.5. Conclusions, and Other Applications

We have derived a model that shows how an imposed change in one parameter will affect other parameters in a federal system of unemployment insurance. The model yields very strong and readily testable predictions for interjurisdictional differences in the paths of these other parameters. Those were tested using a 'difference-in-difference' method (adjusted for other causes) applied to the fiscal role of the payroll tax ceiling in American unemployment insurance. One might believe that a rise in the amount of payroll that is taxed in a system where tax rates can adjust downward to offset this rise would have no effect on taxes; but the theory predicts that total taxes (and benefits, because of the requirement for long-run budget balance in these systems) will rise. Even though the data are quite sparse, a very stringent test produces some support for this prediction.

The analysis speaks to the issue of evaluating the impact of federal (more generally, superior governmental) mandates on outcomes at the state level (at inferior jurisdictions). While a recent burgeoning empirical literature (e.g. Gruber, 1994) has used the same method to perform such evaluations, the approach here offers two potential general improvements. First, the theory makes it clear that superior-government mandates do not affect local outcomes only along the mandated dimension: Because the agents who jointly determine lower-government policy will recontract after the mandate is imposed, other policies will change. Thus other outcomes too will be affected. Second, modeling the specific process of policy determination in each case gives explicit guidelines for empirical work about where to look for larger or smaller impacts of the federal mandate.

A broad range of policy changes is amenable mutatis mutandis to the same kind of modeling and testing that we have done here. Among the possible topics are:

> The impact of changing federal standards for state AFDC payments. While the federal government mandates minimum benefits and implicit taxes, states are free to augment these. What is the impact on states' policy choices when

federal constraints have changed? The answer, and the appropriate empirical analysis, will depend on the interaction of the interested agents – social workers; welfare-rights advocates; taxpayers' groups; and others.[16]

The Tax Reform Act of 1986 abolished the deductibility of state sales taxes from federal personal taxable income. States' responses, in terms of how they changed their reliance on sales versus other taxes, should have depended on the legislative bargaining by agents for groups representing those interests that were most affected by the various taxes used to raise revenue at the state level. Some states will not have been affected by the change, with the impact in other states determined by interactions among these agents.

Several American states have enacted some kind of local tax limitation, in most cases limits on property taxes. These mandates will have different impacts on localities' reliance on alternative sources of revenue depending in predictable ways on how interested parties at the local levels bargain over responses to them. Unlike the example in this study and the two examples listed above, this example offers the possibility of large numbers of lower-level jurisdictions over which to test the hypothesis.

Tariff reductions under the GATT alter the relative gains to different industry groups differently in each signatory country. Because of these changes in their relative bargaining positions they will reach new domestic levels of tariffs and non-tariff barriers on many commodities, not only those directly affected by the GATT reductions. Those equilibria will differ across countries in ways that are predictable.

In any instance where a higher authority changes rules that affect lower authorities the agents involved in determining those and related rules at the lower level will renegotiate a new equilibrium set of outcomes among themselves. The results of the change can be studied by considering bargaining relationships among the interested parties at the lower levels, taking account of the specific policy environment in which the change is imposed. The outcomes of that bargaining should inform us about the empirical correlates of interjurisdictional differences in responses to the superior-government mandate and should condition how we study behavior at lower levels of government.

APPENDIX A
Proof of Lemma 1

For all positive levels of benefits the slope of a representative firm's isoprofit line increases in its unemployment rate. For $u^i = 0$, $e_b^i = [1 - e]/b$. As u^i rises, e_b^i approaches infinity. At $u^i = Umin\{C,w^i\}/\pi Y$ it is undefined. For higher rates, e_b^i increases from negative infinity and approaches zero asymptotically. This means that any two isoprofit lines of firms with different unemployment rates cross at most once, and from this fact the lemma follows.

There are six logical possibilities for the intersection of the three isoprofit lines. Two can be ruled out because if $e_b^i < 0$, then $e_b^j < 0$ for all firms *j* with unemployment rates higher than *i*'s.We consider the remaining four cases in turn.

1. First assume that all three isoprofit curves are positively sloped: e_b^i, e_b^j, $e_b^n > 0$, so all three firms prefer more experience-rating.
   - If $b'' > b'$, then since (b'',e'') is preferred by firm *n*, it must be that $e'' > e^n(b'')$, where $e^n(b'')$ is firm *n*'s isoprofit line through b' evaluated at b''. Since firm *j*'s isoprofit line through (b',e') is everywhere less positively sloped than firm *n*'s, for $b > b'$, $e^n(b) > e^j(b)$; so $e'' > e^j(b'')$ and firm *j* must also prefer (b'',e'').
   - If $b'' < b'$, then firm *i*'s preference implies $e'' > e^i(b'')$, and, since firm *j*'s isoprofit line through (b',e') is everywhere more positively sloped than firm *i*'s, $e'' > e^j(b'')$.
2. If e_b^i, $e_b^j > 0$, but $e_b^n < 0$, then the only way that higher benefits can be preferred by firm *n* is in combination with less experience-rating. But this will never be preferred by firm *i*. If $b'' < b'$, then Case (1) applies.
3. If $e_b^i > 0$ and $e_b^j < 0$, then for *n* and *i* to agree it must be that $b'' < b'$. Firm *n*'s preferences imply that $e'' < e_b^n(b'')$. Since $e_b^j < e_b^n < 0$, for $b'' < b'$, it must be that $e'' < e^j(b'')$.
4. If e_b^i, e_b^j, $e_b^n < 0$, the situation is similar to that of Case (1), except here all three firms prefer less experience rating.

APPENDIX B

State unemployment insurance tax base, 1995

State	Base ($)
Alabama	8000
Alaska	23.800
Arizona	7000
Arkansas	9000
California	7000
Colorado	10.000
Connecticut	10.000
Delaware	8500
District of Columbia	10.000
Florida	7000
Georgia	8500
Hawaii	25.500
Idaho	21.000
Illinois	9000
Indiana	7000
Iowa	14.200
Kansas	8000
Kentucky	8000
Louisiana	8500
Maine	7000
Maryland	8500
Massachusetts	10.800
Michigan	9500
Minnesota	15.300
Mississippi	7000
Missouri	8500
Montana	15.500
Nebraska	7000
Nevada	16.400
New Hampshire	8000
New Jersey	17.600
New Mexico	13.500
New York	7000
North Carolina	13.500
North Dakota	13.400
Ohio	9000
Oklahoma	10.700
Oregon	19.000
Pennsylvania	8000
Rhode Island	16.800
South Carolina	7000
South Dakota	7000
Tennessee	7000
Texas	9000
Utah	16.500
Vermont	8000
Virginia	8000
Washington	19.900
West Virginia	8000
Wisconsin	10.500
Wyoming	11.900

V Discrimination: Preferences for People

One might well ask: What is a section on discrimination doing in a book on labor demand? In most graduate courses in labor economics, the economics of discrimination are taught separately from labor demand; and in two-semester courses, the two topics are often taught in separate semesters. Nonetheless, I believe as Paul Samuelson that even a parrot can do economics: All he needs to do is squawk "supply and demand - supply and demand." Thus it makes sense to consider discrimination under one of these two rubrics; and since discrimination ultimately stems from employers' behavior, either directly or as agents for their customers or other employees, and much of our concern about discrimination is in the labor market, labor demand is an appropriate overarching concept in which to include the study of discrimination. This view seems especially sensible, since the most widely-applied economic theory of discrimination is based on agents' preferences, particularly those of employers; and an alternative theory, of statistical discrimination, is explicitly grounded in employers' behavior.

Employers may be willing to offer different wages to otherwise identical workers whose personal characteristics either accord with their preferences or defy them (Becker, 1957). If most employers feel similarly about a group of workers, their preferences will give rise to equilibrium wage differences between those workers and others. This can arise either because of discrimination against a group of workers, or favoritism toward another group (Goldberg, 1982), although the nature of the long-run equilibria will differ between these two cases. Either way, this view of employers' preferences - of their demand for seemingly non-productive characteristics that workers offer when seeking jobs - means that a worker's characteristics enter into labor demand functions.

Given this view, it would be ideal to treat these non-productive characteristics in the same way as we treat skills - fit them into a formal model of production and derive the extent to which employers substitute between them and groups of skills. That formal approach has not yet been taken, as admittedly it would be quite difficult. Indeed, the literature on discrimination has been limited almost entirely to measuring reduced-form wage and other differentials between groups, adjusted for differences in the groups' members' observable characteristics. Little has been done to infer the sources of discriminatory outcomes - whose preferences they are that give rise to observed discrimination; to infer the productivity of the characteristics that we believe are being discriminated against or favored; to inquire into the distribution of agents' preferences (and thus into their demand for ascriptive characteristics in employment relations); or into how different patterns of a characteristic generate differences in discriminatory outcomes.

Except for Chapter 12 all of the research in this Section tries to add to knowledge in these relatively unexplored areas. Even in those cases in which the specific types of discrimination analyzed do not always stem from outcomes affected by employers' decisions, the studies' focus on preferences does, I believe, provide a useful simulacrum for understanding how employers' preferences can generate discriminatory labor market outcomes. As such, the research described here provides a useful and novel underpinning for the study of labor demand.

Empirical research examining wage differentials between groups viewed as minorities and the "majority" group exploded from the 1970s. Reduced-form measures of adjusted wage differences between the majority and African Americans, Hispanics, women, language minorities, religious minorities and others were produced. Some focus was also on wage differentials arising from differences in height and weight. A few small-scale studies of non-representative populations had produced estimates of unadjusted earnings differences between people of different perceived beauty (Frieze et al, 1991), but there had been no large-scale study of the impact of beauty on earnings using nationally representative samples, and none that considered the economic role of beauty in affecting occupational choice as well as earnings.

Chapter 12 helped reduce that shortage and, indeed, generated a now-substantial literature measuring wage differentials between people of different perceived facial attractiveness. Crucial to these studies is the requirement that people have common standards of beauty; otherwise, there would be no correlation in employers' preferences for this characteristic, so that there could be no wage advantage for good-looking people, since "good-looking" could not be defined. In fact, the evidence is clear that people do agree about what is human beauty, albeit not perfectly, so that we might expect employers' preferences for beauty to alter patterns of employment and wages that would otherwise arise.

Early in my career I realized that entry costs into the sub-field of empirical research on racial discrimination were quite low, so that it would be crowded. With that crowd I doubted that I could add anything of substance and that my time was better spent elsewhere. It took me 25 years to realize that there are interesting substantive questions that go beyond the simple measurement of the impacts of workers' characteristics on wage and employment differences and could instead shed light on the underlying structures that give rise to those reduced-form differentials. Admittedly my interest was initially piqued by seeing that a data set that I had been using for another, unrelated study contained measures of the respondents' looks and by my realization that this could underlie a new study. Quickly, though, I knew that I could go beyond simple measurement and actually think about underlying behavior.

Chapter 12 employs a style of research that has increasingly characterized my work and that I feel is crucial: Using several data sets, often from different economies, to analyze a particular phenomenon. It is too easy with only one data set to "fish" for results (Leamer, 1983; De Long and Lang, 1992), so that it may be appropriate to discount the significance of results in any study that uses only one data set to test some general proposition or describe some allegedly general phenomenon. Having two or more data sets prevents this kind of charade, since a massage on one data set that generates spurious results will generally be unsuccessful in generating the same results on another data set. In a very real sense, two data sets are more than twice as good as one.

Chapter 13 answers a simple "what" question: Do the preferences of discriminating agents react to relative differences in the characteristics that they confront, or do they respond more to absolute differences? Put differently, is it the rank in some scale of a characteristic that matters, or is it the actual extent of the characteristic that affects how it is treated by those who are discriminating? For example, one could imagine that in some future world a long history of intermarriage has reduced the variance in skin tone across the work force (and the effects of skin tone on earnings have already been studied carefully - Hersch, 2008). Would we observe as much difference in outcomes for the lightest or darkest as we do today, in which case one would infer that discrimination is based on relative comparisons? Or would the greater homogeneity of skin tone – the small absolute differences – have led to less discriminatory outcomes based on this characteristic?

Answering these questions is not easy: one requires data that allow for large changes in relative (absolute) differences in a characteristic, while at the same time its absolute (relative) differences remain unchanged. Thus, one essentially needs natural experiments that either shift the distribution of a characteristic up or down without affecting its variance, or alter the variance without affecting the mean of the distribution. These are hard to come by.

Living in the Netherlands for two months each year 2010 through 2012, I was astounded to find that I, a man of average height for his age, was relatively a midget – but only compared to younger people, not to those born in the 1940s like me. The obvious tremendous growth of the average Dutch man's height across cohorts appeared to provide a perfect example of an upward shift in the distribution of some characteristic – maintaining absolute differences while the coefficient of variation of the characteristic decreased. This set off a search for similar natural experiments, and I found two for beauty in contests on game shows (Bélot et al, 2012) and electoral contests (Hamermesh, 2006). By extension, the findings of this section suggest that employers react more to absolute than to rank differences, allowing for a bit of optimism about the likely paths of discriminatory outcomes as a population becomes less heterogeneous.

The research in Chapter 12 raised a large number of questions that involved going behind the simple measurement of the impact of employers' preferences on apparently discriminatory labor market outcomes. The simplest was whether it actually is employers' preferences whose effects we observe, or instead that employers in their hiring are implicitly agents for other actors, perhaps a worker's fellow employees, perhaps the firm's customers. Becker's (1957) theory made the simplifying assumption that employers' preferences generate the observed labor market outcomes, but he realized that employers could merely be representing the preferences of others. Basing the outcomes on employers' preferences was only a convenience in modeling; and although much of American (and other countries') anti-discrimination policies focus on employers' behavior, it is not clear, given our lack of knowledge about the source of discrimination, what the appropriate focus should be, or what focus would be most efficient in reducing discriminatory outcomes.

Very few studies have tried to distinguish among the possible sources of discriminatory outcomes (but see Buffum and Whaples, 1995), perhaps because doing so requires more detailed data than are present in the readily available large-scale data sets that underlie the overwhelming majority of empirical studies of discrimination (including Chapters 12 and part of 13). Chapter 14 was an attempt to remedy this situation by constructing a set of data that allows inferring what agents are responsible for the discrimination that we measure (in this case, discrimination against unattractive lawyers). Aside from providing evidence on this question, the nature of the data set allowed us to examine how employers' preferences create incentives for workers with particular characteristics to sort themselves across occupations (actually, narrow specialties within the general occupation of attorney).

This study arose when we read Wood et al. (1993) and realized that attorneys included in the underlying data set had provided photographs when they matriculated at the law school that generated those data. We knew that because my wife had graduated from that law school and had provided a picture upon matriculation. This gave rise to an ethical question in our research: Should we include my wife in our sample, since we would be having the attractiveness of all the sample participants rated by a panel of raters? We decided not to include her, since she was only one of over 4000 participants and, more important, we did not want people rating somebody we knew so well. The method used in this study – constructing one's own data set by combining information from a variety of sources and constructing much additional information, in this case ratings of the attorneys' beauty – accounted for less than 10 percent of the studies published in the top 3 general journals in economics in the early 1990s. Today it describes over one-third of the publications in those journals (Hamermesh, 2013). This is a welcome methodological change, as abandoning our reliance on pre-packaged data sets enables us, as this study demonstrates, to answer questions that could not otherwise be addressed.

We observe discriminatory outcomes; but what is the nature of the interaction of employers' preferences with the supply of workers bearing a particular characteristic that is discriminated against? Obviously, in the labor market we cannot answer this question, as the required structural estimates are extremely difficult to obtain. Instead, there are other cases, particularly electoral processes, where with information on voters (analogous to employers) and candidates (analogous to workers) we can infer the structure of preferences on the demand side. This requires detailed information on outcomes in relation to the supply of candidates and the characteristics of voters.

In Dillingham et al. (1994) we started a literature that examined how the matching of deciding agents to suppliers' traits affected outcomes (in that case, again, elections), a literature that has been extended with similar methods to judging sports, grading tests and hiring workers. In all cases the issue has been the extent to which a match between a deciding agent's and supplying agent's characteristic alters the deciding agent's decision compared to when there is no match. That is an important issue, but it does not allow us to understand what we mean by discrimination: It, too, merely measures reduced-form outcomes. Chapter 15 goes beyond this by examining how behavioral changes vary with the magnitude of the supply of the particular characteristic when a deciding agent does or does not match a supplier.

Chapter 15 grew out of my concerns about what we mean by discrimination. It also stemmed from my casual observation (and interest in professional gossip) that women nominated for office in the American Economic Association seemed to have a disproportionately high chance of being elected (an observation that was supported by the data we collected for this study). While my casual observation about female success annoyed me, the detailed thinking underlying this study altered my views about what we mean by discrimination and made me hesitate when considering the differential electoral success of members of various demographic groups, both in this narrow, academic context and much more broadly in politics generally and in the labor market.

The literature on matches, including Dillingham et al (1994), is entirely of the standard "what" variety - carefully measuring the magnitude of some effect. The effect, however, is often a subtle reduced-form result of a complex set of interactions between agents on both sides of the market. While it is often difficult to identify the behavior of groups of similar agents in discriminatory situations, one can at least go beyond measuring reduced-form outcomes to consider how the incentives in the market alter the behavior of the agents involved (and how those alterations in turn affect the measured reduced-form outcomes). For example, Chapter 14 demonstrated how attorneys' choices of specialty based on their looks and the productivity of looks in different specialties lead to a different mix of workers than we would observe in a non-discriminatory market, and how that self-selection changes measured wage differentials.

Discrimination also alters occupational choice generally, perhaps crowding workers into particular occupations where there is less discrimination, perhaps excluding them entirely from other occupations. Either way, the wage and employment outcomes that are generated are not the same as would arise from randomly assigning workers to occupations. The question is how important are these changes in behavior by suppliers that are induced by the knowledge that other agents will be discriminating against them (by workers knowing that employers' demands may be discriminatory)? Are they sufficient to make the reduced-form outcomes that we observe much different from what would arise in their absence? The idea is somewhat like the theoretical point of Coate and Loury (1993) that affirmative-action programs will alter the behavior of people they are aimed at protecting.

This possibility has not been addressed in the literature in labor economics, no doubt because it requires pinpointing the induced changes in behavior that might be expected. Like so much else in labor economics, baseball provides a nice mirror for behavior more generally, since it is highly structured and there are data on each player's (agent's) behavior. Chapter 16 takes advantage of this reflection of real-world outcomes to analyze how one group – pitchers in certain minority groups – alter their behavior in response to knowledge that those judging them (umpires, who we can view as analogous to employers) will treat them differently from majority pitchers.

12

Beauty and the Labor Market

He (Aristotle) used to say that personal beauty was a better introduction than any letter.

(Diogenes Laertius, The Lives and Opinions of the Eminent Philosophers)

Discrimination in the labor market has generated immense amounts of research by economists. Many alternative theoretical analyses of the nature of discrimination and a vast empirical literature have been produced (see e.g., Glen Cain's (1986) review). In the United States alone, careful empirical studies of possibly discriminatory outcomes involving blacks, Hispanics, women, linguistic minorities, physically handicapped workers, and no doubt others have been produced.[1] Our purpose here is to offer the first study of the economics of discrimination in the labor market against yet another group - the ugly - and its obverse, possible favoritism for the beautiful. We examine whether there is a reduced-form combination of attitudes toward beauty and a distribution of workers among jobs that generates apparently discriminatory labor market outcomes.

This analysis is interesting in its own right. Every worker brings some physical attractiveness to the labor market along with other attributes, and most are concerned, perhaps inordinately so (Naomi Wolf, 1991), with this aspect of their labor market characteristics. Interest in "lookism, ... the construction of a standard of beauty/attractiveness," is an expression of a belief that people failing to meet that standard are mistreated. Antidiscrimination legislation has been enacted in the United States to prevent denying employment on the basis of "height,

The original version of this chapter was published as: Hamermesh, Daniel S./Biddle, Jeff E. (1994). Beauty and the Labor Market, in: The American Economic Review, 84(5): 1174–1194.

weight and personal appearance," and proposed elsewhere on the basis of "facial features, build and height"; and in the United States a case law in this area is developing and may burgeon under the Americans with Disabilities Act of 1990.[2]

Studying possible discrimination on the basis of looks should also be of broader interest. It is very difficult to construct a research design that allows one to distinguish labor market outcomes arising from discrimination against a group from those produced by intergroup differences in unobserved (by the researcher) productivity. In the case of looks, we may have a better chance of doing so, for we can identify activities in which looks are likely to be more important, and thus where the payoff to beauty (or penalty for homeliness) reflects differences in productivity. In the literature on wage discrimination, attempts to sort out the importance of alternative sources of measured discrimination are quite rare (but see Alan Dillingham et al., 1994).

In section 12.1 we examine some relevant results of social-psychological studies of beauty and human behavior, aiming toward considering whether it is possible to use measures of beauty as if they were objective descriptions. Section 12.2 discusses how beauty might be rewarded in the labor market and how it affects workers' choice of occupations. Section 12.3 describes the three sets of microeconomic data that we use to analyze the role of looks. Section 12.4 tests for the presence of earnings differentials based on looks; section 12.5 examines possible causes of male-female differences in the effects of beauty; and section 12.6 conducts tests aimed at distinguishing the sources of wage differences by looks.

12.1. Background

If there is no common agreement on what constitutes beauty, it makes no sense to consider the role of looks in the labor market. Fortunately, a huge literature exists on this subject, including research by anthropologists, sociologists, and social psychologists, that has recently been ably summarized (Elaine Hatfield and Susan Sprecher, 1986). It seems quite clear that there are few consistent standards of beauty across cultures. Hugely distended lower lips are considered attractive by Ubangi men as were women's bound feet by Manchu dynasty men; and other less extreme examples of differences in standards of beauty across cultures could easily be cited.

Table 12.1

Persistence in Ratings of Beauty, Canadian Quality of Life, 1977, 1979 and 1981 (Percentage Distributions)

A. Distribution of Ratings, 1977–1979 and 1979–1981 Combined

Men (N = 1,504):

	Second-year rating				
First-year rating	1	2	3	4	5
1) Strikingly handsome	0.2	0.9	1.0	0.0	0.0
2) Above average (good looking)	1.4	14.9	15.9	0.7	0.0
3) Average	0.9	15.1	37.5	4.8	0.1
4) Below average (plain)	0.1	0.4	4.0	1.7	0.1
5) Homely	0.0	0.1	0.1	0.1	0.1
1977–1979: $X^2_{[16]} = 151.78$		1979–1981: $X^2_{[16]} = 142.67$			

Women (N = 2,147):

	Second-year rating				
First-year rating	1	2	3	4	5
1) Strikingly handsome	0.4	1.4	0.6	0.0	0.0
2) Above average (good looking)	1.0	14.3	15.8	1.0	0.0
3) Average	0.7	13.3	37.0	4.3	0.4
4) Below average (plain)	0.0	0.8	6.2	2.0	0.2
5) Homely	0.0	0.1	0.2	0.2	0.1
1977–1979: $X^2_{[16]} = 231.13$		1979–1981: $X^2_{[16]} = 169.17$			

B. Summary of Ratings Across Three Years

Both Genders (N = 1,330):

	Absolute deviations from 1977 rating								
			1, 1				2, 2		
1977 rating	0, 0	0,1	Same	Different	0, 2	1, 2	Same	Different	2, 3
1) Strikingly handsome	0.1	0.2	0.8	0.0	0.1	1.1	0.2	0.0	0.1
2) Above average	8.1	13.2	10.4	0.6	0.6	0.9	0.2	0.0	0.0
3) Average	26.3	19.7	6.8	1.0	0.7	0.4	0.1	0.0	0.0
4) Below average	0.3	2.9	3.8	0.2	0.2	0.8	0.2	0.0	0.1
5) Homely	0.0	0.1	0.2	0.0	0.0	0.1	0.2	0.0	0.0
Total:	34.8	36.0	21.9	1.7	1.5	3.2	0.7	0.0	0.2

What is perhaps a bit less obvious is that standards of beauty change over time within the same culture, changes that go beyond preferences and fads in clothing to the question of body type. The Rubens ideal looks much different from her Northern European counterpart walking down the runway at a modern Paris salon. Today's ideal lean Western male would have been viewed as potentially or actually consumptive and a bad match in both labor and marriage markets in 19th-century America. The crucial issue for our purposes is whether standards of attractiveness change slowly enough to allow labor market decisions related to beauty to be planned for a horizon as long as a person's expected working life.

The evidence seems quite clear on this issue: within a culture at a point in time there is tremendous agreement on standards of beauty, and these standards change quite slowly. For example, respondents ranging in age from 7 to 50 who were asked to rank the appearance of people depicted in photographs showed very high correlations in their rankings. Moreover, the ratings of the appearances of a group of individuals photographed at different stages of their adult lives were highly autocorrelated (Hatfield and Spreecher, 1986 pp. 282–83). Today the same facial types are even preferred by people of different races on different continents, perhaps because of the increasing internationalization of media images (*New York Times*, 22 March 1994, p. A6).

Some explicit evidence that, while "beauty is in the eye of the beholder," beholders view beauty similarly is provided by the tabulations in table 12.1. This Canadian survey was conducted in 1977, 1979, and 1981, with different interviewers in each year asked to "categorize the respondent's physical appearance" into one of the five rubrics: strikingly handsome or beautiful; above average for age (good looking); average for age; below average for age (quite plain); and homely. The data have some aspects of a panel, so that many of the respondents were interviewed in two adjacent years, and some appear in all three years.

The matrices of ratings for pairs of adjacent years in the upper part of table 12.1 are highly nonrandom, as shown by the chi- square statistics based on the contingency tables implicit in them. In each there is much more clustering along the prime diagonal than would arise randomly. The lower part of table 12.1 provides information on the constancy of the interviewers' ratings over three biennia. Thirty-five percent of the sample is rated identically in all three years; and nearly 93 percent of the respondents are rated identically in at least two years and only one rating level different in the third year.[3] There is substantial positive correlation in how people rate others' looks.

There has been some examination of some of the labor market correlates of beauty. The best of these is probably Robert Quinn (1978), who generated simple correlations of interviewers' ratings of the looks of respondents who were full-time employees with their incomes using one of the data sets we employ. Incomes were higher among both men and women, the higher the assessment of the respondent's looks was, based on a three-point rating of beauty. The results held for both genders, and there was no evidence of asymmetry in the effect on income of departures from the middle category. A similar study (Patricia Roszell et al., 1989) used the Canadian data underlying table 12.1 to regress 1981 income on 1979 income and a variable rating the respondent's looks, with results implying faster income growth among better-looking respondents.

Several studies have examined correlations of earnings with the appearance of workers in a narrow age or occupational cohort. A recent example is Irene Frieze et al. (1991), who studied earnings of MBAs over the first ten post-degree years. Ratings of beauty based on photographs of the students while in school were correlated positively with both starting and subsequent salaries for males. Among females there was no correlation with starting salary, but more attractive women experienced more rapid salary growth.[4]

A related larger literature has offered photographs and hypothetical résumés of potential workers and asked experimental subjects to choose among these workers for various jobs (Hatfield and Sprecher, 1986). Among men, beauty enhanced the worker's likelihood of being chosen for both clerical and professional/managerial jobs. Beauty helped the women's chances of being selected only for the higher-level clerical jobs.

We can be fairly sure that within the modern industrial world standards of beauty are both commonly agreed upon and stable over one's working life. The evidence also suggests that women's and men's beauty/ugliness might be treated differently in the labor market, so that any empirical study must analyze genders separately. Most important, an examination of the literature makes it clear that there has been little systematic thought about the role of beauty in the labor market; that the empirical analysis of this issue has almost exclusively dealt with very narrow samples; and that it has been limited to tabulations and regressions holding at most one or two variables (usually age) constant.

12.2. Models of Beauty in the Labor Market

One approach to modeling looks-based differences in labor market outcomes is to assume that at least in some occupations attractive workers are more productive than unattractive ones. This advantage could arise from consumer discrimination, with customers preferring to deal with better-looking individuals; or there may be occupations in which physical attractiveness enhances the worker's ability to engage in productive interactions with coworkers. Prima facie evidence supporting this assumption is provided by a recent survey of employers (Harry Holzer, 1993), who were asked, "How important or unimportant is attractive physical appearance (for the job most recently filled)?" Eleven percent responded that appearance was very important, while 39 percent believed that it was somewhat important.

To explore the implications of such a model, consider an economy where each worker *i* is endowed with a vector of productivity-enhancing characteristics X_i and can be classified as either attractive or unattractive. In each of a number of occupations *j* the wage is given by

$$w_{ij} = a_j X_i + b_j \Theta_i$$

where the a_j is a vector of parameters, b_j is positive in some occupations and zero in others, and Θ_i equals 1 if the worker is attractive and 0 otherwise. Workers are assumed to choose the occupation offering the highest wage.

One set of empirical implications of this model involves the distribution of workers across occupations. There will be sorting, in that attractive workers will be observed in greater proportions in those occupations where attractiveness is rewarded. However, segregation by looks will be incomplete; both attractive and unattractive people might be found in any occupation. For example, unattractive workers may choose an occupation where attractiveness adds to productivity if they happen to be well endowed with other characteristics that are valued in that occupation. Likewise, an attractive worker might choose an occupation where attractiveness has no payoff if the choice provides a high relative reward for the worker's particular bundle of other characteristics.

A second set of implications concerns the earnings of attractive versus unattractive workers. If the distribution of X_i is uncorrelated with beauty, attractive workers will on average earn more, whether or not one controls for *X*. Within occupations we will observe a difference between the average earnings of attractive and unattractive people only in those occupations where attractiveness is productive.

An obvious alternative to a model with productivity differences (including those associated with consumer discrimination) generating looks-based differences in outcomes has them resulting from employer discrimination against the unattractive. A Becker-type model involving employers' distaste for unattractive employees produces a looks differential in earnings, but no systematic sorting of workers into occupations on the basis of attractiveness. Further, there is no reason to expect the wage differences between attractive and unattractive workers to differ across occupations.[5]

It thus may be possible to distinguish empirically between a model with looks-based labor market outcomes driven by productivity differences and one in which they arise because of employer discrimination. A practical obstacle to this task is identifying those occupations where attractiveness might plausibly lead to greater productivity. Assuming that a reasonable criterion for identification can be found, however, evidence that attractive people are more heavily represented in such occupations would support the productivity model.

Another test involves a regression like

$$w_i = \beta_0 + \beta_1 X_i + \beta_2 \Theta_i + \beta_3 OCC_i + \beta_4 \Theta_i OCC_i + \varepsilon_i \quad (1)$$

where $OCC_i = 1$ if the worker's occupation has been identified as one where looks are productive, the ε_i are residuals, and the β's are parameters. This regression nests a simple view of occupational crowding, in which confining unattractive workers in certain occupations depresses the wages of all workers in those occupations and thus implies that $\beta_3 > 0$.[6] The productivity model implies $\beta_4 > 0$ and $\beta_2 = \beta_3 = 0$ (i.e., that the worker's looks matter only in those occupations where beauty is important). The employer discrimination model implies that $\beta_2 > 0$ and $\beta_3 = \beta_4 = 0$.

The main focus of our empirical work is to determine whether standard earnings equations yield evidence of a pay difference based on looks. We then try to identify occupations where beauty might be productive in order to examine the extent of labor market sorting by looks and to implement the tests that are implicit in (1).

12.3. Data

Two broad household surveys for the United States and one for Canada provide data on the respondents' looks as well as on the usual labor market and demographic variables of interest to economists. The 1977 Quality of Employment Survey (QES) contains information on 1,515 workers. This survey has the advantage of including great detail about labor market behavior, but the disadvantage of including only labor force participants. The 1971 Quality of American Life

Survey (QAL) contains interviews of 2,164 respondents. For our purposes this study has the advantage of having substantial background information on the respondents, but the disadvantage of containing relatively few variables describing the worker's job. The 1981 Canadian Quality of Life Study (QOL) contains 3,415 observations. This study has none of the disadvantages of the two American data sets and has the additional attraction of providing (for a much smaller subsample that constitutes a three-year panel) three observations on each respondent's looks.

In all three surveys, the interviewer, who visited the respondent in his or her abode, had to "rate (or categorize) the respondent's physical appearance" on the five-point scale shown in table 12.1, along which looks range from strikingly handsome or beautiful to homely.[7] The distributions of the ratings in the three surveys are shown in Table 12.2, (For the Canadian data we present averages based on all the respondents included in the three-year study). Among both men and women, roughly half are rated as average, and many more are rated above-average than are viewed as below-average. Either Canadians are better-looking than Americans, or Canadian interviewers (perhaps the populace generally) are less willing to describe someone as having below-average looks. What is most interesting is that the ratings of women are more dispersed around the middle category. This is a common finding in the social-psychological literature: women's appearances evoke stronger reactions, both positive and negative, than men's (Hatfield and Sprecher, 1986).

Table 12.2

Distribution of Looks: Quality of Employment Survey (QES), 1977; Quality of Life, (QAL), 1971; Canadian Quality of Life (QOL), 1977, 1979 and 1981 (Percentage Distributions)

	QES		QAL		QOL (pooled)	
Category	Men	Women	Men	Women	Men	Women
1) Strikingly beautiful or handsome	1.4	2.1	2.9	2.9	2.5	2.5
2) Above average for age (good looking)	26.5	30.4	24.2	28.1	32.0	31.7
3) Average for age	59.7	52.1	60.4	51.5	57.9	56.8
4) Below average for age (quite plain)	11.4	13.7	10.8	15.2	7.2	8.3
5) Homely	1.0	1.7	1.7	2.3	0.4	0.7
N:	959	539	864	1,194	3,804	5,464

In these samples very few people are rated as strikingly beautiful (handsome) or as homely. We assign these to the nearest category and base all of our estimation on the three-category distinction among above- average, average, and below-average. Even this means that the cell sizes for some of the categories (e.g., people with below-average looks in the QAL) are not very large.

All three surveys offer a variety of measures of earnings. In all of them we chose to calculate hourly earnings as annual earnings divided by 52 times weekly hours.[8] In the analyses involving hourly earnings, all respondents who worked less than 20 hours per week and who earned less than $0.75 per hour in the QAL ($1 per hour in the QES and the QOL) are excluded, as are the self-employed individuals and all those for whom data on the various control variables are unavailable.[9] The empirical work includes only people aged 18–64.

Other variables defined for the analyses of hourly earnings and included in all three data sets are: marital status (which we measure as a zero-one dummy variable, married or not); education, defined as a vector of dummy variables measuring high-school completion, some college, or a college degree or more; and one-digit industry. Self-reported health status is included in all the regressions. Most important, anyone whose health status in the QES is listed as "totally and permanently disabled" or the next most severe category on a seven-point subjective scale is excluded from all the empirical work. In the QAL, a respondent is excluded if health "prevents him/her from doing lots of things," while in the QOL anyone whose self-reported health status is not at least rated as "fair" is excluded.[10] These exclusions minimize any spurious results stemming from a possible correlation between physical appearance and major physical disabilities that reduce productivity in the market.

Our purpose is to isolate the effect of beauty on earnings by controlling for as many other causes of variation in earnings as possible. Inferentially we are thus asking: what is the marginal effect of looks after accounting for all the other causes of variations in earnings that are usually measured? We define the set of regressors quite broadly and try to make them comparable across the three sets of data. In the QES and QOL the data allow the construction of actual labor market experience, years of tenure with the firm, and an indicator of union status. In the former, establishment size is included, while the latter includes firm size. In the QAL, experience is measured as age - schooling - 6. In estimates based on the two American data sets we include dummy variables for race and for location in the American South, while in the QOL we include a vector of variables for Canada's regions and an indicator of whether or not the person speaks English at home.

Finally, the QAL allows us to include measures of the respondents' fathers' occupations, of their early childhood background, and of their immigrant status and that of their parents and grandparents.

12.4. Looks and Earnings

The most interesting economic question involving beauty is probably its relation to an individual's economic success. In section 12.2 we suggested three possible reasons for a premium for beauty or a penalty for ugliness in the labor market: pure employer discrimination, customer discrimination/productivity, and occupational crowding. In order to examine these we need to know first whether earnings differentials based on beauty even exist.

We make no claim to be able to estimate a structural model of a hedonic market for looks. Rather, in the first part of this section we present estimates of standard earnings equations that allow for the possibility of differences in earnings related to looks. In the final part we synthesize the findings to infer what we have learned from this approach about the existence of such earnings differentials. We consider whether such problems as unobservable influences on earnings are correlated with the measures of beauty; whether measurement error clouds our results; and how severe potential problems of simultaneity between earnings and beauty might be.

12.4.1. Estimates of the Relationship of Looks and Earnings

Columns (i) and (iii) of table 12.3 present estimates of earnings equations based on the data from the QES. Columns (i) and (iv) of table 12.4 do the same using data from the QAL, as do columns (i) and (v) of table 12.5 for the QOL. In these and subsequent tables we present the probabilities (p) related to the F statistic testing the joint significance of the variables reflecting individuals' beauty.

Among the six equations, the pair of beauty variables is jointly significantly nonzero at some conventional level in four cases. Moreover, in all six groups people with above-average looks receive a pay premium, ranging from as little as 1 percent to a high estimate of 13 percent (for women in the QAL). In five groups (excluding only women in the QAL), workers with below- average looks receive a pay penalty, ranging from 1 percent to as much as 15 percent. Not all of these individual coefficients are significantly different from zero. However, many are, and the consistency of the pattern across three independent samples suggests that the finding of pay premia and penalties for looks is robust.

Table 12.3

The Impact of Looks on Employees' Earnings: QES, 1977

	Men		Women	
Variable	(i)	(ii)	(iii)	(iv)
Looks:				
Below average	-0.164 (0.046)	-0.162 (0.046)	-0.124 (0.066)	-0.107 (0.071)
Above average	0.016 (0.033)	0.010 (0.034)	0.039 (0.048)	0.035 (0.049)
Obese		0.119 (0.172)		-0.122 (0.134)
Overweight		-0.024 (0.038)		-0.016 (0.058)
Tall		0.027 (0.045)		0.104 (0.114)
Short		-0.105 (0.060)		-0.017 (0.124)
$\bar{R}^2$:	0.403	0.404	0.330	0.327
p on F statistic for beauty variables	0.001	0.001	0.069	0.173
N:	700	700	409	409

Note: The dependent variable is log(hourly earnings); standard errors are shown in parentheses. The equations here also include continuous and indicator variables measuring actual experience (and its square), union membership, health status, marital status, race, years of vocational school, and region, and vectors of indicator variables for educational attainment, tenure with the firm, plant size, city size, and industry. The regressions exclude observations for which data were not available to form these measures and for which weekly hours worked <20, hourly earnings < $1, and age >64 or age <18.

The estimates based on the QES indicate that more attractive people are paid more. However, the premia for good looks are considerably smaller than the penalties for bad looks and are not statistically significant. The results for men are corroborated by the QAL results in table 12.4, with positive estimated coefficients for above-average looks categories and (larger) negative wage penalties for those in below-average looks categories. They are, however, contradicted by the estimates from the QOL in table 12.5. In that sample there is a significant premium for good-looking men, but a tiny and insignificant penalty for men of below-average looks. A similar disagreement exists in the estimates for women. The large penalties for ugliness in the QES are replicated in the Canadian QOL, but are contradicted by a positive coefficient for below-average-looking women in the QAL. There are small premia for above-average-looking women in the QES and QOL, and a large significant premium in the QAL.

The similarity of the premia and penalties across the two genders is also interesting. In the results from the QES they are nearly identical. In the QAL there is a larger penalty for below-average-looking men than for women, but a larger premium for good-looking women. The opposite pattern holds in the QOL. Among people who choose to work at least half time, beauty does not generate very different effects on the earnings of women and men.

Table 12.4

The Impact of Looks on Employees' Earnings: QAL, 1971

	Men			Women		
Variable	(i)	(ii)	(iii)	(iv)	(v)	(vi)
Looks:						
Below average	-0.078	-0.138	-0.079	0.069	0.122	0.061
	(0.069)	(0.081)	(0.069)	(0.073)	(0.095)	(0.073)
Above average	0.065	0.109	0.064	0.128	0.129	0.118
	(0.045)	(0.052)	(0.045)	(0.056)	(0.076)	(0.056)
Short				0.095		0.235
				(0.101)		(0.109)
Tall				0.018		0.251
				(0.066)		(0.214)
Interviewer effects	no	yes	no	no	yes	no
$\bar{R}^2$:	0.371	0.471	0.370	0.283	0.332	0.293
p on *F* statistic for beauty variables	0.124	0.014	0.130	0.072	0.174	0.108
N:	476	476	476	307	307	307

Notes: The dependent variable is log(hourly earnings); standard errors are shown in parentheses. Also included are continuous and indicator variables measuring experience (age – education – 6) and its square, health status, race, marital status, and region, and vectors of indicator variables measuring educational attainment, city size, rural background, immigrant status of the individual and his or her parents and grandparents, father's occupational status, and industry. The regressions exclude observations for which data were not available to form these measures and for which weekly hours worked <20, hourly earnings <$0.75 and age >64 or age <18.

While the results are qualitatively similar in the three samples, one might worry still more about the robustness of the estimates. One concern is that each interviewer might have a different standard for beauty.

These differences could be regarded as a form of measurement error, lowering the efficiency of our estimates and biasing them to the extent that interviewer standards were spuriously correlated with respondents' earnings. To account for any potential problems this might cause, columns (ii) and (v) of table 12.4 and columns (ii) and (vi) of table 12.5 re-estimate these reduced-form earnings equations using interviewer-specific fixed effects for the QAL and QOL, respectively. Among men, the penalty for ugliness increases slightly in both samples; but the changes in the premium for good looks are in opposite directions. Among women the unexpected positive effect of below-average looks in the QAL becomes larger, but none of the other estimates of penalties and premia is affected much. Taken together, the results suggest clearly that the relation between looks and earnings does not arise from idiosyncratic ratings by particular interviewers.[11]

Table 12.5

The Impact of Looks on Employees' Earnings: Canadian QOL, 1981

	Men				Women			
Variable	(i)	(ii)	(iii)	(iv)	(v)	(vi)	(vii)	(viii)
Looks:								
1981	-0.012 (0.052)	-0.027 (0.054)	-0.110 (0.104)		-0.058 (0.063)	-0.072 (0.067)	-0.042 (0.096)	
Average of three years				-0.148 (0.172)				-0.053 (0.120)
Looks above average:								
1981	0.073 (0.028)	0.059 (0.030)	0.019 (0.056)		0.013 (0.027)	0.010 (0.029)	0.016 (0.039)	
Average of three years				0.123 (0.084)				0.068 (0.056)
Interviewer effects	no	yes	no	no	no	yes	no	no
$\bar{R}^2$:	0.302	0.306	0.222	0.228	0.394	0.389	0.487	0.491
p on *F* statistic for beauty variables	0.023	0.099	0.498	0.147	0.540	0.492	0.821	0.348
N:	887	887	350	350	883	883	282	282

Notes: The dependent variable is log(hourly earnings); standard errors are shown in parentheses. Also included are continuous and indicator variables measuring actual experience and its square, health status, union status, non-English speaker, and marital status, and vectors of indicator variables measuring educational attainment, tenure with the firm, firm size, region, and industry. The regressions exclude observations for which data were unavailable to form these measures and for which weekly hours worked <20, hourly earnings <$1, and age >64 or age <18.

Another worry is about variables that are necessarily excluded from some or all of the samples because they are unavailable. Obviously, variables in the latter group cannot be examined here. But in the former group we can consider the impact of excluding the worker's family background and intelligence. Including the family background measures from the QAL, as in table 12.4, lowered the absolute values of the estimated looks premia and penalties by less than 0.005 for men, and by less than 0.02 for women. Had we also included in columns (i) and (iv) of table 12.4 a dummy variable for workers whose intelligence was perceived by the interviewer as being in the top 7 percent, the absolute values of the coefficients for men would fall by 0.002 each, and those for women would fall by 0.006 each. Despite the positive correlation between the subjective measures of intelligence and beauty, the changes are tiny. Adding father's and mother's educational attainment to family background measures in table 12.4 alters the coefficients on the beauty measures by less than 0.001.

Beauty may alter other attributes people bring to the labor market that are not ordinarily considered in economic models. While these effects are difficult to measure, our data permit some exploration of this additional omitted-variable problem. The QOL asks respondents six questions designed to measure their self-esteem, with answers on a four-point scale indicating agreement/disagreement with statements such as, "Those who are always trying to get ahead in life will never be happy." A simple average of these six responses is (weakly) positively correlated with the three-category rating of individuals' looks; and the same measure generates significant positive coefficients when added to the equations underlying columns (i) and (v) in table 12.5. It hardly alters the impacts of the beauty measures, however: In column (i) the estimates become - 0.003 and 0.068, while in column (v) they become - 0.053 and 0.014. Bad looks may produce low self-esteem before the person enters the labor market, and low self-esteem is associated with lower wages; but the measured direct impact of looks on wages is hardly affected by any pre-labor-market effects through self-esteem.

A long, large, and still growing literature (e.g., Paul Taubman, 1975; Robert McLean and Marilyn Moon, 1980; Susan Averett and Sanders Korenman, 1993) has studied the relation between weight or height and earnings. We can test whether our results merely demonstrate the effect on earnings of these few bodily characteristics by including measures of height and weight in the earnings equations. In the QES the interviewer rated the respondent's weight on a five-point scale and estimated the respondent's height in inches, while only height is available in the QAL.[12] For both samples we formed dummy variables based on height, categorizing women as tall if they exceeded 5'9" (6' for men) or short if they were below 5' (5'6" for men). Self-explanatory dummy variables for people who are obese, or only overweight, were constructed for the QES sample.

The results of adding these measures to the earnings regressions are shown in columns (ii) and (iv) of table 3 and columns (iii) and (vi) of table 12.4. Other than wage premia for both short and tall women in the QAL and a penalty for short men in the QES, none of these variables has a coefficient that exceeds its standard error. Most important, including these measures of body type has only a small effect on the coefficients on the ratings of beauty in all four samples – much too small to suggest that the relationship between looks and earnings arises from correlations between appearance and height or weight.

Table 12.6

Stacked Estimates of the Impact of Looks on Hourly Earnings

Sample	Penalty for below-average looks	Premium for above-average looks	$\hat{\beta}_{above} - \hat{\beta}_{below}$	*p* on *F* statistic for looks
Men:				
All three samples	-0.091 (0.031)	0.053 (0.019)	0.144 (0.040)	0.0001
Two U.S. samples	-0.132 (0.039)	0.036 (0.027)	0.168 (0.051)	0.0003
Women:				
All three samples	-0.054 (0.038)	0.038 (0.022)	0.092 (0.048)	0.042
Two U.S. samples	-0.042 (0.049)	0.075 (0.037)	0.117 (0.069)	0.041
Men and women combined:				
All three samples	-0.072 (0.024)	0.048 (0.015)	0.120 (0.031)	0.0001
Two U.S. samples	-0.092 (0.031)	0.046 (0.022)	0.138 (0.041)	0.0002

Notes: The dependent variable is log(hourly earnings); standard errors are shown in parentheses

The Canadian data allow us to examine the effect of the measurement error associated with using only one rating of the beauty of each respondent. For the subset of respondents included in the bottom part of table 12.1 the study provides three independent estimates of beauty. One approach to using this information would create a set of dummy variables for each of the ten combinations of looks ratings based on the threefold classification for each of the three years. This has difficulties in that it produces a few very sparsely occupied cells and generates a different metric from the other results in Tables 12.3–12.5. An alternative, very simple approach averages the dummy variables for above- and below-average looks for each year. Thus, for example, a person who is rated above-average in all three years would have a value of 1 for the combined dummy variable indicating above-average looks and 0 for the below-average variable; for someone rated below-average in one year and average in the other two, the above-average variable equals 0, while the below-average variable equals one-third.

Columns (iii) and (vii) of table 5 present estimates of the same equations as in columns (i) and (v), but now based on the smaller longitudinal sample. Columns (iv) and (viii) replace the one-year dummy variables with the three-year averages. This substitution adds to the significance of the equations for both men and women. Moreover, all four estimated coefficients increase in absolute value, as we would expect if each year's rating contained some degree of measurement error.[13] Obtaining additional information on a worker's beauty provides additional information about his or her earnings.

12.4.2. Synthesis of the Basic Results, Some Criticisms, and an Initial Interpretation

Tables 12.3–12.5 stand on their own and provide the basic evidence for the existence of earnings differentials based on beauty. Nonetheless, it is useful to summarize the results in order to infer what the three sets of data imply are the best estimates of the penalties and premia associated with looks, especially since the individual sets of data are relatively small.

Table 6 presents these summaries for each gender separately and for the entire set of observations, and for all three samples combined and for the two U.S. samples alone. The estimates are from regressions that pool the samples in tables 12.3–12.5 (or tables 12.3 and 12.4 only) and that allow the coefficients on all variables other than the beauty measures to differ across the samples (i.e., analyses that "stack" the regressions). The last column shows that constraining the estimated effects of beauty on earnings to be the same across samples for men and women separately is not rejected by the data; and for each gender both the earnings penalty and premium are significantly nonzero. Indeed, even constraining the effects to be the same for both genders for all three samples is not rejected; and the penalties and premia in both sets of pooled equations are all significantly nonzero.

The results make it clear that there is a significant penalty for bad looks among men. The 9 percent of working men who are viewed as being below average or homely are penalized about 9 percent in hourly earnings, other things equal. The 32 percent who are viewed as having above-average looks or even as handsome receive an earnings premium of 5 percent. Among women there is some evidence of a premium for good looks, with an average effect of about 4 percent; the penalty for bad looks (for the lowest 8 percent of working women) is 5 percent. Among women, neither effect alone is highly significant, though they are jointly significant. The combined results in the bottom two rows suggest a 7–9-percent penalty for being in the lowest 9 percent of looks among all workers, and a 5-percent premium for being in the top 33 percent. While the absolute values of the point estimates of the penalties generally exceed the estimates of the earnings premia, these differences are not significant. There is only weak evidence of asymmetry in how the labor market treats ugliness and beauty.[14]

The third column in table 12.6 combines the premia and penalties from these stacked regressions to estimate the hourly earnings gain to moving from below- to above-average looks. The estimate of 0.120 for the three samples including both men and women is equivalent to the effects on earnings in these (and most other studies) of an extra 1.5 years of schooling. Viewed differently, moving from average to below-average looks would shift the worker from the median of the distribution of earnings to the 43rd percentile; moving to above-average looks would shift him or her to the 53rd percentile. Clearly, while the impacts on earnings of differences in looks are not so great as those of differences in gender, education, or race, they are not trivial.

No doubt there are unobserved factors that might affect productivity and be correlated with looks. For example, greater attractiveness and higher earnings in adulthood may be joint products of a privileged family background. Only the QAL contains variables that allow us to attempt to control for such effects. If family background in general were important, one would expect these partial indicators of it to have a noticeable effect on the estimates. We saw in the previous subsection that they did not, suggesting that the unobservable background measures are unlikely to be biasing our results seriously.[15] This observation and the robustness of the estimated effects of beauty suggest, though they do not prove, that adding still more variables to the list is not likely to alter our conclusions.

There are also potential simultaneity problems with the results. One might argue that they may merely show that the unobserved determinants of productivity generate extra earnings that are used to improve a worker's beauty. This is the conventional problem associated with any hedonic estimation (i.e., holding constant the observables, people with higher wages will choose to invest more in beauty). Alternatively, perhaps the interviewers in these data sets subconsciously bias their ratings of the respondents' beauty because they know, or can intuit, the respondent's earnings.

Three pieces of evidence suggest that these simultaneity problems are not crucial here. First, the social-psychological evidence we mentioned in section 12.1 showed how little individuals' relative physical appearances change during adulthood. This implies that there is limited scope for using unexplained earnings differences to "buy" differences in beauty. Second, if differences in unexplained earnings were used to affect beauty, their persistence over a working life should lead to a greater simultaneity bias among older workers than among younger workers, and thus smaller apparent penalties and premia if we restrict the samples in tables 12.3–12.5 to workers aged 18–30. In fact, all beauty premia and penalties in the QES are larger in this subsample than in the basic estimates in table 12.3. In the other two samples, half the estimates increase in absolute value, while half decrease. There is no evidence of a weaker relation between earnings and beauty among younger workers.

The third bit of evidence addresses the potential problem of interviewers assigning higher ratings to more prosperous respondents. Using the longitudinal data on which columns (iii) and (iv) and columns (vii) and (viii) of table 12.5 are based, we replace the three-year averages of the dummy variables with averages only of the 1977 and 1979 ratings of beauty. If there is a problem of reverse causation from 1981 earnings, it should be less severe when these instruments for beauty in 1981 are used. The estimates become -0.076 and 0.138 for men, and -0.027 and 0.071 for women. For both genders the $\overline{R}^2$ values increase by

0.001 compared to the estimates in columns (iv) and (viii). This standard simultaneity correction does not alter our basic results.[16]

All of these tests reinforce the conclusion that, whatever the causes, people who are better-looking receive higher pay, while bad-looking people earn less than average, other things equal. It is crucial to stress that these penalties and premia reflect the effects of beauty in all its aspects, not merely one of its many components, such as facial structure, bearing, height, weight, or complexion.

12.5. The Absence of Differences by Gender

Particularly surprising in light of some popular discussion (e.g., Wolf, 1991) is the absence of significantly larger penalties and premia, especially the latter, for women than for men. If anything, the evidence goes in the opposite direction: men's looks may have slightly larger effects on their earnings than do women's. One simple explanation might be that our results are a statistical artifact produced because the beauty ratings are a noisier signal of women's physical appearance than of men's. The evidence contradicts this: in the longitudinal part of the QOL the beauty ratings of women are slightly *less* variable over the three years than those of men.

One way that beauty can affect women's labor market success is by influencing their labor force participation. To examine this possibility we estimate probits relating participation to measures of attractiveness for married women in both the QAL and the QOL, and in the longitudinal subsample of the QOL. The coefficients on the beauty measures are shown for the QAL in column (i) and for the QOL in columns (ii)-(iv) of table 12.7. Except when we use the three-year average ratings of beauty in the QOL, the *t*-statistics on the above-average looks ratings are tiny, and the coefficients are always nearly zero. There is only very weak evidence that good-looking women are more likely to be in the labor force than otherwise identical average-looking women.

The effects of below-average looks on women's participation are negative (though insignificantly so) in the QAL; and in the QOL these effects are significantly negative when the current rating of beauty is used (and insignificantly negative when we use the three-year average). The effects are not small. In the QAL the 6 percent of married women with below-average looks are 3-percent less likely to participate than are above-average-looking women. In the QOL the difference in participation rate is 8 per-cent based on the estimates in column (iii) and 11 percent based on the estimates in column (iv) (again illustrating how using several years of ratings of beauty reduces potential downward biases arising from measurement error).[17]

Table 12.7

The Impact of Looks on Married Women's Labor Force Participation (QAL, 1971; QOL, 1981) and on Husband's Education (QES, 1977)

	Probits of participation				Regression of husband's education, QES
	QAL	QOL			
Variable	(i)	(ii)	(iii)	(iv)	(v)
Looks below average:					
1971 (or 1981 or 1977)	-0.168 (0.176)	-0.168 (0.176)	-0.429 (0.245)		*-1.043* (0.369)
Average of 3 years in the QOL				-0.206 (0.318)	
Looks above average:					
1971 (or 1981 or 1977)	-0.034 (0.131)	-0.010 (0.078)	0.020 (0.115)		0.077 (0.308)
Average of 3 years in the QOL				0.245 (0.169)	
Pseudo-$\bar{R}^2$ or $\bar{R}^2$	0.148	0.067	0.082	0.082	0.402
Mean of dependent variable:	0.401	0.524	0.514	0.514	12.63
N:	583	1,287	603	603	199

Notes: Numbers in parentheses are standard errors. In the QAL, the dependent variable equals 1 if the women was employed at the time of the interview. In the QOL, it is whether she stated she was in the labor force on the interview date. Also included in the probits in both samples are indicator variables measuring educational attainment, health status, and age. In the probits based on the QAL, indicator variables for race and the age of the youngest child are also included, as is a measure of family income less the woman's income. In probits based on the QOL, indicator variables describing the number of children are included. In the regression on husband's education from the QES, his age and the wife's educational attainment, age, and health status are also included in the regression.

There is thus some evidence that women select themselves out of the labor force if they are particularly unattractive. However, this selectivity has no important impact on the basic estimates of the effects of looks on earnings (in column (iv) of table 12.4 and column (v) of table 12.5). Correcting for selectivity in the QAL changes the estimated premium associated with above-average looks from 0.128 to 0.130. Accounting for this form of selectivity does not alter the premium in the QOL and changes the earnings penalty from -0.058 to -0.036.

Another possibility is that looks affect women's economic success by altering their opportunities for marriage. Holding constant a woman's age and educational attainment, in all three samples her looks are completely unrelated to her likelihood of being married. They are, however, related to the quality of the husband whom she marries. We use data on husband's education in the QES to estimate regressions that include our standard pair of measures of looks of the married woman (and also her husband's age and her health status, age, and education, to account for assortative mating).[18]

The results, presented in column (v) of table 12.7, also show that above-average looks have essentially no effect on the outcome, in this case on the quality of the husband to whom the woman is matched. However, all else equal, below-average-looking women marry men whose educational attainment is one year less than what the women's own characteristics, including her educational attainment, predict.[19] Women face an additional economic penalty for bad looks in the form of marriage to husbands whose potential earnings abilities are lower.

The results show that the economic penalties facing below-average-looking women are not limited to hourly earnings. Both their success in the marriage market and their likelihood of working outside the home are reduced by their bad looks. No such effects exist for below-average-looking men; and there is no apparent premium in the marriage market or extra effect on participation for either good-looking women or men.

12.6. Sorting, Productivity or Discrimination?

Having demonstrated that the labor market does reward beauty, we now consider the sources of the penalties and premia. The discussion in section 12.2 suggested that to examine these issues we must learn how workers are sorted into occupations and discover how the earnings regressions of tables 12.3–12.5 are affected when the model in (1) is estimated.

A test for sorting requires prior determination of the occupations where looks are likely to enhance productivity. In the absence of a widely accepted objective measure for determining this, we use three independent subjective methods. The first is based on the *Dictionary of Occupational Titles* (DOT) (1977). We assign each worker to a DOT occupation using three-digit occupational codes in both the QES and the QAL and note the DOT measure of "the job's relationship to people." Since physical attractiveness can affect productivity through the worker's interactions with customers or coworkers, we classify jobs with DOT measures that suggest an important role for interpersonal communication as ones where looks are important.[20]

The second method relies on the opinions of eight adults with at least one year of full-time labor market experience who were asked to rate each of the three-digit occupations on a three-point scale: 0, looks are probably not important; 1, looks might be important; and 2, looks are definitely important.[21] If the average rating of the occupation exceeds 0.5, we treat looks as being important in the occupation and form a dummy variable reflecting this average of the subjective ratings.

The third measure uses a survey (Holzer, 1993) of employers' views of the importance of an applicant's appearance in filling the most recent job vacancy. The vacancy's occupational category was also recorded, as was the gender of the applicant hired. We first divided the survey data on the basis of the gender of the worker hired, then compiled for each gender a list of occupations that seemed fairly homogeneous with respect to the importance of appearance and for which there were at least ten observations. For each occupation/gender cell we calculated the percentage of employers responding that appearance was very important or somewhat important and matched these percentages, where possible, to workers from the QES and the QAL.[22]

To split the samples roughly in half, for men we define an occupation as one with "looks important" if more than 40 percent of the employers responded that appearance was important; for women the dividing line is 44 percent. In general, occupations with higher percentages have more contact between workers and customers: sales occupations top the list for men; for women looks are deemed most important in hiring cashiers, receptionists, and waitresses.[23]

If workers sort themselves among occupations/employers based in part on the relative productivity of their beauty, we should observe the highest average rating of individuals' looks in those occupations where our indexes suggest that looks matter most. Table 12.8 presents the fractions of workers in each of the three categories of individuals' looks who work in occupations where looks are important. With three rating schemes for the occupations, two samples, and both genders, we have constructed 12 tests for occupational sorting. Formal tests for sorting yield significant chi-square statistics in only four of the 12 rows. A good way to summarize the results is that all three rating schemes yield a significant relationship between our measures of the importance of beauty in an occupation and the beauty of workers in that occupation in the QAL, but not in the QES. However, in seven of the 12 rows the percentage of workers in jobs where looks are important increases monotonically along the scale of individuals' looks. More important, in ten of them, above-average-looking people are the most likely to be working in occupations where looks are important.

Table 12.8

Occupational Sorting: Percentage of Sample in Occupations with Looks Important

	Own Looks					
	Below average	Average	Above average	Total	X^2	*N*
QES, men:						
DOT	62.6	63.5	64.7	63.7	0.14	700
Subjective	13.2	13.3	11.1	12.7	0.65	700
Employers	46.5	52.2	44.3	49.3	2.14	428
QES, women:						
DOT	76.4	76.2	80.9	77.8	1.16	409
Subjective	21.8	26.2	28.7	26.4	0.96	409
Employers	45.9	45.2	47.1	45.9	0.10	309
QAL, men:						
DOT	40.0	55.6	64.5	56.9	9.00	476
Subjective	17.8	12.9	22.4	16.4	6.50	476
Employers	33.3	61.2	63.3	59.3	7.48	268
QAL, women:						
DOT	67.4	73.9	81.1	75.6	3.61	307
Subjective	34.9	35.3	40.5	37.1	0.87	307
Employers	44.1	44.5	62.6	51.1	8.30	270

Notes: Critical $\chi^2_{[2]}$ values are 5.99 (5-percent level of significance) and 4.60 (10-percent level).

The results in table 12.8 provide some evidence of sorting across occupations by beauty, but it is certainly not strong enough to suggest that occupational crowding is a major factor explaining the looks differential in earnings. It is unclear whether the weakness of the evidence is due to imperfections in our proxies for differences in the importance of beauty among occupations or to the relatively minor role that sorting by beauty plays.

Following (1), we augment the earnings regressions of tables 12.3 and 12.4 with a dummy variable signifying whether or not looks are important in an occupation and with interactions between this variable and the two dummy variables indicating the individual's own looks. As in table 12.8, we base the results on all three measures of occupational beauty. An attempt to capture the spirit of occupational crowding would predict that the occupational dummy variable will have a significant coefficient. A model based on the productivity of beauty in certain occupations implies that the interaction terms will capture the looks differential. The employer-discrimination model predicts that coefficients on all of these additional terms will equal zero, but that individuals' own beauty will affect their wages regardless of occupation.

Table 12.9

Sorting, Looks and the Determination of Earnings: QES, 1977; QAL, 1971

Sample and occupation index	Looks below average	Looks below average x occupation index	Looks above average	Looks above average x occupation index	Occupation index	$\bar{R}^2$
QES, men:						
DOT	-0.177	-0.036	0.041	0.072	0.052	0.405
	(0.058)	(0.095)	(0.042)	(0.069)	(0.041)	
Subjective	-0.162	0.007	0.012	0.051	0.124	0.405
	(0.049)	(0.127)	(0.035)	(0.097)	(0.072)	
Employers	-0.187	-0.112	-0.095	0.103	-0.066	0.410
	(0.076)	(0.107)	(0.057)	(0.084)	(0.049)	
QES, women:						
DOT	-0.174	-0.218	0.023	-0.068	0.032	0.329
	(0.075)	(0.157)	(0.054)	(0.119)	(0.085)	
Subjective	-0.115	-0.037	0.050	-0.036	0.083	0.326
	(0.074)	(0.151)	(0.055)	(0.096)	(0.093)	
Employers	-0.078	-0.013	0.152	-0.312	0.216	0.315
	(0.107)	(0.158)	(0.076)	(0.111)	(0.077)	
QAL, men:						
DOT	-0.102	-0.057	0.070	0.011	0.093	0.373
	(0.107)	(0.142)	(0.056)	(0.089)	(0.055)	
Subjective	-0.097	0.078	0.045	0.089	0.085	0.371
	(0.076)	(0.177)	(0.048)	(0.099)	(0.102)	
Employers	0.145	-0.107	0.124	-0.072	-0.006	0.213
	(0.150)	(0.250)	(0.121)	(0.152)	(0.095)	
QAL, women:						
DOT	0.049	-0.056	0.166	0.175	-0.066	0.282
	(0.088)	(0.159)	(0.063)	(0.130)	(0.088)	
Subjective	0.130	-0.172	O.D75	0.142	-0.053	0.287
	(0.090)	(0.152)	(0.068)	(0.099)	(0.099)	
Employers	0.253	-0.304	0.261	-0.355	0.218	0.272
	(0.153)	(0.229)	(0.127)	(0.162)	(0.117)	

Notes: The dependent variable is log(hourly earnings); standard errors are shown in parentheses. Each regression includes the same additional variables as in the corresponding regression in table 12.3 or 12.4. Those using the occupational indexes based on the DOT and subjective measures also use the same samples. Those using the survey of employers are based on smaller samples: N = 428, 309, 265, and 259.

The results of this test are shown in table 12.9, which presents equations analogous to those in columns (i) and (iii) of table 12.3 (columns (i) and (iv) of table 12.4). For the DOT and subjective measures, the samples are identical to those used in tables 12.3 and 12.4. The coefficients on the main effects representing the respondents' own beauty are not greatly different from what they were in those tables; and the p values on the F statistics testing the pair of variables also differ little from the corresponding estimates in those tables. Even holding constant occupational beauty, below-average-looking workers receive substantial penalties (except, as before, for women in the QAL), and above-average-looking workers receive earnings premia (especially women in the QAL). In the samples using the employer-based estimates of occupational looks, which contain roughly 40-percent fewer observations, the effects of the workers' own looks are significant at least at a low level in three of the four cases.

The main effects of occupational looks exceed their standard errors in six of the 12 equations. The coefficients on the interaction terms exceed their standard errors in ten of the 24 cases. The $\overline{R}^2$ values here are higher for the QES men, lower for the QES women, and higher in one case, lower in the other for both QAL samples than in tables 12.3 and 12.4, while in the reduced samples using the employer-based indexes the $\overline{R}^2$ values are increased in three of the four cases.[24] Taken together, the estimates provide a hint that occupational requirements for beauty may produce independent effects on earnings; but we cannot reject the possibility that they have no effect.

This final exercise demonstrates one thing very clearly: the effects of an individual's own looks on his or her earnings are very robust. That there are earnings premia and penalties for looks independent of occupation suggests that employer discrimination on the basis of looks may lie behind those premia and penalties. That there is some evidence of sorting implies that pure employer discrimination alone does not describe the role of beauty in the labor market; beauty may be productive in some occupations perhaps as a result of customers' preferences.

12.7. Conclusions and Implications

In separate empirical analyses using three sets of household data, we find some evidence of a positive impact of workers' looks on their earnings. The evidence in each sample alone is suggestive but not very strong. When the three samples are combined, however, sample sizes become sufficient to make some fairly clear inferences about the role of beauty in the labor market. Other things equal, wages of people with below-average looks are lower than those of average-looking workers; and there is a premium in wages for good-looking people that is slightly smaller than this penalty. The penalty and premium may be higher for men, but these gender differences are not large. There is also some evidence that the labor market sorts the best-looking people into occupations where their looks are productive.

It is difficult to disentangle the effects of alternative sources of earnings differentials in the data. Nonetheless, our finding that earnings penalties and premia are essentially unaffected when we account for workers' occupations suggests no support for a model of occupational crowding along the dimension of beauty. That there is some occupational sorting by looks provides support for productivity-related discrimination; but the evidence is fairly weak. A related explanation, that there are inherent productivity differences that we do not capture because of omitted variables, cannot be ruled out, though there is some evidence against it. The strongest support is for pure Becker-type discrimination based on beauty and stemming from employer/employee tastes. More light could be shed on these questions by comparative examinations of the relationship between looks and earnings within particular narrowly defined occupations.

Our demonstration shows the magnitude of the incentives that the labor market in North America provides to expend resources on beauty and the mechanisms by which those incentives arise. Whether the same incentives exist in other economies is an obvious topic of interest. The results also lead naturally to further examination of the sources of wage differentials and possible discrimination along various other dimensions, such as physical and mental handicaps. In each case, the method we have developed to aid in distinguishing between productivity/discrimination and occupational sorting can be applied mutatis mutandis to discover the source of other apparently discriminatory outcomes.

13

Tall or Taller, Pretty or Prettier: Is Discrimination Absolute or Relative?

13.1. Introduction

The literature on the economics of discrimination is immense, going back at least to Becker (1957). While research in the area has mostly been empirical - concerned with measuring the ceteris paribus impact of an ascriptive characteristic on some economic outcome, often earnings or wages, a small theoretical literature has made additional fundamental contributions (see the summaries by Cain 1986; Altonji and Blank 1999). With only one exception (Fryer and Jackson 2008), however, the theoretical literature appears to have been unconcerned about how agents form their views of the characteristic against which they discriminate - how they organize their impressions of the characteristic that in turn affect their treatment of members of other groups. The lack of concern with this question in the empirical literature seems to have been complete.

That the question is generally important seems clear. How do wage differences respond to differences in height in the work force, if new cohorts of workers are taller than their predecessors? How would earnings differentials that arise from differences in workers' beauty be altered if workers generally became better-looking? How does the impact of looks on electoral success change if the distribution of candidates' looks changes? Persico et al. (2004), Case and Paxson (2008), Hamer-

---

The original version of this chapter was published as: Hamermesh, Daniel S. (2012). Tall or Taller, Pretty or Prettier: Is Discrimination Absolute or Relative, in: IZA Journal of Labor Economics, 1:2. © 2012 by Springer.

mesh and Biddle (1994), Möbius and Rosenblat (2006), Benjamin and Shapiro (2009) and Berggren et al. (2010) have studied the market responses of these outcomes to differences in the characteristics. None of these studies, nor any other, has considered the general question of how perceptions of the characteristic affect the outcome. With Americans, and especially northern Europeans, becoming taller, the treatment of height as an earnings-enhancing labor market characteristic may change. To the extent that the distribution of looks is changeable by an increasingly affluent and beauty-obsessed public, how those possible changes would affect the returns to beauty is also important.

In this study, I examine these issues on a number of data sets covering several different characteristics and outcomes, with the data coming from the United States and the Netherlands. In several cases I run a "horse race" between models specifying the characteristic as absolute and those specifying it as relative - in percentiles. Where possible, I estimate the kernel density of the characteristic and use kernel estimation to obtain a nonparametric representation of its impact on the outcome, thus obviating spurious results that might arise from the imposition of a particular functional form on the relationship.

This approach seems to be a sensible way of introducing the empirical examination of how perceptions of differences in ascriptive characteristics affect what we view as discriminatory outcomes. No doubt there are other methods of doing so. Whether there is a general answer - a consistent way in which agents form the perceptions that affect how a characteristic alters labor and other market outcomes - is not clear. But by examining several characteristics in a variety of contexts I may be able to shed a bit of light on how perceptions of differences in characteristics (in the empirical examples here, in beauty and in height) affect outcomes that have previously been examined without attention to the nature of the apparent discrimination.

13.2. Modeling the Nature of Responses to Personal Characteristics

In this section I describe the questions of interest generally to provide a guide for future studies, illustrating the general points with the examples I use in subsequent sections. Given a general statistical relationship between some characteristic $X \sim f(X)$ and an outcome Y as:

$$Y = g(X), \tag{1}$$

where I ignore the error term and any conditioning variables in a vector *Z* that might also affect *Y*. In many of the examples here *X* is a measure of beauty that affects some outcome whose desirability increases in *Y*, for example, the likelihood of electoral success. Throughout I assume that *X* is solely ascriptive and that the response of *Y* to it reflects discrimination. I do not inquire (and, indeed, the literature only very rarely considers) whether the response of *Y* to *X* reflects market discrimination or the productivity-enhancing effects of *X*. I follow the literature and assume the former.

The focus throughout is on $\partial Y/\partial X$ and how it changes in response to changes in *f(X)*. In particular, I first examine:

$$\partial(\partial Y/\partial X)/\partial\sigma_X|\mu_X, \tag{2}$$

that is, how the responsiveness of *Y* to changes in *X* is altered when there is a mean-preserving spread in *X*. All of the examinations of this phenomenon relate to beauty. In them, the question is how an outcome responds when there is more dispersion in people's looks, e.g., when the spread between the looks of people at the 90th and 10th percentiles of looks widens. The world does not appear to have generated any exogenous shocks on which we can obtain data that would allow examining such changes directly. I thus need to formulate proxies for the shock in *(2)* that can capture the change.

One way to do this is to note that one could estimate a linear (or log-linear) specification of *(1)* to obtain $(\partial Y/\partial X)$, as is standard practice. If a mean-preserving spread in *X* leaves $\partial Y/\partial X$ unchanged, a re-specification of *(1)* with *X* defined as *C(X)*, the centiles of *X*, would be an inferior description of *g(X)* compared to the linear (or log-linear) specification. In other words, does the relationship *g(X)* describe the responses of *Y* to absolute changes in *X* or to changes in an agent's rank in the distribution of *X*? Taking the beauty example again, I am thus asking whether beauty is better characterized by some absolute scale or by rank in the distribution of beauty. In the empirical sections, absent the desired exogenous shocks to *f(X)*, I follow this approach to infer the shape of *(2)*.

The second issue is the estimation of:

$$\partial(\partial Y/\partial X)/\partial\mu_X|\sigma_X, \tag{3}$$

that is, how the responsiveness of *Y* to *X* changes when there is a variance-preserving increase in the mean of *X*. Using the beauty example, one of two that I use to examine this issue, the question is equivalent to asking whether a given absolute difference in people's looks affects some outcome equally if the average person is bad-looking, average-looking or good-looking. In the case of height, the issue is whether an increase in average height in a population alters the responsiveness of some outcome (earnings is the example here) to absolute differences in height. In this case there are three examples in which shocks unrelated to Y generated such changes. It is a simple matter either to compare estimates of *(1)* obtained from times when μX differs or to examine *(1)* in the presence of simultaneous exogenous shocks to μX across groups.

The difficulty with this entire approach is that *g(X)* may not be linear, not based on centiles or any other simple transformation of *X*, but may instead be some high-powered, non-monotonic and perhaps even discontinuous function of *X*. In the example of beauty, one needs to distinguish between inherently highly nonlinear responses of outcomes to differences in beauty and apparently nonlinear responses that arise because relative differences in looks matter more than absolute differences. While I cannot solve this difficulty generally, in some of the examples the distribution of *X* has sufficient support to allow kernel estimation of *g(X)* and thus to enable me to examine these potential problems.

13.3. The Impact of Changing Variance of a Characteristic

In this section I examine how changes in the distribution of beauty affect the impacts of looks on the success of fund-raisers for a charity, on retention as a participant in a television game show and on electoral success in a professional organization. All three independent examples suggest that absolute differences in looks have bigger effects on outcomes than do relative differences. The superior "performance" of absolute differences is not always large, but taken together the results indicate that future research on the impact of discriminatory tastes should at least proceed from the assumption that discriminating agents care more about absolute than about relative differences in the characteristic against which they discriminate.

13.3.1. The Beauty of Charitable Solicitors

Landry et al. (2006) conducted a field experiment in which solicitors for a charity went door-to-door seeking funds, with different treatments applied randomly to potential target households. As part of the experiment the impacts of solicitors' characteristics, including their physical attractiveness, BMI and personality traits, were also assessed (separately, not by those being solicited). In their published study the authors estimated linear regressions over all the households surveyed, of which over two-thirds contributed nothing. Here I estimate probits describing whether or not a household contributed, then tobits describing that and the amount donated. In the first set of estimated equations I use exactly the same variables as Landry et al., a vector that includes solicitors' beauty as evaluated by ten raters whose assessments were normalized and then averaged. (Thus the mean beauty was 0.06, the standard deviation 0.61[1].) In the second set of estimates I replace each male solicitor's beauty by his percentile in the distribution of male solicitors' looks, and similarly for the female solicitors.

Table 13.1

Charitable donations, field experiment, probit and tobit estimates, $N = 1{,}754^{a}$

	Contribute?		Contributed Amount	
Beauty:				
Absolute:				
Male Beauty	-0.0263		-0.6005	
	(0.042)		(0.936)	
Female Beauty	0.1353		2.6563	
	(0.034)		(0.789)	
Rank:				
Male Beauty/100		-0.0739		-1.6554
		(0.076)		(1.838)
Female Beauty/100		0.2748		5.3858
		(0.070)		(1.599)
Pseudo-R^2	0.0765	0.0760	0.0227	0.0225

[a] The data are from Landry et al. (2006). All equations include as controls a vector of attidudinal variables, indicators of the arm of the experiment and indicators for whether the solicitor was overweight or obese. Standard errors in parentheses below the parameter estimates are clustered on solicitor identification numbers.

Table 13.1 presents the estimates of the two sets of equations, with Columns *(1)* and *(3)* containing the estimates that follow Landry et al. by including absolute beauty measures, Columns *(2)* and *(4)* reporting the results with the beauty variables re-specified as percentiles in the distribution of own-sex beauty. The probit estimates present derivatives showing the impacts of one-unit increases in the independent variables. The estimated standard errors are clustered on the solicitors' identification numbers. As in the original study, male beauty has negative, but quite insignificant effects, while female beauty has significant and quite large positive impacts[2]. (E.g., a two-standard deviation increase in female beauty from the mean in this sample raises the probability that a household contributes to the charity from 0.30 to 0.46.) The explanatory power of the equations containing the absolute measures of beauty exceeds that of the equations containing percentiles, although the differences are small. In this example using market-wide data there is some weak evidence that the absolute effects of the relevant characteristic dominate its relative impacts.

13.3.2. Beauty in a Dutch Game Show, 2002

Belot et al. (2012) describe a television game show in which groups of five people answer questions posed by the quizmaster. At the end of the first round of questions the contestant who earned the most points selects one of the other four group members for expulsion from the group (and from further participation in the show). Belot et al. demonstrate that, holding "productivity" (questions answered) constant, those contestants who were rated (on a 7 down to 1 scale, averaged over ten raters) as being worse-looking were more likely to be expelled. Using these data we can analyze whether the likelihood of expulsion in this round of five players was greater if being relatively worse-looking had the same effect on the probability of expulsion regardless of absolute differences in looks among the players.

The first column in table 13.2 shows the average absolute rating of the beauty of contestants who did not "win" in the first round of the game and were thus eligible for expulsion. The average beauty ratings of these players ranged from 5.73 down to 1.70 on the seven-point scale. Since productivity and/or the "winner's" preferences for expelling other players may depend on characteristics other than beauty, I control for each player's score in the round of questions, a quadratic in the player's age, and an indicator of gender. Column (2) of this table lists conditional logit estimates of the impact of a one-unit increase in the absolute beauty rating on the probability of expulsion. Column *(3)* shows the estimated impact of moving up one in the ranking of beauty among the four "losers" in the round.

There is a substantial difference in the explanatory power of the absolute as opposed to the relative differences in the "losing" contestants' looks on their likelihood of expulsion. The pseudo-R^2 is noticeably higher in the conditional logits based on the specification of differences in beauty as absolute. Column *(4)* presents estimates with both measures (and the controls) included. A likelihood-ratio test comparing this to the conditional logit in Column *(2)* yields $\chi^2(1)=0.62$ $(p=0.43)$; the same test compared to the estimates in Column (3) yields $\chi^2(1)=2.66$ $(p=0.10)$. Although not highly significant statistically, the estimates clearly show that the "losers'" absolute beauty, not their standing in a ranking of beauty, determines how the "winner" of a round in this game treats them.

Table 13.2

Descriptive statistics and conditional logit estimates, Dutch game show, $N=276$ (dependent variable is "sent away")*

	Mean Std. Dev. Range	Parameter estimates		
Beauty				
Absolute	3.52	-0.4911		-0.8525
	(0.69)	(0.2551)		(0.5343)
	[1.70, 5.73]		-0.1346	0.1627
Rank in round	2.50		(0.1002)	(0.2082)
	(1.42)			
Pseudo R^2		0.1678	0.1571	0.1710

* The conditional logits include as controls a vector showing the rank of the person's score in the round, a quadratic in age and an indicator for gender. Standard errors in parentheses below the parameter estimates here and in tables 13.3, 13.5 and 13.6.

Figure 13.1 shows the kernel density of the average beauty ratings of the "losing" contestants in the first round of the game, and Figure 13.2 presents the kernel estimates of its effects on the probability of expulsion. The density is slightly right-skewed, due entirely, as the points in Figure 13.2 show, to the presence of one outlier whose beauty was one standard deviation above that of the second best-looking among the 276 "losing" contestants. That this outlier contestant was expelled from the show explains the strange upturn in the expulsion beauty kernel estimate in Figure 13.2. Ignoring this individual, the kernel estimate implies an especially large penalty to being very bad-looking, so that it is unsurprising that absolute differences in looks describe the relationship better than relative differences.

13.3.3. Economists' Beauty and AEA Elections, 1966–2004

Another example that allows examining the roles of absolute position and rank in the distribution of a characteristic is provided by the data collected and analyzed by Hamermesh (2006). The looks of each candidate in the 78 elections for office (vice-presidents and members of the Executive Committee) in the American Economic Association that were held from 1966 to 2004 were rated by a panel of four incoming economics graduate students, with the average for each rater normalized and then averaged across the four raters. In each four-person election the two candidates obtaining the most votes from the Association's membership won the election. Since candidates' pictures were mailed out with the ballots, the voters at least had the opportunity to choose (discriminate?) on the basis of the candidates' looks. The question is whether they did, and whether any impact of looks worked through the candidate being among the better-looking of the four in his/her election, or whether the absolute extent of differences among the candidates' looks is what mattered for voters' electoral choices.

Column *(1)* in table 13.3 shows the mean, standard deviation and range of the average ratings of each candidate. That the range of the average beauty ratings is large shows that the raters were able to make fairly sharp distinctions among the candidates' looks. Figure 13.3 presents the kernel density of the distribution of the average ratings and suggests that the distribution of the averages (of the four standardized ratings) has an extended right tail.

As in the previous subsection, Column *(2)* of the table shows the conditional logit estimates of the impact of a one standard-deviation increase in absolute beauty, in this case on the probability of winning the election; Column *(3)* shows the estimated impact of a one-unit increase in the rank of the beauty distribution in the election; and Column *(4)* includes both of these variables. Also contained in each equation is a set of controls including, most importantly, the candidate's rank in scholarly productivity among the candidates (measured by lifetime citations in the *Social Science Citation Index* up to the election year), an indicator of gender and whether the candidate had previously held or currently holds high public office[3].

Figure 13.1

Kernel of beauty density, Dutch game show, 2002

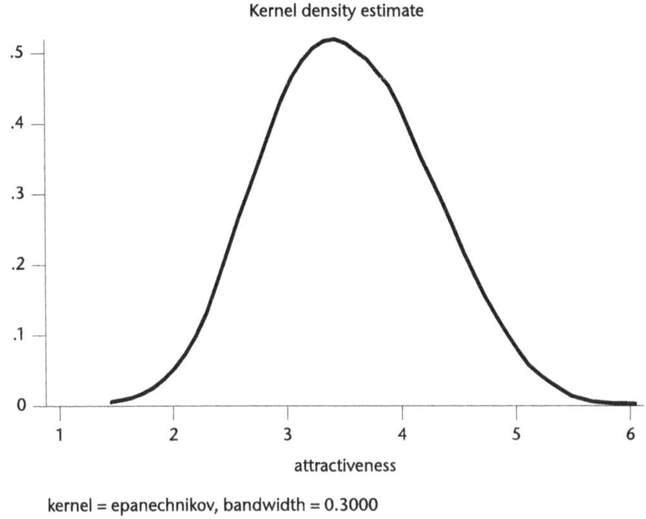

Figure 13.2

Kernel estimation of the effect of beauty on expulsion probability, Dutch game show, 2002

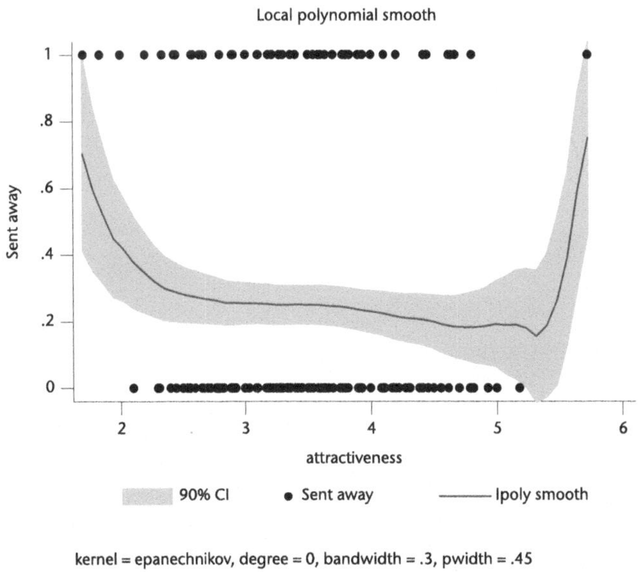

Table 13.3

Descriptive statistics and conditional logit estimates, AEA elections, $N=312$ (dependent variable is "elected")[a]

	Mean / Std. Dev. / Range	Parameter estimates		
Beauty				
Absolute	0.00 (0.71) [-1.80,2.71]	0.3623 (0.2043)		0.5300 (0.4184)
Rank in round	2.50 (1.12)		0.1385 (0.1038)	-0.0981 (0.2123)
Pseudo R^2		0.1846	0.1795	0.1853

a The conditional logits include as controls a quadratic in the candidate's lifetime citations up through the year before the election, and indicators for gender, whether the person had previously held a high-level government position, was in a Top 5 economics department, was not an academic, was African-American or had won a Nobel Prize.

Figure 13.3

Kernel of beauty density, AEA elections, 1966–2004

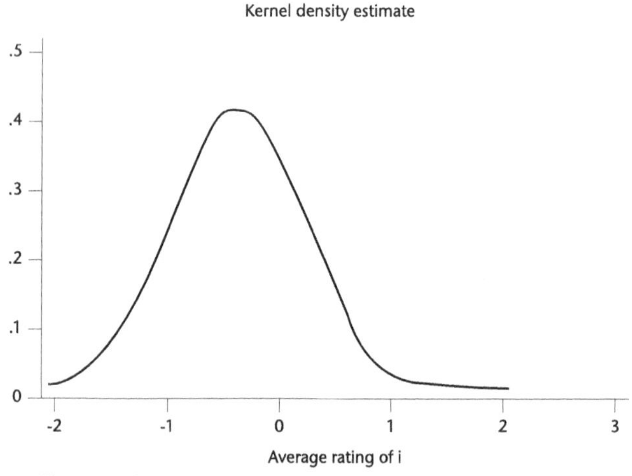

The results are qualitatively remarkably similar to those in the previous subsection. Again the specification of beauty as absolute describes the outcome better than does the candidate's position in the ranking of beauty. The differences are not, however, as large as in the previous example. A likelihood-ratio test comparing the conditional logit in Column *(4)* to the estimates in Column *(2)* yields $\chi^2(1)=0.21$ *(p=0.64)*; the same test compared to the estimates in Column *(3)* yields $\chi^2(1)=1.64$ *(p=0.20)*.

That the results indicate that voters respond to absolute differences in the candidates' looks is also suggested by the kernel estimates shown in Figure 13.4. The response is monotonically increasing over the entire range of the average beauty ratings. It is especially strong, however, as a response to increases in beauty as one approaches the upper tail of looks. This result suggests that here too, and more generally than is possible in the conditional logits, absolute beauty rather than relative position in the distribution of looks determined the outcome.

13.4. The Impact of a Variance-Preserving Increase in a Characteristic's Mean

In this section I examine three natural experiments that allow inferring the impact of an increase in the average of some characteristic that occurs without any change in its variance. I use these to examine whether and how the agents' treatment changes in order to estimate the cross-partial derivative in *(3)*. The first experiment – a change in height in a population – occurred naturally over a period of several decades. The other two – differences in average beauty across small groups of people – were generated by apparently random mixing of the individuals to form those groups. Unlike the previous section, where the examples gave consistent answers to the question, here the results are more mixed.

13.4.1. The Increasing Height of Dutch Men, 1981–2010

Two striking facts stand out about international differences in the distributions of human heights over time: 1) By the middle of the 20th century American males were the tallest in the world; 2) In the early 21st century Dutch males are the world's tallest; and American men have fallen (actually, gained only very slightly in height) far behind their counterparts in most northern European countries[4]. To examine how this striking change altered the relation between earnings and height in the labor market we use two Dutch data sets that allow us to study this question. The focus on the Netherlands is due to the availability of data and to the unusually large and rapid shift in the distribution of heights that occurred there[5].

Figure 13.4

Kernel estimation of the effect of beauty on win probability, AEA elections, 1966–2004

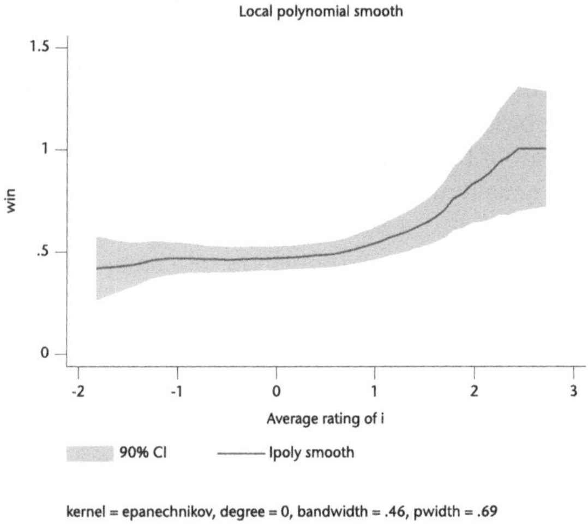

Table 13.4

Descriptive statistics, Dutch household data, men's height (in centimeters), 1981–82 – 2006–2010*

	POLS 1981–82	POLS 1995–96	DNB 1995	DNB 2006–10
Mean	177.92	180.72	181.40	182.30
Std. Dev.	(7.61)	(7.62)	(7.17)	(7.17)
Range	150, 205]	[155, 200]	[160, 206]	[159, 206]
N	2017	1926	1339	872

* Includes only men who are at least 150cm tall and ages 25–59

The Dutch data are from 1981-82, 1995-96, and 2006-10 from two sources: 1) The POLS (*Permanent Onderzoek Leefsituatie*), a household survey from which data are available beginning in 1981, which continued to collect earnings data through the mid-1990s and which also included anthropometric data. Here I use the first two years of the POLS, 1981–82, which like later years only presented data on height in five centimeter categories. I also merge the 1995 and 1996 POLS data to enlarge the sample for the middle of this nearly thirty-year time period; and 2) The DNB Household Survey, a panel study begun in 1993 and continuing through today. I use data from the 1995 wave, to match the POLS data for that period, and independent observations from the most recent waves of the DNB panel, 2006–10. The samples are restricted to men who are at least 150 cm tall and who are between the ages of 25 and 59 inclusive[6].

Some evidence on the startling change in Dutch men's heights is provided in table 13.4, which presents summary statistics for men 25–59 from the POLS and the DNB for each of the three periods, 1981–82, 1995–96 and 2006–10. Over this period the average heights of men in this age group increased by a highly statistically significant 4.3 cm (1.7 inches), an increase in the median height to what would have been about the 75th percentile of Dutch men's heights in 1981–82. It is also worth noting that the means for the two different samples in the mid-1990s are very similar (although the DNB estimate is statistically significantly above the POLS estimate).

The variances are nearly the same in both POLS samples; they are also identical, but lower, in both DNB samples. It is thus fairly likely that that the variance in men's heights did not increase over this period. Assuming that all the information is correct (and the fact that average heights in both 1990s samples are quite similar is encouraging), comparing the 1981–82 POLS to the 2006–10 DNB we can conclude that the assumption of a constant variance is reasonable[7].

Table 13.5

Regression estimates, Dutch household data, men's height, 1981–82 — 2006–10, (dependent variable is ln(annual earnings))*

	POLS 1981–82	POLS 1995–96	DNB 1995	DNB 2006–10
Height:	0.00269	0.00480	0.00467	0.00179
	(0.00105)	(0.00141)	(0.00272)	(0.00339)
Adj. R^2	0.3084	0.2334	0.1949	0.1078
N	2017	1926	1339	872

* The regressions use sample weights. Covariates include a vector of four indicators of educational attainment, a quadratic in age, and an indicator of marital status. Only men who are at least 150cm tall and ages 25–59 are included.

To examine the earnings-height relationship I estimate log-(annual) earnings regressions, controlling for vectors of indicators of educational attainment, a quadratic in age, and marital status, with the results presented in Table 13.5. The estimates for both samples from the mid-1990s are nearly identical. Also, they are remarkably similar to those for 1981–82 - there was very little change in the earnings-height relationship in the POLS data between the early 1980s and the mid-1990s. As a comparison of the two set of results using the DNB data shows, however, the strong relationship observed in the mid-1990s had become smaller by 2010 (although not significantly so due to the larger standard error on the estimate for 2006–10). The earnings-height elasticity dropped from 0.85 to 0.30 in these data over this period. With a linear specification the evidence suggests that the variance-preserving increase in men's heights in the Netherlands sharply reduced the impact of height on earnings.

Figure 13.5

Kernel of height density, DNB 1995

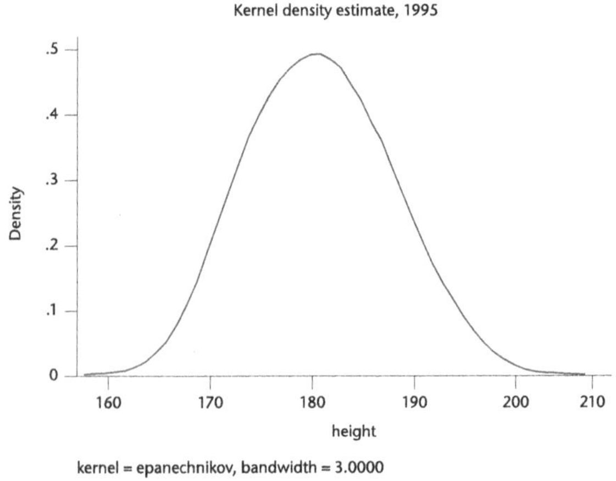

Is the linear specification correct, however? Because information on height was provided in five-centimeter ranges in the POLS data, there are insufficient support points in those data to present meaningful kernel densities and estimates. There are sufficient support points in the DNB data, and Figure 13.5 shows the kernel density of the height measure in the 1995 DNB sample. Comparing it to Figure 13.6, which presents the kernel density for these data for 2006–10, the densities are shaped fairly similarly, with the 2006–10 density shifted rightward, as is also suggested by a comparison of the means and standard deviations in Table 13.4. The kernel estimates of the log-earnings-height relationship for the mid-1990s, shown in Figure 13.7, do not look at all like those shown in Figure 13.8 for 2006–10. In the recent period the relationship rises up to just short of 180 cm – below the mean height, falling thereafter over most of the density in the rest of the range. In the mid-1990s the relationship was increasing much further up the distribution of height.

Figure 13.6

Kernel of height density, DNB 2006–2010

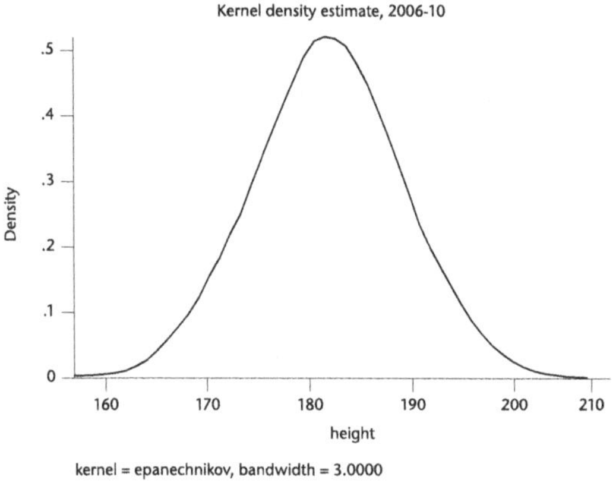

Figure 13.7

Kernel estimation of the effect of height on ln(earnings), DNB 1995

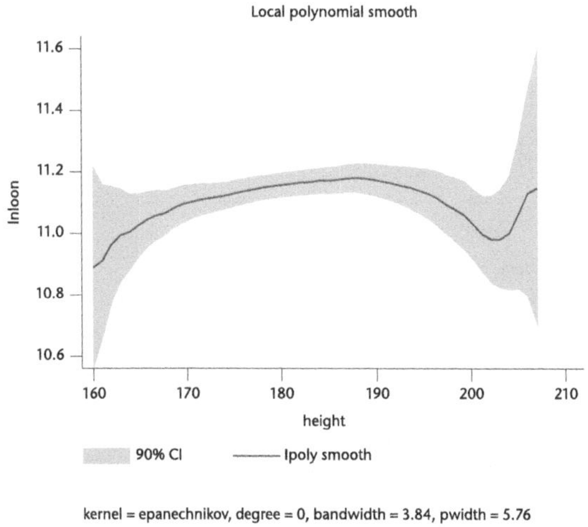

Without any further considerations the results suggest that an increase in the mean of the distribution of this characteristic reduced the cross-partial derivative in *(3)*. It is, however, worth noting that the earnings-height relationship weakened in the most recent sample because it turned flat or even slightly negative at a height slightly above a level that in the early 1980s would have been just above the mean. One explanation for the change might be that in 2006–10 we are observing a market that had not yet adjusted to the long-run equilibrium. It seems likely that employers, presumably those making decisions that led to an earnings-height relationship in 2006–10, were older (and thus shorter) than the average Dutch male ages 25–59. If they did not perceive, or at least did not react to differences in height among potential workers who are substantially taller than they, we would observe an earnings-height relationship shaped exactly like that shown in the kernel estimation shown in Figure 13.8.

Figure 13.8

Kernel estimation of the effect of height on ln(earnings), DNB 2006–10

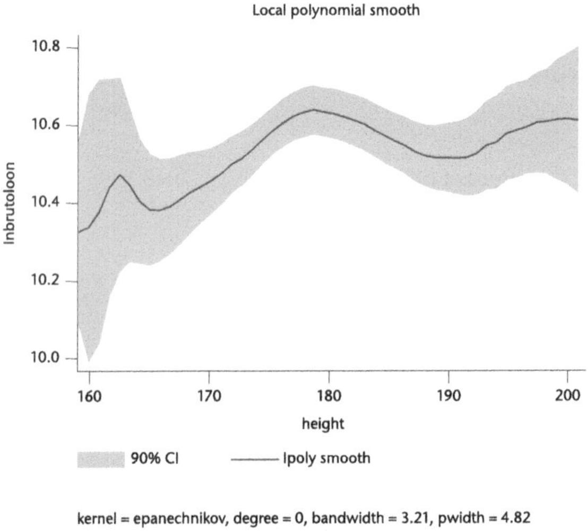

To examine this possibility I separated the 2006–10 DNB sample into half subsamples of workers age 25–42 and ages 43–59 and re-estimated the equation for which results were shown in the last column of Table 13.5. Of course, the men in the sub-sample of older workers are shorter than those in the younger sub-sample (181.05 cm vs. 184.28 cm), and, indeed, the variance is higher in the younger sub-sample. The crucial thing to note is that the parameter estimate of the impact of height on log-earnings in the older sub-sample is 0.0049, nearly identical to the estimates shown in Table 13.5 for the mid-1990s for all men ages 25–59[8]. Among workers in the younger sub-sample the estimated impact of height on log-earnings is –0.0039 in 2006–10. Apparently the market only rewarded the height of older workers, those whose distribution of heights matched more closely that of the people who were likely to have been their employers than did the right-shifted distribution of the heights of younger workers.

Table 13.6

Descriptive statistics and conditional logit estimates, Dutch game show and AEA elections (dependent variable is "sent away" or "elected")*

	Dutch game show		AEA elections	
	Mean / Std. Dev. / Range	Parameter estimates	Mean / Std. Dev. / Range	Parameter estimates
Beauty:				
Own	0.00	−2.8587	0.00	0.3044
	(0.71)	(2.6098)	(0.71)	(0.2097)
	[1.50,5.73]		[−1.79,2.71]	
Average in election	3.50		0.00	
	(0.36)		(0.41)	
	[2.52,4.20]		[−1.01,0.94]	
Interaction:		0.6639		0.2522
Own x Average		(0.7242)		(0.4960)
Pseudo R^2		0.1723		0.1994
N	276		312	

* The conditional logits for the Dutch game show include as controls a vector showing the rank of the person's score in the round, a quadratic in age and an indicator for gender. Those for the AEA elections include as controls the person's share of total citations to the four candidates in the round, and indicators for gender, whether the person had previously held a high-level government position, was in a Top 5 economics department, was not an academic, was African-American or had won a Nobel Prize.

13.4.2. Varying Average Beauty in the Dutch Game Show and the AEA Elections

The winner's decision about whom to "send away" in the Dutch game show and the results of the four-person elections for office in the American Economic Association analyzed in sections 13.2 and 13.3 provide natural experiments for inferring how a one-unit increase in a characteristic, in this case beauty, alters an outcome when the characteristic's mean changes. Columns (1) and (3) of Table 13.6 indicate that there is substantial variation in the average looks of "losing" contestants across games and of candidates across elections. In the game show the range of average looks is nearly five times the standard deviation of the averages, and the range of average looks in the AEA elections is also roughly that relatively large.

I assume that the average looks of participants in an individual game are independent of the outcomes. Indeed, one might imagine that, if anything, the television producers who considered the issue would attempt to keep the averages as close as possible in order to maintain audience interest in the game. That consideration suggests that any inter-game differences in the mean of looks are unplanned. The average looks of candidates in a particular AEA election are almost certainly exogenous: It is difficult to believe that the AEA's Nominating Committee, which selects the candidates, chooses sets of especially good- or bad-looking candidates to match up in a particular election in order to affect the outcome or generate additional voter interest in the process.

I expand the equations whose estimation underlay the results shown in Tables 13.2 and 13.3 to include interactions of the average looks of the candidates in the game or election with the individual participant's or candidate's looks. The focus is on the interaction term – does the impact of a given difference in the looks of candidates change when the average looks in the game or election change.[9] The same controls as before are included, so that only the addition of the interaction terms distinguishes the results of estimating these equations from the results reported in the second columns of Tables 13.2 and 13.3.

As the estimates in Columns (2) and (4) of Table 13.6 show, the impacts of differences in beauty on the probability of being "sent away" are somewhat smaller when the average beauty in a game increases. The interaction term is, however, statistically insignificant (t=0.92). The impact of individual beauty on the probability of election in the AEA is slightly larger when the average candidate is better looking. The change is, however, also quite insignificant statistically (t=0.51) and substantively very minor. The appropriate inference from these results is that, if all the participants' or candidates' beauty increases by the same amount, the impacts of differences in their looks remain unaltered. A change in the mean beauty among the choices facing agents does not change the impact of differences in beauty among those choices.

13.5. Review and Conclusion

The general purpose here has been to introduce the question of how people's perceptions of characteristics against which they discriminate affect the responses of outcomes to differences in the characteristics. We have examined two distinct variations on the usual specifications of models measuring the impacts of personal characteristics that can be viewed as eliciting discriminatory responses by other agents in markets: 1) Whether the responses stem from agents comparing absolute or relative differences in others' characteristics; and 2) Whether changes in the average of a characteristic shared by agents who may be discriminated against affect the responses of the discriminating agents to the remaining differences. I illustrated these general points with examples of personal attractiveness and height. The work is obviously not definitive, but it introduces a question that deserves more consideration in empirical research on discrimination.

The differences between the ability of absolute and relative differences in the characteristic to characterize behavior were not large, but absolute differences in the characteristic consistently described agents' discriminatory responses better than did relative differences. On the second question the results are somewhat more ambiguous. The weak conclusion, however, is that the evidence indicates that responses to remaining differences are not changed when the average of a characteristic increases. In terms of our examples, being equally more attractive than one's competitors enhances positive outcomes by the same amount whether the competitors are bad- or good-looking. Being a few inches taller than other workers has the same positive effect on earnings whether the others are 5'9" or 6'1".

I have shown that, in the context of choices that discriminating agents make between well-defined small sets of individuals among whom they make simultaneous distinctions, i.e., in the studies of the impacts of beauty, the conclusions are unambiguous. The results suggest that the nature of responses to differences in ascriptive characteristics is discernible when we can examine the explicit comparisons that discriminating agents make among those against whom they discriminate. So too, the effects are fairly well determined when the distribution of a characteristic shifts with no change in its variance.

Is there any way to distinguish between the alternatives in these two questions in the more interesting context of labor markets generally rather than in the narrower contexts of charitable solicitations, a game show, elections in a professional organization or the unusually large and rapid increases in height that occurred in one country? Studies based on secondary data describing large national random samples of workers cannot make the required distinctions, as a number of attempts not reported here demonstrate[10]. One possibility would be to construct audit studies in which the characteristics of various lists of job applicants are manipulated to allow inferences about these two issues[11]. Another alternative would be to create laboratory experiments in which groups of agents with appropriately manipulated different characteristics confront other "buying" agents (although the generalizability of any results would be questionable). Yet a third possibility would be econometric case studies of promotion choices (tournaments) in which small numbers of candidates who differ along one of the dimensions analyzed here are included. Overall, given the importance of such characteristics in determining labor market outcomes, it would be worthwhile to understand more about how the structure of perceptions of differences and changes in these characteristics alter individuals' labor market success.

14

Beauty, Productivity and Discrimination: Lawyers' Looks and Lucre

We propose models with an ascriptive characteristic generating earnings differentials and causing sectoral sorting, allowing us to distinguish among sources producing such differentials. We use longitudinal data on a large sample of graduates from one law school and measure beauty by rating matriculation photographs. (1) Better-looking attorneys who graduated in the 1970s earned more than others after 5 years of practice, an effect that grew with experience. (2) Attorneys in the private sector are better-looking than those in the public sector, differences that rise with age. These results support theories of dynamic sorting and customer behavior.

> You could legislate for every kind of discrimination but not this. In everything from jobs to sex the attractive were advantaged, the very plain denigrated and rejected.
>
> (P. D. James, 1995)

14.1. Introduction

Most of the immense empirical literature on discrimination in labor markets has been concerned with the task of measuring earnings gaps (if any) among workers belonging to groups defined on the basis of ascriptive characteristics. This task is complicated by the need to account for differences in productivity. In many studies, especially those con-

The original version of this chapter was published as: Hamermesh, Daniel S./Biddle, Jeff E. (1998). Beauty, Productivity, and Discrimination: Lawyers' Looks and Lucre, in: Journal of Labor Economics, 16(1): 172–201.

centrating on broadly defined groups of workers and based on widely available household surveys, the measures of productivity are disappointingly few given the heterogeneity of the respondents' occupations. Only a handful of studies (e.g., Kahn 1992) makes use of data that are sufficiently detailed to allow the authors to claim that they have purged measured earnings differentials of productivity effects. Having made the measurements, however, empirical studies seldom take the next step of attempting to determine what supports the differentials, although the theoretical literature on discrimination offers a number of possible explanations.[1] There is, then, something of a gap between the theoretical and empirical literatures on labor market discrimination.

In this study, we attempt to bridge that gap while exploring the economic effect of a particular ascriptive characteristic - beauty - that has received almost no attention from economists.[2] Using a rich set of data describing a relatively homogeneous group of workers - graduates of a particular law school - we measure the earnings differential associated with differences in physical attractiveness and then test several hypotheses concerning possible sources of the differential. In the next section, we discuss alternative explanations of wage differentials among workers with different ascriptive characteristics and present a strategy for distinguishing among them empirically. Section 14.3 describes the data used in this study and our method of measuring the characteristic "beauty," while section 14.4 presents evidence of a relationship between beauty and earnings among attorneys. Section 14.5 studies how beauty affects other labor market outcomes for lawyers in an attempt to discover the sources of the beauty/earnings relationship reported in section 14.4.

14.2. Ascriptive Characteristics, Earnings, and Occupational Sorting

Most models of earnings that study the effect of differences in ascriptive characteristics carry with them, usually implicitly, the notion that the size of the effect will differ across sectors of the economy, leading to a sorting of workers related to the characteristic. In models of employer discrimination, for example, the earnings differentials generared by employers' reactions to a characteristic are not expected to emerge among the self-employed, although sorting may drive down their average earnings. Becker-type "taste for discrimination" models also predict greater earnings differences in regulated or monopolized sectors.

Explanations of earnings differentials based on consumer discrimination or unobserved productivity linked to the ascriptive characteristic likewise predict sectoral differences in outcomes associated with the characteristic. Some of the issues can be discussed with the help of a simple model. Assume that there are two sectors in the economy, A and B. Wages of worker *i* in each sector are given by

$$\left.\begin{aligned} W_{Ai} &= a_1 X_{1i} + a_2 X_{2i} + a_3 X_{3i} \\ \text{and} \qquad & \\ W_{Bi} &= b_1 X_{1i} + b_2 X_{2i} + b_3 X_{3i} \end{aligned}\right\} \qquad (1)$$

Characteristics X_1 and X_2 are known to be related to productivity; X_3 is an ascriptive characteristic, which, in keeping with the focus of the subsequent empirical work, we shall call "beauty." All three are uniformly and independently distributed across workers and range between zero and one. Workers choose the sector with the higher wage. Assume that $a_3 > b_3$, that is, beauty is more highly rewarded in sector A than in sector B, and that the other parameters are such that there are workers in both sectors.[3] Under these circumstances, workers of all levels of beauty are found in each sector, but the average level of beauty is higher in sector A.[4]

It is interesting to consider some simple modifications of the above setup that lead to dynamic sorting, the systematic movement of workers from one sector to another as their careers progress, and that can be tested using longitudinal data. One obvious change would allow the relative returns to characteristics to change as the worker acquires labor market experience. A change in the relative return to X_3 would lead to one-way sector switching; for example, if the return to beauty rose faster in A than in B, the more beautiful B workers would switch into A, but no one would switch from A to B.

Two-way switching requires changes in the relative returns to two of the characteristics. Thus, for example, if the return to X_1 falls in sector A relative to the return to beauty, we would observe those more beautiful people in sector B who are poorly endowed with X_1 switching to sector A, while the marginally good-looking worker in sector A who has a lot of characteristic X_1 will switch to sector B. Interestingly, it is possible for two-way switching that is systematically related to X_3 to result from changes only in the relative returns to the other two characteristics. If the return to X_1 in B increases while the return to X_2 in A increases, under most circumstances workers will leave both sectors, with those who move from A to B being less attractive on average than those who stay in A. Those who move from B to A will be more attractive on average than those who remain in B.

The general point is that, in sector A, where looks receive a relatively higher reward, the less attractive workers are on average more "marginal"; that is, they receive lower sector-specific rents. They are thus more likely to switch sectors in response to a relative increase in the return to any characteristic in sector B. Likewise, the more attractive workers in sector B tend to be more marginally attached there and thus more easily attracted into sector A by favorable movements in the relative return in sector A to another characteristic that they possess.

Two-way switching also results if a very simple learning/job shopping component is added to the model (Johnson 1978). Modify wage equations (1) by adding the sector-specific ability variables Θ_{Ai} and Θ_{Bi} to W_{Ai} and W_{Bi}. Assume that the Θ's have zero means, are normally distributed across the population, and are uncorrelated with one another and the X's. Further assume that they are unknown to employers and workers at the point of entry into the labor market but that Θ_{ji} can be revealed by working in sector j for 1 period. Workers live 2 periods and may switch sectors at the end of period 1. The values of the other parameters in (1) are known and unchanging.

A worker who chooses to start in sector A will switch to sector B if $W_{Ai} + \Theta_{Ai} < W_{Bi}$. Under our assumptions, this switch is less likely to occur the higher is the worker's value of X_3. Similarly, among workers who begin in B, those with more X_3 are more likely to make the switch to A. Ignoring discounting, the expected value of a career begun in A is given by

$$V_A = W_A + W_B G\ (W_B - W_A) + \int_{W_B - W_A}^{\infty} [W_A + \Theta_A]\, g(\Theta_A)\, d\Theta_A,$$

and the expected value of starting in B by

$$V_B = W_B + W_A H\ (W_A - W_B) + \int_{W_A - W_B}^{\infty} [W_B + \Theta_B]\, h(\Theta_B)\, d\Theta_B,$$

where $G(\cdot)$ and $H(\cdot)$ are the cumulative distribution functions of Θ_A and Θ_B, and $g(\cdot)$ and $h(\cdot)$ are the corresponding density functions. Workers start their careers in sector A if $V_A > V_B$. Differentiation of $V_A - V_B$ with respect to X_3 shows that, other things being equal, those with higher values of X_3 are more likely to choose A as their first sector. If X_3 is attractiveness, then among junior workers the more attractive are likely to start in A. As workers learn more about aspects of their productivity unrelated to attractiveness, the less attractive will be more likely to switch to B, while the more attractive B workers are the ones more likely to switch to A. Again, this result hinges on the fact that the less attractive workers are more likely to be marginal in A, while the more attractive are marginal in B.

As an empirical matter, the identity of sector A, where X_3 is more highly rewarded, depends on one's hypothesis about the source of the return to X_3. A belief that the differential arises from a general taste by employers for discrimination, as mentioned above, suggests treating self-employment as a separate sector; a preference-based theory of consumer discrimination suggests that occupations involving direct contact with consumers will offer a higher return to X_3; a hypothesis of statistical discrimination implies that we are less likely to observe a return to the characteristic in sectors where productivity is easily measured and the costs of turnover are low; and so on. Once the sectoral divisions implied by a hypothesis are implemented with a particular set of data, testing involves examining differences across sectors in the returns to the characteristic, in its average levels, and in the patterns of intersectoral mobility.

Our empirical analysis is concerned with beauty (the measurement of which we discuss in the next section) and its effects on the earnings and career choices of attorneys. We consider three possible hypotheses about why beauty might lead to higher earnings in this labor market. First, other things being equal, those who hire and promote lawyers may prefer to be surrounded by better-looking colleagues and subordinates. Second, there may be true consumer discrimination, with consumers (clients) preferring better-looking lawyers solely because of the enjoyment of spending time with them, even though their looks do not produce better settlements or judgments. Finally, consumers (clients) may prefer a better-looking lawyer because the lawyer's beauty is itself productive for the consumer. The social-psychological evidence shows (see the studies cited by Hatfield and Sprecher (1986), pp. 82–95) that people find attractive communicators more persuasive than unattractive ones. An attorney who is better able to persuade and convince others, particularly judges and juries, may be producing higher-quality legal services.

To test for employer discrimination we look for differences between self-employed lawyers and those who are employees. To test for the possibility that consumer behavior underlies the labor market outcomes, we divide attorneys into those practicing in the private sector and those in all other types of practice. This division is based on the observation that the duties of a lawyer in the private sector often include a marketing component. The success of a law firm depends on its ability to attract new clients and to keep existing ones, with responsibility for this falling more heavily on the more senior lawyers or partners. A firm deciding to hire or promote a junior attorney will keep this in mind (cf. O'Flaherty and Siow 1995; Lanciers, Rebitzer, and Taylor 1996). If, other things being equal, attractiveness gives a lawyer an edge in marketing to new clients and schmoozing with old ones, and if clients prefer to associate with attractive lawyers, then the latter will generate greater earnings for themselves and their firms. In the public sector, however, the ability to market one's services to clients is unnecessary - the clientele is "captive," and there is no profit motive. Attorneys certainly do not have to worry about attracting clients to maintain their earnings. Thus, if consumers' choices of lawyers lie behind a beauty effect in lawyers' earnings, the effect should be larger for attorneys in the private sector, and private sector attorneys should be more attractive than their public-sector counterparts.

Assuming that we find such differences, it remains to determine whether consumers are basing their decisions on the ascriptive characteristic because they believe it will be productive for them or because they simply prefer it regardless of any monetary gain that it might produce. If the former is true, we may infer that in our example the returns to this characteristic come from better-looking attorneys' greater ability to win monetary or other settlements from judges, juries, and other attorneys rather than from consumers indulging their own taste for discrimination. To study this ultimate question we divide the sample by legal specialization and examine how averages of their beauty differ by specialty within the private sector.

14.3. Data on Lawyers and Their Looks

Law School X (hereafter LSX) is a highly selective institution that has typically matriculated and graduated between 300 and 400 students each year. For many years it has conducted follow-up surveys of its students 5 and 15 years after graduation. The faculty member in charge of this survey has also arranged to have information from the school's records merged with information from the questionnaire. For earlier cohorts of graduates this process provides a record of their scholarly and professional careers from the bachelor's degree through year 15 of legal practice. For more recent cohorts a complete record is provided through year 5 of practice.

Law School X also typically publishes a book of photographs (usually head-and-shoulders pictures) of matriculants in each entering class. While books are no longer extant for all classes, we were able to obtain them for the matriculant classes from 1969 to 1974 (who graduated from 1971 to 1978), and from 1979 to 1984 (who graduated from 1981 to 1988). These photographs underlie the ratings of beauty that provide one of the central bases of this study. Each photograph was copied and mounted on a separate sheet of paper (to prevent contamination from faces nearby on the page) and was rated independently by four different observers: a male under 35, a female under 35, a male 35 or older, and a female 35 or older. Each entering class was rated by a different panel of four.

The raters were asked to place each photograph on the scale: "5, strikingly handsome or beautiful; 4, above-average attractiveness; 3, average; 2, plain, below average in attractiveness; or 1, homely, far below average in attractiveness." Because the photos were examined in 1994, although some were as much as 25 years old, the raters were instructed "to make allowances for the fact that styles and fashions may have changed" and were also told for a person with "a particularly unflattering facial expression, try to imagine how they would look under ordinary circumstances." We obtained ratings of over 4,400 matriculants.

The ideal measure of beauty would account for all of a person's features that make a visual impact on others, including physical characteristics as well as grooming and habitual facial expressions or gestures.[5] A photograph captures only facial features and to some extent grooming, and captures them imperfectly, as when photos are "flattering" or "unflattering." The errors thus introduced into our beauty measure, however, are unlikely to be systematically related to any of the economic outcomes on which we focus.[6] Also, the use of a measure of beauty based on rating photographs has one important advantage over the interviewer rating measure in the data used by Hamermesh and Biddle (1994), for the rater's assessment of attractiveness cannot be contaminated by other information about the subject obtained during an interview (e.g., by socioeconomic status).

Table 14.1.

Description of Ratings of Beauty

A. Average Pairwise Correlation Coefficients, Graduates Used in Analysis (Number of Observations)

	Men	Women
Year 5 sample	0.405 (1,567)	0.398 (401)
Year 15 sample	0.446 (623)	

B. Coefficients (and Their SEs) from Regression of the 62 Pairwise Correlation Coefficients on Raters' Characteristics

	Coefficients
Young male	0.0114 (0.0230)
Young female	0.0050 (0.0232)
Older female	-0.0509 (0.0230)
$\bar{R}^2$	0.085

C. All Matriculants: Mean Standardized Rating (No. of Observations)

	Year 5 Sample	Year 15 Sample
Respondents:	0.0088 (2,469)	0.0224 (1,245)
Men	-0.0455 (1,903)	-0.0254 (1,097)
Women	0.2046 (566)	0.3769 (148)
Nonrespondents	-0.0115 (1,917)	-0.0287 (971)

The notion that beauty can systematically affect economic outcomes is predicated on the assumptions that a person's beauty changes very slowly and that there are common standards of beauty in the population. The leading study examining the first assumption is Adams (1977), who had panels of observers rate photographs of the same people taken at ages 16–20, 30–35 and 45–50. The correlations of the ratings of facial attractiveness, the relevant measure for our study, across pictures (and within raters) were 0.87 for women across the first two pictures (0.63 formen), 0.93 (0.51) across the second and third pictures, and 0.79 (0.59) between the first and third pictures.

These results suggest a tremendous persistence of beauty over an even wider range of the life cycle than the ages 22–40 that constitute the span for the typical respondent in the LSX data.

The existence of common standards of beauty at a moment in time will be reflected in a positive correlation between different raters' assessments of the same subject. Panel A of table 14.1 shows average pairwise correlations of around 0.40 between panel members' ratings of the matriculants who responded to the year 5 and year 15 surveys. Cronbach's α for the ratings by a four-person panel was typically 0.75 in these classes.[7] This is somewhat lower than the extent of agreement in ratings of Looks reported for more heterogeneous samples (Zebrowitz, Montepare, and Lee 1993), but it still suggests substantial agreement among the raters about the appearance of the matriculants.[8]

It is also worth knowing whether the existence and strength of the correlation between a pair of ratings depends on the demographic characteristics of the raters. Panel B of table 14.1 addresses this question. We regressed the correlation coefficients between pairs of ratings of the same set of photographs on indicator variables of the sex and age of the two raters. The results show, for example, that the extent of agreement between older males (the excluded category) and younger females does not differ significantly from that between older males and younger males.

The correlations between older female raters and others tend to be lower than those between other pairs, but they are still uniformly positive and highly significant. There is a shared element across all four groups' perceptions of attractiveness. That this shared perception of what is attractive exists should hardly surprise well-read economists: were there no agreement about beauty, Keynes's (1936, chap. 12) metaphor likening choosing shares of stock to "newspaper competitions in which the competitors have to pick out the six prettiest faces from a hundred photographs, the prize being awarded to the competitor whose choice most nearly corresponds to the average preferences of the competitors as a whole" would make no sense.

To create a single beauty measure for each attorney, we averaged the four ratings. These averages were then standardized within each entering class, so that within each class beauty has a mean of zero and a variance of one. Standardization is a response to the fact that in some panels one rater gave consistently higher ratings than those in other panels (although ratings that were correlated with others in the same panel). These "generous" panelists would tend to raise the average beauty measure for all members of the class relative to other classes. Standardization corrects for this, under the assumption that all classes are drawn from the same population with respect to beauty.

Panel C of table 14.1 presents the mean standardized beauty ratings and sample sizes for each survey separately by respondent status. Respondents in both surveys are more attractive than nonrespondents, and the difference in average attractiveness is greater in the survey at year 15 than at year 5, as one would expect if looks have some ultimate positive effect on success and success increases the probability of response. The difference in year 5 between respondents and nonrespondents is tiny, however, and even at year 15 it is not significant. This suggests that we need not be too concerned about sample selection in this case.[9]

Table 14.1 shows a striking result: the average attractiveness rating of male respondents is well below that of the female respondents. The difference in the average ratings of beauty is independent of the sex of the person doing the rating, and such large average differences are not observed in most of the psychology literature. While the average beauty of men in the sample was approximately the same in the two cohorts of matriculants, the women in the earlier cohort were rated as substantially better-looking than their female successors (as can be seen by comparing the average ratings for women in the year 5 and year 15 samples). This difference across cohorts may reflect favorable treatment of beauty in the admissions process in the late 1960s (since pictures were not usually included in applications in the later cohort), and/or it may result from good-looking women's greater beliefs during the 1960s that their beauty would pay off in the legal profession. Whatever the reasons, the differences make it essential that all the analyses be performed separately by sex and cohort. Since there were very few female matriculants in the late 1960s and early 1970s at LSX, this means that some of the results are based only on male attorneys.

The LSX surveys provide large amounts of information on the respondents' backgrounds, performance, and activities in law school, their career histories, and their current work activities and environments. Questions have been changed, added, or dropped over the years. Thus in defining the samples to be used in the analyses, we traded off the desire for more information on each respondent against the loss of observations because some information was unavailable for some respondents (or even for entire graduating classes). Unless the loss of observations from adding another variable was very small, we generally chose to restrict the information and retain a larger sample.

Table 14.2.

Means (and SD) of Important Variables

	Year 5 Sample				Year 15 Sample – Men, Classes from 1970s
	Men, Classes from:		Women, Classes from:		
	1970s	1980s	1970s	1980s	
Real wage (1982–84$):					
Year 1	29,124	34,287	27,877	33,834	29,056
	(8,055)	(10,588)	(7,367)	(10,949)	(8,125)
Year 5	46,859	52,053	44,541	47,782	46,214
	(14,830)	(19,594)	(17,879)	(18,475)	(13,390)
Year 15	...	...	...	...	116,965
					(82,374)
Class rank	175.04	167.63	188.74	186.74	175.4
Law journal	0.219	0.256	0.220	0.245	0.218
Office ≥ 50 attorneys	0.312	0.580	0.329	0.536	0.404
Public sector	0.305	0.197	0.243	0.127	0.098
No. of jobs through year 5	1.69	1.82	1.78	1.89	1.65
	(0.83)	(0.83)	(0.86)	(0.89)	(0.82)
No. of jobs through year 15	...	...	...	...	2.19
					(1.30)
N	778	789	82	319	623

In analyzing the year 5 samples we use two sets of variables: (1) personal, educational, and first-job characteristics, a vector P_1, including indicator variables for race; type of college (Ivy League or Seven Sisters; public in the state where LSX is located; other public); years of post baccalaureate experience before law school and whether a master's or doctorate was obtained in this period; whether the person was on a law journal at LSX or argued in a moot-court competition; class rank; whether he or she held a judicial clerkship after law school; and whether the first job was in the private sector. Also included in P_1, mainly as a proxy for unmeasured quality, is the number of jobs held between graduation and year 5.[10] (2) Year 5 job characteristics, J_5, including years of practice in the private sector; a vector of indicator variables for the size of the metropolitan statistical area where the person works; another vector for the number of other attorneys in the office (16–49; 50–149; >149); and an indicator of whether the person was working in the private sector. In studying the year 15 respondents we also include the vector J_{15}, containing the same variables as J_5 but observed at year 15.

The year 5 surveys contain retrospective information on income from the first post-law-school job, W_1, and the current income from the principal job in year 5, W_5. From the year 15 surveys we use income from the principal job in year 15, W_{15}.[11] The measures of W_5 and W_{15} are reports of current earnings, but that of W_1 is retrospective and may contain more sampling error. That potential problem is likely, however, to be very small for this population of professional workers for whom the initial salary is probably quite salient. Each nominal wage is deflated by the consumer price index for the year for which it is reported, so that all comparisons are in constant (1982–84) dollars.

One should note throughout this discussion and in sections 14.4 and 14.5 that the sample is remarkably homogeneous. All the matriculants performed very weil as undergraduates, and all received essentially the same basic training at the same law school. Bearing that in mind, we show in table 14.2 the means and standard deviations of some of the major variables. The 1970s cohorts were more likely to be working in the public sector, legal aid, or nonprofit institutions in year 5 than their 1980s counterparts and less likely to be working in large law firms. They held significantly fewer jobs during the first 5 years after law school, perhaps a reflection of the rapid growth in demand for attorneys in the 1980s (see Rosen 1992), perhaps of intercohort differences in *Sitzfleisch*.[12]

Despite their observational homogeneity, the samples exhibit a remarkably typical extent of underlying heterogeneity. The variance (and coefficient of variation) of earnings increases sharply between years 5 and 15, reflecting the "fanning out" that is observed in age-earnings profiles generally (Mincer 1974). At years 1 and 5 there are small but significant sex differences in earnings, a fact noted for a sample of lawyers by Wood, Corcoran, and Courant (1993). Finally, like workers generally, these attorneys settle into jobs as they age: between graduation and year 5 they hold 0.65 additional jobs (a 15% turnover rate per annum), but in the next 10 years on average only 0.54 additional jobs are obtained (only a 5% annual turnover rate).

14.4. The Effect of Beauty on Earnings

In this section we consider whether a relationship between attractiveness and earnings exists in this market, how it differs by sex and cohort, and how it evolves over workers' careers. Tables 14.3 and 14.4 examine the earnings-beauty relationship for men and women and for each cohort separately. The estimated coefficients on the variables in the vectors P_1 and J_5 are presented in table 14.Al. Given the observational homogeneity of the samples, these regressions account for surprisingly large fractions of the intrasample variance in earnings; indeed, the plethora of information that we have on the respondents' characteristics accounts for as much of the variance in earnings as is

Table 14.3.

Estimates of Log(Earnings) Regressions, Year 5 Samples, Men

	Dependent Variable			
	W_1	W_1	W_5	W_5
A. All classes (N = 1,567):				
Standardized beauty	0.0198 (0.0100)	0.0131 (0.0079)	0.0310 (0.0094)	0.0257 (0.0079)
P_1	No	Yes	No	Yes
J_5	No	No	No	Yes
$\bar{R}^2$	0.111	0.231	0.032	0.349
B. 1970s classes (N = 778):				
Standardized beauty	0.0183 (0.0100)	0.0167 (0.0099)	0.0495 (0.0128)	0.0431 (0.0114)
P_1	No	Yes	No	Yes
J_5	No	No	No	Yes
$\bar{R}^2$	0.022	0.061	0.020	0.235
C. 1980s classes (N = 789):				
Standardized beauty	0.0214 (0.0137)	0.0053 (0.0116)	0.0104 (0.0139)	0.0068 (0.0104)
P_1	No	Yes	No	Yes
J_5	No	No	No	Yes
$\bar{R}^2$	0.096	0.377	0.016	0.474

Notes: Each regression here and in tables 14.4 and 14.5 also includes indicator variables for each graduating class. P_1 includes race; type of undergraduate college; years of post baccalaureate experience before law school; whether advanced degree before law school; whether on a law journal; whether in courtroom competitions; unusually fast or slow completion of law school; class rank; whether held clerkship in first year; first job private; number of jobs years *0–5*. J_5 includes number of years in the private sector; vector of dummy variables for metropolitan statistical area size; whether in the public sector or legal aid; vector of dummy variables for number of attorneys in office.

standard in similar equations describing much more heterogeneous samples (e.g., Current Population Surveys).

The coefficients on the beauty variable in the earnings regressions are small for both sexes during the first post-law-school year. Indeed, they differ little by sex or by cohort, with a 2 SD increase in the standardized rating producing an insignificant increase in wages of around 3%. The estimates lead to the general inference that there is a small and weak positive relationship between beauty and initial earnings even holding constant a wide array of job and personal characteristics.

In the year 5 earnings regressions for men, the coefficient on the beauty variable is positive and significant, whether or not the large vector of control variables is added. A 2 SD increase in attractiveness is associated with about a 10% increase in earnings. The estimated effect of beauty

Table 14.4.

Estimates of Log (Earnings) Regressions, Year 5 Samples, Women

	Dependent Variable			
	W_1	W_1	W_5	W_5
A. All classes (N = 401):				
Standardized beauty	0.0237 (0.0157)	0.0096 (0.0144)	0.0425 (0.0220)	0.0138 (0.0184)
P_1	No	Yes	No	Yes
J_5	No	No	No	Yes
$\bar{R}^2$	0.153	0.321	0.043	0.378
B. 1970s classes (N = 82):				
Standardized beauty	0.0326 (0.0393)	0.0143 (0.0445)	0.0797 (0.0556)	0.0135 (0.0613)
P_1	No	Yes	No	Yes
J_5	No	No	No	Yes
$\bar{R}^2$	-0.014	-0.018	-0.001	0.205
C. 1980s classes (N = 319):				
Standardized beauty	0.0219 (0.0171)	0.0139 (0.0149)	0.0347 (0.0239)	0.0087 (0.0194)
P_1	No	Yes	No	Yes
J_5	No	No	No	Yes
$\bar{R}^2$	0.142	0.379	0.051	0.428

Note: See note to table 14.3.

on female lawyers' earnings is also positive with or without the control variables, but, because of the very small number of women in the 1970s cohort, the estimates are imprecise and insignificant. Least absolute distance regressions yield essentially the same inferences as the ordinary least squares estimates presented in table 14.4. Also, specifications with beauty measured by a set of dummy variables do not indicate any asymmetry or nonlinearity in the relationship between beauty and earnings.[13]

In the 1980s cohort the coefficients on beauty in the year 5 earnings regressions are much smaller but never negative. Among men the coefficient is significantly less than in the 1970s cohort at year 5 ($t = 2.35$ on the difference between the estimates in the final column of table 14.3). This change is not part of a generalized decline in returns to the attributes that affect earnings: as a comparison of the first two columns in table A1 shows, the effect of most of the other variables that affected the earnings of young attorneys increased over this decade.

Table 14.5.

Estimates of Log (Earnings) Regressions, Year 15 Samples, Men ($N = 623$)

	Dependent Variable			
	W_1 (1)	W_1 (2)	W_5 (3)	W_5 (4)
Standardized beauty	0.0073 (0.0100)	0.0069 (0.0113)	0.0442 (0.0135)	0.0388 (0.0126)
P_1	No	Yes	No	Yes
J_5	No	No	No	Yes
$\bar{R}^2$	0.023	0.042	0.021	0.241
	W_{15} (1)	W_{15} (2)	W_{15}* (3)	
Standardized beauty	0.0829 (0.0259)	0.0629 (0.0207)	0.0542 (0.0202)	
P_1	No	Yes	Yes	
J_5	No	Yes	Yes	
J_{15}	No	Yes	Yes	
$\bar{R}^2$	0.022	0.413	0.445	

Notes: See note to table 14.3. J_{15} includes number of years in the private sector; vector of dummy variables for metropolitan statistical area size; whether public sector or legal aid; vector of dummy variables for number of attorneys in office.

* Adds Year 15 annual hours to J_{15}.

The smaller beauty coefficient in the year 5 earnings regression for the 1980s cohort is more curious in light of the results in table 14.5, which presents estimates like those in panel B of table 14.3, but for the slightly smaller sample of lawyers from the 1970s cohort for whom all the data in the vectors P_1, J_5 and J_{15} are available. The conclusions about year 5 earnings in the broader sample from the 1970s cohort are repeated in the estimates for this reduced sample that are presented in the top half of table 14.5. The bottom tableau shows the relationship between beauty and earnings at year 15. (The estimates of the coefficients on the vectors P_1, J_5 and J_{15} are presented in table 14.A2.) Column 3 of the bottom tableau of table 14.5 presents the same equation as column 2, but with year 15 annual hours included as an additional characteristic. Comparing the coefficients in the two equations, we can infer that better-looking lawyers work longer hours at year 15, but most of the effect of beauty on earnings is a pure wage effect, not simply a matter of bringing in more business at the same hourly pay. In this cohort, better-looking midcareer attorneys were billing at higher rates, not just billing more hours.[14] By the time the 1970s cohort was well established in legal practice, an attorney whose appearance in a photograph taken on average nearly 20 years earlier placed him 1 SD below the mean of looks was earning around 12% less per annum than one whose looks at that time put him 1 SD above the mean.[15]

From the late 1970s to the late 1980s the relationship between beauty and earnings among starting associate attorneys diminished, but over the same period the relationship grew stronger within the cohort that had entered the profession in the 1970s. An interaction between experience and the effect of beauty on an attorney's earnings might explain the second phenomenon, but not the first. The two changes might be linked to the rapid growth in demand for lawyers' services in the late 1980s, particularly if its effect differed across the two cohorts. Interestingly, that appears to have been the case. Among professionals age 30–34 with advanced degrees, Current Population Survey data show that between 1979–83 and 1989–93 the wages of full-time attorneys rose relative to those of college professors by 15%, those of health professionals by 11%, those of natural scientists by 16%, and those of engineers by 16%.[16] At the same time the relative earnings of attorneys ages 40–44 were 5% and 28% lower than those of professors and health professionals, respectively, in 1989–93 than in 1979–83, and only 4% and 2% higher than those of natural scientists and engineers, suggesting there was less excess demand for older lawyers.

In many law firms older attorneys are responsible for attracting and retaining clients, and their good looks might work to their advantage in this area. It may be that firms responded to the increase in demand for legal services mainly by hiring more young associates to produce the legal output for the growing number of clients whom the more senior attorneys were attracting. Under these circumstances the importance of young lawyers' ability to produce high-quality work under the direction of a senior attorney may have grown relative to their future ability to market the firm's services.[17]

The difference between cohorts in the effect of beauty is also consistent with the notion that the effect of a characteristic early in the career affects its subsequent effect. This statement about the time path of the return to a characteristic as a cohort ages is similar in a complex earnings function to the observation by Baker, Gibbs, and Holmstrom (1994) that the subsequent level of wages in a firm's cohort of workers depends on the state of the labor market early in its career. It is also consistent with the more conventional notion (Berger 1985) that a cohort's size affects its wages over its entire working life. Finally, it may be that whatever led to the diminution of the beauty coefficient at year 5 between the 1970s and 1980s cohorts also lowered the rate at which the effect of beauty on earnings typically grows as attorneys change duties over their careers. This would lead to the coefficient on earnings for the 1980s cohorts at year 15 being lower than what we observed for the 1970s cohorts at year 15. A good test of the alternative explanations and analogies can regrettably only come from data available in 1996–2003 on the earnings of the 1980s cohort at year 15 of their careers.

In all of our subsamples there is a positive relationship between beauty and earnings, and among men in the 1970s cohort and for the sample of men as a whole the relationship is statistically significant. It might be argued that this relationship reflects simultaneity in the determination of beauty and earnings. One possible form of simultaneity between earnings and beauty, caused by high-paid workers using their earnings to "buy beauty," is obviously not a problem here, as our measures reflect the subjects' appearance several years before they entered the labor market. A more subtle simultaneity might arise if both beauty and economic success are linked to the students' socioeconomic background, as when more affluent parents invest more in their children's looks, and when economic success is correlated across generations. This could be a significant problem in a population with a fairly wide range of parents' incomes, as children of the poor may lack access to proper diets, health care, and so on. Our sample, however, is quite homogeneous and is made up of students at a single prestigious law school who come mostly from middle- to upper-middle-class families. It seems unlikely that there would exist more than a negligible correlation between parents' income and child's beauty over the range of family backgrounds in our samples. Nonetheless, in an attempt to account for this we added to the earnings regressions a measure of the fraction of law-school costs defrayed by the student's parents. Including this proxy for parents' wealth had essentially no effect on the coefficients of the beauty measure.

It might also be argued that the beauty coefficients in the earnings regressions capture a correlation between beauty and other productivity-enhancing characteristics that have been omitted from the equations. Concerns about omitted-variable bias arc mitigated considerably by our inclusion of a very rich set of measures

Table 14.6.

Effects of Beauty on Pre-Labor-Market Outcomes

	Men, Classes from:		Women, Classes from:	
Dependent Variable	1970s	1980s	1970s	1980s
Class rank	3.655 (3.793)	3.097 (3.706)	-10.647 (12.402)	3.317 (5.067)
Moot court	-0.0144 (0.0104)	-0.0026 (0.0136)	0.0047 (0.0098)	0.0234 (0.0187)
Law journal	0.0016 (0.0142)	-0.0143 (0.0167)	-0.0368 (0.0403)	0.0436 (0.0234)
Judicial clerkship	-0.0065 (0.0112)	-0.0303 (0.0125)		-0.0208 (0.0208)
First job in large firm (50+ lawyers)	0.0307 (0.0227)	0.0245 (0.0188)		0.0450 (0.0277)

Notes: For class rank the table lists regression coefficients of the standardized beauty measure. For the other four dependent variables the effects of a 1 SD increase in the standardized ratings of beauty are presented. The regressions for class rank also include dummy variables for race, undergraduate college, before-law-school degrees, and a continuous measure of before-law-school experience. The probits for law journal and moot court include these measures and class rank, while the probit for attaining a clerkship includes these measures and all three other dependent variables listed in this table. The probit for obtaining one's first job in a large firm includes these measures and all four other dependent variables. The clerkship probit was not estimated for the 1970s cohort of women because only 3 of the 82 respondents obtained clerkships, and the pro bit on first job was not estimated for this group because the question was only asked of them in the year 15 interview.

correlated with ability, including undergraduate performance, class rank in law school, participation in moot-court competitions and law journals, and firm size. It is possible to test directly for a correlation between beauty and those indicators of ability that we can measure, and thus perhaps get some indication of whether beauty is correlated with productivity-enhancing characteristics that we cannot observe.

Table 14.6 shows the effect of a 1 SD increase in the standardized beauty ranking on class rank (with a higher number implying a lower class rank), the probability of participating in a moot-court competition, and the probabilities of being on a law journal and of obtaining a judicial clerkship. Also included is a probit on whether the person's first job was in a large law firm (≥50 attorneys), presumably the kind of firm that has the pick of more able attorneys. Of the 18 coefficients in the table, only one is significant at conventional levels. The only consistent suggestion – and it is a very weak one, with no coefficients significant even at the 90% level of confidence – is that beauty may steer attorneys toward the larger firms where average salaries are higher. A general reading of the evidence in this table, however, leaves little room for inferring that there is much correlation between beauty and pre-labor market indicators of ability.

These considerations suggest that, while other interpretations of the positive coefficient of beauty in the earnings regressions are possible, a causal relationship running from looks to earnings stands as the most plausible. The possibility remains that the causal relationship is partly indirect, so that the attractiveness of young attorneys induces them to make investments that we cannot measure. If this were true, the coefficients on the beauty variables in this section would not correspond to the coefficients on beauty in the model of section 14.2 since they would not represent the increase in earnings that would occur if an attorney's looks and nothing else were to change. They would still, however, reflect outcomes arising in a world where greater beauty leads to higher earnings.

14.5. Sorting and the Sources of Wage Effects

While we have demonstrated the existence of a large and growing effect of beauty on earnings in one cohort of attorneys, the more interesting and more general question is what the evidence implies about the sources of this return. The explanations in section 14.2 suggested the existence of distinct sectors in the labor market and predicted both differences in the returns to beauty across them and systematic sorting of workers related to their beauty. One explanation based on some form of employer discrimination implied that a beauty effect will not be found among the self-employed since there is ipso facto no employer who can discriminate. The sample used to generate the earnings equations reported in table 14.3 includes 60 male lawyers in private solo practice. We augmented the year 5 earnings regressions for men with an indicator variable identifying these self-employed attorneys and an interaction between that variable and the beauty measure. A negative value of the interaction would be consistent with employer discrimination, but we find instead that this term is positive, although statistically insignificant.[18] A test of the hypothesis that the sum of the coefficients on the interaction term and the main effect of beauty equals zero is rejected at the 90% level of confidence. Thus an examination of the small group of self-employed lawyers in our sample provides no evidence that employer discrimination explains the effect of beauty on earnings. If anything, beauty pays off more for self-employed junior attorneys than for employees.

To begin considering the potential role of consumer discrimination or productive beauty, we divided the sample between attorneys practicing privately or in the public sectors. (The latter includes those working for government-prosecutors, staff attorneys for government agencies, etc.; legal-aid lawyers, and those who categorize their practice as "other," most of whom probably work for nonprofit organizations.) The first panel of table 14.7 shows for the 1970s classes the means of the standardized average beauty ratings in each sector at years 5 and 15. Male private-sector attorneys are more attractive on average than are male public-sector attorneys at both 5 and 15 years after graduation. Moreover, the gap between the two sectors grows over the 10 years. In the very small sample of women the public-sector lawyers are more attractive at year 5, while at year 15 those in the private sector are better-looking.[19]

To study more closely the phenomenon of two-way switching that was described by the model in section 14.2 we divided the sample of male lawyers into four groups: those in the public sector in years 5 and 15 (public stayers), in the private sector in both years (private stayers), in the private sector in year 5 but the public sector in year 15 (private leavers), and those in the public sector in year 5 and the private sector in year 15 (public leavers). We estimate a multinomial logit model including variables describing performance in law school to discover whether the probability of membership in these groups was systematically related to beauty. The results in the second panel of table 14.7 show that private stayers (the comparison group) are more attractive than public stayers. Furthermore, lawyers who left the private sector between years 5 and 15 are less attractive than those who remained, while lawyers who switched from the public sector are more attractive than those who stayed.[20]

Could differences across the sectors in the premia earned by more attractive attorneys explain this pattern of mobility? We examine this possibility in table 14.8, which reports results of separate earnings regressions estimated for men in the 1970s classes in private- and public-sector practices. These results may also shed light on possible employer discrimination, as public employers, shielded from competition, would

Table 14.7.

Effects of Beauty on Attorney's Transition between Sectors

	Mean Standardized Beauty		
	Men		Women
Year 5:			
Private sector	-0.014 (731)		0.329 (64)
Public sector	-0.098 (134)		0.522 (34)
Year 15:			
Private sector	0.018 (707)		0.474 (59)
Public sector	-0.212 (86)		0.423 (24)
	Multinomial Logits		
	Private 15 Public 5,	Public 15 Private 5,	Public Both
Standardized Beauty	0.2279 (0.1559)	-0.4656 (0.2559)	-0.1820 (0.1394)
Pseudo-R^2		0.040	
N		785	
p on beauty coefficients		0.059	

Notes: The base group contains those attorneys who practiced in the private sector in both years 5 and 15. Each arm of the logit function also includes dummy variables for the person having been on a law journal, engaged in a court competition and tenure in clerkship, and the continuous variable for class rank. The number of observations is included in parentheses after each mean. Parenthetical values for standardized beauty are standard errors.

have more freedom to indulge their tastes for attractive employees. In both years, but especially at year 15, the variance in earnings among attorneys in the public sector is much lower and is reflected in the lower $\bar{R}^2$ in the regressions describing the public sector. Despite this, the coefficient on beauty is slightly higher in the public sector in year 5 and lower in year 15, although the differences are not statistically significant. Some caution should be exercised in interpreting these results, for the beauty coefficient in one sector may not represent the premium that would be paid to the average worker in the other sector if he or she switched sectors. This selectivity may be a problem, but we showed in table 14.6 that beauty is not significantly correlated with a number of ability measures that might affect sectoral choice.

Taken at face value, the results in table 14.8 show that the beauty premia in the two sectors are equal in percentage terms, since the equations describe the logarithms of earnings. Average earnings are lower in the public sector, however, with the gap at year 15 being very large. This implies that, while the public- and private-sector beauty premia at year 5 are roughly the same in dollar terms, by year 15 a 1 SD increase in average beauty is worth $3,200 to the average public-sector attorney, but $10,200 to the average private-sector attorney.[21]

A rising absolute premium for beauty in the private sector could lead to sectoral switching linked to beauty. For example, consider a model in which experience as an attorney builds human capital that raises the potential earnings of all attorneys in both sectors at known rates, with the rate of increase being faster for potential private-sector earnings

Table 14.8.

Log (Earnings) Regressions, Year 15 Samples, Men

	Private		Public	
	W_5	W_{15}	W_5	W_{15}
Mean earnings ($)	47,642 (15,270)	122,812 (81,144)	39,926 (12,026)	49,682 (12,725)
Standardized beauty	0.0515 (0.0130)	0.0851 (0.0223)	0.0668 (0.0279)	0.0636 (0.0356)
$\bar{R}^2$	0.110	0.150	0.065	0.012
N	717	658	128	84

Notes: Regressions include the same variables as those in the multinomial logits in Table 14.7 as well as indicator variables for graduating class. Standard deviations are in parentheses below means, standard errors below coefficients.

(adding sector-specific human capital would not alter the main conclusions). Also assume, as seems reasonable, that some attorneys receive an individual-specific psychic benefit from public-sector work that remains constant in each period. Finally, assume that a premium is paid to more attractive workers that is equal across sectors in percentage terms. It will then be rational for some workers to begin in the public sector because of the psychic reward but then switch to the private sector as the absolute earnings difference between the two sectors grows. Other things being equal, more attractive public-sector attorneys are more likely to make this switch, and make it sooner, because for them the absolute earnings difference between the two sectors is larger at every moment in time. If one adds to the model unexpected, sector-specific shocks to potential earnings net of beauty, either demand shocks affecting all workers in the sector or individual-specific shocks, more attractive public-sector workers are more likely to move in response to positive shocks to private-sector earnings, and less attractive private-sector workers are more likely to move in response to positive shocks to public-sector earnings. This arises because of the greater marginality of the less attractive workers in the private sector and of the more attractive public-sector workers, as we discussed in the model of section 14.2.[22]

The combined evidence of tables 14.7 and 14.8 accords with the notion that beauty is productive in private attorneys' efforts to attract and retain clients (consumers), an activity that becomes more important with experience. Additional evidence supporting this interpretation, at least for men, is presented in table 14.9. It shows separately for the 1970s and

Table 14.9.

Effects of a 1 SD Increase in Standardized Beauty on the Probability of Early Parnership, 1970s and 1980s Classes

	Men, Classes from:		Women, Classes from:	
	1970s	1980s	1970s	1980s
Mean probability	0.284	0.065	0.255	0.036
Standardized beauty	0.0511	0.0123	-0.0268	-0.0166
	(0.0168)	(0.0072)	(0.0453)	(0.0067)
Pseudo-$\bar{R}^2$	0.191	0.151	0.424	0.192
N	714	749	51	280

Note: Each probit also includes indicator variables for the person having been on a law journal, engaged in a court competition, held a judicial clerkship, size of the law firm, and continuous variables for class rank and years in the private sector between graduation and year 5. Standard errors are in parentheses.

1980s cohorts the effect of an increase in standardized average beauty on the probability of the unusual event that the attorney becomes a partner in a law firm by year 5 (early partnerships were rare but much more frequent among 1970s graduates than among the 1980s graduates). The estimates are derived from probits on samples limited to private-sector attorneys. Among men in both cohorts the statistically significant point estimates imply that a 1 SD increase in attractiveness increased the probability of early partnership by over 20%. The results for women, in contrast reveal one of the few significant differences in the effect of beauty by sex that we have found: greater attractiveness among women lowers their chances of early partnership.[23]

In sum, by five years after law-school graduation attorneys have sorted themselves so that those in the private sector are better-looking than those in the public sector, a sorting that continues between years 5 and 15. The beauty premia are roughly equal in monetary terms in the two sectors at year 5, but if we also consider the option value of location in the private sector produced because beauty raises the chances of promotion, we can perhaps explain the sectoral differences in attractiveness at year 5. The widening gap in the dollar returns to beauty can account for the movement of more attractive public-sector workers to the private sector that we observe occurring between years 5 and 15.

In the earnings regressions in table 14.8 we also found that the percentage returns to being on a law journal and to a higher class rank rise in the private sector relative to the public sector, while the returns to having held a clerkship rise relatively in the public sector.[24] As the model of section 14.2 suggests, with these relative changes moving in opposite directions we would observe flows of workers of different beauty even if sectoral differences in the returns to beauty did not change over time.

The greater rewards for attractiveness in the private sector are consistent with the notion that choices by consumers (clients) help to support the return to beauty in the market for attorneys. However, as we discussed earlier, there are two conceptually distinct reasons consumers might wish to hire more attractive attorneys. The first is the desire to indulge a taste for spending time with better-looking people; the second is a belief that better-looking attorneys will generate greater financial gains for them as a result of the discriminatory attitudes of judges, juries, or adversaries. The two possibilities are not mutually exclusive. The latter might explain why the return to beauty in the public sector, while apparently lower than in the private sector, is still positive: opportunities for advancement in the public sector are likely to be enhanced by greater success in front of judges and juries. The final task of this section is to search for additional evidence on the question of whether beauty is productive for attorneys.

If more attractive lawyers are more productive in the sense of being more persuasive, our model suggests that they will be disproportionately represented in legal specialties where their beauty could assist them in generating more favorable judgments for clients. The data set allows us to make at least a rough attempt at determining whether this occurs. Graduates from classes after 1979 were asked how they spend their work time. Based on the attorney's most frequent activity, an experienced attorney used the 24 possible responses to classify the respondents into the four categories of litigation, corporate/finance, regulation/administrative, and other.[25] (Results based on the percent distributions of each respondent's work time differed little.) Since litigators deal with judges and juries more than do attorneys in other specialties, we would expect them to be better looking.

The first two parts of table 14.10 present average standardized beauty ratings by sex for each of the four groups of specialties chosen by attorneys from the 1980s cohort who practiced in the private sector at year 5. For both sexes in this cohort the litigators are indeed the most attractive

Table 14.10.

Means and Standard Deviations of Means of Beauty by Specialty, 1980s Classes Year 5, 1970s Classes Year 15

	Litigation	Corporate and Financial	Regulation and Administrative	Other
A. Men, 1980s cohort year 5:				
Mean beauty	0.0099	-0.0577	-0.1311	-0.0525
	(0.0724)	(0.0511)	(0.0938)	(0.0780)
N	133	366	113	145
B. Women, 1980s cohort year 5:				
Mean beauty	0.2506	0.2168	0.0032	0.0500
	(0.1580)	(0.0967)	(0.1455)	(0.1122)
N	56	126	46	57
C. Men, 1970s cohort year 15:				
Mean beauty	0.1180	-0.0295	-0.0285	0.0411
	(0.0698)	(0.0571)	(0.0897)	(0.0784)
N	225	303	127	149

among the four groupings. The same interspecialty differences exist among men from the 1970s cohort at year 15, with litigators again being better-looking than those in other specialties. The results thus accord with the productivity hypothesis (put differently, with the hypothesis that the ultimate source of the earnings advantage is with judges, juries, and other lawyers who treat better-looking advocates especially well), but none of the differences between the average beauty in any pair of specialties is statistically significant at conventional levels.

The division of specialties into those where beauty is more or less likely to affect the pecuniary outcomes of legal cases is subjective. To carry this approach one step further in an objective manner we performed an analysis of variance of the standardized average beauty ratings by sex across each of the 24 legal specialties. The p-values describing the F-statistics for these analyses were 0.22 among male attorneys and 0.54 among female attorneys at year 5 in the 1980s cohort. Among male attorneys at year 15 in the 1970s cohort, the p-value is 0.33. This objective classification of lawyers by specialty implies very clearly that average beauty differs little across legal specialties. We may conclude that our possibly crude measures of specialization generate at most only weak evidence that attorneys sort themselves by specialty in ways that are consistent with their believing that beauty produces more advantageous outcomes for their clients.

14.6. Conclusions

We have demonstrated how one particular ascriptive characteristic – beauty – is related to wages in one profession. The richness of our data has allowed us to examine longitudinal variation in the returns to beauty and to be particularly careful to avoid simultaneity problems with a characteristic that could partly be affected by income. The evidence strongly suggests that beauty is not merely correlated with but actually causes differences in earnings. In the cohort of attorneys who graduated from law school in the early to mid-1970s, the effect of beauty on earnings grew as they matured in their practices. The absence of any effect in the cohort of attorneys who graduated in the early and mid-1980s may stem from the temporary tightness of the legal labor market or from changes in society's attitudes about this characteristic.

Several possible causes of the effect of beauty on professional earnings suggest themselves, including employer discrimination, customer discrimination, and discrimination by judges/juries that makes beauty productive for attorneys. The absence of greater returns to beauty among employed as compared to self-employed lawyers suggests that we can rule out employer discrimination. That the effect is generated by clients preferring to engage better-looking attorneys is supported by the finding that the monetary return to beauty rises especially rapidly in the private sector, by the fact that more attractive men obtain partnerships early, and by attorneys switching between the public and private sectors based partly on looks.

We cannot distinguish very well whether clients' choices result from their pure taste for discrimination or from their correct belief that judges, juries, and other attorneys treat better-looking advocates more favorably, so that engaging a good-looking lawyer will generate pecuniary gains for the client. Indeed, both causes may operate. The notion that the ultimate source of the effect of beauty on earnings is a generalized preference for good looks that is diffused among all those involved in the legal system is consistent with the existence of a positive return to beauty even in the public sector, but the absence of good evidence of sorting between legal specialties based on looks points more toward pure customer discrimination.

More important than our demonstration of beauty's effect on earnings is the approach that we have indicated and followed for determining the source of that effect, an approach that is relevant for the study of any ascriptive characteristic. Simply demonstrating that some characteristic generates effects in the labor market, as has become standard in studies of labor market discrimination, is not enough. If we are concerned about those effects, we cannot assume that employers are the ultimate cause simply because they are the proximate cause. Instead, we need to determine the ultimate cause to discover whether public-policy intervention is required and, if so, how to target it efficiently and equitably so as to alter any detrimental labor market effects of the particular characteristic.

There is a large literature on workers' sorting themselves across fields/areas/industries depending on the relative returns to some particular characteristics that they may possess. We have extended models of that type to account for the dynamic sorting that occurs as the returns to characteristics in different sub markets change over time or as information is revealed to workers about their relative productivity in different sectors. We find empirical support for the standard implication that workers choose that type of work where the payoff to the characteristic with which they are relatively well endowed is the greatest, but we also generate evidence that dynamic sorting occurs in directions consistent with changes in the relative returns to the characteristic (in this case, beauty). This analysis could be fruitfully applied to examining patterns of dynamic sorting by race and sex to study the effect of discrimination on the basis of those characteristics. Other areas of labor market behavior, for example, risk-taking in occupational choice, where the returns differ across sectors and change as workers age, could also be examined using this approach.

15

What is Discrimination? Gender in the American Economic Association, 1935–2004

Fifty years ago Gary S. Becker (1957) set out the definition of discrimination used by economists today: a premium required to interact with a member of some group when that person is, except for group membership, identical to other individuals who are not discriminated against. This concept has generated an immense empirical literature designed to measure the extent of market discrimination (see, e.g., Francine D. Blau and Lawrence M. Kahn, 2000, on gender discrimination). This study presents an example that seems to indicate irrational discrimination against one group (men) and in favor of women. We show, however, that the same facts are consistent with rational preferences in favor of women, or with irrational discrimination against this seemingly favored group.

15.1. Initial Results

We illustrate this proposition with a particularly stark example of apparent gender discrimination - a female advantage in elections of officers of the American Economic Association. We know (Alan E. Dillingham et al., 1994) that women had an advantage in election to office in a much smaller association of economists. In elections to confer an

The original version of this chapter was published as: Hamermesh, Daniel S./Donald, Stephen G. (2006). What Is Discrimination? Gender in the American Economic Association, 1935-2004, in: The American Economic Review, 96(4): 1283-1292.

honorific in another association, however, female economists were treated identically to males with objectively identical qualifications (Hamermesh and Peter Schmidt, 2003). To shed light on general issues of discrimination, we examine the determinants of the outcomes of elections from 1935 through 2004 in the AEA, where there are far more voters than in any other election in the profession. We relate them to the candidates' ascriptive characteristics and a measure of their scholarly impact. The results suggest the difficulty of identifying the causes and even the direction of discrimination.

Beginning with officers whose terms started in 1935, each year the AEA has sent its members slates of four nominees for each of two positions as vice-president, and four nominees for each of two positions on the Executive Committee, to take office beginning the next calendar year (year *t*).[1] Those elected have some (consultative) decision-making power over the affairs of the Association and hold offices that many might view as prestigious. Lists of candidates and winners of these four-person elections, beginning with 1935, form the basis of the dataset used here.

Figure 15.1.

Percent Female among Candidates and Winners, AEA Elections 1935–2004

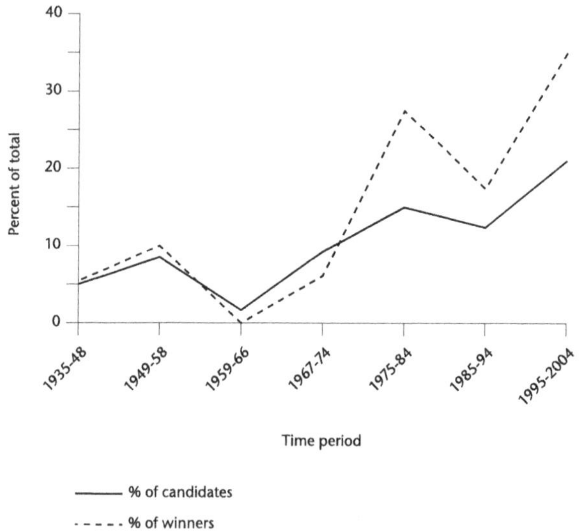

Information on the representation of women on the ballots and among the winners is presented in Figure 15.1. (The event is winning or losing an election and has a probability of 0.50.) The figure makes it strikingly clear that since the early 1960s an increasing fraction of candidates have been female. It also demonstrates that since the early 1970s female candidates have had a substantially better chance of winning these elections than have male candidates.

15.2. Other Factors Affecting Electoral Outcomes

The information presented in Figure 15.1 ignores the impact of other observable characteristics that may have made women more attractive candidates than their male counterparts.Because of difficulties in obtaining some of the measures, we concentrate here on elections from 1959 to 2004. As measurable indicators of the candidates' potential appeal, we include

- *Honorable* – whether the candidate ever held a governmental position that carries with it the designation "honorable."[2] We include this measure to examine whether the publicity attached to such positions, or perhaps the recognition that they convey of the candidate's competence, affects her/his electoral chances.
- *Affiliation* – including measures of whether the candidate is affiliated with a "Top 5" institution (Harvard, MIT, Princeton, Chicago, or Stanford) and whether she/he is not an academic.
- *Race* – whether the candidate is an African American.
- *Field* – whether the candidate is a theorist or econometrician. This designation is clearly impressionistic, so that any results on this measure must be interpreted carefully.
- *Distinction* – whether the candidate is a future Nobel Prize winner.[3] This measure is less relevant for elections during the last decade of our sample, given the likely lags between recognition by the local (American) profession and by the Swedish Nobel Committee.

All but the last of these characteristics have been readily available to the voters, as the Association has been enclosing an information sheet with a brief vita along with the ballot, and has even included pictures since at least the mid-1960s.

We also construct a measure of scholarly impact: the number of citations each candidate receives to her/his work, a variable designed to indicate standing in the profession around the time of the election when the voters are considering candidates' qualifications. Among candidates for office in the elections from 1968 to 2004, we found citations in year $t - 2$ (the most recent complete calendar year in which impressions on the voters could have been made). For the elections for office from 1959 to 1967 we sum citations in years $t - 4$, $t - 3$, and $t - 2$.[4] In all cases we calculate the candidates' share of citations among the nominees for the particular offices. Thus, if all candidates in a four-person election were identical along this dimension, each would obtain a value of 0.25 for this measure. This measure indicates the relative importance of the candidates' work in the eyes of the profession as a whole.[5]

While the ascriptive measures we use are not orthogonal to each other, it is nonetheless interesting to examine how candidates' unconditional chances of electoral victory differ by their characteristics. The upper part of Table 15.1 presents statistics – the means and their associated standard errors – describing in columns 1–3, respectively, the shares of candidates having each characteristic, their success probability, and the average share of citations of candidates in the category. The most striking feature is that for all but the first two characteristics listed in the table the probability of success does not differ significantly from 0.50. There is no evidence from the average outcomes that being at a Top 5 institution or outside academe, or being an African American, a theorist or econometrician, or a future Nobel Prize winner, is significantly related to the likelihood of victory in these elections.

Only two characteristics – gender, and having held or currently holding a high-level government position – have a significant relation to the likelihood of winning. Seventy percent of "honorable" candidates are elected, significantly different from 50 percent ($t = 2.84$, $p < 0.01$); 74 percent of female candidates emerged victorious from their elections, also significantly different from 50 percent ($t = 3.68$, $p < 0.001$). The average female candidate and the average honorable candidate have far below the average fraction of citations, 0.25, in any given election. Indeed, only 3 of the 46 female candidates had at least 25 percent of citations in their election. If scholarly impact matters, the advantage for women illustrated in Figure 15.1 understates the extent to which they have been favored in these elections.

The bottom part of Table 15.1 shows clearly that scholarly impact does matter. Each successively lower quartile of candidates by citation share has a successively lower probability of electoral victory, and the probabilities are nearly symmetric around 0.50. The chance that a candidate in the top quartile of citation shares wins an election differs from 50 percent by about the same (statistically significant) amount as does that of a candidate in the bottom quartile, and similarly for candidates in the second and third quartiles of the distribution of the shares of citations.

15.3. Estimating a Model of the Determinants of Electoral Success

Given the institutional arrangements governing the elections, any estimation procedure must account for the fact that there are exactly two winners in each four-person election. Thus, standard binary choice models (probits or logits) on observations on the individual candidates cannot be used to describe the outcomes. Although they correctly constrain each candidate's chances of election to be on the open unit interval, they cannot impose this basic institutional restriction. The appropriate way to think about the elections is as a choice among six (${}_4C_2$) possible pairs of candidates, only one pair of which can be victorious. Taking this view, conditional multinomial logit (CML) estimation (Jeffrey M. Wooldridge, 2002, pp. 500 *passim.*) would appear to be an appropriate way to estimate the determinants of the electoral results.

We describe each pair by the sum of its members' characteristics, e.g., number female, sum of the two candidates' shares of citations. CML estimates of the determinants of electoral victory in each of the 92 elections, 1959 to 2004, are presented in columns 1 and 2 of Table 15.2. The estimates corroborate and even strengthen the inferences from the descriptive statistics presented in Table 15.1. A candidate's share of citations has a significant positive effect on her/his electoral chances, as do gender and having held or currently holding a high-level government position. Moreover, the implied *t*-statistics on the coefficients of the variables "female" and "honorable" are larger than the *t*-statistics from Table 15.1 testing the hypotheses that the variable means differ from 0.50. This is not surprising, given that the share of citations raises the probability of election and is less than 0.25 in each of these groups. These three measures alone produce significant effects on the probability of election. As with inferences from the descriptive statistics, none of the other variables significantly affects electoral probabilities, although theorists and

Table 15.1.

Fractions of Candidates by Type and their Winning Chances and Shares of Citations, 92 Contested AEA Elections 1959–2004 ($N = 368$)[a]

Characteristic	(1) Share of candidates	(2) Win probability[b]	(3) Share of citations[c]
Female	0.125	0.739* (0.065)	0.102** (0.011)
Honorable	0.125	0.696* (0.069)	0.196** (0.023)
Top 5 school	0.370	0.574 (0.043)	0.320** (0.016)
Nonacademic	0.092	0.471 (0.087)	0.151** (0.025)
African American	0.046	0.412 (0.123)	0.087** (0.029)
Theory/econometrics	0.209	0.416 (0.057)	0.305** (0.020)
Future Nobelist	0.103	0.605 (0.080)	0.414** (0.029)
Share of citations:			
Top quartile		0.620* (0.051)	0.495** (0.012)
Second quartile		0.533 (0.052)	0.283** (0.004)
Third quartile		0.456 (0.052)	0.166** (0.003)
Bottom quartile		0.391* (0.051)	0.057** (0.003)

a Standard errors of means in parentheses.

b If candidates in the group had the same chance of electoral victory as the average candidate, each mean in this column would be 0.50. An asterisk denotes the mean is significantly different from 0.50.

c If candidates in the group had the same scholarly impact as the average candidate, each mean in this column would be 0.25. Double-asterisks denote the mean is significantly different from 0.25.

econometricians do suffer some electoral disadvantage, while faculty members at Top 5 institutions reap some advantage.[6]

While this estimation method solves the problem of constraining the winners' electoral chances, in our case it is likely to fail to satisfy one of its central assumptions, the independence of irrelevant alternatives.

Since each of the winners is also included in two of the other five pairs of potential outcomes, it is extremely difficult to believe that the unobservables describing a particular pair of candidates are uncorrelated with the unobservables describing all five other pairs. Thus, we need to develop an estimator that constrains the winners' electoral probabilities and also accounts for dependence among the pairs of outcomes. The required multinomial multiple-response (MMR) estimator does not appear to have been addressed before (although a related econometric issue was modeled by David E. Bloom and Christopher L. Cavanaugh, 1986).[7]

Model the underlying desirability of candidate *j* in election *i* as:

$$(1) \qquad y^*_{ji} = x_{ji}\,\beta + \varepsilon_{ji}\,.$$

Let the indicator for the pair of candidates who won the election be $z_i\ \{j,\ l\}$ for $j \neq l$, where $z_i\ \{j,\ l\} = z_i\ \{l,\ j\}$. Then the contribution of election i to the likelihood function is:

$$(2)\ L_i = \prod_{j=1}^{4} \prod_{l>j}^{4} \Pr\left(z_i\{j,\ l\} = 1 \mid x\ \right)^{z_i\{j,\ l\}},$$

where

$$\sum_{j=1}^{4} \sum_{l>j}^{4} z_i\ \{j,\ l\} = 1.$$

The issue is one of calculating the probabilities $\Pr(z_i\{j,\ l\} = 1 \mid x)$. Assume that the ε_{ji} are independent random variables. This assumption implies that the errors are independent across individual candidates. Arbitrarily ordering the observations so that candidates 1 and 2 win the four-person election, for a general distribution of the error terms,

$$(3)\ \Pr\ (z_i\ \{1,\ 2\} = 1 \mid x)$$
$$= \Pr\left(y^*_{1i} > y^*_{3i}\,,\ y^*_{1i} > y^*_{4i}\,,\ y^*_{2i} > y^*_{3i}\,,\ y^*_{2i} > y^*_{4i} \mid x_i\right)$$
$$= \Pr\left(\{ y^*_{1i} > y^*_{wi} \} \cap \{ y^*_{2i} > y^*_{wi} \} \mid x_i\right),$$

where $y^*_{wi} = \max\ \{y^*_{3i}, y^*_{4i}\}$. Noting that the probabilities can be written as expectations of indicator functions $(1(\cdot))$, and substituting from (1), we can rewrite (3) as

$$(4)\ \Pr\ (z_i\ \{1,\ 2\} = 1 \mid x)$$
$$= E\left(1(\{ y^*_{1i} > y^*_{wi} \}) \cdot 1\ (\{ y^*_{2i} > y^*_{wi} \}) \mid x_i \right),$$
$$= E\left(E\left(1(\{ \varepsilon_{1i} > y^*_{wi} - x_{1i}\,\beta \}) \mid\ y^*_{wi} \right) \cdot E\left(1\ (\{ \varepsilon_{2i} > y^*_{wi} - x_{2i}\,\beta \}) \mid\ y^*_{wi} \mid x_i\right),$$
$$= E\left((1(- H(y^*_{wi} - x_{1i}\,\beta)) \cdot (1 - H(y^*_{wi} - x_{2i}\,\beta)) \mid x_i\right),$$

where H is the cumulative distribution function of ε_{ji}. The particular estimator depends on the assumptions about the nature of the distribution of the ε_{ji}.

This technique for modeling MMRs would appear to be applicable to elections in which there is more than one winner and more candidates than winners.[8] The general technique is applicable to estimating the determinants of responses in any case in which there is a fixed number $K > 1$ of slots that must be filled from among a fixed number $N > K$ of choices. As an example, this approach fits quinella bets on horse races perfectly.[9]

We assume that the errors ε_{ji} in (1) are independent $N(0, 1)$, generating a probit-type estimator. The specific form is derived in the Appendix, along with that for a logit-type estimator.[10] The results of estimating the determinants of the electoral outcomes are presented in columns 3 and 4 of Table 15.2. They are qualitatively like those using CML: the impacts of each independent variable on the desirability index, y^*_{ji}, do not change much compared to the CML specifications. The implied t-statistics are roughly the same and, as with those specifications, none of the other covariates approaches statistical significance. Using this estimation procedure, only the three variables "female," "honorable," and "share of citations" significantly increase a candidate's electoral chances.[11] Clearly, and regardless of estimation method and other controls, women have been favored in these elections.[12]

Figure 15.1 suggested that something happened in the early to mid-1970s to alter electoral outcomes increasingly to favor female candidates. There is some evidence (John M. McDowell et al., 2001) that female economists' probability of tenure, conditional on an entry-level academic appointment, rose in the early 1980s, so this structural break may be part of a larger change in the profession's treatment of women. To examine this possibility, we reestimated the models in columns 1 and 3 of Table 15.2 over each of a large number of pairs of subperiods, beginning with the pair 1959–1966 and 1967–2004, and ending with the pair 1959–1996 and 1997–2004. Only for the pairs of subsamples, in which the earlier period is taken as ending anywhere from 1968 to 1975, do the coefficient estimates differ significantly across the two subperiods. The highest likelihood ratio is for a structural break between 1974 and 1975, and we use the latter subperiod here.[13] Before the mid-1970s, women's chances of being elected, given their other measurable characteristics, did not differ from those of men. Thereafter, women had an electoral advantage.

Table 15.2.

Conditional Multinomial logit (CML) and Multinominal Multiple Response (MMR) Estimates of the Determinants of Electoral Victory, AEA Elections[a]

	(1)	(2)	(3)	(4)	(5)	(6)	(7)	(8)
	1959–2004				1975–2004			
Estimator:	CML		MMR		CML		MMR	
Characteristic								
Female	1.732	1.699	1.359	1.349	2.270	3.674	1.744	2.622
	(0.377)	(0.380)	(0.306)	(0.322)	(0.472)	(0.987)	(0.360)	(0.604)
Share of citations	3.526	3.336	2.771	2.680	3.606	3.557	2.892	2.871
	(0.681)	(0.750)	(0.455)	(0.546)	(0.906)	(0.902)	(0.672)	(0.682)
Honorable	1.071	1.018	0.843	0.782	0.689	0.705	0.581	0.597
	(0.357)	(0.380)	(0.280)	(0.306)	(0.418)	(0.420)	(0.353)	(0.356)
Top 5 school		0.271		0.225				
		(0.253)		(0.205)				
Nonacademic		0.156		0.040				
		(0.442)		(0.307)				
African American		0.087		0.139				
		(0.602)		(0.379)				
Theory/econometrics		0.500		0.332				
		(0.305)		(0.272)				
Future Nobelist		0.270		0.118				
		(0.423)		(0.292)				
Female* no. of women in other election						-1.649		-1.089
						(0.849)		(0.570)
Log *L*	-139.89	-137.85	-140.64	-138.72	-88.41	-88.41	-88.41	-88.41
Number of candidates	368				240			

a Standard errors in parentheses.

Columns 5 and 7 in Table 15.2 show the estimates of the CML and MMR models for 1975 to 2004. The parameter estimates are not hugely different from their counterparts in columns 1 and 3, although with both estimators the statistical significance of honorable status is diminished. Both female and the share of citations, however, have large and highly significant effects on a candidate's chances of victory during the subperiod 1975–2004. When the five other covariates included in the estimates in columns 2 and 4 in the table were added to the models presented in columns 5 and 7, none had a parameter estimate larger than its standard error. This vector of additional covariates neither added significantly to the model's ability to describe the outcomes nor affected, in any major way, the estimated impacts of the three variables included in columns 5 and 7.

A final possibility is that there is crowding on the ballot – that the presence of a candidate in the other election with the same characteristic (e.g., more women) reduces the electoral chances of other candidates with that characteristic. The raw data strongly suggest that this is the case for female candidates. The 16 female candidates on the ballot between 1975 and 2004, who had no women candidates on the ballot in the other election, had a 0.94 probability of winning. The 20 women who had one female candidate in the other election had a 0.80 probability of victory, while only one of the three women who were candidates simultaneously with two women in the other election on the ballot won their elections.

To examine this issue in more detail, we successively reestimated the model in columns 1 and 3 for the subsample 1975–2004 to allow for this possibility for women and honorable candidates, and the model in columns 2 and 4 for those variables and for candidates from Top 5 schools, nonacademics, theorists/econometricians, and future Nobel laureates. For example, in the case of female candidates, the number of women on the ballot in the vice-presidential election in a particular year was interacted with the female indicator for candidates in the Executive Committee election in that year. For the covariates other than female, none of the effects came close to achieving statistical significance, nor did any alter our inferences about the importance of gender, citations and honorable status, and the unimportance of the other covariates, in determining outcomes.

For women candidates, the effect is substantial and statistically significant at nearly the 5-percent level, as the CML estimates in column 6 and the MMR estimates in column 8 show. When a woman is on the ballot and there are female candidates in the other election, her chances of winning are diminished. If there are two female candidates in the other election (the most yet nominated in any four-person election), the parameter estimates imply that her chance of victory differs little from that of an otherwise identical male candidate.[14] The results suggest that there is crowding in voters' behavior toward female candidates. With just one female candidate on each ballot, however, both women retain an advantage over male candidates. The median voter does not prefer electing just one ("token") female officer.

15.4. Gender Discrimination by Whom?

The means in Table 15.1 and the estimates in Table 15.2 show a clear electoral disadvantage for male candidates which developed in the 1970s. The first and simplest interpretation of the evidence is that women became the benefactors of reverse discrimination by the Association's electorate as the preferences of an unchanging median voter changed.

Figure 15.2.
Membership, Voter Turnout and Nominating Committee, 1935–2004

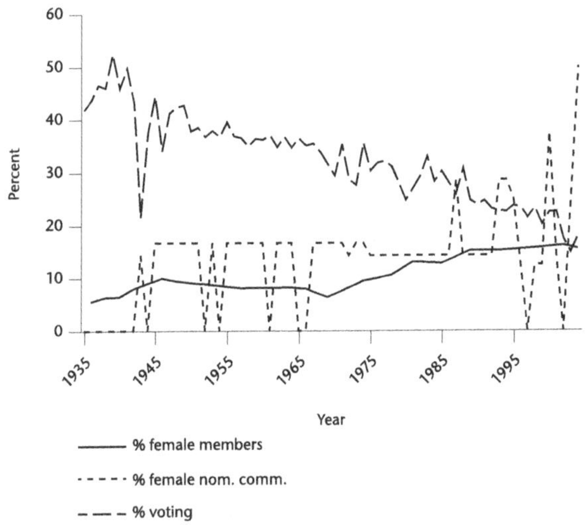

Another possibility is that the apparent reverse discrimination results from our having excluded measures of relevant productive characteristics (because we lack data on them). These might include organizational ability, willingness to accomplish tasks on time, and ability to interact productively with colleagues in reaching decisions; and they might be possessed in greater amounts by female candidates and therefore confer an advantage on them in the eyes of the voters.[15] If this were true, the change in electoral outcomes to favor women in the mid-1970s would require arguing that the electorate became more aware of the role of these unmeasurable characteristics, that their importance increased, and/or that gender differences in endowments of them rose.

A third possibility is that the identity of the median voter changed toward someone who is more likely to favor female candidates, perhaps a female voter. Since we cannot observe individual ballots, we cannot be certain about the gender of voters in this Association; but we can use information from the Association's *Directories* or *Handbooks* to infer the share of women in the potential electorate, the AEA membership. Taking all the available issues beginning in 1936, we sampled members' names randomly and in each case tried to infer from their first names whether they were men or women. While classification problems mean that measurement error is added to sampling error, there is no reason to believe that the estimates are biased downward. The sample sizes are such that, ignoring possible measurement error, the standard errors of the estimated means never exceed 1.1 percent.

Figure 15.2 presents our best estimates of the representation of women in the Association's membership. While women's share of AEA membership has grown, even today women account for no more than one-sixth of the members. The growth in female representation since the 1960s (which occurred exclusively in the 1970s and 1980s) may mean that the gender identity of the median voter, and perhaps her/his preferences, changed over this period.[16]

The percentage of female AEA members did not differ that greatly between the 1960s and the early 1980s, rising from about 8 percent to about 13 percent. Could this small increase have made such a huge difference in electoral outcomes? Voter participation in these elections is not large, as Figure 15.2 shows: during the 1970s turnout hovered around 30 percent, far more than twice the percentage female membership. Until the mid-1980s, the median voter must then have been male.

In the end, we cannot determine the ultimate cause of the development of the electoral advantage of women in this association. All the facts together, however, militate toward an interpretation that the median voter's (probably a male's) attitude toward gender in these elections changed in the early 1970s and yielded the apparent reverse discrimination that we have observed for three decades. Interestingly, this change occurred shortly after the enactment of Title IX - the profession's concerns filtered through its political system at roughly the same time as those of the national body politic.

We cannot tell whether the change in the mid-1970s represents irrational discrimination or a rational realization of what may be women's unobservable productive characteristics. The central finding is that, regardless of the underlying cause, the median voter appears to desire more female officers than she/he has had the opportunity of choosing in most years, but her/his desire for female candidates is not lexicographic.

Since 1974 women have accounted for only 16.2 percent of all candidates. Indeed, even during the last ten years of the sample women comprised only 21.5 percent of the candidates. Although these percentages have exceeded women's representation in the Association's membership, the suppliers of candidates - the nominating committees - might be viewed as having supplied too few female candidates to satisfy the voters' revealed preferences to vote for women. From this viewpoint, one could interpret the evidence presented here not as reverse discrimination, either irrational or rational, *in favor* of women by the electorate, but rather as discrimination *against* women by the suppliers of candidates for office in the Association - the nominating committees and the Association presidents who have selected them.[17] This possible undersupply of female candidates does not result from a lack of women among those who choose the candidates - the AEA nominating committees. Figure 15.2 also presents the percentage of women on the nominating committee for the election of officers in each year. There was one woman on the committee in most years between 1945 and 1966 (out of between five and seven members), and in every year from 1967 through 1986 there was exactly one woman, a percentage representation at least as high as their representation among the AEA membership. Since then, the number of women on the committee has fluctuated from zero to four (out of seven or eight members). Since the mid-1960s women have usually been better represented among the suppliers of candidates than in the Association as a whole, although only in the mid-1970s did the representation of women on the ballot increase rapidly, albeit not enough to satisfy the median voter.

15.5. Conclusions – Implications for Studying Discrimination

We have examined the determinants of victory in contested elections to office in the AEA. The estimates show that, while standard measures of scholarly impact affect outcomes, so does the gender of the candidate, an effect that became apparent only beginning in the mid-1970s. Coupled with very small changes in the gender mix of the electorate, this change suggests that the preference for women, given their representation on the ballot, probably arose from changing preferences among male voters. The results of these elections suggest the existence of reverse discrimination, rational or irrational, in favor of women. The apparent demand for more female candidates than have generally been provided may also mean that the Association's leaders have discriminated against women by failing to nominate them in numbers sufficient to satisfy the preferences of the electorate for female officers.

This conclusion may satisfy the priors of many observers of this Association and of labor markets generally. What if, however, we had shown that women's (or some other group's) electoral chances were significantly below 50 percent and that they were at least proportionately represented among the nominators and nominees? Would the analogous inference, that the suppliers of candidates had failed to accommodate voters' preferences and had been nominating too many women, be as appealing? Put in the context of labor markets, if we measured market discrimination against a minority group, an argument analogous to the one made here might point out that the outcome simply satisfies the tastes of the median consumer given the supply of labor by the minority group. In sum, the ambiguities in inferring what these differences in outcomes imply should hardly reassure anybody who has thought about issues of discrimination in this profession, in the electoral process, or in labor markets.

APPENDIX

Specific Functional Forms for the Multinomial Multiple-Response Estimator

In the case where $\varepsilon_{ji} \sim N(0,\ 1)$, we can use the symmetry of the normal distribution to specify equation (4) as

$$\text{(A1)}\qquad E\left(\left(1-\Phi(y^*_{wi}-x_{1i}\beta)\right)\cdot\left(1-\Phi(y^*_{wi}-x_{2i}\beta)\right)\mid x_i\right)$$
$$=E\left(\Phi(x_{1i}\beta-y^*_{wi})(\Phi(x_{2i}\beta-y^*_{wi})\mid x_i\right).$$

Letting candidates 1 and 2 in each election be the winners, we can write

$$\Pr\ (z_i\{1,2\}=1\mid x)$$
$$=\int \Phi(x_{1i}\beta-y^*_{wi})\,\Phi(x_{2i}\beta-y^*_{wi})\times\Phi(y^*_{wi}-x_{4i}\beta)\,\varphi(y^*_{wi}-x_{3i}\beta)\,dy+$$
$$\times\int \Phi(x_{1i}\beta-y^*_{wi})\,\Phi(x_{2i}\beta-y^*_{wi})\times\Phi(y^*_{wi}-x_{3i}\beta)\,\varphi(y^*_{wi}-x_{4i}\beta)\,dy.$$

The log-likelihood is then

$$\text{(A2)}\qquad \log L(\beta)$$
$$=\sum_{i=1}^{n} z_i\{1,2\}\log(\Pr\{1,2\}=1|x_i).$$

In the case of the extreme value distribution the error term is distributed

$$\varepsilon\sim g(\varepsilon)=\exp(-\varepsilon)G(\varepsilon),$$
$$G(\varepsilon)=\exp(-\exp(-\varepsilon)).$$

A typical expression is then

$$\exp(x_{3i}\beta)/[\exp(x_{1i}\beta)+\exp(x_{3i}\beta)+\exp(x_{4i}\beta)],$$

and the left-hand side of (A1) reduces to

$$E(G(y^*_{wi}-x_{1i}\beta)\,G(y^*_{wi}-x_{2i}\beta))$$
$$=[\exp(x_{3i}\beta)+\exp(x_{4i}\beta)]/$$
$$[\exp(x_{1i}\beta)+\exp(x_{2i}\beta)+\exp(x_{3i}\beta)+\exp(x_{4i}\beta)].$$

We then have

$$\begin{aligned}
&\Pr(z_i\{1, 2\} = 1 \mid x) \\
&= 1 - [\exp(x_{3i}\beta) + \exp(x_{4i}\beta)] / [\exp(x_{1i}\beta) \\
&\quad + \exp(x_{3i}\beta) + \exp(x_{4i}\beta)] - [\exp(x_{3i}\beta) \\
&\quad + \exp(x_{4i}\beta)] / [\exp(x_{2i}\beta) + \exp(x_{3i}\beta) \\
&\quad + \exp(x_{4i}\beta)] + [\exp(x_{3i}\beta) \\
&\quad + \exp(x_{4i}\beta)] / [\exp(x_{1i}\beta) + \exp(x_{2i}\beta) \\
&\quad + \exp(x_{3i}\beta) + \exp(x_{4i}\beta)].
\end{aligned}$$

The log-likelihood function is calculated using these expressions in (A2).

16

Strike Three: Discrimination, Incentives, and Evaluation

Tests of labor market discrimination typically compare labor market outcomes (e.g., wages, promotion rates) across groups and, after controlling for worker productivity, assign any residual differences to discrimination. But what if an evaluator who discriminates along the dimension being studied subjectively determines a worker's measured productivity, as is true in all but the simplest piece-rate environments? A worker subjected to such biased evaluations might appear less productive, which ordinarily would justify a lower wage. However, in this case the econometrician would underestimate, or perhaps even miss altogether, instances of labor market discrimination when they in fact exist.

A subtler complication is that workers, anticipating biased evaluations, may alter their behavior in ways intended to minimize its impact. For example, a police officer can either: 1) write traffic citations (the number of which can be objectively measured), or 2) investigate crimes (which is subject to performance review by a higher-ranking officer). If the officer has sufficient discretion, a biased evaluation in the second activity would lead the officer to alter the allocation of her time. Presumably, a positive bias would cause the officer to spend more time investigating crimes, and vice versa. Such bias-induced shifts in behavior further complicate the identification problem in assessing the impact of discrimination in labor markets.

This study addresses both of these issues, using detailed data on the evaluation, observed strategies and performances of Major League

The original version of this chapter was published as: Parsons, Christopher A./Sulaeman, Johan/Yates, Michael C./Hamermesh, Daniel S. (2011). Strike Three: Discrimination, Incentives, and Evaluation, in: American Economic Review, 101: 1410–1435. © 2011 by American Economic Association.

Baseball (MLB) players. Our focus is on racial/ethnic bias, specifically between the umpire (evaluator) and the pitcher (worker), although the arguments we develop apply to any type of subjective bias.[1] We pay particular attention to the race/ethnicity "match" of the umpire and pitcher, which occurs when, for example, a black umpire evaluates a black pitcher, as opposed to evaluating a white or Hispanic pitcher.

Our first observation is that pitchers who match the race/ethnicity of the homeplate umpire appear to receive slightly favorable treatment, as indicated by a higher probability that a pitch is called a strike, compared to players who do not match. Although this confers an advantage to some players at the expense of others, the effect we document here is small, on average affecting less than a pitch per game. Much more interesting are situations *when* and *where* the effects are strongest. Roughly one-third of the ballparks we study contained a system of computerized cameras (QuesTec) used to evaluate the umpires, comparing their ball/strike calls to a less subjective standard. Umpires have strong incentives to suppress any bias in such situations, as the QuesTec evaluations are important for their own career outcomes. With such *explicit* monitoring, evidence of any race or ethnicity preference vanishes entirely.

We find similar effects with *implicit* monitoring; when a game is well attended (and presumably more closely scrutinized), or when the pitch is pivotal for an at-bat, race/ethnicity matching again plays no role in the umpire's evaluation. In situations where the umpire is neither explicitly nor implicitly monitored, the effect of the bias is considerable. As an example, a Hispanic pitcher facing a Hispanic umpire in a low-scrutiny setting (e.g., no cameras, poorly attended) receives strikes on 32.5 percent of called pitches, which drops to 30.0 percent if a black umpire is behind the plate.

Such direct effects are magnified when pitchers adjust their strategies in response to biased evaluations. Like the multitasking police officer mentioned previously, a pitcher can alter his behavior to make himself either more immune, or more exposed, to the umpire's judgment. Specifically, pitches thrown near the borders of the strike zone (e.g., over one of home plate's corners) are called balls nearly as frequently as they are called strikes. They constitute a "fuzzy" region where the umpire can employ maximum subjectivity. Because such pitches are more difficult for batters to hit than those thrown directly into the strike zone, we would expect pitchers aware of favorable treatment to throw disproportionately to this fuzzy region. We find exactly this. Pitchers who match the umpire's race/ethnicity attempt to "paint the corners," throwing pitches allowing umpires the most discretion. This tendency is much stronger in low-scrutiny situations, when umpires face a lower cost of indulging their preferences.

At the end of both exercises, we are left with two specific conclusions. First, incentives matter. Unless provided strong incentives not to do so, umpires appear to allow the pitcher's race or ethnicity to influence their subjective judgments. This leads to a small, but nontrivial, direct effect on the game, simply by increasing the probability that a pitch is called a strike. Second, pitchers appear to understand these incentive effects and take measures to protect themselves by avoiding situations requiring a high degree of subjectivity when facing a downward bias.

The results also lead to two general conclusions. First, these results show that when worker productivity is measured subjectively, and when such measurements are biased by discrimination, the usual tests for discrimination are biased toward finding nothing. We illustrate the size of this bias in our sample of baseball pitchers. Second, they illustrate the need to be aware of the manner in which discrimination in one facet of evaluation can lead market participants to alter their behavior in other dimensions.

Baseball offers several advantages when studying discrimination. First, because every pitch is potentially subject to the home-plate umpire's discretion when it is thrown (several hundred times per game), there is sufficient scope for racial/ethnic discrimination to be expressed, as well as for it to affect games' outcomes significantly. In addition, the very large number of independent pitch-level observations involving the interaction of different races/ethnicities allows us not only to explore umpires' preference for players of their own race/ethnicity, but also to examine preferences toward other races/ethnicities.[2] An additional feature of baseball data is that, unlike other sports where a group dynamic among officials may alter the expression of individual biases, the home-plate umpire is exclusively responsible for calling every pitch in a typical baseball game.[3]

The most fortunate aspect of the dataset is that it allows us to develop several independent proxies for the scrutiny of the umpire's decisions, and in so doing, to test for the existence of price-sensitive discrimination by umpires. The time period that we analyze, 2004–2008, is special, because only during this time were a portion of the ballparks outfitted with computers and cameras to monitor umpires' ball/strike calls. Because umpires are randomly assigned to venues, observing differences in their behavior between parks with and without monitoring technology makes a convincing case that properly placed incentives can have the desired effect. These results allow us not only to describe how biases can influence subjective performance valuations, but also to offer prescriptive suggestions to minimize their impact.

Several studies (e.g., Luis Garicano, Ignacio Palacios-Huerta, and Canice Prendergast 2005; Eric W. Zitzewitz 2006; and Thomas J. Dohmen 2008) have examined home-team preferences by referees/judges in various sports, and another, Michael A. Stoll, Steven Raphael, and Harry J. Holzer (2004), examines racial match preferences in employment generally. Our study most closely resembles Joseph Price and Justin J. Wolfers' (2010) work on NBA officiating crews' racial preferences. Although the first part of our empirical analysis corroborates their findings (but for a different sport), we are mainly interested in *when* or *where* racial/ethnic bias is most likely to be observed. Here, we offer two insights. First, we show that discrimination is price sensitive, so that making it more costly reduces its expression. Second, we show that, when quantifying how players are affected by biased performance evaluations, the direct effect is only part of the story. Because players will alter their strategies in response, even situations that are seemingly insulated from a biased evaluator (e.g., non-called pitches in baseball games) are affected.

This research adds to a large literature on racial discrimination in sports, specifically in baseball, going back at least to Anthony H. Pascal and Leonard A. Rapping (1972), James D. Gwartney and Charles T. Haworth (1974), and Gerald W. Scully (1974), and recently J. C. Bradbury (2007) generally, with others dealing with particular racial/ethnic issues (Clark Nardinelli and Curtis J. Simon 1990, David W. Findlay and Clifford E. Reid 1997, and Rodney D. Fort and Andrew M. Gill 2000). It includes studies of such outcomes as productivity, wages, customers' approbation of players, selection for honors, and others. There is some evidence of wage disparities among baseball players of different races, but the results are mixed, e.g., Lawrence M. Kahn (1991). The conclusions of racial discrimination (or lack thereof) in this literature depend upon each player's productivity being accurately measured, as measured productivity is typically the crucial control variable. We suggest questioning this central assumption: If officials' judgments are themselves subject to racial/ethnic bias, adjusting for differences in the returns to *measured* productivity will not enable us to obtain proper measures of the extent of discrimination.

The results allow us to think about the deeper question of measuring discrimination generally. If, as we show here, the match to the race/ethnicity of their evaluator affects evaluations of workers, then the measured productivity of the worker will depend on the nature of that match. This difficulty has serious implications for measuring discrimination and is another manifestation of the difficulty of identifying discrimination pointed out by Stephen G. Donald and Daniel S.Hamermesh (2006).

In the next section we describe the pitch- and game-level data and explain our classification of umpires' and players' races/ethnicities. We analyze individual pitches in Section II and in Section III show that umpires express these preferences strongly only in times of low scrutiny. We examine the indirect impact of discrimination on pitchers' strategies in Section IV. Section V shows the overall effects on pitchers' performances and derives the size of the effects of biased performance evaluation on the measurement of wage discrimination generally and for the example of pitchers' salaries.

16.1. Data

16.1.1. *Pitches*

There are 30 teams in Major League Baseball, with each team playing 162 games in each regular season. During a typical game each team's pitchers throw about 150 pitches, so that approximately 700,000 pitches are thrown each season. We collect pitch-by-pitch data from ESPN.com for every regular-season MLB game from 2004–2008.[4] Our final dataset consists of 3,524,624 total pitches. For each pitch we identify the pitcher, pitcher's team, batter, batter's team, catcher, pitch count, score, inning, and pitch outcome. We classify each pitch into one of seven exhaustive and mutually exclusive categories: Called strike, called ball, swinging strike, foul, hit into play, intentional ball or hit by pitch. We supplement each pitch observation with other relevant information, including the stadium name, home team, away team, and the identities and positions of all four umpires.

16.1.2. *Player and Umpire Race/Ethnicity*

We next classify each position player, pitcher, and umpire who appears in our dataset as white, Hispanic, black, or Asian. To begin this task, we collect country of birth for every player and umpire.[5] Players or umpires are classified as Hispanic if they were born in: Colombia, Cuba, Curaçao,

Table 16.1.
Summary Statistics of Pitches

	Pitch outcomes, 2004–2008 (percentage distributions)							
	Total pitches	Called strike	Called ball	Swinging strike	Foul	In play	Intentional ball	Hit by pitch
All	3,524,624	17.09	36.56	8.98	17.08	19.41	0.63	0.25
Pitcher								
White ($N = 861$)	2,544,515	17.19	36.48	8.77	17.10	19.58	0.64	0.24
Hispanic ($N = 278$)	793,797	16.86	36.77	9.57	17.03	18.86	0.64	0.27
Black ($N = 37$)	89,355	16.24	36.68	9.71	17.54	19.07	0.52	0.24
Asian ($N = 39$)	96,957	17.12	36.81	8.87	16.59	19.70	0.64	0.27
Batter								
White ($N = 1,147$)	1,813,768	17.37	36.90	9.11	16.92	18.84	0.58	0.28
Hispanic ($N = 493$)	1,061,115	16.81	35.91	8.72	17.35	20.31	0.68	0.22
Black ($N = 187$)	571,563	16.65	36.67	9.17	17.08	19.50	0.70	0.23
Asian ($N = 46$)	78,178	17.63	36.80	7.44	17.35	19.88	0.71	0.19
Umpire								
White ($N = 91$)	3,215,949	17.09	36.55	8.97	17.09	19.41	0.64	0.25
Hispanic ($N = 5$)	111,524	17.06	36.80	8.87	16.97	19.33	0.70	0.27
Black ($N = 6$)	197,151	17.13	36.63	9.00	16.99	19.44	0.59	0.22

Dominican Republic, Mexico, Nicaragua, Panama, Puerto Rico, or Venezuela. Players from Japan, South Korea, and Taiwan are classified as Asian. We classify an additional 69 players using an *AOL Sports* article which lists every African-American player on an MLB roster at the beginning of the 2007 season.[6] We also utilize a similar list of past and present Hispanic players in MLB from Answers.com.[7] All remaining unclassified players and umpires are classified by visual inspection of pictures found in Internet searches.[8] Three of the race/ethnic groups are represented among umpires (there are no Asian umpires in MLB), and all four are represented among pitchers.

Table 16.1 presents the distributions of the pitch outcomes. The first row of the table summarizes all pitches, while subsequent rows subdivide pitches based on the race/ethnicity of the pitcher, the batter, and the home plate umpire, respectively. Approximately 46 percent of pitches elicit a swing from the batter, hit the batter, or are intentionally thrown out of the strike zone. Our pitch-level analysis focuses on the 54 percent of pitches (1.89 million) that result in called strikes or balls, since these alone are subject to evaluation by the home-plate umpire. Of these, about 32 percent are called strikes, and the rest are called balls.

The table also reports the number of pitchers, batters, and home-plate umpires in each of the four race/ethnicity categories. The percentages of white pitchers (70 percent) and batters (61 percent) are lower in our sample than the percentage of white umpires (89 percent). On the other hand, Hispanics, constituting 23 percent of pitchers and 26 percent of batters, are underrepresented among umpires (only 5 percent). Black pitchers, batters, and umpires make up 3 percent, 10 percent, and 6 percent of the samples, respectively. Asian players constitute 3 percent of pitchers and 2 percent of batters.

16.1.3. Pitch Location

For approximately one-third of the games played in the 2007 season and all those played in 2008, we collected from PITCHf/x several additional variables. PITCHf/x, a computerized technology owned by Sportvision, uses two cameras to record the path of a pitch from the pitcher's hand to home plate.[9] The parameters measured and calculated using this technology include: 1) the pitch type, determined using MLB's proprietary neural net classification algorithm, 2) the estimated pitch location when it crosses the home plate relative to the center of the front of the home plate, and 3) the top and bottom of the strike zone as determined by the PITCHf/x operator.[10]

16.1.4. Pitcher Performance

For each starting pitcher's appearance in each game, we collect from box scores the number of innings pitched, the numbers of hits, runs, and home runs allowed, walks, strikeouts, and earned runs (downloaded from the ESPN Website). We also obtain the final score of the game to identify the winning and losing teams.

Table 16.2.

Summary of Umpires' Called Pitches by Umpire-Pitcher Racial/Ethnic Match, MLB 2004–2008

	Pitcher race / ethnicity				
	White	Hispanic	Black	Asian	Total percent called strikes
Umpire race / ethnicity					
White					
Pitches	2,319,522	726,137	81,251	89,039	
Called pitches	1,244,523	389,411	42,986	47,973	
Called strikes	398,673	122,441	13,194	15,269	
Percent called strikes	32.03	31.44	30.69	31.83	31.86
Hispanic					
Pitches	80,956	24,844	2,559	3,165	
Called pitches	43,632	13,299	1,374	1,760	
Called strikes	13,857	4,194	429	549	
Percent called strikes	31.76	31.54	31.22	31.19	31.68
Black					
Pitches	144,037	42,816	5,545	4,753	
Called pitches	77,472	23,035	2,922	2,561	
Called strikes	24,900	7,195	886	784	
Percent called strikes	32.14	31.24	30.32	30.61	31.86
Total percent called strikes	32.03	31.43	30.69	31.75	31.86

16.2. Called Pitches and Umpire-Pitcher Matches

Table 16.2 reports for each pitcher/umpire racial/ethnic combination the number of pitches thrown, the number of called pitches, the number of called strikes and the percentage of called pitches that are strikes. About two-thirds of the called pitches in our sample occur when the umpire and pitcher share the same race/ethnicity (mostly white pitcher/white home-plate umpire). While the percentage of pitches that are called is similar in situations where the umpire's and pitcher's race/ethnicity match and in situations where they do not (53.7 percent), a central difference is that the percentage of called pitches that are strikes is higher when they match (32.0 percent) than when they do not (31.5 percent).

The summary statistics in Table 16.2 ignore possible differences inherent in the quality or "style" of pitchers by race/ethnicity. They also ignore the possibly different outcomes generated by nonrandom assignment of pitchers to face different opponents, and of umpires to games played by particular teams.[11] To account for these and other potential difficulties, our central test for umpires' discrimination in calling strikes is the specification:

$$\text{(1)} \qquad \text{I(Strike | Called Pitch)}_i = \gamma_0 + \gamma_1 UPM_i + \gamma_2 \text{Controls}_i + \varepsilon_i,$$

where the dependent variable is an indicator of whether a called pitch is a strike, the γ are parameters, ε is a well-behaved error term, and i indexes pitches. The main explanatory variable of interest is *UPM*, an indicator of whether the umpire (*U*) and pitcher (*P*) match (*M*) on race/ethnicity. In almost all of our tests, we include fixed effects for each pitcher, umpire, and batter so that *UPM* reflects the *marginal* effect of a racial/ethnic match between the home-plate umpire and pitcher. That is, because any player or race-specific effects are swept out by the fixed effects, umpires' bias is identified purely via the interaction term, *UPM*.

In addition to these, we employ a number of control variables. Pitch-count indicators, which record how many balls and strikes have accrued during a particular at-bat, are crucial because pitchers alter the location of their pitches based on the ball-strike count. Inning indicators are also included, because pitchers are usually less fatigued early in games, and because a "relief" pitcher often replaces a pitcher who starts the game in later innings, with a different (often reduced) accuracy.[12] Home-field bias is captured by top-of-the-inning indicators, which account for which team is pitching. Lastly, we include the pitcher's score advantage (defined as the number of runs, potentially negative, by which the pitcher's team is ahead).

Table 16.3.1.

Effects on Called Strikes of the Relationship between Pitcher and Umpire Race/Ethnicity, MLB 2004–2008

Pitchers Umpire	White All (1)	Black All (2)	Hisp. All (3)	All White (4)	All Black (5)	All Hisp. (6)
Panel A. Main parameter estimates						
Black umpire	−0.0005	0.0004	−0.0010			
	(0.0019)	(0.0105)	(0.0031)			
Hispanic umpire	−0.0045	0.0097	0.0079			
	(0.0024)	(0.0127)	(0.0049)			
Black pitcher				−0.0148	−0.0157	−0.0027
				(0.0023)	(0.0103)	(0.0125)
Hispanic pitcher				−0.0072	−0.0089	0.0020
				(0.0009)	(0.0034)	(0.0054)
Observation	1,365,660	47,285	425,731	1,676,942	103,429	58,305
R^2	0.031	0.031	0.030	0.028	0.025	0.030
Fixed effects	P	P	P	U	U	U

Pitchers Umpires	All All (7)	All All (8)	All All (9)
UPM	0.0024	0.0021	0.0016
	(0.0013)	(0.0017)	0.0017)
Observations		1,838,676	
R^2	0.031	0.091	0.091
Fixed effects	P	PU	PUB

Table 16.3 presents the results of estimating equations where the pitcher's and umpire's race/ethnicity are allowed to influence the likelihood of a called strike. All the estimates are based on linear-probability models (but probit estimates present the same picture) with heteroskedasticity-robust standard errors. The first three columns show specifications separately for white, black, and Hispanic pitchers, respectively, controlling for umpire race/ethnicity and pitcher fixed effects. The next three columns show separate equations for white, black, and Hispanic umpires, respectively, controlling for pitcher race/ethnicity and umpire fixed effects. The final three columns include all pitchers and umpires, with each column adding successive vectors of fixed effects, including in the final column pitchers, umpires, and batters.

Table 16.3.2.

Effects on Called Strikes of the Relationship between Pitcher and Umpire Race/Ethnicity, MLB 2004–2008 (continued)

	Strikes		
Balls	0	1	2
Panel B. Coefficients on pitch count indicators in the specification in column 9			
0		−0.226	−0.355
		(0.001)	(0.001)
1	−0.023	−0.190	−0.326
	(0.001)	(0.001)	(0.001)
2	0.042	−0.151	−0.289
	(0.002)	(0.002)	(0.001)
3	0.206	−0.060	−0.257
	(0.003)	(0.003)	(0.002)

2nd	3rd	4th	5th	6th	7th	8th	9th	Top of inning	Pitcher's score advantage
Panel C. Coefficients on inning indicators and pitcher's score advantage in the specification in column 9									
-0.010	-0.024	-0.032	-0.032	-0.034	-0.025	-0.024	-0.018	0.006	0.002
(0.001)	(0.001)	(0.001)	(0.001)	(0.001)	(0.001)	(0.002)	(0.002)	(0.001)	(0.004)

Notes: All estimates are based on linear-probability models with heteroskedasticity-robust standard errors in parentheses, here and in Tables 16.4-16.6. UPM indicates whether the umpire and pitcher match on race/ethnicity. The control variables whose coefficients are reported in panels B and C are included in all the estimates. Pitcher's Score Advantage is the number of runs, potentially negative, that the pitcher's team is ahead at the time of the pitch. Top of Inning is an indicator equaling 1 if the home team is pitching. *P*, *U*, and *B* represent pitcher, umpire, and batter fixed effects, respectively. Standard errors in parentheses.

There is some, albeit weak, evidence of favoritism by umpires for pitchers who match their race/ethnicity. For example, column 1 shows that Hispanic umpires judge white pitchers more harshly than do white umpires (the omitted indicator variable), but that they judge Hispanic pitchers more favorably (column 3). Similarly, column 4 shows that white umpires, the overwhelming majority, judge minority pitchers more harshly than they judge white pitchers. Taking the results in column 9 with the full sets of control variables and fixed effects as the best description of the underlying behavior, however, it is quite clear that there is no generally significant impact of the match on umpire evaluations ($p = 0.34$).

Although the results with the broadest sets of fixed effects do not suggest a significant effect of the umpire-pitcher match, the point estimate implies that a given called pitch is approximately 0.16 percentage points more likely to be a strike if the umpire and pitcher match race/ethnicity. The likelihood that a given called pitch is called a strike is 31.9 percent. Thus when the umpire matches the pitcher's race/ethnicity, the rate of called strikes rises by one-half percent above the rate when there is no match.[13]

16.3. Biased Evaluation When Bias Is Costly

One might examine the results in Table 16.3 and conclude that, while the point estimates are interesting, their statistical insignificance means that there is very little here. Given an economist's view that agents acting out their preferences will react to the price of an activity, however, it is worthwhile examining the impacts of umpire-pitcher matches as the price of discrimination changes. We begin by asking what factors affect the price of expressing racial or ethnic discrimination. Studies of cognitive behavior indicate that presenting the biased party with counterexamples of the stereotype of interest can reduce the severity and/or frequency of the biased behavior (Stephanie A. Goodwin et al. 2000; Irene V. Blair 2002). In other words, simply making conscious a subconscious bias imposes a sufficient psychological cost to mitigate its expression. Another mechanism is to increase the visibility of the biased party's behavior, potentially exposing the offender to social or legal penalties. Here we proxy the price of discrimination by the extent to which an umpire's evaluations of pitchers will be scrutinized. We employ three different measures to examine whether a higher price of discrimination reduces the extent to which umpires engage in discriminatory behavior.

The first source of scrutiny is QuesTec, a computerized monitoring system intended to evaluate the accuracy and consistency of home-plate umpires' judgments. From 2004–2008, QuesTec had been installed in 11 of MLB's 30 ballparks.[14] QuesTec's Umpire Information System (UIS) consists of four cameras that track and record the location of each pitch, providing information about the accuracy and precision of each umpire's ball and strike calls. Despite opposition from some umpires and players (perhaps most memorably, pitcher Curt Schilling's assault on a camera after a poor outing), the QuesTec system served as an important tool to evaluate umpires during our sample period. According to the umpires' union's agreement with MLB, QuesTec is the primary mechanism to gauge umpire performance. If more than 10 percent of an umpire's calls differ from QuesTec's records, his performance is considered substandard, which can influence his promotion to "crew chief," assignment to postseason games, or even retention in MLB.[15]

Because QuesTec is installed in roughly one-third of ballparks, and because umpiring crews are rotated randomly around the league's ballparks, virtually every umpire in our dataset calls a substantial number of pitches in parks with and without QuesTec.[16] Additionally, both the umpires' and teams' schedules change every year, exposing each umpire to a wide cross-section of batters and pitchers in both types of parks. Throughout the analysis we test whether greater scrutiny – the possibly higher cost of bias in subjective evaluation of pitches in QuesTec parks – leads umpires to call strikes "by the book." Any role that racial/ethnic (or any other) preferences play in influencing pitch calls should be mitigated if costs of being judged substandard are imposed, as through QuesTec. Some pitchers may, however, react differently from others in response to QuesTec.[17] For that reason, in all of the estimates in this part (and hereafter) we include fixed effects not only for each pitcher, umpire and batter, but also for the presence or absence of QuesTec in each game, i.e., pitcher-QuesTec fixed effects, umpire-QuesTec fixed effects, and batter-QuesTec fixed effects.

Figure 16.1.

Race and Called Strike Percentages in QuesTec and Non-QuesTec Ballparks

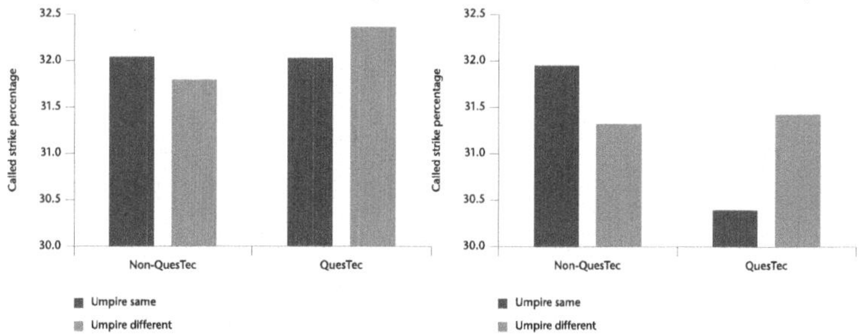

Figure 16.1 graphs the average percentages of called pitches that are strikes in ballparks with and without QuesTec, for white and minority pitchers respectively. The effect of monitoring on umpires' behavior is apparent, with both white and minority pitchers being judged differently by umpires of matched race/ethnicity, depending on whether the pitch is thrown in a park with QuesTec installed. The difference

in the called-strike percentage between QuesTec and non-QuesTec parks is significant for both white and minority pitchers.

Table 16.4.

Effects on Called Strikes of Explicit Monitoring of Umpires, MLB 2004–2008

	QuesTec (1)	Non-QuesTec (2)	All (3)
Umpire-pitcher match (UPM)	−0.0048	0.0059	0.0059
	(0.0027)	(0.0022)	(0.0022)
QuesTec × UPM			−0.0107
			(0.0035)
Observations	679,979	1,158,697	1,838,676
R^2	0.089	0.088	0.088

Notes: All estimates are based on linear-probability models with heteroskedasticity-robust standard errors in parentheses, here and in Tables 4-6. UPM indicates whether the umpire and pitcher match on race/ethnicity. The control variables whose coefficients are reported in panels B and C are included in all the estimates. Pitcher's Score Advantage is the number of runs, potentially negative, that the pitcher's team is ahead at the time of the pitch. Top of Inning is an indicator equaling 1 if the home team is pitching. P, U, and B represent pitcher, umpire, and batter fixed effects, respectively. Standard errors in parentheses.

Figure 16.2.

Race and Called Strike Percentages by Game Attendance

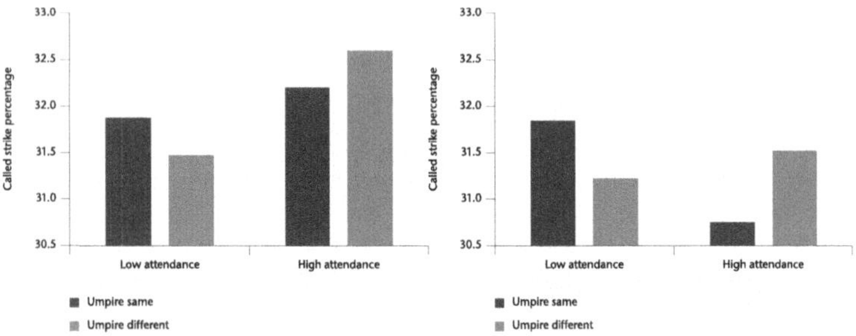

Note: Low (high) attendance games are those with percentage attendance below (above) the median.

Table 16.4 contains the results of estimating (1) separately for QuesTec and non-QuesTec parks, with controls for inning, pitch count, pitcher score advantage, and top of the inning.[18] The results are striking: in ballparks with the UIS, shown in column 1, the coefficient on *UPM* is –0.48 percentage points and is not significantly different from zero. In parks without QuesTec, shown in column 2, the same coefficient is 0.59 percentage points per pitch ($p = 0.007$). These differences make clear why *UPM* is not significant in the aggregate sample. The effects found in Table 16.3 averaged the statistically significant positive impact of an unscrutinized match (non-QuesTec) with a statistically insignificant negative impact of a scrutinized match (QuesTec) that is nearly as large. Thus, in the presence of price-sensitive discrimination, we should expect the point estimates in Table 16.3 to be low, since the entire sample consists of a mix of high- and low-scrutiny games. Specifically, QuesTec covers about 37 percent of pitches, so that the average result from Table 16.3 is easily reconciled: $(0.37)(-0.48) + (0.63)(0.59) = 0.19$, close to the 0.16 estimate obtained with a comparable set of fixed effects.

Column 3 of Table 16.4 presents the results when the QuesTec indicator is interacted with *UPM*. When the pitcher and umpire match race/ethnicity, pitching in a QuesTec ballpark reduces the likelihood that a called pitch is ruled a strike by over 1 percentage point, more than offsetting the favoritism shown by umpires when QuesTec does not monitor them. Each effect is highly significant, implying that umpires implicitly allow their apparent preference for matched pitchers to be expressed when the pitches underlying their decisions are not recorded.

QuesTec is an explicit monitoring technology. Implicit monitoring can have similar effects, suggesting that even subtle incentive mechanisms can have desirable effects on otherwise discriminatory outcomes. The two measures for implicit scrutiny of umpires are crowd attendance (scaled by stadium capacity) and the "importance" of the pitch.[19]

The idea for the first is simple. Having many fans close to home plate presumably exposes the umpire to their scrutiny – a badly called pitch is unlikely to go unnoticed.[20] Figure 16.2 confirms that crowd attendance, like QuesTec, dramatically alters umpire behavior. A game is defined as "well attended" if the crowd attendance is above the median percentage capacity in this sample, roughly 70 percent. Compared to well-attended games, umpires calling poorly attended games appear to favor pitchers of matched race/ethnicity. In the case of white pitchers, both minority and white umpires tend to call fewer strikes in poorly attended games, but the reduction in strikes called by minority umpires is over three times larger. The same effect is seen to an even greater degree among minority pitchers. During well-attended games, matching minority umpires call about 0.8 percent *fewer* strikes. They call 0.7 percent *more* strikes in poorly attended ones, a net effect of over 1.5 percentage points.

Table 16.5.

Effects on Called Strikes of Implicit Monitoring of Umpires, MLB 2004–2008

	High attendance (1)	Low attendance (2)	All games (3)
Panel A. Distinguishing by game attendance			
UPM	−0.0034	0.0064	0.0036
	(0.0025)	(0.0024)	(0.0019)
Well attended (>69% capacity)			0.0059
			(0.0012)
Well attended x UPM			−0.0037
			(0.0015)
Observations	902,261	936,415	1,838,676
R^2	0.089	0.088	0.088

	Terminal (4)	Non-terminal (5)	All pitches (6)	Early inning (7)	Late inning (8)
Panel B. Distinguishing by terminal count and inning					
UPM	−0.0026	0.0031	0.0031	0.0044	0.0023
	(0.0027)	(0.0021)	(0.0018)	(0.0031)	(0.0022)
Terminal count *UPM			−0.0058	−0.0086	−0.0038
			(0.0014)	(0.0024)	(0.0017)
Observations	427,136	1,411,540	1,838,676	641,053	1,197,623
R^2	0.175	0.042	0.088	0.095	0.085

		UPM interacted with				
	UPM	QuesTec	Well attended	Terminal count	Observations	R^2
Panel C. Combining explicit and implicit monitoring proxies						
All pitches (9)	0.0089	−0.0102	−0.0035	−0.0058	1,838,676	0.088
	(0.0024)	(0.0036)	(0.0015)	(0.0014)		

Notes: Low (high) attendance games are defined as games with percentage attendance below (above) the median. A terminal count is defined as a count with three balls and/or two strikes. Standard errors in parentheses.

In columns 1 and 2 of panel A in Table 16.5, we show the results of estimating (1) separately for well- and poorly-attended games respectively. Each equation includes the same battery of controls as in Table 16.4, i.e., pitcher, umpire, and batter fixed effects, pitch counts, and inning indicators. As with the QuesTec results, the *UPM* variable is significant (p = 0.008) only in poorly attended games, with an effect of 0.64 percentage points per pitch. During well-attended games there is no significant effect of an umpire-pitcher racial/ethnic match and, as before, the point estimate is negative. Column 3 generalizes the results by aggregating all games and interacting *UPM* with the indicator for a game's being well attended. In a poorly attended game, a pitch called by an umpire of the same race/ethnicity as the pitcher is 0.36 percentage points more likely to be judged a strike than when the umpire and pitcher do not match. If the game is well attended, this racial-match effect is eliminated: a pitch is no more likely to be called a strike if the pitcher and umpire match race/ethnicity. The results for this completely different proxy for the price of discrimination are qualitatively identical to those obtained for the QuesTec/non-QuesTec distinction.

Figure 16.3.

Race and Called Strike Percentages in Terminal Non-Terminal Counts

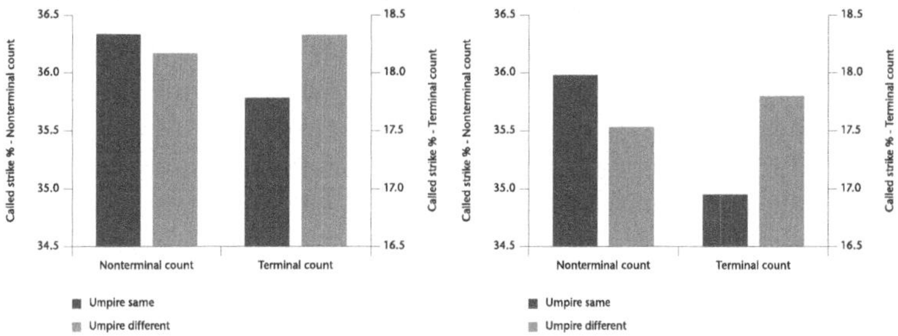

A third proxy for the scrutiny of umpires varies many times within each game. We separate pitches into two categories, "terminal" and "nonterminal." A pitch is potentially terminal if the umpire's next judgment can terminate the batter's plate appearance. Specifically, a pitch that is thrown with two strikes and/or three balls is potentially terminal, as a third strike or fourth ball terminates the at-bat. In such situations, the umpire's judgment is likely to be scrutinized more heavily by the pitcher, batter, catcher, managers, and fans. An initial glimpse into the effects of this distinction is shown in Figure 16.3. Here we observe the same contrast as for the previous two proxies for scrutiny, as umpires appear to favor pitchers with whom they match only in nonterminal counts, when scrutiny is likely to be reduced.

Columns 4 and 5 of panel B of Table 16.5 show estimates of (1) separately for terminal and non-terminal pitches, with pitcher, umpire and batter fixed effects and the usual set of control variables. We consider pitches of differing importance separately, with the result that the coefficients of *UPM* have opposite signs. For pitches that cannot be terminal, the estimated coefficient of *UPM* is 0.31 percentage points (p = 0.15) - umpires favor pitchers who match their own race/ethnicity. For potentially terminal pitches, where scrutiny of the umpire is likely to be greater, umpires appear to judge pitchers of their own race/ethnicity (insignificantly) more harshly than unmatched pitchers. In column 6 all pitches are aggregated, and *UPM* is interacted with an indicator for potentially terminal pitches. The results mimic those implicit in the estimates in columns 4 and 5, as the coefficient on the interaction term is negative and significant at better than the 1 percent level.

In columns 7 and 8 we consider another source of within-game variation in implicit scrutiny. We assume that, because umpires' evaluations are more likely to be pivotal late in games, scrutiny in the first few innings is likely to be comparatively less. We thus designate the first third (three innings) of a game as "early," and the remainder "late." We expect that a terminal count will have a stronger effect on the outcome of a pitcher-umpire racial/ethnic match in early innings. Comparing the results across the two columns, we see that this is the case, with the magnitude of the interaction between terminal count and *UPM* being over twice as large in early as in late innings (–0.86 versus –0.38 percentage points).

Our proxies for scrutiny are not redundant. The correlation between QuesTec and attendance percentage is small, and because the type of pitch (terminal or nonterminal) is a within-game measure, it is necessarily uncorrelated with either between-game measure. It is therefore not surprising that, when all three interactions are included simultaneously in panel C, everything remains significant with nearly identical magnitudes as in panels A and B.

Before proceeding to issues of robustness, we briefly address whether the *UPM* effect is due to positive bias for pitchers who match the umpire's race/ethnicity (i.e., favoritism), or to negative bias against those who do not match. Answering this question in our context is difficult, because ball and strike calls are inherently subjective (compare this to tennis, where the definition of a shot being "in" or "out" is completely objective, allowing, for example, computerized instant replay to reverse the judge's calls). Absent an objective standard on strike calls, we cannot precisely quantify the bias' direction; but comparing umpires' behavior between QuesTec and non-QuesTec ballparks provides some illumination.

If one accepts the premise that umpires exercise special care in QuesTec parks, the strike percentage there, although not perfect, is closer to the desired benchmark of objectivity that would permit the desired calculation. For each of the nine possible race/ethnic combinations, we compare the called strike percentage in QuesTec parks (the quasi-objective benchmark) to that in non-QuesTec parks. First, all three cases of a match (e.g., white-white) show a higher called strike percentage in non-QuesTec parks, which suggests favoritism in less scrutinized situations. Second, five of the six cases of nonmatch show a lower called strike percentage in non-QuesTec parks, which suggests negative bias. Such a two-sided pattern not only justifies the use of an aggregate *UPM* variable in Tables 16.3–16.5; it also demonstrates that the effect is symmetric and pervasive across nearly every possible combination. However, we do not focus further on the positive/negative bias distinction, because baseball – and indeed all games with winners and losers – is a zero-sum game. It is *relative* treatment that matters most, just as in labor markets generally it is disparate treatment, not the difficult-to-identify distinction between the absence of favoritism and the presence of negative bias, that underlies so much case law.

16.3.1. Other Matches

An umpire influenced by the race of the pitcher may also be influenced by that of the batter or the catcher, especially because in the latter case, the umpire is in continuing close contact. We find little evidence to support this argument. In the same types of regressions as in Tables 16.3–16.5, but with new matching variables, there is some very weak evidence that matched batters receive the type of preferential treatment experienced by matched pitchers; but the magnitudes are much smaller in every case and are generally statistically insignificant. Evidence for similar catcher-umpire matches is even weaker. For the purposes of our analysis, umpires appear almost exclusively focused on pitchers. Their matches with other relevant players do not affect their judgments. This may be because the pitchers are being judged constantly throughout the game, while other players are not. But, no doubt, one could put forth other explanations consistent with the absence of effects for batters.

16.3.2. Postseason

The three proxies for scrutiny have the advantage of splitting the sample of called pitches into two large groups, generating the statistical power required to detect subtle differences in called strike probabilities. There are many additional cross-sectional tests one could perform, e.g., comparing playoff to regular season games (because the former are likely to be particularly scrutinized), but such thin cross-sectional comparisons contain almost no power. For example, we replicate the analysis in panel C of Table 16.5, aggregating playoff and regular season games, and including interaction terms for postseason pitches with the coefficients of interest (unreported). There is only the weakest of evidence that playoff situations reduce further the expression of umpire bias (the interaction of postseason with *UPM* is negative, as expected, but the p-value is 0.74). We encounter a similar problem when, for example, examining particularly "important" games, such as those pivotal for playoff races late in the season.

16.3.3. Umpire and City Characteristics

It may be that umpires' measurable characteristics (beyond their race/ethnicity) and those of the city where a game is played explain our results. We collected demographic information on each umpire from a variety of sources and include his age and experience, and in many cases both his state of birth and residence. For each ballpark we also obtain the racial/ethnic breakdown of the surrounding metropolitan statistical area.

We find no evidence that the racial composition of an umpire's birthplace or residence predicts his propensity to penalize non-matching players, but there is some weak evidence that bias is more likely among younger and less experienced umpires. The coefficient on *UPM* in a respecification of (1) among the upper half of umpires ranked by experience is less than half its magnitude in estimates for umpires in the lower half of the distribution. If (1) is reestimated separately for the 18 "crew chiefs," veterans selected for their seniority and performance, the point estimate of the coefficient on *UPM* is nearly zero. This evidence is consistent with models of selection or learning. Perhaps discriminating umpires are not promoted and are dropped from the ranks. Alternatively, experience may teach umpires to restrain their own biases, although, if so, it is unclear why learning should be as slow as it apparently is.

We also reestimated the basic equation for blacks, and for Hispanics, separately, adding in each case main effects and interactions with *UPM* of the percentage of the minority group in the metropolitan area where the ballpark is located. Among blacks the interaction was positive, but statistically insignificant; among Hispanics it was negative and also statistically insignificant. Our conclusions are not affected by the racial/ethnic mix of the team's catchment area.[21]

16.3.4. Gaming the System

Perhaps managers are implicitly both aware of these preferences and able to act upon them. Because the majority of umpires are white, there is a distinct advantage for a team with one or more minority pitchers (particularly starting pitchers) to have QuesTec in its home park. We found no information about how teams were awarded QuesTec in their home parks, or whether they could influence this choice. A second possibility is that teams receiving QuesTec systems traded for minority pitchers from teams whose parks were not similarly equipped.

Although we have no direct evidence, some simple calculations suggest that either possibility may have merit. For visiting pitchers, the percentage of pitches thrown in QuesTec parks is nearly identical for whites and minorities (37.4 and 37.9 respectively). This is to be expected, because on average, teams play approximately the same fraction of opponents whose home stadiums contain QuesTec. Thus, there is no evidence that visiting managers adjust their pitching lineups to minimize the exposure of their minority pitchers to the subjective bias of a white umpire. Home pitchers tell a different story. Minority home pitchers throw 39.2 percent of their pitches in QuesTec parks, compared to only 35.5 percent for white pitchers.

Home minority pitchers are more likely to be in QuesTec environments, which can only be the case if their home ballpark has QuesTec. This is consistent with either initial nonrandom assignment of QuesTec to teams with a disproportionate number of minority pitchers, with transactions that increase the fraction of minority pitchers for teams already equipped with QuesTec, or with game-time lineup juggling by home teams. Although we cannot distinguish among these alternatives, this evidence is interesting in suggesting that biased evaluations in one area (e.g., called strikes) may have unintended consequences in other areas (e.g., the allocation of minority pitching talent). Note that none of these possibilities alters the significance or interpretation of the previous results, as all regressions control for player ability, umpire tendencies, and the presence or absence of QuesTec.

16.4. The Effects of Biased Evaluations on Agents' Strategies

The pitch-level evidence makes very clear that direct effects on pitch outcomes are small. Of course, one can construct specific examples where the estimated direct effect is fairly large: a black pitcher throwing a *nonterminal* pitch in the *early innings* of *poorly attended* games in a *non-QuesTec* ballpark gains over 6 percentage points by matching (41.4 versus 35.2 percent called strikes). But in most situations, the direct impact on called pitches is not large.

Indirect effects on players' strategies may, however, have larger impacts on the outcomes of plate appearances and games. The dynamic between a pitcher and batter is clearly affected by each party's beliefs about the umpire's evaluation in the event of a called pitch. If a pitcher expects favoritism, he will incorporate this advantage into his strategy, perhaps throwing pitches that allow the umpire more discretion.

This in turn may change the batter's optimal behavior. If the batter expects such pitches to be called strikes, he is forced to swing at "worse" pitches, which reduces the likelihood of getting a hit.[22] To appreciate more fully such induced changes in strategy, for all the starting pitchers for whom such data are available (over 500,000 pitches), we augment the pitch-level data with the dataset on pitch characteristics.[23] This level of detail allows addressing the extent to which pitchers alter their strategies (e.g., location and type of pitch) when facing a biased subjective evaluation.

Panel A of Table 16.6 summarizes the two location variables of interest: 1) the horizontal pitch distance, and 2) the pitch height. The first is the distance (in feet) from the center of home plate. (The slightly negative mean value for this variable reflects the tendency to avoid hitting or pitching inside to batters, most of whom are right handed.) The second is calculated as the pitch's vertical distance from the center of the strike zone, which is set by the computer operator to be between the batter's waist and knee (typically 2.5 feet above the ground). That this region varies among batters is not a problem, as all of the analyses include batter fixed effects.

Pitches in certain locations are almost always called one way or the other. This is apparent in Figure 16.4, which shows the location of all called strikes. A strike generally corresponds to the elliptical region centered around the plate and slightly below the batter's waistline. We define three concentric ellipses corresponding to: 1) the *inside* of the strike zone, 2) the *edge* of the strike zone, located just outside the center region, and 3) the complement to both regions, denoted as *outside*. Figure 16.4 shows the *inside*, an ellipse with major axis equal to 2 feet, and a minor axis equal to 1.6 feet. The *edge* is bordered by the *inside* and the *outside*, a larger ellipse with major axis 2.6 feet and minor axis 2.2 feet.

Table 16.6.

Pitch Location, Type, and the Effects of Pitcher-Umpire Racial/Ethnic Matches, MLB 2007–2008

	Mean	Quantiles:	5th	25th	50th	75th	95th
Panel A. Pitch locations (distance from home-plate center), 2007–2008, N = 538,194							
	-0.04		-1.53	-0.68	-0.04	0.60	1.44
	-0.11		-1.60	-0.69	-0.10	0.48	1.36

By location			By type				
Inside	Edge	Outside	Change-up	Curveball	Fastball	Slider	Other
Panel B. Percentage distributions of pitches by type, 2007–2008, N = 533,150							
39.55	19.98	40.47	13.43	10.88	57.48	13.52	4.69

	QuesTec (1)	Non-QuesTec (2)	All games (3)
Panel C. Effects on probability of pitch in the edge of the strike zone			
UPM	-0.0005	0.0095	0.0095
	(0.0047)	(0.0042)	(0.0042)
QuesTec x UPM			-0.0102
			(0.0063)
Observations	199,085	339,109	538,194
R^2	0.001	0.001	0.001

	QuesTec (4)	Non-QuesTec (5)	All Games (6)
Panel D. Effects on probability of a curve ball			
UPM	0.0033	0.0128	0.0125
	(0.0032)	(0.0029)	(0.0028)
QuesTec x UPM			-0.0087
			(0.0043)
Observations	195,777	337,373	533,150
R^2	0.020	0.021	0.021

Notes: The sample consists of all pitches (called and noncalled, excluding intentional balls) thrown by starting pitchers. In panel A the pitch location is the Cartesian coordinate, where the origin is the intersection of the vertical line from the center of the home plate and the horizontal line equidistant to the top and the bottom of the strike zone. The information is from PITCHf/x. Standard errors in parentheses.

We experimented with several alternative sizes for these ellipses, and none changes the basic results. Panel B of Table 16.6 summarizes the distribution of pitches by region. Roughly 40 percent are thrown in each of the *inside* and *outside* regions, with the balance in the *edge*.

Pitches thrown to each region generate different outcomes. A called pitch in the *inside* region will be a strike almost 87 percent of the time. Thus, a pitch thrown in this region is associated with little uncertainty. Similarly, a pitch thrown in the *outside* region has very little chance of being called a strike (3.8 percent), resulting in even less uncertainty about the call. A pitch thrown to the *edge* region, however, is called a strike 44.3 percent of the time, generating nearly the maximum uncertainty possible for a binomial variable. The *edge* region allows the umpire the greatest discretion.

Figure 16.4.

Called Strikes by Distance from Home-plate Center, 2007–2008 (*N = 144,990*)

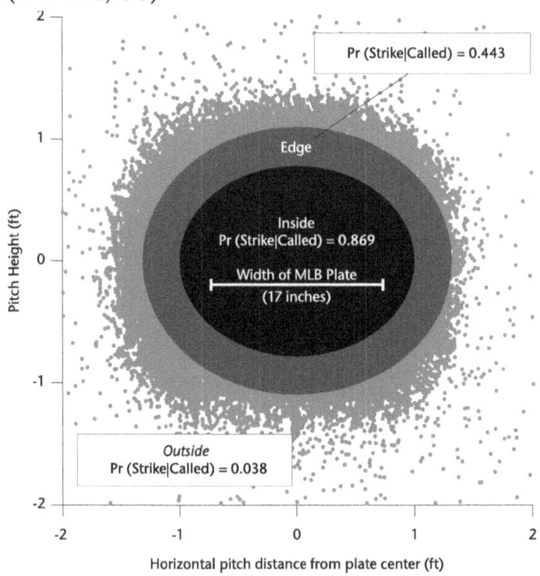

Given this distinction, it is comforting that the *edge* is where the effects of the previous sections occur. Matches in the *inside* are associated with an increase in the called strike percentage of only 0.3 percentage points, from 86.7 percent (no match) to 87 percent (match). The *outside* shows no difference at all. The percent called strikes in the *edge* is 43.6

absent a match, compared to 44.5 percent with a match. If pitchers understand this advantage, then we can predict that a matching pitcher will throw more pitches to the *edge*, where his advantage (courtesy of a biased umpire) is maximized. This aids the pitcher, because pitches to this region are considerably more difficult for the batter to hit.

Panel C of Table 16.6 presents the results of regressions similar to (1), except: 1) we include *all* pitches thrown by starting pitchers, not just called pitches, as was required for the previous analysis; and 2) the dependent variable indicates whether a pitch is thrown to the *edge*. As before, we include fixed effects for each pitcher, umpire, and batter, as well as all count and inning indicators. The first column shows the result for pitchers in QuesTec parks, where we see that a race/ethnicity match between the pitcher and umpire has virtually no effect on pitch location. In non-QuesTec parks, the situation changes drastically. Matches lead to a 0.95 percentage-point increase in the probability of throwing to the middle region, representing a 5 percent increase relative to the base nonmatch rate of 19.7 percent. The third column aggregates all observations, where the magnitude of the interaction term is over 1 percent ($p = 0.10$).

By throwing pitches that can reasonably be called as either balls or strikes, matching pitchers gamble on the fact that this region offers them an advantage. Panel D of Table 16.6 shows a related, but distinct, finding. Its interpretation requires some institutional detail. The most common pitch in baseball is the *fastball* (about 58 percent of our sample), which travels in a mostly straight line from the pitcher's hand toward home plate. Skilled pitchers, however, can place spin on pitches, causing them to deviate from a straight trajectory. Pitches with substantial "break" end their flights with dramatic dips that are notoriously difficult to hit solidly. Adding this vertical element also makes these pitches more difficult to judge.[24] As with pitches to the *edge*, judging a curveball requires subjectivity, which is the source of a matching pitcher's advantage. If matching pitchers are aware of a biased umpire, we would expect them to throw more breaking pitches.

The first column in panel D shows that, in QuesTec parks, a match is associated with a slight preference for breaking balls. In non-QuesTec parks, the magnitude quadruples to 1.28 percent ($p < 0.001$). The aggregation of all pitches in column 3 tells the same story. Matching in parks without explicit monitoring leads pitchers to select pitches allowing umpires the most discretion, enabling them to maximize their advantage stemming from the umpire's bias. While panel D makes the distinction only between curveballs and other pitches, the result is nearly identical if we distinguish between all breaking pitches (e.g., sliders, cutters) and fastballs.

An unpublished Appendix, available from the first author, presents a simple game-theoretic model that formalizes the intuition for the results in Table 16.6. It shows that, when pitchers expect a racial/ethnic match with the umpire to result in more called strikes, their optimal response is to select pitch locations away from the center of the plate (as shown in Table 16.6). Intuitively, the umpire's bias reduces the penalty for throwing *edge* pitches that are difficult for the batter to hit.

The results and the general theory seem relevant for examining the effect of bias on agents' behavior in a variety of contexts. For example, in the literature on racial profiling (e.g., John Knowles, Nicola G. Persico, and Petra E. Todd 2001, and Persico 2002), while the search data in the empirical literature do not allow examining these indirect effects, the theory demonstrates that they will arise. On the reverse side, the theory of affirmative action (Stephen Coate and Glenn C. Loury 1993) demonstrates that antidiscriminatory policies will produce indirect effects on agents' behavior.

In the larger labor market, the history of occupational segregation is replete with examples of discrimination in occupational choice altering agents' labor market behavior to their own detriment. The exclusion of Jews from property ownership in the late Middle Ages, the exclusion of African Americans from most of the railway trades until the 1950s, and perhaps even the "glass ceilings" in corporate hierarchies, all resulted in crowding into occupations (see Barbara R. Bergmann 1971) that was an indirect effect of bias in other occupations. Our work merely provides a specific example of these effects that allows them to be identified more clearly than in the broader labor market context.

16.5. Measures of Performance and the Measurement of Discrimination

The preceding discussion implies that, conditional on swinging, the batter is less likely to get a hit when the umpire and pitcher match. This implication suggests analyzing a variety of game-level performance measures for each starting pitcher to infer the total of the direct and indirect effects of bias on performance. Table 16.7 examines each starting pitcher's hits allowed, runs given up, and wins (per game).[25] Because the sample shrinks by nearly three orders of magnitude compared to the pitch-level results, our ability to detect relatively subtle effects is greatly reduced. Nonetheless, for both groups (non-Hispanic whites in panel A, minorities in panel B), pitchers' outcomes along all three game-level performance measures are superior in matching situations. Non-Hispanic white starting pitchers who match win 1.7 percentage points more often in non-QuesTec parks, which reverses to negative 3 percentage points in QuesTec parks. The "QuesTec effect" of 4.6 percentage points is nearly significant ($p = 0.08$). For minority starting pitchers, the similar gap is even larger, at 12.9 percentage points ($p = 0.06$), although there are only 74 matches in QuesTec parks.

Table 16.7.

Estimated Effects on Performance of Umpire and Starting Pitcher Racial/Ethnic Match, $N = 12{,}127$ Games, MLB 2004–2008

	Umpire-pitcher racial match	N	Win	Hits allowed	Runs allowed
Panel A. White pitchers					
QuesTec	Match	5,953	0.347	6.190	3.215
	Nonmatch	605	0.377	6.109	3.179
	Diff		−0.030	0.081	0.036
			(0.021)	(0.102)	(0.092)
Non-QuesTec	Match	10,491	0.351	6.174	3.154
	Nonmatch	1,003	0.334	6.240	3.234
	Diff		0.017	−0.066	−0.080
			(0.016)	(0.073)	(0.069)
	Diff-in-diff		−0.046	0.147	0.116
			(0.026)	(0.126)	(0.115)
Panel B. Minority pitchers					
QuesTec	Match	74	0.257	6.284	3.581
	Nonmatch	2,313	0.356	6.006	3.179
	Diff		−0.099	0.278	0.402
			(0.052)	(0.297)	(0.276)
Non-QuesTec	Match	119	0.370	5.891	3.185
	Nonmatch	3,696	0.340	6.080	3.223
	Diff		0.030	−0.189	−0.038
			(0.045)	(0.226)	(0.214)
	Diff-in-Diff		−0.129	0.466	0.440
			(0.069)	(0.373)	(0.349)

Note: Standard errors in parentheses.

Several other aggregate performance measures show the same patterns. Both groups give up fewer hits in matching situations in non-QuesTec parks, whites by about 1 percentage point, minorities by about 2 percentage points. As before, each pattern reverses in QuesTec parks. A similar pattern is seen along additional performance metrics. Figure 16.5 shows several of them, again for non-QuesTec parks and for white and minority pitchers separately. Presented as percentage changes from their baseline levels (Table 16.7 presented differences in levels), the vast majority improve in match situations. From the starting pitcher's perspective, a racial/ethnic match with the umpire helps his earned runs (fewer), hits (fewer), walks (fewer), and home runs (fewer). Only strikeouts go in the opposite direction. One might expect little effect for strikeouts, which, at least in the fraction that are called third strikes, require bias on a terminal count, which we have already shown does not occur.

To the extent that pay is based on measured productivity, our findings of small direct and larger indirect effects of racially/ethnically disparate treatment carry important implications for measuring the extent of discrimination in baseball and in labor markets generally. In particular, they imply that estimates of the extent of discrimination will be understated, even controlling for standard measures of performance.

Consider a simple earnings equation:

$$W_i = \alpha M_i + \beta P_i^* + \upsilon_i, \tag{2}$$

where W is the logarithm of earnings, M an indicator of minority status, P^* is worker i's true productivity, and υ a random error in the determination of earnings. The parameter α is the true effect of minority status on earnings when productivity measurements are free of bias. Assume that the majority workers' productivity is measured without bias, but that minority workers are subject to a negative bias in their assessment by evaluators, which leads to a shortfall of their measured productivity P below their true productivity:

$$\begin{aligned} P_i &= P_i^* - \varphi, \text{ if } M = 1; \\ P_i &= P_i^*, \text{ if } M = 0, \end{aligned} \tag{3}$$

$\varphi > 0$. Then we can rewrite (2) to obtain an estimating equation in observables:

$$W_i = [\alpha + \beta\varphi]M_i + \beta P_i + \upsilon_i, \quad \text{or}$$

$$W_i = \alpha' M_i + \beta P_i + \upsilon_i. \tag{2'}$$

The standard estimate of earnings discrimination adjusted for productivity differences, α', has a positive bias in the amount $\beta\varphi$.

To obtain some feel for the size of this bias in the particular case that we have examined, we can simulate the wage effects using the estimates of φ underlying Figure 16.5 and estimates of β from three studies of MLB that examined pitchers and used at least some of these outcomes as determinants of salaries. We are essentially estimating the reduction in minority pitchers' salaries as a result of the average amount of bias arising during the 2004–2008 seasons due to umpire-pitcher racial/ ethnic matches. Kahn (1993, Table A2) estimates equations like (2′) using a set of outcome measures that can be conformed to ours by including the percentage of games won and ERA. Making reasonable assumptions about the means of these outcomes for starting pitchers in 2004–2008, applying the effects in Figure 16.5, and using his parameter estimates yields an estimated bias of $\beta\varphi = 0.034$. Mark P. Gius and Timothy P. Hylan (1996, Table 16.6.2) use strikeouts/inning, walks/inning, and winning percentage, all of which are also conformable with our outcome measures. The same method based on their parameter estimates produces an estimate of $\beta\varphi = 0.012$. Finally, using the estimates for starting pitchers by Anthony C. Krautmann, Elizabeth F. Gustafson, and Lawrence Hadley (2003), the estimate of $\beta\varphi = 0.074$.[26]

Figure 16.5.

Effects of Umpire-Pitcher Racial/Ethnic Match on Pitcher Performance, Non-QuesTec Ballparks, MLB 2004–2008 (*N* = *15,308*)

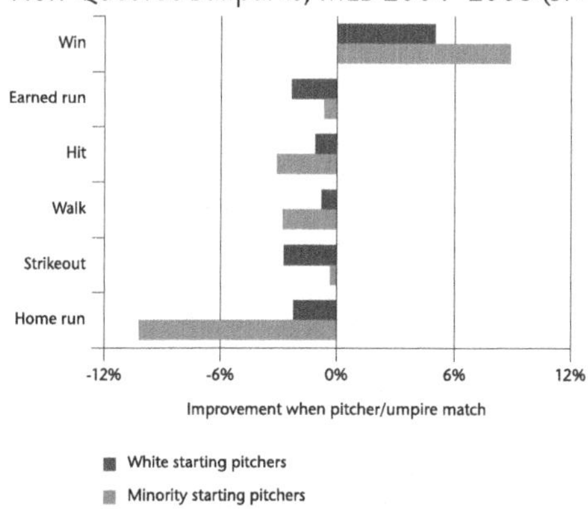

While we have demonstrated the extent of bias to estimated discrimination in earnings that arises because of biased evaluations of MLB pitchers, this effect is probably smaller than would be observed for workers generally. The scope for the expression of racial/ethnic preferences of umpires for/against pitchers is almost surely far less than in most workplaces. Evaluations of pitchers are made discretely and very frequently – when a pitch is thrown. These are not one-shot comments made at most monthly at the evaluator's leisure. Also, as our demonstrations of reduced bias when there is greater scrutiny suggest, there are quite stringent external limits on the expression of bias against unmatched pitchers. The relative lack of such limits in the general workplace suggests that the example here may provide a lower bound on the extent of bias to estimates of disparate outcomes generally.

The general point, that bias will affect measures of productivity, is not new (see, e.g., Glen G. Cain 1986). It is, however, generally ignored in the scholarly literature measuring the wage effects of discrimination. In the huge industry of employment litigation, standard practice is to adjust wages using measures of supervisors' evaluations of workers. As we have shown, even in a very controlled and highly scrutinized environment, these can be biased against minorities. Our results suggest that this bias must be accounted for whenever one wishes to measure racial/ethnic disparities in rewards in the workplace.

16.6. Conclusions

The analyses of individual pitches and game outcomes suggest that baseball umpires express racial/ethnic preferences in their decisions about players' performances.

Pitches are slightly more likely to be called strikes when the umpire shares the race/ethnicity of the starting pitcher, an effect that is observable only when umpires' behavior is not well monitored. The evidence also suggests that this bias has substantial effects on pitchers' measured performance and games' outcomes. The link between the small and large effects arises, at least in part, because pitchers alter their behavior in potentially discriminatory situations in ways that ordinarily would disadvantage themselves (such as throwing pitches directly over the plate). As in many other fields, racial/ethnic preferences work in all directions – most people give preference to members of their own group. In MLB, as in so many other fields of endeavor, power belongs disproportionately to members of the majority-white-group.

The type of discrimination that we have demonstrated is disturbing because of its implications for the sports labor market. In particular, minority pitchers are at a significant disadvantage relative to their white peers, *even in the absence of explicit wage discrimination by teams*. Although some evidence suggests such explicit discrimination exists, i.e., there is a wage gap among baseball players of different races, the fact that almost 90 percent of the umpires are white implies that the *measured* productivity of minority pitchers may be downward biased. Implicitly, estimates of wage discrimination in baseball that hold measured productivity (at least of pitchers) constant will understate its true size.

More generally, our results suggest caution in interpreting any estimates of wage discrimination stemming from equations relating earnings to race/ethnicity, even with a large set of variables designed to control for differences in productivity. To the extent that supervisors' evaluations are among the control variables included in estimates of wage discrimination, or even if they only indirectly alter workers' objective performances, their inclusion or their mere existence contaminates attempts to infer discrimination from adjusted racial/ethnic differences in wages. If racial/ethnic preferences in evaluator-worker matches are important, standard econometric estimates will generally understate the magnitude of racial/ethnic discrimination in labor markets.

While the specific evidence of racial/ethnic match preferences is disturbing, our analysis of the expression of discrimination should be encouraging: When their decisions matter more, and when evaluators are themselves more likely to be evaluated by others, our results suggest that these preferences no longer manifest themselves. Indeed, these findings imply that the particular impacts of racial/ethnic match preferences in baseball may now have been vitiated, since beginning in 2009 all ballparks are equipped with QuesTec or similar technologies.[27] Clearly, raising the price of discrimination in the labor market generally is more difficult; but our results may suggest analogous measures that might have the desired effects.

VI Where Has Research on Labor Demand Been? Where Is It Going?

This volume has dealt with labor demand, which is typically viewed as the other side of the scissors that determines wage and employment in labor markets. Its sub-title is "The Neglected Side of the Market," a neglect that I believe was demonstrated from the 1960s through the early 1990s (Stafford, 1986; Hamermesh, 1993), and has perhaps been even clearer in the past fifteen years. An interesting question, especially in light of what I hope is the demonstration here that a lot of interesting research has been produced in this area, is why it has been neglected relative to research on labor supply. I can see several reasons, both mechanical and intellectual.

I do not wish to be chauvinistic; but like it or not, and no doubt this is a transitory phenomenon that will change as this century progresses, the bulk of the leading research in economics has been conducted by American researchers. And, as I have shown elsewhere (Hamermesh, 2007), that research has unfortunately used American data. The United States has been a leader in generating data on individuals and households. The American Panel Study of Income Dynamics was the first of its kind (beginning in 1968), and it has inspired similar panels in Germany, the United Kingdom, Australia, Korea and other countries. Household data, which are designed to analyze questions about labor supply, have been readily accessible to American empirical economists.

Data on establishments and firms in the United States have been much less readily accessible. Indeed, the U.S. has arguably been in the *derrière garde* of generating sets of data on companies that are accessible to researchers. These have only recently (in the past two decades) become available; and even they can be used only if one has access to a restricted center where the data are housed. In the United States we seem much more concerned about privacy issues for companies than for individuals, a concern that has partly conditioned the availability of different kinds of data. That has made these data much less readily usable by researchers than household-based data have been.

The differential accessibility of individual and firm data has conditioned research on labor demand. Indeed, it explains why the studies in Sections III.3 and III.4 relied on data that I collected by hand from employers, and why, to study a question that would have been much better answered with data on employers, I had, *faute de mieux*, to rely on household data (Section IV.10). In short, the studies here reflect the availability of data in the U.S. and, to a lesser extent, in other nations too.

One major intellectual difficulty with doing research on labor demand is that many more policy initiatives that might be studied by labor economists have unsurprisingly to do with labor – i.e., workers. That being the case, analyzing issues using data describing individuals makes more sense if one is predominantly interested in policy: It is, after all, the behavior of individuals that will, at least in a partial equilibrium context, be changed by the policies in which one is interested.

A second intellectual reason for the imbalance in research has to do with the belief, perhaps the truth, that the supply of labor to firms is perfectly elastic, at least in the not too long long-run. That being the case and if, as is the case with many economists, our intellectual concerns are with wage rather than employment determination, neglecting the demand side again makes sense. Given the tremendous influence of Chicago-style labor economics on the intellectual underpinnings of this sub-field (e.g., the work of Lewis, Mincer and Becker), the focus on wages is perhaps not surprising.

This combination of mechanical and intellectual reasons has led labor economists and those interested in labor issues to focus much more on the analysis of labor supply than on labor demand. Indeed, in the second decade of the 21st century we have seen two active prongs of research on labor supply: A focus on highly mathematical, theory-based studies of individual and family labor supply behavior (following up on the survey by Blundell and MaCurdy, 1999) and a nearly atheoretical approach focusing on the causal impacts of policies on hours of work (e.g., Bosch and van der Klaauw, 2012).

These two prongs are not visible to anywhere nearly the same extent in the much sparser set of studies of labor demand or even of employers' discrimination. Indeed, theory-based research of the sort typified by Section III.1 or IV.7 is just no longer being done. Of course, one cannot expect the methods of thirty years ago to be applied today in what one hopes is a discipline that is progressing; but, unlike in the study of labor supply, no advance in methodology, both theoretical or econometric, has been apparent in studying labor demand. Instead, albeit with many fewer examples, general issues of labor demand have been analyzed using atheoretical approaches that search for exogeneity to analyze the impacts of shocks to labor demand to study particular policies (e.g., IV.8 of this volume).

This paucity of theory-based research on labor demand does not mean that progress has not been made (beyond the advances in the chapters included in this volume). Indeed, over the last two decades a number of useful studies have been published using the "search for exogeneity" approach. A particularly clever, albeit narrow example was provided by Angrist (1996). Examining day-to-day variation in the extent to which low-skilled Palestinian laborers were allowed into Israel proper during the first *intifada*, the study teased out the impact of that variation on the employment and wages of Israeli workers.

During World War II the rate at which men were drafted for military service differed across American states. In those states where more men were called up for military duty, their scarcity in the civilian sector resulted in a greater increase in the demand for female workers. Acemoglu et al (2004) showed that in those states there were greater increases in women's wages. As the theory of labor demand predicts, there was also a negative relation between wages and employment. Without linking it to a specific structural parameter, the study implicitly estimated the elasticity of factor price of female labor *at that particular time*.

Other studies have used this approach to infer responses to policy. While the results may not be readily transferable to labor markets in rich countries, examining policies in developing countries has the virtue that in many cases the range of policy variation is much greater than is usually observed in the United States and other richer and, regrettably for our purposes, more rigid, in terms of changes in policy, economies. Thus Kugler and Kugler (2009) examine the impact on employment demand in manufacturing of legislated changes in payroll tax rates in Colombia. The payroll tax rate averaged 47 percent in 1982, but in 1996 it averaged 60 percent. This 13 percentage-point shock to this part of labor costs reduced employment on average by 6 percent. Moreover, the declines in employment were largest in the manufacturing companies on which the largest increases in payroll taxes were imposed. The implied elasticity of labor demand complements the immense earlier work (summarized in Hamermesh, 1993,

Chapter 3) that produced estimates of this parameter, but these new estimates vitiate any concerns about exogeneity that might bother someone about the earlier literature.*

A different aspect of the theory of labor demand is what is implied about its responsiveness to shocks to product demand. The "older-fashioned" studies of factor demand estimated the degree of returns to scale, both short- and long-run, explicitly in the context of the formal models on which they were based. While recent research has paid less attention to structure, some recent efforts, typically aimed at inferring the responses of local labor markets, have allowed inferences about returns to scale in the demand for labor (e.g., aus dem Moore and Spitz-Oener, 2012).

Even in the area of discrimination, where an immense amount of research has focused on measuring wage differentials independent of any concern about causation, the exogeneity approach has recently used random variation of assignment of agents in very large samples of data to infer the "demanders'" preferences for agents of different types. Thus Section V.16 and the other research cited there, while not directly linked to preferences, implicitly offers evidence on the reduced-form impacts of differences in agents' preferences for groups of suppliers of different ethnicities/races.

With all the studies presented in this volume, and with the many (not myriad) others that have been produced over the past forty years, what can we be confident that we really know? Perhaps foremost is the simple fact that the demand curve for labor slopes down – the demand elasticity for workers and hours is negative. This fundamental fact means that policies that raise the cost of an hour of labor will reduce the demand for hours. As much as we would like to see policies such as higher minimum wages, higher overtime penalties and others have no negative impact on total hours worked, it is absolutely clear that they do have negative impacts. That they do so differentially across the work force is also clear – the constant-output demand elasticity is lower for more skilled workers and, in general, for workers with more human capital embodied in them – be it more experience, more general education or more (firm- or occupation-) specific training.

We also know that most of the movement in employment is churning – the replacement of workers who leave their jobs voluntarily. We also have learned, as the studies in Sections III.3 and III.4 demonstrate,

* Interestingly, the estimates in this study fall well within the interquartile range of the estimates in the studies summarized there.

that this replacement occurs quickly – lags in the adjustment of employment demand are fairly short, especially compared to lags in investment. Also, employers adjust employment in lumps – apparently at least some of the costs of adjustment are fixed.

All of these findings, some of which are apparent in the chapters in this volume, should condition the application of labor market policies. They suggest that there is no "free lunch" in regulating the wages and non-wage monetary benefits of work. We can apply policy aimed at certain groups, and it may increase their wages, employment and/or hours; at the same time, however, it will alter employment and hours in other groups, to their detriment. Obversely, wage subsidies can be used to increase employment in targeted groups, but here too substitution among groups of workers will alter the employment and hours of workers in groups that are not targeted.

We know from an immense literature that employers' preferences, or at least employers' expressions of their customers' and employees' preferences, alter the distribution of wages and employment along a variety of dimensions. These have included race, ethnicity, gender, sexual orientation, religion, weight and others. Several chapters in this volume have extended the list of dimensions to include workers' physical beauty, a category that is less immutable than gender or race, but perhaps at least as fixed as religion or weight. Aside from the prurient interest in it, these studies have demonstrated that beauty does generate substantial, but limited payoffs in the labor market; and it has enabled us to examine how altering the distribution of workers' characteristics that employers confront alters the returns to those characteristics. The studies here also pose the deeper question of what we mean by discrimination and point out in greater detail than heretofore the link between studying discrimination and studying labor demand.

While the studies here and many others have advanced our knowledge of labor demand, a very large amount of work needs to be done before we can even say that we have advanced the literature as far as it has been advanced in the area of labor supply. Obviously the theoretical basics (such as used in Sections III.1 and IV.7) should be adapted for use in country- and industry-specific contexts; but that kind of research, while crucial for answering specific questions, will not lead to the qualitative advances that have characterized the academic literature to date. Instead, what are needed are studies that base themselves in theory – that can generate estimates of parameters that have some link to theory – but that at the same time answer fundamental questions about *why* some phenomenon occurs.

The theoretical analysis of static labor demand is well-grounded, and we are unlikely to see many further developments in this area. Applications of the theory to large samples of establishment-based data, however, are the next step in this area. Most of what we think we know about the fundamental parameters describing labor demand is based on highly aggregated data. Some research has been done on this topic using microeconomic data, but much more is needed; and with the growth of establishment-based microeconomic data sets, that kind of research is now doable.

Studies of dynamic labor demand are less well developed. While the questions here are probably less important for understanding labor markets, given the apparent rapid adjustment of labor demand, the slow adjustment of investment to shocks means that studying spillovers from adjustment of capital to the adjustment of labor is worthwhile. Research on this issue has been conducted off and on for nearly fifty years, beginning with Nadiri and Rosen (1969), but it is only recently that the microeconomic data have become available to allow some initial, most interesting research in this important area (Asphjell et al, 2014).

In the case of policy in the area of labor demand it is not enough to study how a particular policy in a particular area at a particular time alters employment and/or hours. It is true that there are many types of policies that have not been extensively studied, such as the topic covered in Section IV.9; but even among those that have been well studied, merely showing that X affects Y in the particular context has very little predictive value. The effects of any policy are altered by slight variations in different sets of policy parameters that render particularistic estimates of very little general use. What is needed, within the desire to show causation, is a link between the parameters that underlie the policy and its impacts in the context being studied. With that link one can then use the particular to move to the general. Without it, and no matter how elegantly and clearly one demonstrates that a particular policy generates an outcome, one cannot use a specific example to describe what one believes to be a general phenomenon. I like to think that the studies in Section IV, while in each case specific to time and place, have at least to some extent generated results that are linked to fundamental parameters and thus applicable in other times and locations.

The study of discrimination has been pervaded by questions of "how much," with almost no study of "why?" or "what affects what?". The studies in Sections V.13, V.15 and V.16 move toward answering these questions, but they admittedly make only small strides. Feld et al (2013) goes part-way in the proper direction, trying to infer the extent to which apparently discriminatory differentials result from discrimination against a minority or favoritism toward a majority group. More studies like that are necessary if the study of discrimination is to be more than particularistic and, even more important, if it can be linked structurally to the theory of labor demand which must surely at least partly underlie discriminatory outcomes in labor markets.

I do not expect to see huge thrusts of research on labor demand in the next two decades, at least if we define labor demand as the type of work spanned by the studies in Sections III and IV of this volume. Nonetheless, questions about policy in the area of labor demand do arise occasionally in all economies, and these are likely to stimulate academic research that generates results that are broadly applicable and that attract academic and policy attention worldwide. More likely is the development of research on labor market discrimination that recognizes the link that I have outlined here between that strand of research and the demand for labor, thus placing the study of discrimination in its roots in the theory of employers' behavior – which is, after all, the theory of labor demand broadly defined.

Notes

Chapter 1

1 These statements are, respectively, by Eli Ginzberg, "Dimensions of Youth Unemployment," April 5, 1979, unpublished; Alice Yohalem, Hearings before the Joint Economic Committee of Congress, 95:2, June 7, 1978, p. 255; and Alice Rivlin, Hearings before the House Budget Committee, February 21, 1978, p. 53.

2 Freeman (1979) and Welch (1979) show that there has been substantial adjustment in relative wages of youths over the past fifteen years, and Morse (1980) indicates that, except for black males, teenage wage rates did adjust well between 1960 and 1970. However, Johnson (1980) presents arguments why one might, in the face of this evidence, believe the youth labor market is not entirely free of wage rigidity. Consistent with this view, King (1979) presents tentative evidence of some effect of increased female participation on youth unemployment.

3 The studies looking at substitution by age are Anderson (1977), Freeman (1979), Grant (1979), Johnson-Blakemore (1979), and Welch-Cunningham (1978).

4 Sato and Koizumi (1973) lay out the relationships among the substitution and complementary elasticities.

5 For adult males, and increasingly too for adult females, the evidence is fairly clear that supply elasticities are nearly zero (see Borjas and Heckman, 1978). For other groups this assumption is less tenable.

6 For a description of the construction of the data see Grant (1979).

7 Even this fairly fine disaggregation of the work force may involve some inadmissible aggregations. For example, aggregation of youths 14–19 and 20–24 may be incorrect. Nonetheless, the broader categorization is all that the data source allows; in any event, finer disaggregations simply did not give estimates of the C_{ij} that are consistent with theory.

8 See Denny and Fuss (1977) for the methods of testing for weak separability in the context of the translog approximation.

9 Berndt (1980) demonstrates that when labor-capital separability is inappropriately implicitly assumed, the resulting cross-price elasticities of demand for factors are overestimated and the own-price elasticities of demand are underestimated.

10 Those studies, however, only show that blue-collar labor and capital are *p*-substitutes, a result which follows automatically once one finds that white-collar labor and capital are *p*-complements. Further, because most previous studies, including Grant (1979) and Anderson (1977), present elasticities of substitution, their finding that each labor type is a p-substitute for capital is not necessarily in conflict with our finding on their *q*-complementarity.

11 In an attempt to extend our work beyond manufacturing we estimated the capital stock in the entire private nonfarm economy in each SMSA by prorating the manu-

facturing capital stock by the ratio of hours worked. The capital stock measure was entered into equations (1). The results were disappointing: The significance of the estimated γ_{ij} dropped sharply. It would appear that data limitations make it impossible to derive useful cross-section estimates of labor-labor substitution parameters outside manufacturing, since, as we have shown for manufacturing, a capital measure must be included where none is available.

12 Between May 1967 and May 1979 the share of the labor force accounted for by white women 25+ grew from 0.243 to 0.268, roughly a 10% increase. Data by age, race, sex and industry cannot be obtained for each year, but we can note that, as a percentage of full-time employees in manufacturing, women increased from 23.9% to 25.7% between 1967 and 1977. (Computed from *Current Population Reports*, P-60, nos. 60 and 118.)

13 Though we wish to simulate employment effects, our estimates are based on man-hours of inputs. Assuming, as is standard in the literature, that the exogenous change produces no long-run change in the relative prices of persons and hours, our estimates are appropriate for simulating the longrun effect of the influx of women.

14 This discussion is modelled after that in Johnson (1980).

Chapter 2

1 Hatanaka (4, pp. 238–242) computed the cross-spectrum of the aggregate layoff *rate* and the aggregate *level* of industrial production. This comparison makes little economic sense, for the layoff rate, like the other components of net employment change, is related by the logarithmic derivative of a simple Cobb-Douglas production function to the change in output rather than to its level. The only rationale for this comparison must be as an examination of two of the NBER business cycle indicators. Because of the difficulties of identifying leads in the cross-spectrum from lags which are 180 degrees out of phase, however, it is not even clear that Hatanaka's estimate of the lead-lag relationship is a good test of these two indicators.

2 The limited number of complete cycles available in most data is what really limits the usefulness of spectral techniques at low frequencies. In twenty years of data we may have only three or four complete cycles and may not be able to make inferences about the process generating the data. For an explicit discussion of this point see (9, p. 289) and (5, p. 251).

3 This latter assumption seems justified on the basis of other work I have done on this subject. In a simultaneous equation model in which seasonal changes are held constant I found that the level of quits appears to depend only on the level of unemployment. The validity of this assumption as it regards seasonal changes can be substantiated by spectral analysis. If we find that the spectra of the series on quits in different industries are similar to each other, yet different in shape from the spectra of output changes or the other gross employment change series for the industry, we might infer that they are related to some factor or factors not specific to any particular industry.

4 Ulman (7) examines the level of quits and that of wages for a cross section of industries and cites union pressure in high-wage industries as causing wages in those industries to be greater than the marginal product of labor in those industries. This excess is a rent to workers in these industries and gives them an incentive to remain at their present jobs. Such an explanation sheds no light, however, on interindustry differences in the behavior of gross changes in employment over time.

5 See (5, pp. 256–257) for a discussion of prewhitening and recoloring and (4) for derivations of the more basic results of spectral analysis.

Chapter 3

1 Other studies have examined (1) with $I > 1$ under varying degrees of generality about the lags of the inputs and about the Z_j. Thus Daniel Hamermesh (1969) examined gross employment changes; Frank Brechling (1975) and Matthew Shapiro (1986) studied the joint adjustment of employment and capital; and Robert Topel (1982) specified joint adjustment of inventories and employment. M. I. Nadiri and Rosen (1969) included all of these variables.

2 There has been some discussion of more general adjustment processes of other inputs. Michael Rothschild (1971) studied the adjustment of capital; Alan Blinder (1981) and Andrew Caplin (1985) examined (*S, s*) models of inventories, essentially assuming both fixed and increasing variable costs of adjustment. Aside from Stephen Peck (1974), who analyzed investment in (very lumpy purchases of) electricity-generating plants, the few empirical studies based on these models use only aggregated data.

3 In other areas only the second part of this approach seems important. Most investment goods and consumer durables purchases are inherently lumpy. This means that the major question of interest should be the nature of the aggregation of lumpy purchases that generates paths of the observed aggregates.

4 I exclude a linear term in $\dot{L}$. Were it included, its only effect on the path would be to change the target; were it alone included, it would not be optimal for the firm to lag adjustment of labor demand.

5 I ignore the issue of employment-hours substitution and assume here that hours per worker are fixed. (See Robert Hart, 1984). Some of the labor hoarding that is apparent in the empirical results clearly reflects variations in hours per worker, on which data are unfortunately not available.

6 Factor prices are not available in my main source of data. Also, there is some evidence that they are less important in affecting short-run labor-demand fluctuations than are expectations about output (Richard Freeman, 1977).

7 No major strikes occurred in this company during the 53 months covered by the employment data. A few plants were shut down by strikes for less than one week, but this does not seem to have affected production worker employment or monthly output in the seven plants.

8 Under alternative (9) the number of parameters is one greater for both (4) and (5) because of the inclusion of a_2.

9 I present results using only the one-month forecast of output and the expected change three months beyond that. Inclusion of a six-month forecasted change did not add to the quality of the fitted equations for any of the plants. Also, because the estimates of (5) for Plant 7 never converged no matter what starting values or algorithms were chosen, results are presented only for six individual plants. The seventh plant is included in the pooled data and in the estimates based on the aggregate of all plants.

10 We can study the specification errors induced into the equations by the absence of wage data by examining Figure 3.1 around the one time in the sample period when a substantial amount of wage information became available (when a new collective bargaining contract was negotiated). In only one of the seven plants was there a sharp fluctuation (drop) in employment during that month, and in only one of the other plants did employment fluctuate (drop) during the prior month. It is unlikely that the parameter estimates or inferences about the adjustment paths are greatly affected by the absence of wage data.

11 In all cases the procedure MAXLIK in GAUSS is used to find the maxima of the likelihood functions. The particular algorithm chosen is the Davidon-Fletcher-Powell method. The starting values for the parameters were the OLS estimates of (4), with $K = 0$ and $\sigma_\varepsilon = 1$.

12 I examined first-order autocorrelation in (5) by considering a weighted average

of the errors in (5a) and (5b) (with weights $1 - \hat{p}_t$ and $\hat{p}_t$). There was no significant serial correlation in any of the estimates of (5).

13 As a first approximation to a general model a term in L_{t-1} was added to (5b). It did not significantly raise the likelihood values in the pooled data, and it did so in estimates for only one of the six plants.

14 No such turnover data are available for the sample period used in estimating (4) and (5).

15 The VAR models were estimated with four lags of the dependent variable and the current value and four lags of the independent variable.

16 The unpublished output data were provided by Kenneth Armitage of the Board of Governors of the Federal Reserve. Unlike in the plant-level data, there is substantial seasonality in the output data for these industries. (About one-third of the variation in output is accounted for by a bivariate regression of Y_t on Y_{t-12}). Despite this, the estimates presented here are based on seasonally unadjusted data to maintain comparability with the previous section. The inability to discriminate between models of adjustment costs is not affected when the models are reestimated on seasonally adjusted output data.

17 Consider the following example of how this might occur. With fixed adjustment costs, in a simplified model employment change in a plant will be zero if output change $y < K$ and $y > -K$, and be some multiple of y if $|y| \geq K$. Let y be distributed uniformly over the interval $[y^* - a, y^* + a]$, with $\Pr(y = y') = 1/2a$ on this interval and $a > K$. I assume $y^* > 0$, so average output is rising. Then:

$$E(y|\,|y| \geq K) = ay^* / [a - K].$$

A mean-preserving spread in y involves an increase in a, which implies a decrease in $E(y|\,|y| \geq K)$ if $y^* > 0$. For a given aggregate change in output, an increase in the dispersion of output change across sub-units reduces the absolute value of the average output change among those units that are varying employment. Since the average change in employment is a multiple of $E(y|\,|y| \geq K)$, its absolute value is also reduced even though y^* has not changed.

18 See Nickell, 1979; Simon Burgess, 1988; Hamermesh, 1988, and Katharine Abraham and Susan Houseman, 1987.

19 The U.S. plant-closing law, P. L. 100–379, provides that employers must give 60 days' advance notice to workers for plant closings and for layoffs expected to last more than six months, if more than 100 workers are involved.

Chapter 4

1 This tradition is mostly restricted to Europe (see also Bentolila and Bertola, 1990), while modelling adjustment based on net costs is more prevalent in North America. One possible reason for this difference may be the greater concern in Europe with policies that impose hiring and firing costs on the employer.

2 Even in the depressed U.S. economy of 1981, the last year for which data were collected, the average monthly quit rate in manufacturing was 1.3%. (Employment and Earnings, February 1982.)

3 That this is a non-profit hospital does not present problems, so long as we can assume that the hospital minimizes (adjustment and other) costs.

4 This restriction may impart errors to the estimated path of employment if the adjustment of hours is slow. We know, however (see Hamermesh, 1993, Chapter 7), that hours are adjusted more rapidly than employment, suggesting that these errors are likely to be small. Even with these errors, there is no reason to conclude that the assumption generates biases in any estimates of the relative sizes of gross and net costs.

5 Good data are not available for the United States after 1981; but earlier evidence for the United States is corroborated by more recent data for other countries, including for Canada by Picot and Baldwin (1990).

6 The twelfth-order lag captures seasonal covariation between employment and revenue. An alternative, including monthly dummy variables in the equations, did not alter the conclusions based on the estimation of (5').

7 This short-sightedness is clearly a step back from the forward-looking model of (3); but such models cannot be solved analytically under lumpy costs. The behavioural implications gained by allowing for the possible realism of nonconvex costs come at the expense of some of the realism about expectations.

8 Estimating the equation in levels generates very small changes in the parameters and has no qualitative effect on the results.

9 Equations that included first-order lags of revenue in Plants *j* and *k* in the equation for Plant *i* were also estimated. The pairs of terms in $Y_{j,t-1}$ and $Y_{k,t-1}$ were not jointly significant in any of the three equations, and their inclusion had very minor effects on the estimates of λ and β_Q.

10 These are autoregressions of deviations from the series means.

11 A variety of initial values and all the algorithms in the MAXLIK procedure in GAUSS were used. In every case the likelihood functions failed to converge. As the results for the eventual solution suggest, the failures stemmed from the flatness of the likelihood functions along the dimension K_H.

12 Not surprisingly, deriving any implications about adjustment paths in such a model is extremely difficult. Moreover, given the problems in estimating even the lumpy-costs model with the particular, very short microeconomic time series used here, attempting to estimate a more general model would be a fruitless exercise.

13 These are discussed in Hamermesh (1993, Chapter 8), Nickell (1979), Abraham and Houseman (1989), and Bentolila and Bertola (1990) are just a few who link these policies to differences in adjustment speeds.

Chapter 5

1 A simple regression of log employment on the quit rate and a time trend yields

$$\log(L) = \underset{(307.6)}{1.17} + \underset{(25.45)}{0.924}{*}T(\times 1000) + \underset{(18.83)}{1.20}{*}Q, \qquad \bar{R}^2 = 0.931,$$

where Q is the seasonally adjusted quarterly quit rate, and we list *t*-statistics here and throughout the paper in parentheses. The simple correlation of log(L) and Q is *0.63*. The extent of the responsiveness of quits to the availability of jobs is shown in Hamermesh (1969) using data for small industries from 1958 to 1966, in which the elasticity of the quit rate with respect to aggregate unemployment was *-2·6*.

2 That quits and fires are logically separate categories that can usefully be distinguished is clear (McLaughlin 1991). By using the published data, we implicitly rely on each employer's classification of separated workers into the two main categories, quits and layoffs. The only incentive for biases in the data could arise if employers mistakenly believe that what they list on the forms submitted to the Bureau of Labor Statistics, a federal agency, will somehow affect their state unemployment insurance taxes. Since no individual workers' names are listed on these forms, this seems highly unlikely. No doubt employers might misreport some separations; but systematic errors seem very unlikely.

3 The two studies only have access to time-series on accessions and separations, the latter of which include voluntary quits and the endogenous layoffs. They are thus incapable, as Burgess and Nickell explicitly recognize, of linking their modelling of the representative firm's choices to the estimates.

4 See the description in the statistical section of any issue of the *Monthly Labor Review* before 1983.

5 Seasonally adjusted versions of all of the variables are used. Standardized forms of each variable, $Z^* = (Z/\bar{Z})-1$, where $\bar{Z}$ is the mean of Z, were used in the estimation.

The discounting parameter β was set equal to *0.98* prior to estimation, an average annual real interest rate of nearly 8%. The results were insensitive to changes in β.

6 The *J*-statistic is distributed χ^2 with degrees of freedom equal to the number of instruments minus the number of estimated parameters. For starting values of θ_{11} and θ_{12} that are each positive or each negative, we found two different local optima. We report here the estimates at the global optimum.

7 In model III the other structural parameters are

$$\alpha_1 = 8 \cdot 192; \quad \alpha_{11} = 0 \cdot 113; \quad \alpha_{12} = 0 \cdot 0032.$$
$$(1{\cdot}75) \qquad (0{\cdot}48) \qquad (5{\cdot}84)$$

While we cannot be sure that A is positive-definite, since we do not estimate α_{22}, the positive point estimates of the other three parameters are good indications that this fundamental description of technology is valid in these data.

8 A recent example of such comparisons is Abraham and Houseman (1989).

Chapter 6

1 See Hamermesh (1993, Chapter 4) for a summary and critical discussion of this literature.

2 This is essentially the decomposition used in the establishment data collected by the U.S. Bureau of Labor Statistics from 1958 through 1981.

3 The figure is simplified by omitting vacant jobs. It is based on people and jobs and necessarily ignores intensity of effort (including hours worked in each job and effort per hour).

4 One might add the term $2M$ to $H + X$, where M is the number of jobs created and destroyed within the firm independent of any hiring or separations that have occurred.

5 Three studies (Cramer and Koller (1988); Anderson and Meyer (1994), Burgess *et al.* (1994)) have used establishment data to examine employment changes and worker flows, though none has accounted for internal mobility, and none has information on types of flows of workers.

6 Deaths of firms are excluded from the sample, which may bias downwards the measures of job and labor turnover.

7 The raw estimates imply $J^C - J^D = 2.6$ percent, which does not satisfy the identity (3). To obtain the identity we adjusted $H1$ and $X2$ by adding respectively $\delta_1\ H1$ and $\delta_2\ X2$. The optimal weights δ_i are those that minimize the quadratic loss function $\delta_1^2 + \delta_2^2$, subject to $(1 + \delta_1) H1 - (1 + \delta_2) X2 = H - X + M3 - M4$.

8 The measure of labor turnover is the sum of hires and separations and may double-count movements of workers.

Chapter 7

1 See the studies by Hashimoto-Mincer (1971), Welch (1974), Mincer (1976) and Siskind (1977). Part of this sensitivity may be due to the mixing of supply and demand elements in a single equation, a problem which the work in section II seeks to overcome. Only Welch-Cunningham (1978) has a sound basis in the theory of factor demand, and that study has problems in its efforts to disaggregate teen labor into three subgroups to find substitution elasticities within the teenage group.

2 Clearly, there may be some "bunching" of the distribution at the minimum. For our argument to be valid, we only require that a higher minimum causes a greater truncation of the distribution.

3 For the private nonfarm sector and each of the larger industries the time trends in (1') were positive and significant. All the coefficient estimates on the adult unem-

ployment variable were negative and significant. To account for simultaneous-equations bias, (1') for the private nonfarm sector was reestimated using an instrumental estimate for teen wages in the relative price and the *MINT* variables. (The instrumental equation included *MIN*, *DUMS*, and teenage and adult population. The coefficient of the minimum wage in this equation was .032; its t-statistic was 1.58.) The reestimation of (1') yielded a relative price elasticity of -2.41 (t = -2.34), but a much lower elasticity on *MINT*, -.027 (t = -.42).

4 To examine whether induced reductions in employment elsewhere affect employment in a specific sector, *MINT* for the private nonfarm sector was added to the equations for each of the three industries. In no case was the coefficient on this variable significantly different from zero, nor did its addition ever change the coefficient on *MINT* in Table 7.3 by more than one standard error.

5 Since coverage and the legislative minimum are separate issues, we experimented with separate variables for each. The logs of the fraction of teen employment covered and the ratio of the minimum wage to teen labor costs were entered in (1'). For retail trade and the private nonfarm sector only did $\hat{\sigma}_e$ decrease. In all four cases the larger effects were through the relative minimum; their elasticities were -.21, -.14, -.21 and -.43 for the four equations, and they were significantly negative except for services. The other coefficients in the equations changed only slightly.

6 The output measure is gross domestic business product deflated by the gross domestic product deflator. These series were from the CITIBASE file.

7 In the system in which only homotheticity has been imposed, the coefficient on *MINT*, along with its t-statistic, is -.056 (-1.13).

8 We know from Grossman (1980) that increases in the minimum wage have only slight effects on wages above the minimum. Insofar as young workers have less human capital, this evidence for the assertion that attention be directed toward the effect of higher minima on the employment of youths corroborates our result.

9 As a check on the validity of using capital stock and user cost series together with labor input and price data constructed from an entirely different source, it is worth reporting some statistics describing these data. The mean shares are .0619, .6263, and .3118 for youths, adults, and capital, respectively. Moreover, the mean annual full-time earnings seem quite reasonable in light of previous work.

10 This undoubtedly results from the instability induced by the small share of costs accounted for by young labor. As shown in Grant-Harnermesh (1981), it is difficult to get sensible parameter estimates from systems like (4) when the average shares become small.

11 Implicit in the calculations of η_{YY} and η_{YA} based on (6) is the assumption that the effective minimum wage stays unchanged as *WY* varies.

12 The estimates could also be based on (1'). However, the restrictions of that specification (exclusion of terms in output and the untested constraint that wage elasticities for teens and adults be equal) make it less interesting than (2) or the translog system for this purpose.

13 The implied η_{YY} is calculated as σ_{YY} (-9.53) times the share of teens (.033). This latter is calculated as teens' share of labor earnings from Section 7.2 times labor's share from Section 7.3. η_{AT} is just σ_{YA} (. 966) times . 033.

14 This latter is derived by assuming that one-third of all teens earn the minimum or less, that their average wage is half that of other teens, and that teens' share of output is 3.3 percent.

15 The t-statistics presented in Table 7.5 are calculated using the standard errors of $\partial ET \ / \ \partial MINT$, $\partial ET \ / \ \partial WT$ and $\partial EA \ / \ \partial WT$: the only stochastic measures used in estimating the substitution effects. The scale effect is stochastic only when I set $\partial ET \ / \ \partial Q = \partial EA \ / \ \partial Q = \hat{\gamma}$ in which case its $t = 4.35$, that of $\hat{\gamma}$.

16 Ashenfelter-Smith (1979) built a model that suggests firms will decrease compliance as the effective minimum rises. While they present no direct evidence on this, they do show the widespread nature of noncompliance.

Chapter 8

1 Ehrenberg and Schumann (1982), Hart (1987), and Owen (1989) discuss in detail the relevant issues and survey available research. Recent examples of work on this topic include Trejo (1991, 1998) and Hunt (1999).

2 See, for example, Hart and Wilson (1988) and König and Pohlmeier (1989).

3 MaCurdy et al. (1997) also analyze California's daily overtime law, but their approach differs in important ways from ours. For example, they rely on cross-sectional comparisons between California workers and other workers, whereas we examine how the work schedules of California men responded to changes in overtime coverage.

4 Much of the information in this section comes from California Industrial Welfare Commission (1994) and from discussions with Karla Yates of that Commission and Daniel Comet of the California Department of Industrial Relations. In no way does this imply, however, that these agencies or individuals necessarily endorse or agree with any of the statements made here.

5 As of 1994, other states that imposed some type of a daily overtime penalty were Alaska, Colorado, Nevada, Oregon, and Wyoming. In most cases, however, these overtime laws cover only a few narrowly defined industries and lack the broad scope of California's law.

6 In order to facilitate alternative work schedules, changes made after 1985 gave certain workers the option to relax overtime pay requirements. For example, by a two-thirds vote of the appropriate employment unit, manufactunng workers could adopt a ten-hour daily overtime standard and health care workers could adopt a twelve-hour daily standard. Employers complained that the conditions required to implement these alternative work schedules were very difficult to satisfy, however, and relatively few work groups opted to adopt such schedules.

7 Put differently, the statutory overtime premium creates a kink in the cost function at eight hours of daily work, and this kink induces some firms that would otherwise assign overtime instead to adopt the corner solution of an eight-hour workday.

8 The questionnaire asks, "How many days a week does ... usually work at this job?" and "How many hours per week does ... usually work at this job?" Imputing daily hours using these questions does not appear to influence our findings. For 1985 and 1991, when both direct and imputed measures of daily work hours are available, the two measures are highly correlated and produce similar estimation results. Nor does it matter whether we round off our imputed measure of daily hours to the nearest integer. We report here the estimates obtained without rounding. In other words, if imputed daily hours are 8.23, we treat the worker as having 0.23 overtime hours per day and we categorize his workday as "longer than eight hours" rather than as "exactly eight hours." The results are similar, however, when we recalculate these variables after first rounding imputed daily hours to the nearest integer.

9 The results are similar, however, when Western states outside of California are included in the control group (which is not surprising because these states have relatively small populations and the daily overtime penalties that do exist are narrow in coverage).

10 See Gruber (1994), Gruber and Poterba (1994), and Yelowitz (1995) for other recent applications of the "difference-in-difference" and "difference-in-difference-in-difference" estimators.

11 Throughout we report least-squares estimates, but probit estimates of overtime incidence and tobit estimates of overtime hours imply similar effects of California's overtime law.

12 Notice that even in 1973, before the daily overtime penalty became mandatory for them, California men worked long hours less frequently than did men in other states. If the sources of this initial difference are difficult to observe and control

for, then cross-sectional comparisons of California men and other men in 1985 - after California's law was extended to male workers - will not identify the effects of the daily overtime penalty. It is for this reason that we adopt the strategy of comparing the changes that California men and other men experienced between 1973 and 1985. As for why the incidence of daily overtime was relatively low for California men even before they were subject to the state overtime law, two explanations come to mind. First, in 1973, California's economy was depressed compared to the rest of the country. (See the relevant data on unemployment rates provided in footnote 14.) Second, to maintain internal equity, some California firms in 1973 may have offered male employees the same daily overtime premium that these firms were legally required to pay their female employees.

13 In using changes for women to account for California-specific shocks, our specification assumes that such shocks produce the same percentage-point change in the overtime incidence of men and women. This assumption results in conservative estimates of the effects of California's daily overtime penalty. An alternative assumption is that the regionspecific shocks produce the same proportional change in the overtime incidence of men and women. Triple-difference estimates using this alternative assumption imply even larger estimated effects of California's overtime law, because women work long hours much less frequently than men do, and, therefore, the rise in the overtime incidence of California women (relative to other women) between 1973 and 1985 is bigger when measured in proportional rather than in absolute terms.

14 The overall U.S. unemployment rate climbed from 4.9% in May 1973, to 7.2% in May 1985, whereas the California unemployment rate rose only slightly over the same period, from 7.0% to 7.3%. Between 1985 and 1991, neither unemployment rate changed much, with 1991 rates of 7.7% for California and 6.9% for the nation as a whole.

15 The double- and triple-differences for 1985–1991 are sizeable in economic terms, despite our inability to rule out at conventional levels of statistical significance that these effects are zero. This issue reappears throughout the study, because the precision of our estimates will allow us to detect only relatively large effects. Even for a state as populous as California, monthly CPS data on labor market outcomes contain considerable sampling error. Card (1992) encountered the same problem in his analysis of California's 1988 minimum-wage hike.

16 We do not control for union membership, because this information is collected for only a quarter of the observations in the 1985 and 1991 CPS data (so including a union indicator in the regressions would drastically reduce our sample sizes). This omission is unlikely to affect our results, however, because rates of unionization and the decline in these rates over time were very similar in California and the control states. Between 1973 and 1985, for example, unionization rates for the male workers in our samples fell from 37.8% to 23.3% in California and from 38.0% to 23.5% in the other regions.

17 The industry categories are durable goods manufacturing; nondurable goods manufacturing; transportation, communication, and other public utilites; wholesale trade; retail trade; finance, insurance, and real estate; business and repair services; personal services; entertainment and recreation services; and professional and related services. The occupation categories are sales workers; clerical workers; service workers; crafts workers; operators, including transportation workers; and laborers. Recall that workers from certain industries (such as agriculture and construction) and occupations (such as managers and professionals) have already been excluded from the sample because these sectors are exempt from the overtime pay regulation.

18 Indeed, for employees working five days per week and an unchanging number of hours each day, overtime hours are the same whether defined according to an eight-hour daily standard or a forty-hour weekly standard. Of the California men in our 1973 sample who worked more than eight hours per day (which is the

group directly affected by the expansion of state overtime law that occurred in 1980), 51% worked exactly five days per week.

19 The propensity for California men to work long workdays without exceeding a forty-hour workweek grew from 1% in 1973 to 3% in 1985 and 1991, and, in all three years, this propensity is similar for men in non-Western states as for men in California. The propensity is slightly higher for women than it is for men, but the important point is that such work schedules are uncommon for all groups in all years.

20 The CPS information on daily schedules pertains to "usual" daily hours of work. So, in Table 8.7, we employ the corresponding data on usual weekly hours of work.

21 Compliance with federal overtime law is far from perfect, with one estimate suggesting that it is as low as 80% (Ehrenberg and Schumann (1982)).

Chapter 9

1 Conducted by the Confederación Española de Organizaciones Empresariales (Eironline (2003)).

2 The regulatory framework described in this section was in effect at the time the data used in the empirical part were collected (May 2003). In December 2003, the Portuguese Labor Law was heavily modified. Very unfortunately, no survey on the timing of work in firms has been conducted since the legislative changes occurred.

3 By contrast, in 2007 in the U.S. the average worker in manufacturing worked 4.2 hours of overtime in a typical week *(Economic Report of the President* (2008)), which could not, given the annual maximum, have occurred in Portugal for *any* worker.

4 Although this is by no means a general rule, since weekend hours are not necessarily overtime hours, the overtime pay premium for weekend work (100 percent) puts a *de facto* cap on what collective bargaining rules will stipulate. The absence of a unique well-defined penalty for work at any given time is analogous to the frequent absence of a well-defined overtime penalty noted for the U.K. by Hart and Ruffell (1993).

5 The exact starting and ending hours of night work may be set differently by collective agreement. The law stipulates that work done over an 11-hour interval that contains 7 consecutive hours within the 10PM–7AM interval may be considered night work if that is so agreed (art. 29-2).

6 Some recent examples of uses of data from the *QP* are Portugal and Cardoso (2006) and Varejão and Portugal (2007).

7 The survey was conducted in France, Germany, the Netherlands, Portugal, Spain and the United Kingdom as part of an EU-funded project on operating hours, working time and employment. A summary of the findings can be found in Delsen et al. (2007), where a chapter specific on the Portuguese results is included (Castro and Varejão (2007)). Although the same basic questionnaire was used in all countries, the annex we use was specific to Portugal. Because no other country that fielded the EU-COWE obtained information on the number of workers present at each hour of the week, currently the questions we ask can only be answered using Portuguese data.

8 Four size classes and seven industry groups were considered for stratification of the sample. The four size strata are: 1–19, 20–249, 250–499 and 500 or more employees. The seven industry strata are: Primary sector, secondary sector, construction, distributive services, producer services, social services, and personal services.

9 These figures are available from the third author upon request.

10 While the term tempogram, and figures for typical workdays, have been used in recent studies based on household time-diary surveys (e.g., Michelson and Crouse (2004)) unsurprisingly given the novelty of our data set none has been generated for establishments.

11 Whether the firm-based or individual-based tempogram is more accurate is not clear. Part of the differences may be due to different coverage of workers by sec-

tor. Regardless, it has become standard in the literature on measurement error in labor-related data to assume that the employer-provided information is correct (e.g., Bound et al. (1994)).

12 Even though the firm time-use survey gives us the number of workers at every time of day-week, we cannot from there trace the identity or characteristics of individual workers across each hour of the week. Indeed, knowing that the firm has, for example, 20 workers from midnight to 4AM is compatible with having just 20 workers at that time, or having 80 workers, each working one single hour (or any situation in-between). The firm-based survey does not identify individual workers.

13 These are the years 1986 to 2002 (with the exception of 1990 and 2001, for which the data are not available).

14 The introduction of fixed effects in the face of the cut in the standard workweek in 1996 would cause biases in our estimates of production parameters in the 2003 cross section only if those effects varied with the distribution of employment in 2003, which seems highly unlikely, but in any case is not testable.

15 The own-quantity elasticity of complementarity is $[a_{ii} + s_i^2 - s_i]/s_i^2$; the cross-quantity elasticity is $1 + a_{ij}/s_i s_j$., where s is the share of the input in total labor cost.

16 To obtain the share of earnings at times *N* we multiply weekday night hours, *WN*, by 1.25, daytime weekend hours, *ED*, by 2, and weekend night hours, *EN*, by 2.5, and compare the result to its sum with daytime weekday hours, *WD*. Thus assuming the same base wage rate at all times, the share of earnings at times *D* is $(1.25 \times WN + 2 \times ED + 2.5 \times EN)/(WD + 1.25 \times WN + 2 \times ED + 2.5 \times EN)$.

17 As Trejo (1991) shows for overtime penalties, some, in this case unknown amount of any change in the penalty would be dissipated as workers' supply decisions adjust to changing incentives. To the extent that this would be important we thus overstate the impacts of the policy changes discussed here. The wage penalty rate Θ is computed as the weighted average wage rate mandated for the four pay regimes described in the previous section. The base wage rate (paid weekday daytimes) was rescaled to 1. We used as weights the number of hourly slots to which each of the pay regimes applies.

Chapter 10

1 One example of this kind of response is the introduction of bills requiring prior notification of a plant closing. The most recent version, the "Labor-Management Notification and Consultation Act," 99:1, H.R. 1616, mandated at least 90 days' prior notification of a permanent layoff or a plant closing involving more than 50 workers. This bill came within five votes of passage in the House of Representatives in 1985.

2 I assume, following Farber (1983), that unionized jobs must be rationed.

3 Obviously, there are other firms and workers whose relationship lasts longer than they expected. They thus experience unexpectedly high returns on their joint investment. For that reason estimates of unexpected losses may be viewed as measures of the size of the lower tail of the distribution of returns to firm-specific investment. Since many social policies focus on the lower tails of various distributions, e.g., income, weeks employed, and on providing incentives to avoid such losses, this approach is consistent with the analysis of labor market policy.

4 In a quite different context, that of union-management relations, Alchian (1982) stresses the importance of specific quasi rents in calculating losses when a contractual relationship is severed.

5 That there are such skills is suggested by Shaw (1984).

6 All that is required for the results to go through is that $B'' < C''$.

7 If the assumption of identical utility functions is abandoned, some results that are qualitatively similar to those developed below can still be derived. For exam-

ple, make the specific assumption that workers and firms have different utility functions, both characterized by constant relative risk aversion, with the functions defined over increments to wealth. One can then show that the amount of firmspecific investment will be reduced if either $R(T_W)$ or $R(T_F)$ decreases from a starting point where $R(T_W) = R(T_F)$.

8 This is a simplifying assumption designed to ease the exposition; the results do not depend on it.

9 The argument that management hides information to prevent shirking is the obverse of the argument presented here. Only senior workers can shirk effectively, since junior workers are interchangeable with new hires. Senior workers who do shirk, though, can have their wages cut and still have an incentive to remain in the firm. The combination of shirking-wage cuts for senior workers is precisely the issue discussed in the text; and if we do not observe any flattening of the wage-tenure profile, we may assume that unusual amounts of shirking do not occur and that workers have little information. Moving outside the game-theoretic approach, one might ask why management does not provide information to workers as a way of inducing wage concessions. Some such behavior may occur; but, if it does, the concessions should be greatest among the most senior workers, who are earning the largest quasi rents. Here too, the empirical work tests how important and successful this kind of tactic is.

10 See Mincer-Jovanovic (1981) for an example of linking these profiles to patterns of firm-specific investment. While the argument here and in most of the literature has based the wage-tenure profile on investment in firm-specific training, one might inquire whether a similar link could be established in a model of bonding such as Lazear's (1981). If both parties' horizons suddenly shorten in such a model, new workers will be less willing to forgo current wages in exchange for higher wages later. Indeed, with a sufficiently short horizon workers will not sacrifice any current wages, and the profile will be flat. Thus, the bonding model seems observationally equivalent to the model developed here; in both, a flattening of the wage-tenure profile implies that workers have acquired substantial information. However, it has substantially different implications from the specific-investment model about the nature of the social costs of adjustment. Yet another possibility is that the wage-tenure relationship is based on a search model, with workers who are badly matched leaving firms quickly, so that the more senior workers are seen to earn rents to their earlier fortuitous match. (See Marshall-Zarkin (1984) for an approach to wage-tenure profiles based on this view.) If this is the underlying cause of the wage-tenure relationship, our inferences from changing wage-tenure profiles to changes in the path of firm-specific investment are incorrect.

11 Bartel-Borjas (1981) were aware of the role of specific training in separations, but they did not focus on the wage-tenure profile's relation to time remaining on the job as we do below.

12 An alternative approach, which would yield the same results if estimated over the same observations, would estimate wage growth each year before displacement as a function of tenure on the job. That would require successive complete vectors of data on each observation. Because fewer observations would be available, I examine instead how the cross-section wage-tenure profile changes as the date of separation approaches.

13 See Congressional Budget Office, *Dislocated Workers: Issues and Federal Options*, July 1982, Chapter 3, for a discussion of various approaches to defining displacement.

14 While tenure in a particular job is available more often in this panel, that measure does not reflect firm-specific investment very well. Consider two workers, one with the firm for five years on five separate jobs, each lasting a year, the other in the firm for one year on the same job. Though each has tenure of one year on the job, the appropriateness of using total tenure is apparent.

15 Yet another problem limiting the sample size is the restriction of the data to household heads. Since some small fraction (below 10 percent) of the households change heads each year, and since the data of interest are reported for household heads, observations must be discarded because the information on tenure and other variables cannot be linked to the date of displacement.

16 As people separated involuntarily in 1977–1981 are included in the sample, wage rates are made comparable across calendar time for $T - i, i = 1, ..., 4$, by inflating using the growth in private nonfarm hourly earnings between the time the worker's wage is observed and 1980.

17 Union relative wage effects ranged from 18 to 31 percent; the rate of return to schooling was around 4 percent; the premium for white workers was between 5 and 18 percent; men received 31 to 45 percent higher pay than otherwise identical women workers; and the premium for being outside the South ranged from 0 to 18 percent.

18 Only for year $T - 1$ was the t-statistic on the quadratic term in TN greater than one in absolute value. (For that regression the coefficients were 0.0175 ($t = 1.99$) on TN, and -0.00037 ($t = -1.09$) on TN^2.)

19 One possibility that might explain the apparent lack of flattening is that the linear, and even quadratic forms of *TN* too, misspecify the equation, and that newer workers must be treated separately. To examine this, I reestimated (9) for each of the four samples, first including a dummy variable for workers with at most one year of tenure, then including a dummy variable for those with at most two years of tenure. Only one of these eight variables added significantly to the equations' explanatory power, and in no case did their addition change the inference that there is little flattening of the profile as involuntary separation approaches.

20 Equations (9) were also estimated separately for years $T - 1, ..., T - 4$ for the samples disaggregated by union status, and disaggregated by reason for involuntary separation. Only for $T - 4$ was the hypothesis that the layoff-displaced subsamples could be pooled rejected at the 5 percent level of confidence, and only for $T - 1$ for the union-nonunion disaggregation was the hypothesis rejected even at the 10 percent level.

21 Had we made the specific assumption of different constant-relative-risk-aversion utility functions, the results would unambiguously imply that neither s^* nor t^* changed, so that the displacement was a surprise to both parties.

22 This conclusion corroborates the sense of surprise expressed by workers and their representatives when plants close. One local union president discussed how his employer expanded for several years and then, "... we were notified that in three weeks we would be shut down. The people in the town were quite shocked .... It completely caught us off guard." (James Savoy, "Statement," House Subcommittee on Labor-Management Relations, 98:2, *Hearings*, May 4, 1984.)

23 This range brackets the estimates of the rate of depreciation of on-the-job training in Johnson (1970).

24 Because Mincer-Jovanovic use OLS estimation, the simulated quit rate becomes negative for high values of tenure in the firm. I arbitrarily restricted q to be nonnegative in the simulations.

25 One should note that, because the estimates in Section 10.5 are based only on those who remain with the firm until it closes, the calculation of the total gross social cost of the lost firm-specific capital is an underestimate. Workers who leave also may reap below-average returns on their prior investments. All we calculate here is the value of the worker's share of specific human capital for those *workers who remain* in the firm until it closes.

26 Since these estimates exclude lost fringe benefits, particularly losses of unvested pension benefits, even they underestimate the workers' losses of future remuneration that was specific to their previous jobs.

27 There is some weak evidence for the United States (Folbre et al, 1984; Addison-Portugal, 1986) that the state laws do reduce the costs borne by displaced workers.

Chapter 11

1 A detailed discussion of the mechanics of these laws is contained in Hamermesh (1977).

2 The evidence in Figure 11.1 suggests that the congressional response has clearly not been motivated by concerns about erosion of the tax base. While solvency considerations are part of the explanation of the timing of increases in the ceiling, that should not affect our theoretical or empirical work, since we concentrate on interstate differences in reactions to the changed ceiling.

3 An increase above the current $7,000 ceiling was proposed in 101st Congress, H.R. 3896, in 102nd Congress, H.R. 1367 and 4727, and most recently in a very modest change recommended by the Advisory Council on Unemployment Compensation (1996).

4 Adams (1986) examined the determination of the parameters of states' UI tax policy generally, treating each state as a laboratory independent of any effects of federal mandates.

5 That it is difficult to revisit continuously issues on the federal political agenda lends further credence to the assumption that state governments expect federal policy to remain unaltered.

6 That partial experience rating generates cross-subsidies is clear from evidence in Anderson and Meyer (1993) and elsewhere. What is less clear is the direction of those subsidies, which doubtless differs among jurisdictions depending on exactly the kind of bargaining that we outline in this section.

7 Halpin (1978) provides evidence that greater experience rating leads employers to contest more claims.

8 For some direct evidence that workers recognize this effect see AFL-CIO (1975), which adopted a resolution recommending, 'Eliminating experience rating altogether or, at the very least, reducing the minimum range between maximum and minimum tax rates, prohibiting zero rates ...'

9 We also normalize political power with employment, implicitly assuming that each firm has one vote in the policy process.

10 The second-order condition requires that the worker's indifference curve be more concave than the median firm's isoprofit line. The more risk-averse workers are, the more likely it is that this condition will be satisfied.

11 It is worth contrasting our results with the standard median-voter theory underlying the flypaper effect puzzle. Rather than having a single median voter, we have interest-group bargaining. The median firm determines crucial aspects of the preferences of one party, but cannot choose the outcome. Secondly, unlike increased spending on a public good, the impact on the median firm of changes in the tax ceiling is intrinsically affected by the distribution of firms. This latter fact is true even when wages are endogenous to the policy process. Proposed resolutions of the flypaper effect puzzle have moved in each of these directions.

12 Compared to truly exogenous events or mandates, such as those evaluated by Card (1990), it is hardly natural or experimental. It is, however, no less natural or experimental than many of the events that have been analyzed in this literature.

13 It is worth noting that in North Dakota in 1972; Alabama, New Jersey and New Mexico in 1978; and Arkansas, Delaware, Michigan, Vermont and Wisconsin in 1983 the state tax ceiling was raised from C_{T-1} to a level above C^* at T. Such behavior is inconsistent with the model in Section 3, but it may be consistent with the solution to a temporary problem of state UI systems in the late 1970s and early 1980s, namely the very high indebtedness of some state systems to the federal government. By the 1980s these debts carried increasingly substantial penalties. With rigidities in state tax systems, raising the base by more than was mandated could have been viewed by all employers as a way of raising additional taxes to pay off the debt to the federal UI trust funds and reduce interest penalties. To examine this hypothesis we estimated a probit relating whether the state raised its ceiling by more than required

by the federal mandate to the ratio of its outstanding debt to its annual UI taxes (with time indicator variables included). The sample includes all states where $C_{T-1} < C^*$ in 1978 and 1983. The results showed that a higher debt made constrained jurisdictions significantly more likely to raise the ceiling by more than the federal government required. Indeed, while a constrained (BELOW) state with no debt had only a 7 percent probability of going beyond the required increase, the state with the largest proportional debt had a 50 probability of raising its ceiling beyond the federal mandate.

14 These results and those in Table 11.3 are changed only minutely if the District of Columbia is dropped from the analysis in recognition of its unusual position in the American federal system.

15 Similarly, replacing TAXES by total tax rates on both sides of (5) does not alter our conclusions.

16 We are indebted to Rebecca Blank for these insights into the arcana of the American AFDC system.

Chapter 12

1 Examples of each are, respectively, Francine Blau and Andrea Beller (1992), George Borjas and Marta Tienda (1985), David Bloom and Gilles Grenier (1992), and Melissa Famulari (1992).

2 Quoted by Fred Siegel, "The Cult of Multiculturalism," New Republic, 18 February 1991, p. 38, from an official document from Smith College. The city of Santa Cruz, California, enacted and subsequently repealed an ordinance banning such discrimination (New York Times, 13 February 1992, p. A18). The foreign legislation was proposed in the Philippine Congress, reported by the Associated Press, 13 December 1992. The case law and the Americans with Disabilities Act are discussed by Tony McAdams et al. (1992). A recent case is Hodgdon v. Mt. Mansfield Company, 6 November 1992, in which the Vermont Supreme Court ruled that a chambermaid's lack of upper teeth qualified as a handicap protected under the state's Fair Employment Practices Act.

3 Given the distributions across the five categories in 1977 in this three-year sample, 20 percent would randomly be classified identically in all three years, and 79 percent would be randomly classified identically in two years and only one category different in the third. With a sample of 1,330 people, the probabilities of observing the outcomes in this part of Table I are infinitesimally tiny.

4 An unpublished work in the late 1970's by Robert Frank of Cornell University correlated earnings of recent Cornell graduates with ratings of their appearance (from pictures) by a group of current undergraduates.

5 Such a model would predict a disproportionate representation of attractive workers in certain industries (i.e., those shielded from competition). The literature on occupational crowding has often assumed that preference-based employer discrimination is occupation-specific, which in our case would imply that employers experience a visceral reaction only when contemplating the presence of an attractive or unattractive employee in certain occupations. It is hard to know how one might identify such occupations a priori (although the employee's physical proximity to the employer at work might be one factor).

6 It is not clear what an occupational-crowding model would imply about β_2 and β_4. The literature usually presumes that occupational segregation will be incomplete; but it has not produced a rigorous, canonical model that generates predictions about the relative wages of different types of workers in the same occupation.

7 These are the only broadly based surveys we could find that contain information on looks and earnings. A number of other surveys, including one interesting proprietary data set used in a (racial) discrimination case by Mark Killingsworth,

contain information on the worker's general appearance. This measure seems more likely to be influenced by income than the physical appearance measures that are available in our samples.

8 All the equations were reestimated using annual earnings, with weekly hours included as an independent variable. None of our conclusions is changed qualitatively by this modification.

9 Note that in 1971 in the United States the minimum wage was \$1.60 per hour, and in 1977 it was \$2.30. In Canada in 1981 the federal minimum was \$3.50, and some provincial minima were even higher. The disqualifications on the wage rate are thus designed to exclude those observations for which measurement errors are likely. Excluding the small fraction of workers whose estimated hourly wage is far below statutory minima does not imply any selectivity on a characteristic that is correlated with looks. In the QAL, for example, there is no relation at even the 20-percent level of significance between the beauty measures and the probability of exclusion from the sample for this reason. Even if there were, the fraction of people so excluded is below 5 percent of the sample.

10 Of the respondents in the QES between the ages of 18 and 64 this disqualified 10; from the QAL, 126; and from the QOL, 18.

11 One related possibility is that interviewers of different sexes rate respondents differently. This possibility is also handled by using interviewer fixed effects. It is not likely to be a problem in any case, since 95 percent of the respondents in the two American samples were interviewed by women. A related problem is that there may be differences in the interviewers' ability to classify workers of different races. Not surprisingly, given that the overwhelming majority of the respondents are white, the estimates in Tables 12.3 and 12.4 change only minutely when African-Americans are deleted from the sample.

12 The rating scale for weight (in descending order) was: "obese," "overweight," "average for height," "underweight," and "skinny." Among women (men), 3.2 (0.7) percent were rated obese, 19.6 (17.4) percent were rated overweight, 65.8 (72.7) percent were considered average, 11.2 (8.5) percent were rated underweight, and 0.2 (0. 7) percent were rated skinny.

13 There are other ways of combining the three ratings. For example, assume that each interviewer assigns a rating along the five-point scale based on her estimate of underlying beauty, *B*. For a homely person, for example, the data in Table 12.2 imply that the person is in the lowest 2.5 percent of the population. Assuming that *B* is normally distributed, the best estimate of that person's *B* is $\hat{B} = E(B|B < N^{-1}(0.025))$. Similar inferences can be drawn based on partitioning the normal density for each of the other ratings using the population percentages in Table 12.2. An estimate of a respondent's true beauty is B^*, the average of the three independent estimates of $\hat{B}$. Using B^* rather than $\hat{B}$ as a measure of beauty generates improvements in goodness of fit and increases in the absolute values of estimated coefficients similar to those associated with columns (iii) and (iv) and with columns (vii) and (viii).

14 Remember that hourly earnings were calculated using actual weekly hours, but assuming that all workers spent the same number of weeks employed. The QES and QOL provide data on weeks of layoff (in the last year in the QES, two years in the QOL). We estimated Tobit regressions of the determinants of weeks of layoff (for the roughly 7 percent of males who reported having been laid off) including controls for education level, experience, union status, tenure with the firm, and firm or establishment size. In both samples the *t* statistics on the dummy variable for above-average looks were below 0.5 in absolute value. Bad looks raised the probability of layoff and lengthened its duration, with *t* statistics of 1.54 in the QES (1.40 in the QOL). This provides additional evidence for the conclusion that there is some asymmetry in the effect of looks on earnings. However, note from Table 12.2 that below-average looks are much less frequent than above-average

looks in these ratings, so that any asymmetry in our results may be due more to how beauty is rated than to how the market treats beauty.

15 We are indebted to Bob Willis for suggesting this point.

16 The same conclusion is reached if we replace 1981 ratings of beauty with ones predicted from regressions using all the information contained in the 1977 and 1979 ratings. Despite this evidence, one might still argue that serial correlation in earnings creates a simultaneity between current earnings and lagged ratings of beauty. Under usual assumptions about serial correlation in earnings, however, one would not find, as we do, that the results using the 1977 and 1979 ratings in the small longitudinal sample are at least as strong as those using the 1981 data only.

17 Not surprisingly, similar probits on men's laborforce participation yielded no relationship between looks and the probability of participation. These results and those for women are qualitatively the same when we use linear regressions instead of probits to describe participation.

18 The underlying data on education are listed in seven categories, not single years of schooling. We assign years of schooling to these categories (5, 8, 10, 12, 14, 16, and 17) and base the regressions on these. Ordered probits based on the seven categories yield the same qualitative conclusions.

19 Regressions for the education of wives in the QES generated estimated effects of -0.11 and 0.13 years on the dummy variables indicating their husbands' looks, with *t* statistics below 0.8 in absolute value. The sorting of economic outcomes in marriage appears to be related to beauty only for women.

20 We rely on the fifth digit of the DOT code, which can take nine different values according to whether the job involves "mentoring," "negotiating," "instructing," "supervising," "diverting," "persuading," "speaking, signaling," "serving," or "taking instructions, helping." We treat all but the last as indications that interpersonal interaction is an important aspect of the occupation.

21 The 28 pairwise correlations of the ratings of the 504 occupations ranged from 0.36 to 0.61, with a mean of 0.47.

22 The survey targeted employers of low-education workers. As a result there were too few observations in several broad occupation cells to calculate occupational beauty ratings, preventing many QES and QAL sample members from being included in this part of the analysis.

23 Complete information on the occupational rankings is available upon request from the authors.

24 A more straightforward test simply includes a vector of dummy variables for one-digit occupations in the basic equation for both samples and genders. The coefficients on the dummy variables for below- and above-average looks are hardly altered in size or significance. Among the QES men (women), the coefficients (analogous to those in columns (i) and (iii) of Table 12.3) become -0.156 and 0.014 (-0.100 and 0.026). Among the QAL men (women), the coefficients (analogous to those in columns (i) and (iv) of Table 12.4) become -0.059 and 0.062 (0.068 and 0.115). Taking this approach to its logical extreme (and losing between one-fourth and one-half of the degrees of freedom in each model), we reestimated the equations with separate dummy variables for each three-digit occupation. The results for men in both samples are essentially unchanged in this extension; for women the parameter estimates maintain their signs, but their absolute values are cut in half.

Chapter 13

1 The mean differs slightly from zero because better-looking solicitors appear to have contacted more households, and each observation is a household.

2 There is no effect of solicitors' beauty on the size of the contribution conditional

on it being positive. The impact of female solicitors' beauty in these data works through its inducements to make some contribution.

3 Estimates of these equations that did not include these controls, and other estimates that include the share of citations instead of the rank in this measure, yield the same conclusions about the relative importance of absolute and relative differences in beauty.

4 See Komlos and Lauderdale (2007) for evidence, and http://www.thedailyshow.com/watch/thu-June-21-2007/stature-of-liberty for a humorous popular presentation of this phenomenon.

5 We restrict the analysis here to men to avoid concerns about the changing labor force participation of Dutch women. Suffice it to note, however, that Dutch women's heights in these samples also rose significantly and sharply over these periods. We use men 25–59 to avoid including those who may not have reached their full adult height or who may have begun to shrink.

6 In the four years of the POLS that are used here this restriction excludes seven men. It excludes seven men from the DNB in 1995, and one man from the DNB in 2010. I supplement the 2010 sample going backward through 2006 with men who did not appear in the 2010 wave. No individual appears more than once in the 2006–10 sub-sample that we use here. Of the 872 men used in that sub-sample, 449 are observed in 2010, 136 in 2009, 83 in 2008, 109 in 2007 and 95 in 2006.

7 We can reject the hypothesis that the means of the two distributions are the same (t=23.54). Given the sample sizes, we cannot reject the hypothesis that the variance of the distribution was unchanged over this period.

8 Re-estimating the model for the DNB 1995 sample only on workers ages 29 through 45 (presumably a random sample of those who would reach 43 through 59 in 2009, the average year in which members of the 2006–10 sample were observed), the estimated impact of height is even larger than it was for this cohort in 2009.

9 Since the average probability of being sent away is always 0.25, and that of election is always 0.5, the main effect of average looks in a game or an election cannot be included in the specification of the conditional logits.

10 I examined the impacts of absolute and relative rankings of heights on earnings in the Dutch data and the American Time Use Survey, with nearly identical results for specifications of height as absolute or relative. Similarly ambiguous results were produced for the impact of beauty on earnings in recent German data, and for estimates of the impact of immigrants' skin color on earnings (using data on skin color previously used by Hersch 2008).

11 See, however, Heckman (1998) for a discussion of audit studies and some of their difficulties. Despite concerns about whether asking businesspeople to spend time evaluating resumés of phony applicants is even ethical, there seems to be no shortage of researchers willing to undertake this type of study.

Chapter 14

1 Some authors, such as Borjas and Bronars (1989) and Buffum and Whaples (1995), concentrate on measuring one particular form of discrimination (by consumers and by fellow employees, respectively).

2 The relationship between beauty and economic success has, however, received substantial attention from the news media. See, e.g., Jane Brody, "The Ideal Face Transcends Culture," New York Times (March 22, 1994), p. A6, or ABC's television news program 20/20 (November 4, 1994).

3 Differences across sectors in the returns to the same characteristic in a competitive equilibrium are discussed by Heckman and Scheinkman (1987) and Rosen

(1983). Only under very restrictive assumptions on how characteristics enter sector-specific production functions will one observe equalization of returns across sectors.

4 If we assume instead that X_3 is a dichotomous characteristic, it is possible to have workers of both types in both sectors, with the majority of the high X_3 workers in sector A. Adding more sectors and characteristics to the model does not change the basic conclusion that workers will sort into sectors that pay a greater reward to the attributes that they possess.

5 Langlois and Roggman (1990) discuss the psychology of perceptions of beauty.

6 The photographs of many of the classes in our study were taken by a photographer provided by the law school. In other years students submitted a picture, most often from a college yearbook, which once again may have been the work of an institutionally provided photographer. There is thus little chance that a correlation between students' socioeconomic background and photo quality could arise because higher-income students bought the services of better photographers.

7 For 2 of the 12 years only two raters were used. As in the other cases, an average rating was formed from this reduced number of constituents.

8 Current unfamiliarity with styles of dress from the late 1960s could have led to greater heterogeneity in the ratings of members of the early cohort. In fact, however, Cronbach's α and the average pairwise correlations among the raters were both slightly *higher* for the earlier cohort.

9 This result also holds if we disaggregate respondents and nonrespondents by sex: the differences in average beauty are independent of respondent status among both men and women.

10 Excluding this last measure has virtually no effect on any of the estimates of the coefficients of the beauty variables in the regressions of the next section. Similarly, only tiny changes are produced if we add yet another measure of ability to the equations, a composite of the matriculant's adjusted undergraduate gradepoint average and LSAT score.

11 Both W_5 and W_{15} are based on answers to questions about "net (pretax) earnings" from the "principal position."

12 This differs from Spurr and Sueyoshi's (1994) finding of little difference across these cohorts in turnover rates among a group of lawyers with more heterogeneous backgrounds.

13 Although indicator variables for the size of the firm where the attorney's first job was located have significant positive effects on year 5 earnings, their inclusion has almost no effect on the sizes or significance of the beauty effects in these equations and those of Tables 14.4 and 14.5.

14 Data on annual hours worked are not available in the year 5 surveys for classes that graduated before 1976, so that we cannot examine this equation for the 1970s cohort in year 5. For men (women) in the 1980s cohort, reestimating the final equation in Table 14.3 (Table 14.4) does not alter the conclusion about the insignificant effect of beauty at year 5.

15 If we include only W_5 and the vector J_{15} in an equation relating W_{15} to beauty, we again find that the coefficient on beauty in this cohort increased as it aged.

16 The calculations are based on the usual weekly earnings of all full-time workers in these occupations who had at least 18 years of schooling (after 1991, more than an M.A.) from the 1979-93 Outgoing Rotation Groups of the Current Population Survey.

17 Another possibility is that the beauty coefficient varies with firm size at year 5. The coefficient is slightly, but not significantly, smaller in firms with 50+ attorneys, but this difference and the growing share of attorneys in the later cohorts who are located in large firms do almost nothing to explain the differences in the beauty coefficients at year 5 between the 1970s and 1980s cohorts.

18 The main effect of beauty had a coefficient of 0.025 (SE of 0.008), the coefficient on the main effect of solo practice was -0.033 (0.040), and the coefficient on their interaction was 0.034 (0.037).

19 The average attractiveness of all attorneys in this subsample rose between years 5 and 15 because those who left the practice of law during this interval were significantly less attractive than those who continued to practice. As the dynamic sorting model of Section II shows, this could result from the rising wage effect of attractiveness with experience in the legal profession noted in Section III accompanied by a decline in the relative returns to other characteristics.

20 Caroline Hoxby (personal communication, July 26, 1995) observed that this result could be an artifact of low beauty ratings having been assigned to men who were poorly dressed for their pictures and who also had a preference for public-sector jobs, with well-dressed men being rated higher and preferring private-sector jobs. It is true that the average beauty rating was significantly lower among the 30% of men in the 1970s cohort who did not wear a tie in their photograph. However, the distributions of attorneys in the four categories listed in Table 14.7 were remarkably similar among the better- and the worse-dressed groups (83% of the former, 81% of the latter were in the private sector in both years). Moreover, if we limit the sample to those who wore ties, the standardized average beauty ratings in the four sectoral categories in Table 14.7 were .096, .093, -.429, and -.021 - somewhat stronger support for our hypothesis than is provided by the full sample. As an additional check, in other regressions based on part B of Table 14.3 the tie variable had absolutely no effect on the impact of standardized beauty on earnings.

21 Whether the average public-sector worker could expect to see both his salary and the monetary premium associated with his attractiveness rise following a move to the private sector depends in part on the extent to which sectoral differences in salary reflect a compensating differential or instead differences in the observed and unobserved productivity of workers located in the two sectors (Goddeeris 1988). Our earnings regressions, which include detailed controls for productivity, still indicate a 25% shortfall in the earnings of public-sector attorneys by year 15. (Notice that this difference is far below the raw earnings difference - 158% - between attorneys in the two sectors at year 15.) Also, holding constant year 5 earnings, lawyers who switched from the public sector earned considerably more in year 15 than those who stayed, while those who left the private sector earned much less than those who stayed there. This suggests very strongly that the average public-sector lawyer who switched to the private sector in year 15 would experience a substantial earnings gain.

22 Sauer (1996) analyzes the job mobility of attorneys in the context of a formal model of search.

23 Adding marital status and the presence of children at the time of law-school graduation to these probits does not qualitatively affect the conclusions. Moreover, the coefficients on marital status have *t*-statistics far below one in absolute value. It is true, however, that more attractive female attorneys were also more likely to be married at year 5, while attractiveness did not significantly affect male attorneys' probability of being married. Since we are not analyzing the effect of beauty on the marriage market, the absence of any effect of marital status on partnership, either directly or indirectly through beauty, makes further pursuit of the issue irrelevant for this study.

24 The growing returns are presumably due to skills that enabled the person to qualify for the law journal or achieve a higher class rank, not to those achievements per se.

25 Respondents who stated that their practice was mainly debtor/creditor, civil rights, criminal law, domestic relations, or torts and personal injuries were classed as being mainly in litigation. Those who listed themselves as being in antitrust, corporate, employee benefits, estates, or securities law were classified as being in corporate/finance; attorneys whose specialties were banking, com-

munications, energy, environmental, or immigration law were classified as being in regulation/administrative law. Those in other specialties were included in the catch-all category "other."

Chapter 15

1 Until the late 1930s, the position of president of the Association was also contested. Since no women were nominated for that office during those years, we ignore elections for president.

2 Under U.S. federal practice anyone with a judgeship, a seat in Congress, or the rank of assistant secretary or higher in the executive branch receives this honorific.

3 Insignificant results and no effects on the estimated impacts of other variables were obtained when another indicator of distinction, prior receipt of the John Bates Clark Medal, was included in the estimation.

4 Using several years' citations in the early years of the sample is necessary to reduce the sampling error resulting from the relative paucity of journals catalogued in those years. The citation counts are from the on-line *Social Science Citation Index* and include all self-citations and citations to the author regardless of her/his order in the authorship. This database has citations for individual years beginning only with 1955.

5 We use citations in the most recent complete calendar year for most of this sample. Hamermesh et al. (1982) show that, even in the context of an outcome that is clearly cumulative, going beyond recent citations adds little to the ability to describe variations in the outcome.

6 If one incorrectly specifies a simple probit model, the inferences about the effects of the determinants of the elections do not differ qualitatively very much from those implicit in the results in Table 15.2.

7 We use this term based on Wooldridge's (2002) usage for the standard case where only one of out *N* possible choices can be made.

8 There is a substantial literature on elections in multimember electoral districts. The theoretical literature has examined voting patterns given preferences (Elisabeth R. Gerber et al., 1998), while the empirical literature has focused on characteristics of winners without formally examining the elections' determinants (e.g., Richard Niemi et al., 1985).

9 Other examples include admissions to many educational institutions (e.g., the U.S. military academies, many medical schools), some scholarship competitions, winning the three medals awarded among the eight finalists in many Olympic track and swimming events, and choosing some investment portfolios.

10 The maximum-likelihood estimates produced under the assumptions about the error terms that generate the logit-type estimator are qualitatively the same as those for the probit-type estimator.

11 One possible omission is the simultaneous presence of candidates from the same institution, which describes 7 percent of the sample. An indicator for this occurrence had a negative, albeit not statistically significant, effect on the probability of electoral victory. Its impacts on the estimated coefficients in column 4 were tiny, raising each absolute value slightly and lowering slightly their standard errors. A measure of the candidates' years since the Ph.D. degree was quite insignificant statistically (and negative) and had a tiny influence on the other coefficients.

12 We can provide a hint at the predictive value of the model using the two elections for officers. The models in Table 15.2 appear to work well. In the election for vice-presidents for 2005, the winners' score in the CML model was third highest (out of the six), although all six scores were very close together. In the MMR model, the winners' scores ranked them (a close) second and third. In the election for Executive Board for 2005, the winners' score far exceeded the scores of the other five possible

pairs, and the winners' scores in the MMR model were also far above the losers'. In the 2006 elections, both methods predicted that the eventual winners would be the top two choices in the elections for vice-presidents and for Executive Board.

13 Using the methodology of Donald W. K. Andrews (1993), the maximum of the likelihood-ratio (LR) statistics testing for a break in all coefficients is not quite significant at usual levels. If, however, we test for a break in the coefficient on the female variable alone, the test-statistic is significant, with the highest LR statistic for a break between 1974 and 1975.

14 The 1974 elections were the first in which at least one woman appeared in both elections. If that year is added to the estimation, the estimated effect of crowding becomes slightly stronger and more significant statistically.

15 Psychological research shows that women score higher in personality inventories on such characteristics as restraint, friendliness, and personal relations (Joan Guilford et al., 1976, p. 108; James N. Butcher and Paolo Pancheri, 1976, pp. 224–25).

16 The data provide an interesting perspective on how World War II changed the gender composition of the profession. While the membership of the AEA grew steadily, World War II saw a sharp rise in the fraction female, from 6.4 percent in 1940 to 9.9 percent in 1946 (with "Edna the Economist" perhaps an analog to "Rosie the Riveter"). Absent a *Directory* or *Handbook* between 1948 and 1957, we cannot tell whether, as Claudia D. Goldin (1991) showed generally, women left the profession disproportionately after the war or whether the old patterns of inflow reasserted themselves.

17 One reader argued that lumpiness and the thinness of the distribution of qualified female candidates might have induced this apparent undersupply of female candidates. This explanation is logically possible, but even restricting the choice set to female full professors in the top 17 public university economics departments, the Ivy League, Stanford, Chicago, and MIT in 2002, there were 31 women (calculated from James Hasselback, 2002).

Chapter 16

1 Pitches are subject to the umpire's discretion (are "called") only when the batter does not swing, rendering necessary a judgment of whether the pitch was a "ball" or a "strike."

2 The data also include a small number of Asian pitchers, but because there are no Asian umpires, we exclude them in our analysis. Given their trivial numbers, however, their inclusion gives nearly identical results in every instance.

3 Umpires can be positioned behind home plate or at first, second, or third base. The home-plate umpire occasionally appeals to either the first- or third-base umpire, but this is a relatively infrequent occurrence, and in any case is usually initiated by the home-plate umpire himself to help determine if the batter swung at the ball.

4 The pitch-by-pitch information is from: http://sports.espn.go.com/mlb/playbyplay?gameId=NNNNNNNNN&full=1, where NNNNNNNNN represents the nine-digit game ID. The first six digits correspond to the year, month and date of the game. The box score information is from http://sports.espn.go.com/mlb/boxscore?gameId=NNNNNNNNN.

5 Player's country of birth information can be found at http://www.baseball-reference.com/bio/. Umpire's country of birth information can be found at http://mlb.mlb.com/mlb/official_info/umpires/roster.jsp.

6 The complete list can be found at http://Blackvoices.aol.com/Black_sports/special/_a/african-americanplayers-in-mlb/20070413095009990001.

7 The complete list can be found at http://www.answers.com/topic/list-of-hispanic-players-in-major-leaguebaseball.

8 For a few umpires, no pictures were available on the Internet. For each of them we

watched past games in which the umpires worked to ascertain their race/ethnicity. Any such classification is necessarily ambiguous in a number of cases. To the extent that we have inadvertently classified pitchers, umpires, or batters in ways different from how they might be treated on the field, this will introduce classical measurement error into the matches and thus reduce the strength of any results that we generate.

9 The information is provided by the MLB free of charge at: http://gd2.mlb.com/components/game/mlb/.

10 The operator sets a horizontal line at each batter's belt as he settles into the hitting position, and the PITCHf/x software adds four inches up to define the top of the zone. For the bottom of the zone, the PITCHf/x operator sets a horizontal line at the hollow of each batter's knee. More information on PITCHf/x's parameters can be found at: http://fastballs.wordpress.com/category/pitchfx-glossary/ and http://webusers.npl.illinois.edu/~a-nathan/pob/tracking.htm.

11 Examination of umpires' schedules indicates that, while umpires typically travel as a four-person crew throughout much of the year, crews are randomly assigned across teams, ballparks, geography, and league (American or National). Furthermore, umpires rotate in a specific order, i.e., each serves as the home-plate umpire exactly every fourth game, resulting in random assignment of umpires to starting pitchers.

12 With pitcher fixed effects, this second reason for inning indicators is obviously subsumed.

13 As a check on this issue, we reestimated the model including sequentially the race/ethnic match between the first-, second-, and third-base umpire and the pitcher. None of these extensions materially changes our conclusions.

14 QuesTec was installed in the ballparks of the Anaheim Angels, Arizona Diamondbacks, Boston Red Sox, Cleveland Indians, Oakland Athletics, Milwaukee Brewers, Houston Astros, New York Mets, Tampa Bay Devil Rays, Chicago White Sox, and New York Yankees.

15 An umpire's evaluation is not based solely on QuesTec. If an umpire falls below the QuesTec standards, his performance is then reviewed by videotape and live observation by other umpires to determine his final evaluation score. No such measures are taken, however, if an umpire meets the QuesTec standards.

16 The fraction of games in which QuesTec was installed was virtually identical for all umpires in our sample, differing for the few umpires calling only a handful of games.

17 For example, New York Mets pitcher Tom Glavine, known as a "finesse" pitcher who depends on pitches close to the strike zone border, complained publicly that QuesTec's influence on umpire calls forced him to change his style (Associated Press, July 9, 2003). Glavine reports that he was told, "(umpires do) not call pitches on the corners at Shea (his home ballpark) because they (the umpires) don't want the machine to give them poor grades."

18 The direct effect of being in a QuesTec park is, of course, not directly observable, being subsumed in the pitcher-QuesTec fixed effects.

19 We scale by stadium capacity to minimize the impact of differences between stadium sizes. If we assume that stadiums populate relatively uniformly, attendance/capacity is a good proxy for the number of fans close enough to judge pitch location. In any case, this scaling makes little difference in our results. If instead we use attendance, all coefficients of interest remain highly significant.

20 Percentage attendance may also proxy the popularity of the participating teams or the importance of a particular game. Thus, not only might the umpire be exposed to more scrutiny from the additional fans present at well-attended games, but he may also face added scrutiny in the form of larger television audiences and increased air time given to game highlights.

21 The overwhelming majority of minority pitchers are Hispanic. We have aggregated them, but some are white Hispanics, while others are black Hispanics. To allow

for the possibility that the two different groups of minority umpires might treat Hispanic pitchers who match their own characteristics differently from other Hispanic pitchers, we visually inspected the pitchers' pictures, divided the Hispanic aggregate into white and black groups, and consequently redefined *UPM*. This reclassification had almost no effect on the estimates produced in Tables 16.3–5. Implicitly, Hispanic and other umpires treat Hispanic pitchers the same regardless of the pitcher's racial identity. We also investigated whether American-born Hispanic pitchers were treated differently from Hispanic pitchers born outside the US, and found no evidence that the pitcher's birthplace affected expressed racial/ethnic bias by umpires. As we cannot rule out the possibility that we have incorrectly classified the Hispanic pitchers, this analysis may be subject to a classic "errors-in-variables" bias. That problem, if it exists, would reduce the likelihood of finding a significant relationship, as pointed out in Fort and Gill (2000).

22 Examining the coefficients on the count indicators in Table 16.3 illustrates the intuition. When the pitcher has a substantial advantage in the count, he has little incentive to throw a "hittable" pitch, i.e., one near the middle of the plate. Instead, he usually throws pitches near the corners that are both less likely to be hit if the batter swings, and less likely to be called strikes if the batter does not. Such behavior translates into sizable advantages for pitchers depending on the count. In 2004, batters got a hit 33 percent of the time when the count was 2–1 (two balls and one strike) but dropped to less than 18 percent when the count was 1–2.

23 The number of pitches differs slightly across the panels because of difficulties in classifying by location and type. Jowei Chen (2007) used these data for a single season as controls to examine racial bias in MLB umpires' calls.

24 A Google search for "umpire" and "calling a curveball" generates dozens of links to articles and advice to umpires wishing to master the evaluation of this difficult pitch.

25 We tabulate each starting pitcher's win decisions rather than whether the team actually wins the game. If one considers this second measure instead, the differences are similar, although the overall mean is 0.5 by construction. (The mean for wins is lower in the text table because relief pitchers are frequently awarded decisions.)

26 We use the means in this sample as the baselines. For the fraction of games won, 0.37; for ERA, 4.44; for strikeouts/inning by starting pitchers, 0.75; and for walks/inning, 0.43. We can take the estimates of the bias as examples here to infer the dollar impacts of this subtle form of discrimination. In 2006, the midpoint of our sample, the average salary of starting pitchers in MLB was $4.8 million. A bias to the estimated effect of minority status on compensation of starting pitchers of between 1 and 8 percent suggests that those pitchers are underpaid relative to white pitchers by between $50,000 and $400,000 per year.

27 See "Ball-Strike Monitor May Reopen Wounds" (Alan Schwarz, New York Times, March 1, 2009, electronic version available at http://www.nytimes.com/2009/04/01/sports/baseball/01umpires.html.)

References

Introduction by the Editors

Bargain, O., Immervoll, H., Peichl, A., Siegloch, S. (2012). Distributional consequences of labor-demand shocks: the 2008–2009 recession in Germany, in: International Tax and Public Finance, 19(1): 118–38.

Brück, T., Haisken-DeNew, J. P., Zimmermann, K. F. (2006). Creating Low Skilled Jobs by Subsidizing Market-Contracted Household Work, in: Applied Economics, 38(8): 899–911.

Hamermesh, D., Soss, N. (1974). An economic theory of suicide, in: Journal of Political Economy, 82(1): 83–98.

Hamermesh, D. (2014). Do labor costs affect companies' demand for labor?, in: IZA World of Labor 2014: 3 doi: 10.15185/izawol.3

Hamermesh, D. (1993). Labor Demand, Princeton, NJ: Princeton University Press.

Hamermesh, D. (1986). The Demand for Labor in the Long Run, in: Ashenfelter, O., Layard, R. (Eds.), Handbook of Labor Economics, Amsterdam: North-Holland, Chapter 8.

Krause, A., Rinne, U., Zimmermann, K.F. (2012). Anonymous job applications in Europe, in: IZA Journal of European Labor Studies, 1(5).

Neumark, D. (2014). Employment effects of minimum wages, in: IZA World of Labor 2014: 6 doi: 10.15185/izawol.6

Peichl, A., Siegloch, S. (2012). Accounting for Labor Demand Effects in Structural Labor Supply Models, in: Labour Economics, 19(1): 129–38.

Rinne, U. (2014). Anonymous job applications and hiring discrimination, in: IZA World of Labor 2014: 48 doi: 10.15185/izawol.48

Riphahn, R. T., Thalmaier, A., Zimmermann, K. F. (1999). Schaffung von Arbeitsplätzen für Geringqualifizierte, Gutachterliche Stellungnahme im Auftrag des Bundesministeriums für Arbeit und Sozialordnung, IZA Research Report No. 2.

Schneider, H., Zimmermann, K. F., Bonin, H., Brenke, K., Haisken-DeNew, J. P., Kempe, W. (2002). Beschäftigungspotenziale einer dualen Förderstrategie im Niedriglohnbereich, Gutachten im Auftrag des Ministeriums für Arbeit und Soziales, Qualifikation und Technologie des Landes Nordrhein-Westfalen, IZA Research Report No. 5.

Stewart, J. (2014). The importance and challenges of measuring work hours, in: IZA World of Labor 2014: 95 doi: 10.15185/izawol.95.

Part II

Becker, G. (1957). The Economics of Discrimination, Chicago: University of Chicago Press.
Blau, F. (2012). Gender, Inequality, and Wages, New York: Oxford University Press.
Easterlin, R. (2010). Happiness, Growth and the Life Cycle, New York: Oxford University Press.
Hamermesh, D. (1993). Labor Demand, Princeton, NJ: Princeton University Press.
Hamermesh, D. (2002). International Labor Economics, in: Journal of Labor Economics, 20(4): 709–32.
Hamermesh, D., Hassink, W., van Ours, J. (1996). Job Turnover and Labor Turnover: A Taxonomy of Employment Dynamics, in: Annales d'Économie et de Statistique, 41–42: 21–40.
Heckman, J., Pages-Serra, C. (2004). Law and Employment: Lessons from Latin America and the Caribbean, Chicago: University of Chicago Press.
Hicks, J. (1932). The Theory of Wages, London: Macmillan.
Letterie, W., Pfann, G., Verick, S. (2010). On Lumpiness in the Replacement and Expansion of Capital, in: Oxford Bulletin of Economics and Statistics, 72(3): 263–81.
Marshall, A. (1920). Principles of Economics, London: Macmillan.
Shapiro, C., Stiglitz, J. (1984). Equilibrium Unemployment as a Worker Discipline Device, in: American Economic Review, 74(3): 433–44.
Stafford, F. (1986). Forestalling the Demise of Empirical Economics: The Role of Microdata in Labor Economics Research, in: Ashenfelter, O., Layard, R. (Eds.), Handbook of Labor Economics, Amsterdam: Elsevier, 387–423.
Thomas, J. (2002). Is Lumpy Investment Relevant for the Business Cycle?, in: Journal of Political Economy, 110(3): 508–34.
Winkelmann, L., Winkelmann, R. (1998). Why Are the Unemployed So Unhappy? Evidence from Panel Data, in: Economica, 65(257): 1–15.

Introduction to Part III

Davis, S., Haltiwanger, J. (1992). Gross Job Creation, Gross Job Destruction and Employment Reallocation, in: Quarterly Journal of Economics, 107(3): 819–63.
Dunne, T., Roberts, M., Samuelson, L. (1989). The Growth and Failure of Manufacturing Plants, in: Quarterly Journal of Economics, 104(4): 671–98.
Ferguson, C. (1971). The Neoclassical Theory of Production and Distribution, London: Cambridge University Press.
Granger, C., Hatanaka, M. (1964). Spectral Analysis of Economic Time Series, Princeton, NJ: Princeton University Press.
Gould, J. (1968). Adjustment Costs in the Theory of Investment of the Firm, in: Review of Economic Studies, 35(1): 47–55.
Grant, J. (1979). Substitution among Labor, Labor and Capital in U.S. Manufacturing. Unpublished Ph.D. Dissertation, Michigan State University.
Griliches, Z. (1969). Capital-Skill Complementarity, in: Review of Economics and Statistics, 51(4): 465–68.
Hamermesh, D. (1969). A Disaggregative Econometric Model of Gross Changes in Employment, in: Yale Economic Essays, 9(2): 107–45.
Hamermesh, D. (1993). Labor Demand, Princeton, NJ: Princeton University Press.
Holt, C., Modigliani, F., Muth, J., Simon, H. (1960). Planning Production, Inventories and Work Force, Englewood Cliffs, NJ: Prentice-Hall.
Lazear, E., Spletzer, J. (2012). Hiring, Churn and the Business Cycle, in: American Economic Association, Papers and Proceedings, 102(3): 575–79.
Nerlove, M. (1964). Spectral Analysis of Seasonal Adjustment Procedures, in: Econometrica, 32(3): 241–86.
Oi, W. (1962). Labor as a Quasi-Fixed Factor of Production, in: Journal of Political Econ-

omy, 70(6): 538–55.
Pfann, G., Palm, F. (1993). Asymmetric Adjustment Costs in Non-linear Labour Demand Models for the Netherlands and UK Manufacturing Sectors, in: Review of Economics Studies, 60(2): 397–412.
Pfann, G., Verspagen, B. (1989). The Structure of Adjustment Costs for Labour in the Dutch Manufacturing Sector, in: Economics Letters, 29(4): 365–71.

Chapter 1

Allen, R. G. D. (1938). Mathematical Analysis for Economists, London: Macmillan.
Anderson, J. (1977). Labor Force Age Structure Changes and Relative Wages, Harvard University, unpublished paper.
Anderson, R. (1979). On the Accuracy of Estimated Factor Demand Elasticities in Flexible Functional Form Demand Models, Michigan State University, Econometrics Workshop Paper No. 7906.
Berndt, E. (1980). Modelling the Simultaneous Demand for Factors of Production, in: Hornstein, Z. (Ed.), The Economics of the Labor Market, London: Her Majesty's Stationery Office.
Berndt, E., Christensen, L. (1974). Testing for the Existence of a Consistent Aggregate Index of Labor Inputs, in: American Economic Review, 64: 391404.
Borjas, G., Heckman, J. (1978): Labor Supply Estimates for Public Policy Evaluation, in: Proceedings of the Industrial Relations Research Association, 31: 320–31.
Christensen, L., Jorgenson, D., Lau, L. (1973). Transcendental Logarithmic Production Frontiers, in: this REVIEW, 55: 28–45.
Denny, M., Fuss, M. (1977). The Use of Approximation Analysis to Test for Separability and the Existence of Consistent Aggregates, in: American Economic Review, 67: 404–18.
Freeman, R. B. (1979). The Effect of Demographic Factors on Age-Earnings Profiles, in: Journal of Human Resources, 14: 289–318.
Freeman, R., Medoff, J. (1978). The Youth Labor Market Problem: An Overview, NBER, unpublished paper.
Grant, J. H. (1979). Substitution among Labor, Labor and Capital in U.S. Manufacturing, Michigan State University, unpublished Ph.D. dissertation.
Hamermesh, D., Grant, J. H. (1979). Econometric Studies of Labor-Labor Substitution and their Implications for Policy, in: Journal of Human Resources, 14: 518–42.
Johnson, G. E. (1980).The Theory of Labor Market Intervention, in: Economica, 47: 309–29.
Johnson, G. E., Blakemore, A. (1979). The Potential Impact of Employment Policy on the Unemployment Rate Consistent with Non-Accelerating Inflation, in: American Economic Association, 69: 119–23.
King, A. (1979). The Effect of Illegal Aliens on Unemployment in the United States, University of Texas-Austin, unpublished paper.
Morse, L. (1980). Unemployment and Relative Wage Adjustment among Black and White Teenagers, The Urban Institute, unpublished paper.
Sato, R., Koizumi, T. (1973). On the Elasticities of Substitution and Complementarity, in: Oxford Economic Papers, 25: 44–56.
Welch, F. (1979). Effects of Cohort Size on Earnings, in: Journal of Political Economy, 87: 565–98.
Welch, F., Cunningham, J. (1978). Effects of Minimum Wages on the Level and Age Composition of Youth Employment, in: this REVIEW, 60: 140–45.

Chapter 2

Bureau of Labor Statistics (1966). Employment and Earnings Statistics for the United States 1909-66, Washington: United States Government Printing Office, 1312(4).
Eckaus, R. S. (1964). Economic Criteria for Education, in: this Review, 46: 181-90.
Federal Reserve System, Board of Governors (1962). Industrial Production, 1957-59 Base, Washington: United States Government Printing Office.
Granger, C. W. J., Hatanaka, M. (1964). Spectral Analysis of Economic Time Series, Princeton: Princeton University Press.
Nerlove, M. (1964). Spectral Analysis of Seasonal Adjustment Procedures, in: Econometrica, 32: 241-86.
Oi, W. Y. (1962). Labor as a Quasi-Fixed Factor of Production, in: Journal of Political Economy, 70: 538-55.
Ulman, L. (1965). Labor Mobility and the Industrial Wage Structure in the Postwar United States, in: Quarterly Journal of Economics, 79: 73-97.
Wallis, K. F. (1965). Description of a Computer Program for Spectral Analysis of Economic Time Series, unpublished paper.
Wold, H. O. (1967). Review of Granger and Hatanaka, Spectral Analysis of Economic Time Series, in: Annals of Mathematical Statistics, 38: 288-93.

Chapter 3

Abraham, K., Houseman, S. (1987). Employment Security and Employment Adjustment, in: Proceedings of the Industrial Relations Research Association, 40: 44-54.
Blinder, A. (1981). Retail Inventory Behavior and Business Fluctuations, in: Brookings Papers on Economic Activity, 2: 443-505.
Brechling, F. (1975). Investment and Employment Decisions, Manchester: Manchester University Press.
Burgess, S. (1988). Employment Adjustment in U.K. Manufacturing, in: Economic Journal, 98: 81 -103.
Caplin, A. (1985). The Variability of Aggregate Demand with (S, s) Inventory Policies, in: Econometrica, 53: 1395-409.
Eisner, R., Strotz, R. (1963). Determinants of Business Investment, in: Commission on Money and Credit, Impacts of Monetary Policy, Englewood Cliffs, NJ: Prentice-Hall, Chapter 2.
Fair, R. (1969). The Short-Run Demand for Workers and Hours, Amsterdam: North-Holland.
Fair, R. (1984). Specification, Estimation and Analysis of Macroeconometric Models, Cambridge: Harvard University Press.
Feldstein, M. (1976). Temporary Layoffs in the Theory of Unemployment, in: Journal of Political Economy, 84: 937-58.
Freeman, R. (1977). Manpower Requirements and Substitution Analysis of Labor Skills, in: Research in Labor Economics, 1: 151-85.
Gennard, J. (1985). Job Security: Redundancy Arrangements and Practices in Selected OECD Countries, Paris: OECD.
Goldfeld, S., Quandt, R. (1976). Techniques for Estimating Switching Regressions, in: Goldfeld, S. M., Quandt, R. (Eds.), Studies in Nonlinear Estimation, Cambridge, MA : Ballinger, Chapter 1.
Gordon, R. (1979). The 'End-of-Expansion' Phenomenon in Short-Run Productivity Behavior, in: Brookings Papers on Economic Activity, 2: 447-61.
Gould, J. (1968). Adjustment Costs in the Theory of the Firm, in: Review of Economic Studies, 35: 47-56.
Hamermesh, D. (1986). The Demand for Labor in the Long Run, in: Ashenfelter, O., Layard, R. (Eds.), Handbook of Labor Economics, Amsterdam: North-Holland, Chapter 8.

Hamermesh, D. (1988). The Demand for Workers and Hours and the Effects of Job Security Policies: Theory and Evidence, in: Hart, R. (Ed.), Employment, Unemployment and Labor Utilization, London: Unwin Hyman.
Hamermesh, D. (1969). A Disaggregative Econometric Model of Gross Changes in Employment, in: Yale Economic Essays, 9: 107–46.
Hart, R. (1984). The Economics of Non-Wage Labour Costs, London: Allen & Unwin.
Holt, C., Modigliani, F., Muth, J., Simon, H. (1960). Planning Production, Inventories and Work Force, Englewood Cliffs, NJ: Prentice-Hall.
Nadiri, M. I., Rosen, S. (1969). Interrelated Factor Demand Functions, in: American Economic Review, 59: 457–71.
Nickell, S. (1984). An Investigation of the Determinants of Manufacturing Employment in the United Kingdom, in: Review of Economic Studies, 51: 529–57.
Nickell, S. (1986). Dynamic Models of Labour Demand, in: Ashenfelter, O., Layard, R. (Eds.), Handbook of Labor Economics, Amsterdam: North-Holland Press, Chapter 9.
Nickell, S. (1979). Unemployment and the Structure of Labour Costs, in: Journal of Monetary Economics, 1(1): 187–222.
Peck, S. (1974). Alternative Investment Models for Firms in the Electric Utilities Industry, in: Bell Journal of Economics, 5: 420–60.
Rosen, S. (1968). Short-Run Employment Variation on Class-I Railroads in the U.S., 1947–1963, in: Econometrica, 36: 511–29.
Rothschild, M. (1971). On the Cost of Adjustment, in: Quarterly Journal of Economics, 85: 605–22.
Sargent, T. (1978). Estimation of Dynamic Labor Demand Schedules under Rational Expectations, in: Journal of Political Economy, 86: 1009–44.
Shapiro, M. (1986). The Dynamic Demand for Capital and Labor, in: Quarterly Journal of Economics, 101: 513–42.
Topel, R. (1982). Inventories, Layoffs, and the Short-Run Demand for Labor, in: American Economic Review, 72: 769–87.
Trivedi, P. K. (1985). Distributed Lags, Aggregation and Compounding: Some Econometric Implications, in: Review of Economic Studies, 52: 19–35.

Chapter 4

Abraham, K., Houseman, S. (1989). Job security and work force adjustment: how different are U.S. and Japanese practices?, in: Journal of the Japanese and International Economies, 3: 500–21.
Bentolila, S., Bertola, G. (1990). Firing costs and labour demand: how bad is Eurosclerosis?, in: Review of Economic Studies, 57: 381–402.
Burgess, S., Dolado, J. (1989). Intertemporal rules with variable speed of adjustment: an application to UK manufacturing employment, in: Economic Journal, 99: 347–65.
Goldfeld, S., Quandt, R. (1976). Techniques for estimating switching regressions, in: Goldfeld, S., Quandt, R. (Eds.), Studies in Nonlinear Estimation, Cambridge, MA: Ballinger.
Gould, J. (1968). Adjustment costs in the theory of investment of the firm, in: Review of Economic Studies, 35: 47–55.
Hamermesh, D. (1989). Labor demand and the structure of adjustment costs, in: American Economic Review, 79: 674–89.
Hamermesh, D. (1993). Labor Demand, Princeton, NJ: Princeton University Press.
Holt, C., Modigliani, F., Muth, J., Simon, H. (1960). Planning Production. Inventories and Work Force, Englewood Cliffs, NJ: Prentice-Hall.
Holtz-Eakin, D., Rosen, H. (1991). Municipal labor demand in the presence of uncertainty: an econometric approach, in: Journal of Labor Economics, 9(3): 276–93.
Lucas, R. E. (1967). Optimal investment policy and the flexible accelerator, in: International Economic Review, 8: 78–85.
Nadiri, M. I., Rosen, S. (1969). Interrelated factor demand functions, in: American Economic Review, 59: 457–71.

Neftçi, S. (1984). Are economic time series asymmetric over the business cycle?, in: Journal of Political Economy, 92: 307–28.
Nickell, S. (1979). Unemployment and the structure of labour costs, in: Carnegie-Rochester Conference Series on Public Policy, 11: 187–222.
Nickell, S. (1986). Dynamic models of labour demand, in: Ashenfelter, O., Layard, R. (Eds.), Handbook of Labour Economics, Amsterdam: North-Holland Press.
Oi, W. (1962). Labor as a quasi-fixed factor of production, in: Journal of Political Economy, 70: 538–55.
Pfann, G., Palm, F. (1993). Asymmetric adjustment costs in nonlinear labour demand models for the Netherlands and UK manufacturing sectors, in: Review of Economic Studies, 60: 397–412.
Picot, G., Baldwin, J. (1990). Patterns of quits and layoff in the Canadian economy, in: Canadian Economic Observer.
Sargent, T. (1978). Estimation of dynamic labor demand schedules under rational expectations, in: Journal of Political Economy, 86: 1009–44.

Chapter 5

Abraham, K., Houseman, S. (1989). Job security and work force adjustment: how different are US and Japanese practices?, in: Journal of the Japanese and International Economies, 3: 500–21.
Burgess, S. (1993). Cyclical behaviour of employment in the UK: the role of endogenous adjustment costs, in: van Ours, J., Pfann, G., Ridder, G. (Eds.), Labor Demand and Equilibrium Wage Formation, Amsterdam: North-Holland.
Burgess, S., Nickell, S. (1990). Turnover in UK manufacturing, in: Economica, 55: 295–318.
Davis, S., Haltiwanger, J. (1992). Gross job creation, gross job destruction and employment, in: Quarterly Journal of Economics, 107: 819–64.
Gallant, A. R. (1987). Nonlinear Statistical Models, New York: John Wiley.
Hamermesh, D. (1969). A disaggregative econometric model of gross changes in employment, in: Yale Economic Essays, 9: 107–45.
Hamermesh, D. (1993). Labor Demand, Princeton, NJ: Princeton University Press.
Hamermesh, D. (1995). Labour demand and the source of adjustment costs, in: Economic Journal, 105: 620–34.
Hansen, L. (1982). Large sample properties of generalized method of moments estimators, in: Econometrica, 50: 1029–54.
Hussey, R. (1992). Nonparametric evidence on asymmetry in business cycles using aggregate employment time series, in: Journal of Econometrics, 51: 217–31.
Lockwood, B., Manning, A. (1993). The importance of kinked adjustment costs: some evidence from UK manufacturing, in: van Ours, J., Pfann, G., Ridder, G. (Eds.), Labor Demand and Equilibrium Wage Formation, Amsterdam: North-Holland.
McLaughlin, K. (1991). A theory of quits and layoffs with efficient turnover, in: Journal of Political Economy, 99: 1–29.
Nickell, S. (1984). An investigation of the determinants of manufacturing employment in the United Kingdom, in: Review of Economic Studies, 51: 529–57.
Nickell, S. (1986). Dynamic models of labour demand, in: Ashenfelter, O., Layard, R. (Eds.), Handbook of Labor Economics. Amsterdam: North-Holland.
Pfann, G., Palm, F. (1993). Asymmetric adjustment costs in non-linear labour demand models for the Netherlands and UK manufacturing sectors, in: Review of Economic Studies, 60: 397–412.
Sargan, D., Bhargava, A. (1983). Testing residuals from least squares regression for being generated by the Gaussian random walk, in: Econometrica, 51: 153–74.

Chapter 6

Anderson, P., Meyer, B. (1994). The Extent and Consequences of Job Turnover, in: Brookings Papers on Economic Activity, Microeconomics, 177-248.
Burgess, S., Nickell, S. (1990). Turnover in UK Manufacturing, in: Economica, 55: 295-318.
Burgess, S., Lane, J., Stevens D. (1994). Job Flows Worker Flows and Churning, Center for European Policy Research, unpublished paper.
Caballero, R., Engel, E., Haltiwanger, J. (1995). Aggregate Employment Dynamics: Building from Microeconomic Evidence, in: National Bureau of Economic Research, Working Paper No. 5042.
Cramer, U., Koller, M. (1988). Gewinne und Verluste von Arbeitsplätzen in Betrieben - der Job-Turnover, Ansatz, in: Mitteilungen aus der Arbeitsmarkt- und Berufsforschung, 21: 361-77.
Davis, S., Haltiwanger, J. (1990). Gross Job Creation and Destruction: Microeconomic Evidence and Macroeconomic Implications, in: NBER Macroeconomics Annual, 5: 123-68.
Davis, S., Haltiwanger, J. (1992). Gross Job Creation, Gross Job Destruction and Employment Reallocation, in: Quaterly Journal of Economics, 107: 819-63.
Dunlop, J. (1957). The Task of Contemporary Wage Theory, in: Taylor, G., Pierson, F. (Eds.), New Concepts in Wage Determination, New York: McGraw Hill.
Dunne, T., Robert, M., Samuelson, L. (1989). The Growth and Failure of U.S. Manufacturing Plants, in: Quarterly Journal of Economics, 104: 671-98.
Hamermesh, D. (1989). Labor Demand and the Structure of Adjustment Costs, in: American Economic Review, 79: 674-89.
Hamermesh, D. (1993). Labor Demand, Princeton University Press.
Hamermesh, D. (1995). Labor Demand and the Source of Adjustment Costs, in: Economic Journal, 105: 620-634.
Hassink, W., van Ours, J., Ridder, G. (1994). The Role and Prevalence of Internal Labour Markets: An Empirical Investigation, in: Vrije Universiteit Research Memorandum, 1994-2044.
Jovanovic, B. (1979). Job Matching and the Theory of Labor Turnover, in: Journal of Political Economy, 87: 972-90.
Leonard, J. (1987). In the Wrong Place at the Wrong Time, in: Lang, K., Leonard, J. (Eds.), Unemployment and the Structure of Labor Markets, New York: Basil Blackwell.
Leonard, J., van Audenrode, M. (1993). Corporatism Run Amok: Job Stability and Industrial Policy in Belgium and the United States, in: Economic Policy, 17: 355-400.
Lockwood, B., Manning, A. (1994). The Importance of Kinked Adjustment Costs: Some Evidence from U.K. Manufacturing, in: van Ours, J., Pfann, G., Ridder, G. (Eds.), Labor Demand and Equilibrium Wage Formation, Amsterdam: North-Holland Press.
Nickell, S. (1986). Dynamic Models of Labour Demand, in: Ashenfelter, O., Layard, R. (Eds.), Handbook of Labor Economics, Amsterdam: North-Holland Press.
Sargent, T. (1978). Estimation of Dynamic Labor Demand Schedules under Rational Expectations, in: Journal of Political Economy, 86: 1009-44.

Introduction to Part IV

Abraham, K., Farber, H. (1987). Job Duration, Seniority and Earnings, in: American Economic Review, 77(3): 278-97.
Biddle, J., Hamermesh, D. (1990). Sleep and the Allocation of Time, in: Journal of Political Economy, 98(5): 922-43.
Brown, C. (1982). The Effects of the Minimum Wage on Employment and Unemployment, in: Journal of Economic Literature, 20(2): 487-528.
Burda, M., Hamermesh, D., Weil, P. (2008). The Distribution of Total Work in the EU and USA, in: Boeri, T., Burda, M., Kramarz, F. (Eds.), Working Hours and Job Sharing in the EU and USA, New York: Oxford University Press, 11-91.

Card, D., Krueger, A. (1995). Myth and Measurement: The New Economics of the Minimum wage, Princeton, NJ: Princeton University Press.
Costa, D. (2000). Hours of Work and the Fair Labor Standards Act: A Study of Retail and Wholesale Trade, 1938–1950, in: Industrial and Labor Relations Review, 53(4): 648–64.
Ehrenberg, R. (1972). Fringe Benefits and Overtime Behavior, Lexington, MA: Heath Lexington.
Hamermesh, D. (1977). Jobless Pay and the Economy, Baltimore: Johns Hopkins University Press.
Hamermesh, D. (1996). Workdays, Workhours, Work Schedules: Evidence for the United States and Germany, Kalamazoo, MI: The W.E. Upjohn Institute.
Hamermesh, D. (1999). The Timing of Work over Time, in: Economic Journal, 109(1): 37–66.
Kletzer, L. (1989). Returns to Seniority after Permanent Job Loss, in: American Economic Review, 79(3): 536–43.
Minimum Wage Study Commission (1981). Report, Volumes I-V, Washington: GPO.
Neumark, D., Wascher, W. (2008). Minimum Wages, Cambridge, MA: MIT Press.
Ruhm, C. (1991). Are Workers Permanently Scarred by Job Displacements?, in: American Economic Review, 81(1): 319–24.
Trejo, S. (1991). The Effects of Overtime Pay Regulation on Worker Compensation, in: American Economic Review, 81(4): 719–40.

Chapter 7

Ashenfelter, O., Smith, R. (1979). Compliance with the Minimum Wage Law, in: Journal of Political Economy, 87: 333–50.
Berndt, E., Christensen, L. (1974). Testing for the Existence of a Consistent Aggregate Index of Labor Inputs, in: American Economic Review, 64: 391–404.
Brown, C., Gilroy, C., Kohen, A. (1981). Effects of the Minimum Wage on Youth Employment and Unemployment, in: Minimum Wage Study Commission, Report, Volume V.
Freeman, R. (1979). The Effect of Demographic Factors on Age-Earnings Profiles, in: Journal of Human Resources, 14: 289–318.
Grant, J., Hamermesh, D. (1981). Labor Market Competition Among Youths, White Women and Others, in: Review of Economics and Statistics, 63: 354–60.
Grossman, J. B. (1980). The Impact of the Minimum Wage on Other Wages, in: Mathematica Policy Research, unpublished paper.
Hamermesh, D. (1976). Econometric Studies of Labor Demand and their Application to Policy Analysis, in: Journal of Human Resources, 11: 507–25.
Hamermesh, D. (1981). Employment Demand, the Minimum Wage and Labor Costs, in: Report to the Minimum Wage Study Commission.
Hamermesh, D., Grant, J. (1979). Econometric Studies of Labor - Labor Substitution and their Implications for Policy, in: Journal of Human Resources, 14: 518–42.
Hashimoto, M., Mincer, J. (1971). Employment and Unemployment Effects of Minimum Wages, Columbia University, unpublished paper.
Johnson, N., Katz, S. (1970). Continuous Univariate Distributions, Houghton Mifflin, New York.
Meyer, R., Wise, D. (1981). Discontinuous Distributions and Missing Persons: The Minimum Wage and Unemployed Youth, NBER Working Paper No. 711.
Mincer, J. (1976). Unemployment Effects of Minimum Wages, in: Journal of Political Economy, 84: 87–104.
Siskind, F. (1977). Minimum Wage Legislation in the United States, in: Economic Inquiry, 15: 135–38.
Welch, F. (1974). Minimum Wage Legislation in the United States, in: Economic Inquiry, 12: 285–318.
Welch, F., Cunningham, J. (1978). Effects of Minimum Wages on the Level and Age Composition of Youth Employment, in: Review of Economics and Statistics, 60: 140–5.

Chapter 8

California Industrial Welfare Commission (1994). Chronological History of the 8-Hour Day in California, Staff Report.

Card, D. (1992). Do Minimum Wages Reduce Employment? A Case Study of California, 1987–1989, in: Industrial and Labor Relations Review, 46: 38–54

Card, D., Sullivan, D. (1988). Measuring the Effect of Subsidized Training Programs on Movements In and Out of Employment, in: Econometrica, 56: 497–530.

Ehrenberg, R. (1971). Fringe Benefits and Overtime Behavior, Lexington, MA: D.C. Heath.

Ehrenberg, R., Schumann, P. (1982). Longer Hours or More Jobs?, Ithaca, NY: ILR Press.

Gruber, J. (1994). The Incidence of Mandated Maternity Benefits, in: American Economic Review, 84: 622–41.

Gruber, J., Poterba, J. (1994). Tax Incentives and the Decision to Purchase Health Insurance: Evidence from the Self-Employed, in: Quarterly Journal of Economics, 109: 701–33.

Hamermesh, D. (1993). Labor Demand, Princeton, NJ: Princeton University Press.

Hamermesh, D. (1996). Workdays, Workhours and Work Schedules: Evidence for the United States and Germany, Kalamazoo, MI: W.E. Upjohn Institute.

Hart, R. (1987). Working Time and Employment, Boston: Allen and Unwin.

Hart, R., Wilson, N. (1988). The Demand for Workers and Hours: Micro Evidence from the U.K. Metal Working Industry, in: Hart, R. (Ed.), Employment, Unemployment, and Labor Utilization, Boston: Unwin Hyman.

Hunt, J. (1999). Has Work-Sharing Worked in Germany?, in: Quarterly Journal of Economics, 114: 117–48.

Kinoshita, T. (1987). Working Hours and Hedonic Wages in the Market Equilibrium, in: Journal of Political Economy, 95: 1262–77.

Konig, H., Pohlmeier, W. (1989). Worksharing and Factor Prices: A Comparison of Three Flexible Functional Forms for Nonlinear Cost Schemes, in: Journal of Institutional and Theoretical Economics, 145: 343–57.

Lewis, H. G. (1969). Employer Interests in Employee Hours of Work, Chicago: University of Chicago.

MaCurdy, T., Bhattacharya, J., DeLeire, T. (1997). Overtime Compensation in California: Shifting from the 8-Hour Day to the 40-Hour Week, Palo Alto, CA: Stanford University.

Owen, J. (1989). Reduced Working Hours: Cure for Unemployment or Economic Burden?, Baltimore: Johns Hopkins University Press.

Topel, R. (1998). Analytical and Empirical Knowledge in Labor Economics, in: Haltiwanger, J., Manser, M., Topel, R. (Eds.), Labor Statistics Measurement Issues, Chicago: University of Chicago Press.

Trejo, S. (1991). The Effects of Overtime Pay Regulation on Worker Compensation, in: American Economic Review, 81: 719–40.

Trejo, S. (1998). Does the Statutory Overtime Premium Discourage Long Workweeks?, Santa Barbara, CA: University of California.

Yelowitz, A. (1995). The Medicaid Notch, Labor Supply, and Welfare Participation: Evidence from Eligibility Expansions, in: Quarterly Journal of Economics, 110: 909–39.

Chapter 9

Bound, J., Brown, C., Duncan, G., Rodgers, W. L. (1994). Evidence on the Validity of Cross-sectional and Longitudinal Labor Market Data, in: Journal of Labor Economics, 12: 345–68.

Bresnahan, T. F., Ramey, V. A. (1994). Output Fluctuations at the Plant Level, in: Quarterly Journal of Economics, 109: 593–624.

Burda, M. C., Hamermesh, D., Weil, P. (2008). The Distribution of Total Work in the EU and US, in: Boeri, T. (Ed.), Working Hours and Job Sharing in the EU and USA: Are

Europeans Lazy? Or Americans Crazy?, New York: Oxford University Press, 11-91.
Castro, A., Varejão, J. (2007). Operating Hours, Working Time and Employment in Portugal, in: Delsen, L. (Ed.), Operating Hours and Working Times: A Survey of Capacity Utilization and Employment in the European Union, Heidelberg: Physica, 147–67.
Delsen, L., Bosworth, D., Gross, H., Muñoz de Bustillo y Llorente, R. M. (2007): Operating Hours and Working Times: A Survey of Capacity Utilization and Employment in the European Union, Heidelberg: Physica.
Economic Report of the President (2008). Washington: Government Printing Office.
Eironline (2003). www.eurofound.europa.eu/eiro/2003/country/spain.htm.
Hamermesh, D. (1993). Labor Demand, Princeton, NJ: Princeton University Press.
Hamermesh, D. (1996). Workdays, Workhours and Work Schedules: Evidence for the U.S. and Germany, Kalamazoo, MI: W.E. Upjohn Institute.
Hamermesh, D. (1999). The Timing of Work over Time, in: Economic Journal, 109: 37–66.
Hamermesh, D. (1999a): Crime and the Timing of Work, in: Journal of Urban Economics, 45: 311–30.
Hart, R. A., Ruffel, R. J. (1993). The Cost of Overtime Hours in British Production Industries, Economica, 60: 183–201.
Instituto Nacional de Estatistica de Portugal (INE) (2001). Inquérito à Ocupação do Tem 1999, Lisbon: INE.
Kostiuk, P. F. (1990). Compensating Differentials for Shift Work, in: Journal of Political Economy, 98: 1054–75.
Mayshar, J., Solon, G. (1993): Shift Work and the Business Cycle, in: American Economic Association, Papers and Proceedings, 83: 224–8.
Michelson, W., Crouse, D. (2004). Examining Large-Scale Time-Use Files through Graphic Representation, in: electronic International Journal of Time Use Research, 1, 85–100.
Morrison, C. J., Berndt, E. (1981). Short-Run Labor Productivity in a Dynamic Model, in: Journal of Econometrics: 16, 339–65.
Nickell, S. (2008). Is the U.S. Labor Market Really That Exceptional? A Review of Richard Freeman, in: Journal of Economic Literature, 46: 384–95.
Portugal, P., Cardoso, A. R. (2006). Disentangling the Minimum Wage Puzzle: An Analysis of Worker Accessions and Separations, in: Journal of the European Economic Association, 4: 988–1013.
Rosen, S. (1974). Hedonic Prices and Implicit Markets: Product Differentiation in Pure Competition, in: Journal of Political Economy, 82: 34–55.
Shapiro, M. (1995). Capital Utilization and the Marginal Premium for Work at Night, University of Michigan, unpublished paper.
Stafford, F. (1980). Firm Size, Workplace Public Goods and Worker Welfare, in: Siegfried, J. (Ed.), The Economics of Firm Size, Market Structure and Social Performance, Washington: Federal Trade Commission.
Trejo, S. J. (1991). The Effects of Overtime Pay Regulation on Worker Compensation, in: American Economic Review, 81: 719–40.
Varejão, J., Portugal, P. (2007). Employment Dynamics and the Structure of Adjustment Costs, in: Journal of Labor Economics, 25: 137–65.
Winston, G. (1982). The Timing of Economic Activities, New York: Cambridge.

Chapter 10

Abowd, J., Ashenfelter, O. (1981). Anticipated Unemployment, Temporary Layoffs, and Compensating Wage Differentials, in: Rosen, S. (Ed.), Studies in Labor Markets, Chicago, IL: University of Chicago Press.
Addison, J., Portugal, P. (1986). The Effect of Advance Notification of Plant Closings on Unemployment, University of South Carolina, unpublished paper.
Alchian, A. (1982). First National Maintenance vs. National Labor Relations Board, UCLA, unpublished paper.

Altonji, J., Shakotko, R. (1985). Do Wages Rise with Job Seniority?, in: National Bureau of Economic Research, Working Paper No. 1616.
Baldwin, R. (1984). Rent-Seeking and Trade Policy: An Industry Approach, in: Weltwirtschaftliches Archiv, 120: 662–77.
Bale, M. (1976). Estimates of Trade-Displacement Costs for U.S. Workers, in: Journal of International Economics, 6: 245–50.
Bartel, A., Borjas, G. (1981). Wage Growth and Job Turnover: An Empirical Analysis, in: Rosen, S. (Ed.), Studies in Labor Markets, Chicago, IL: University of Chicago Press.
Farber, H. (1983). The Determination of the Status of Union Workers, in: Econometrica, 51: 1417–37.
Folbre, N., Leighton, J., Roderick, M. (1984). Plant Closings and Their Regulation in Maine, 1971–1982, in: Industrial and Labor Relations Review, 37: 185–96.
Freeman, R. (1980). The Exit-Voice Tradeoff in the Labor Market, in: this Journal, 94: 643–74.
Gennard, J. (1985). Job Security: Redundancy Arrangements and Practices in Selected OECD Countries, Paris, France: OECD, unpublished paper.
Glenday, G., Jenkins, G. (1984). Industrial Dislocation and the Private Cost of Labor Adjustment, in: Contemporary Policy Issues, 2: 23–36.
Jacobson, L. (1978). Earnings Losses of Workers Displaced from Manufacturing Industries, in: Dewald, W. (Ed.), The Impact of International Trade and Investment on Employment, Washington, DC: GPO.
Jenkins, G., Montmarquette, C. (1979). Estimating the Private and Social Opportunity Cost of Displaced Workers, in: Review of Economics and Statistics, 61: 342–53.
Johnson, G., Youmans, K. (1971). Union Relative Wage Effects by Age and Education, in: Industrial and Labor Relations Review, 24: 171–9.
Johnson, T. (1970). Returns from Investment in Human Capital, in: American Economic Review, 60: 546–60.
Kiefer, N., Neumann, G. (1979). An Empirical Job-Search Model, with a Test of the Constant Reservation-Wage Hypothesis, in: Journal of Political Economy, 87: 89–108.
Lazear, E. (1981). Agency, Earnings Profiles, Productivity and Hours Restrictions, in: American Economic Review, 71: 606–20.
Marshall, R., Zarkin, G. (1984). The Effect of Job Tenure on Wage Offers, Duke University, unpublished paper.
Mincer, J. (1974). Schooling, Experience and Earnings, New York, NY: National Bureau of Economic Research.
Mincer, J., Jovanovic, B. (1981). Labor Mobility and Wages, in: Rosen, S. (Ed.), Studies in Labor Markets, Chicago, IL: University of Chicago Press.
Mitchell, O. (1982). Fringe Benefits and Labor Mobility, in: Journal of Human Resources, 17: 286–98.
Neumann, G. (1978). The Direct Labor Market Effects of the Trade Adjustment Assistance Program, in: Dewald, W. (Ed.), The Impact of International Trade and Investment on Employment, Washington, DC: GPO.
Sandell, S. (1980). Job Search by Unemployed Women: Determinants of the Asking Wage, in: Industrial and Labor Relations Review, 33: 368–78.
Sandell, S., Shapiro, D. (1985). Age Discrimination and Labor Market Problems of Displaced Older Male Workers, in: Southern Economic Journal, 52: 90–102.
Shaw, K. (1984). A Formulation of the Earnings Function Using the Concept of Occupational Investment, in: Journal of Human Resources, 19: 319–40.
Topel, R. (1984). Equilibrium Earnings, Turnover, and Unemployment, in: Journal of Labor Economics, 2: 500–22.
Viscusi, W. K. (1980). Sex Differences in Worker Quitting, in: Review of Economics and Statistics, 62: 388–98.
Wachter, M. (1984). The Training Component of Growth Policies, in: Wachter, M., Wachter, S. (Eds.), Removing Obstacles to Economic Growth, Philadelphia, PA: University of Pennsylvania Press.

Chapter 11

AFL-CIO (1975). Policy Resolutions Adopted by the Eleventh Constitutional Convention, AFL-CIO, Washington, DC.
Adams, J. (1986). Equilibrium taxation and experience rating in a federal system of unemployment insurance, in: Journal of Public Economics, 29(1): 51–77.
Advisory Council on Unemployment Compensation (1996). Collected Findings and Recommendations: 1994-1996, ACUC, Washington, DC.
Anderson, P., Meyer, B. (1993). Unemployment insurance in the United States: layoff incentives and cross subsidies, in: Journal of Labor Economics, 11(1): 70–95.
Bailey, S., Connolly, S. (1998). The flypaper effect: identifying areas for further research, in: Public Choice, 95(3–4): 335–61.
Becker, G. (1983). A theory of competition among pressure groups for political influence, in: Quarterly Journal of Economics, 108(2): 371–400.
Brechling, F. (1977). The incentive effects of the US unemployment insurance tax, in: Research in Labor Economics, 1: 41–102.
Card, D. (1990). The impact of the mariel boatlift on the Miami labor market, in: Industrial and Labor Relations Review, 43(2): 245–57.
Courant, P., Gramlich, E. (1990). The impact of the tax reform act of 1986 on state and local fiscal behavior, in: Slemrod, J. (Ed.), Do Taxes Matter? The Impact of the Tax Reform Act of 1986, Cambridge, MA: MIT Press, 243–75.
FitzRoy, F., Hart, R. (1985). Hours, layoffs and unemployment insurance funding: theory and practice in an international perspective, in: Economic Journal, 95(3): 700–13.
Grossman, G., Helpman, E. (1994). Protection for sale, in: American Economic Review, 84(4): 833–50.
Gruber, J. (1994). The incidence of mandated maternity benefits, in: American Economic Review, 84(3): 622–41.
Halpin, T. (1978). Three Essays on the Effects of Experience Rating in Unemployment Insurance, Michigan State University, unpublished PhD dissertation.
Hamermesh, D. (1977). Jobless Pay and the Economy, Baltimore: Johns Hopkins Press.
Hamermesh, D. (1990). Unemployment insurance, short-time compensation and labor demand, in: Research in Labor Economics, 11: 241–69.
Hamermesh, D., Scoones, D. (1996). Multilevel 'general policy equilibria': evidence from the American unemployment insurance tax ceiling, in: National Bureau of Economic Research, Washington, DC, Working Paper no. 5578.
Inman, R. (1989). The local decision to tax: evidence from large US cities, in: Regional Science and Urban Economics, 19(3): 455–91.
Poterba, J. (1994). State budgetary responses to fiscal crises: the effects of budgetary institutions and politics, in: Journal of Political Economy, 102(4): 799–821.
Topel, R. (1984). Experience rating of unemployment insurance and the incidence of unemployment, in: Journal of Law and Economics, 27(1): 29–60.

Introduction to Part V

Becker, G. (1957). The Economics of Discrimination, Chicago: University of Chicago Press.
Bélot, M., Bhaskar, V., van de Ven, J. (2012). Beauty and the Sources of Discrimination, in: Journal of Human Resources, 47(3): 851–72.
Buffum, D., Whaples, R. (1995). Fear and Lathing in the Michigan Furniture Industry: Employee-Based Discrimination a Century Ago, in: Economic Inquiry, 32(2): 234–52.
Coate, S., Loury, G. (1993). Will Affirmative-Action Policies Eliminate Negative Stereotypes?, in: American Economic Review, 83(5): 1220–40.
Bradford De Long, J., Lang, K. (1992). Are All Economic Hypotheses False?, in: Journal of Political Economy, 100(6): 1257–72.

Dillingham, A., Ferber, M., Hamermesh, D. (1994). Gender Discrimination by Gender: Voting in a Professional Society, in: Industrial and Labor Relations Review, 47(4): 622–33.
Frieze, I., Olson, J., Russell, J. (1991). Attractiveness and Income for Men and Women in Management, in: Journal of Applied Social Psychology, 21(3): 1039–57.
Goldberg, M. (1982). Discrimination, Nepotism and Long-Run Wage Differentials, in: Quarterly Journal of Economics, 97(2): 307–19.
Hamermesh, D. (2006). Changing Looks and Changing 'Discrimination': The Beauty of Economists, in: Economics Letters, 93(3): 405–12.
Hamermesh, D. (2013). Six Decades of Top Economics Publishing: Who and How, in: Journal of Economic Literature, 51(1): 162–72.
Hersch, J. (2008). Profiling the New Immigrant Worker: The Effects of Skin Color and Height, in: Journal of Labor Economics, 26(2): 345–86.
Leamer, E. (1983). Let's Take the Con Out of Econometrics, in: American Economic Review, 73(1): 31–43.
Wood, R., Corcoran, M., Courant, P. (1993). Pay Differences among the Highly Paid; The Male-Female Earnings Gap in Lawyers' Salaries, in: Journal of Labor Economics, 11(3): 417–41.

Chapter 12

Averett, S., Korenman, S. (1993). The Economic Reality of 'The Beauty Myth', in: National Bureau of Economic Research, Cambridge, MA, Working Paper No. 4521.
Blau, F., Beller, A. (1992). Black-White Earnings over the 1970s and 1980s: Gender Differences and Trends, in: Review of Economics and Statistics, 74(1): 276–86.
Bloom, D., Grenier, G. (1992). Earnings of the French Minority in Canada and the Spanish Minority in the United States, in: Chiswick, B. (Ed.), Immigration, language, and ethnicity, Washington, DC: American Enterprise Institute Press, 373–409.
Borjas, G., Tienda, M. (Eds.) (1985). Hispanics in the U.S. economy, New York: Academic Press.
Cain, G. (1986). The Economic Analysis of Labor Market Discrimination: A Survey, in: Ashenfelter, O., Layard, R. (Eds.), Handbook of labor economics, Amsterdam: North-Holland, 693–785.
Dictionary of Occupational Titles (1977). Washington, DC: U.S. Government Printing Office.
Dillingham, A., Ferber, M., Hamermesh, D. (1994). Gender Discrimination by Gender: Voting in a Professional Society, in: Industrial and Labor Relations Review, 47(4): 622–33.
Famulari, M. (1992). The Effects of a Disability on Labor Market Performance: The Case of Epilepsy, in: Southern Economic Journal, 58(4): 1072–87.
Frieze, I., Olson, J., Russell, J. (1991). Attractiveness and Income for Men and Women in Management, in: Journal of Applied Social Psychology, 21(3): 1039–57.
Hatfield, E., Sprecher, S. (1986). Mirror, mirror ...: The importance of looks in everyday life, Albany, NY: State University of New York Press.
Holzer, H. (1993). Multi-City Study of Urban Inequality, Michigan State University, unpublished paper.
McAdams, T., Moussavi, F., Klassen, M. (1992). Employee Appearance and the Americans with Disabilities Act: An Emerging Issue?, in: Employee Responsibilities and Rights Journal, 5(4): 323–38.
McLean, R., Moon, M. (1980). Health, Obesity, and Earnings, in: American Journal of Public Health, 70(9): 1006–9.
Quinn, R. (1978). Physical Deviance and Occupational Mistreatment: The Short, the Fat and the Ugly, Institute for Social Research, University of Michigan, unpublished paper.
Roszell, P., Kennedy, D., Grabb, E. (1989). Physical Attractiveness and Income Attainment Among Canadians, in: Journal of Psychology, 123(6): 547–59.
Taubman, P. (1975). Sources of inequality in earnings, Amsterdam: North-Holland.
Wolf, N. (1991). The beauty myth, New York: Anchor.

Chapter 13

Altonji, J., Blank, R. (1999). Race and gender in the labor market, in: Ashenfelter, O., Card, D. (Eds.), Handbook of labor economics, Amsterdam: Elsevier, 3143–259.
Becker, G. (1957). The economics of discrimination, Chicago: University of Chicago Press.
Belot, M., Bhaskar, V., van de Ven, J. (2012). Beauty and the sources of discrimination, in: The Journal of Human Resources, 47: 851–72.
Benjamin, D., Shapiro, J. (2009). Thin-slice forecasts of gubernatorial elections, in: Review of Economics and Statistics, 91: 523–36.
Berggren, N., Jordahl, H., Poutvaara, P. (2010). The looks of a winner: Beauty and electoral success, in: Journal of Public Economics, 94: 8–15.
Cain, G. (1986). The economic analysis of labor market discrimination: A survey, in: Ashenfelter, O., Layard, R. (Eds.), Handbook of labor economics, Amsterdam: North-Holland, 693–785.
Case, A., Paxson, C. (2008). Stature and status: Height, ability and labor-market outcomes, in: Journal of Political Economy, 116: 499–532.
Fryer, R., Jackson, M. (2008). A categorical model of cognition and biased decision making, in: Berkeley Electronic Journal of Theoretical Economics, 8.
Hamermesh, D. (2006). Changing looks and changing 'discrimination': The beauty of economists, in: Economics Letters, 93: 405–12.
Hamermesh, D., Biddle, J. (1994). Beauty and the labor market, in: American Economic Review, 84: 1174–94.
Heckman, J. (1998). Detecting discrimination, in: Journal of Economic Perspectives, 12: 101–16.
Hersch, J. (2008). Profiling the new immigrant worker: The effects of skin color and height, in: Journal of Labor Economics, 26: 345–86.
Komlos, J., Lauderdale, B. (2007). Underperformance in affluence: The remarkable relative decline in U.S. heights in the second half of the 20th century, in: Social Science Quarterly, 88: 283–305.
Landry, C., Lange, A., List, J., Price, M., Rupp, N. (2006). Toward an understanding of the economics of charity: Evidence from a field experiment, in: Quarterly Journal of Economics, 121: 747–82.
Möbius, M., Rosenblat, T. (2006). Why beauty matters, in: American Economic Review, 96: 222–35.
Persico, N., Postlewaite, A., Silverman, D. (2004). The effect of adolescent experience on labor market outcomes: The case of height, in: Journal of Political Economy, 112: 1019–53.

Chapter 14

Adams, G. (1977). Physical Attractiveness Research: Toward a Developmental Social Psychology of Beauty, in: Human Development, 20: 217–39.
Baker, G., Gibbs, M., Holmstrom, B. (1994). The Wage Policy of a Firm, in: Quarterly Journal of Economics, 109: 881–920.
Berger, M. (1985). The Effect of Cohort Size on Earnings Growth: A Reexamination of the Evidence, in: Journal of Political Economy, 93: 561–73.
Borjas, G., Bronars, S. (1989). Consumer Discrimination and Self-Employment, in: Journal of Political Economy, 97: 581–605.
Buffum, D., Whaples, R. (1995). Fear and Lathing in the Michigan Furniture Industry: Employee-Based Discrimination a Century Ago, in: Economic Inquiry, 32: 234–52.
Goddeeris, J. (1988). Compensating Differentials and Self-Selection: An Application to Lawyers, in: Journal of Political Economy, 96: 411–28.
Hamermesh, D., Biddle, J. (1994). Beauty and the Labor Market, in: American Economic Review, 84: 1174–94.

Hatfield, E., Sprecher, S. (1986). Mirror, Mirror ...: The Importance of Looks in Everyday Life, Albany, NY: SUNY Press.
Heckman, J., Scheinkman, J. (1987). The Importance of Bundling in a Gorman-Lancaster Model of Earnings, in: Review of Economic Studies, 54: 243–55.
James, P. D. (1995). Original Sin, New York: Knopf.
Johnson, W. (1978). A Theory of Job Shopping, in: Quarterly Journal of Economics, 92: 261–78.
Kahn, L. (1992). The Effects of Race on Professional Football Players' Compensation, in: Industrial and Labor Relations Review, 45: 295–310.
Keynes, J. M. (1936). The General Theory of Employment, Interest and Money, New York: Harcourt, Brace & World.
Landers, R., Rebitzer, J., Taylor, L. (1996). Rat Race Redux: Adverse Selection in the Determination of Work Hours, in: American Economic Review, 86: 329–48.
Langlois, J., Roggman, L. (1990). Attractive Faces Are Only Average, in: Psychological Science, 1: 115–21.
Mincer, J. (1974). Schooling, Experience and Earnings, New York: National Bureau of Economic Research.
O'Flaherty, B., Siow, A. (1995). Up-or-Out Rules in the Market for Lawyers, in: Journal of Labor Economics, 13: 678–708.
Rosen, S. (1983). A Note on Aggregation of Skills and Labor Quality, in: Journal of Human Resources, 18: 425–31.
Rosen, S. (1992). The Market for Lawyers, in: Journal of Law and Economics, 35: 215–46.
Sauer, R. (1996). Job Mobility and the Market for Lawyers, Tel Aviv: Tel Aviv University, unpublished paper.
Spurr, S., Sueyoshi, G. (1994). Turnover and the Promotion of Lawyers, in: Journal of Human Resources, 29: 813–42.
Wood, R., Corcoran, M., Courant, P. (1993). Pay Differences among the Highly Paid: The Male-Female Earnings Gap in Lawyers' Salaries, in: Journal of Labor Economics, 11: 417–41.
Zebrowitz, L., Montepare, J., Lee, H. K. (1993). They Don't All Look Alike: Individuated Impressions of Other Racial Groups, in: Journal of Personality and Social Psychology, 65: 85–101.

Chapter 15

Andrews, D. W. K. (1993). Tests for Parameter Instability and Structural Change with Unknown Change Point, in: Econometrica, 61(4): 821–56.
Becker, G. S. (1957). The economics of discrimination, Chicago: University of Chicago Press.
Blau, F. D., Kahn, L. M. (2000). Gender Differences in Pay, in: Journal of Economic Perspectives, 14(4): 75–99.
Bloom, D. E., Cavanagh, C. L. (1986). An Analysis of the Selection of Arbitrators, in: American Economic Review, 76(3): 408–22.
Butcher, J. N., Pancheri, P. (1976). A handbook of cross-national MMPI research, Minneapolis: University of Minnesota Press.
Dillingham, A. E., Ferber, M. A., Hamermesh, D. (1994). Gender Discrimination by Gender: Voting in a Professional Society, in: Industrial and Labor Relations Review, 47(4): 622–33.
Gerber, E. R., Morton, R. B., Rietz, T. A. (1998). Minority Representation in Multimember Districts, in: American Political Science Review, 92(1): 127–44.
Goldin, C. D. (1991). The Role of World War II in the Rise of Women's Employment, in: American Economic Review, 81(4): 741–56.
Guilford, J. S., Zimmerman, W. S., Guilford, J. P. (1976). The Guilford-Zimmerman temperament survey handbook: Twenty-five years of research and application, San Diego: EdITS Publishers.

Hamermesh, D., Johnson, G. E., Weisbrod, B. A. (1982). Scholarship, Citations and Salaries: Economic Rewards in Economics, in: Southern Economic Journal, 49(2): 472–81.
Hamermesh, D., Schmidt, P. (2003). The Determinants of Econometric Society Fellows Elections, in: Econometrica, 71(1): 399–407.
Hasselback, J. (2002). The 2002-2003 economics faculty directory, Upper Saddle River, NJ: Prentice-Hall.
McDowell, J. M., Singell, L. D., Ziliak, J. P. (2001). Gender and Promotion in the Economics Profession, in: Industrial and Labor Relations Review, 54(2): 224–44.
Niemi, R., Hill, J., Grofman, B. (1985). The Impact of Multimember Districts on Party Representation in U.S. State Legislatures, in: Legislative Studies Quarterly, 10(4): 441–55.
Wooldridge, J. M. (2002). Econometric analysis of cross section and panel data, Cambridge, MA: MIT Press.

Chapter 16

Answers.com (2007). List of Hispanic Players in Major League Baseball. http://www.answers.com/topic/list-of-hispanic-players-in-major-leaguebaseball.
Bergmann, B. R. (1971). The Effect on White Incomes of Discrimination in Employment, in: Journal of Political Economy, 79(2): 294–313.
Black Voices (2007). African American Players in the MLB. http://Blackvoices.aol.com/Black_sports/special/_a/african-americanplayers-in-mlb/20070413095009990001.
Blair, I. V. (2002). The Malleability of Automatic Stereotypes and Prejudice, in: Personality and Social Psychology Review, 6(3): 242–61.
Bradbury, J. C. (2007). The Baseball Economist: The Real Game Exposed, New York: Dutton.
Cain, G. G. (1986). The Economic Analysis of Labor Market Discrimination: A Survey, in: Ashenfelter, O., Layard, R. (Eds.), Handbook of Labor Economics, New York: Elsevier Science, 693–785.
Chen, J. (2007). What Does Baseball Teach Us about Reducing Racial Discrimination? Evidence from Two Natural Experiments, unpublished paper.
Coate, S., Glenn, C. L. (1993). Will Affirmative-Action Policies Eliminate Negative Stereotypes?, in: American Economic Review, 83(5): 1220–40.
Dohmen, T. J. (2008). The Influence of Social Forces: Evidence from the Behavior of Football Referees, in: Economic Inquiry, 46(3): 411–24.
Donald, S. G., Hamermesh, D. (2006). What Is Discrimination? Gender in the American Economic Association, NBER Working Paper No. 10684.
Economic Association (1935-2004). American Economic Review, 96(4): 1283–92. ESPN. 2004-2008. MLB Box Score. http://sports/espn.go.com/mlb/boxscore?gameId=NNNNNNNNN, where NNNNNNNNN represents the nine-digit game ID.
ESPN (2004–2008). MLB Play By Play. http://sports.espn.go.com/mlb/playbyplay?gameId=NNNNNNNNNN&full=1, where NNNNNNNNN represents the nine-digit game ID.
Findlay, D. W., Reid, C. E. (1997). Voting Behavior, Discrimination and the National Baseball Hall of Fame, in: Economic Inquiry, 35(3): 562–78.
Fort, R., Gill, A. M. (2000). Race and Ethnicity Assessment in Baseball Card Markets.
Journal of Sports Economics, 1(1): 21–38.
Garicano, L., Palacios-Huerta, I., Prendergast, C. (2005). Favoritism under Social Pressure, in: Review of Economics and Statistics, 87(2): 208–16.
Gius, M. P., Hylan, T. R. (1996). An Interperiod Analysis of the Salary Impact of Structural Changes in Major League Baseball: Evidence from Panel Data, in: Fizel, J., Gustafson, E., Hadley, L. (Eds.), Baseball Economics: current Research, Westport, CT: Praeger, 77–84.
Goodwin, S. A., Gubin, A., Fiske, S. T., Yzerbyt, V. Y. (2000). Power Can Bias Impression Processes: Stereotyping Subordinates by Default and by Design, in: Group Processes

and intergroup Relations, 3(3): 227–56.
Gwartney, J., Haworth, C. (1974). Employer Costs and Discrimination: The Case of Baseball, in: Journal of Political Economy, 82(4): 873–81.
Kahn, L. M. (1991). Discrimination in Professional Sports: A Survey of the Literature, in: Industrial and Labor Relations Review, 44(3): 395–418.
Kahn, L. M. (1993). Managerial Quality, Team Success, and Individual Player Performance in Major League Baseball, in: Industrial and Labor Relations Review, 46(3): 531–47.
Knowles, J., Persico, N., Todd, P. (2001). Racial Bias in Motor Vehicle Searches: Theory and Evidence, in: Journal of Political Economy, 109(1): 203–29.
Krautmann, A. C., Gustafson, E., Hadley, L. (2003). A Note on the Structural Stability of Salary Equations: Major League Baseball Pitchers, in: Journal of Sports Economics, 4(1): 56–63.
Major League Baseball (2006–2008). Major League Umpire Roster. http://mlb.mlb.com/mlb/official_info/umpires/roster.jsp.
Major League Baseball (2007–2008). PITCHf/x Pitch Location Dataset. http://gd2.mlb.com/components/game/mlb/.
Nardinelli, C., Simon, C. (1990). Customer Racial Discrimination in the Market for Memorabilia: The Case of Baseball, in: Quarterly Journal of Economics, 105(3): 575–95.
Parsons, C., Sulaeman, J., Yates, M. C., Hamermesh, D. (2011). Strike Three: Discrimination, Incentives, and Evaluation: Dataset, in: American Economic Review. http://www.aeaweb.org/articles.php?doi=10.1257/aer.101.4.1410.
Pascal, A. H., Rapping, L. A. (1972). The Economics of Racial Discrimination in Organized Baseball, in: Pascàl, A. H. (Ed.), Racial discrimination in Economic Life, Lexington, MA: Lexington Books.
Persico, N. (2002). Racial Profiling, Fairness, and Effectiveness of Policing, in: American Economic Review, 92(5): 1472–97.
Price, J., Wolfers, J. (2010). Racial Discrimination among NBA Referees, in: Quarterly Journal of Economics, 125(4): 1859–87.
Scully, G. W. (1974). Pay and Performance in Major League Baseball, in: American Economic Review, 64(6): 915–30.
Sports Reference (2004–2008). Players by Place of Birth. http://www.baseball-reference.com/bio/.
Stoll, M. A., Raphael, S., Holzer, H. J. (2004). Black Job Applicants and the Hiring Officer's Race, in: Industrial and Labor Relations Review, 57(2): 267–87.
Zitzewitz, E. (2006). Nationalism in Winter Sports Judging and Its Lessons for Organizational Decision Making, in: Journal of Economics and Management Strategy, 15(1): 67–99.

Concluding Thougths

Acemoglu, D., Autor, D., Lyle, D. (2004). Women, War and Wages: The Effect of Female Labor Supply on the Wage Structure at Midcentury, in: Journal of Political Economy, 112(3): 497–551.
Angrist, J. (1996). The Short-run Demand for Palestinian Labor, in: Journal of Labor Economics, 14(3): 425–53.
Asphjell, M., Letterie, W., Nilsen, Ø., Pfann, G. (2014). Sequentiality versus Simultaneity: Interrelated Factor Demand, in: Review of Economics and Statistics.
Blundell, R., MaCurdy, T. (1999). Labor Supply: A Review of Alternative Approaches, in: Ashenfelter, O., Card, D. (Eds.), Handbook of Labor Economics, Amsterdam: Elsevier, 3: 1559–695.
Bosch, N., van der Klaauw, B. (2012). Analyzing Female Labor Supply: Evidence from a Dutch Tax Reform, in: Labour Economics, 19(3): 271–80.
Feld, J., Salamanca, N., Hamermesh, D. (2013). Endophilia or Exophobia? Beyond Discrimination, in: National Bureau of Economic Research, Working Paper Number 19471.
Hamermesh, D. (1993). Labor Demand, Princeton University Press.
Hamermesh, D. (2002). International Labor Economics, in: Journal of Labor Economics,

20(4): 709–32.
Hamermesh, D. (2007). Viewpoint: Replication in Economics, in: Canadian Journal of Economics, 40(3): 715–33.
Kugler, A., Kugler, M. (2009). Labor Market Effects of Payroll Taxes in Developing Countries: Evidence from Colombia, in: Economic Development and Cultural Change, 57(2): 335–358.
Nadiri, M. I., Rosen, S. (1969). Interrelated Factor Demand Functions, in: American Economic Review, 59(4): 457–71.
aus dem Moore, J. P., Spitz-Oener, A. (2012). Bye Bye, G.I. - The Impact of the U.S. Military Drawdown on Local German Labor Markets, in: SFB649 Humboldt University Discussion Paper 2012-2024.
Stafford, F. (1986). Forestalling the Demise of Empirical Economics: The Role of Microdata in Labor Economics Research, in: Ashenfelter, O., Layard, R. (Eds.), Handbook of Labor Economics, Amsterdam: Elsevier, 1: 387–423.

Index

A

B

C

D

E

F

G

H

I

J

K

L

Q

R

S

T

U

V

W

Y

About the Author...

Daniel S. Hamermesh is Professor in Economics, Royal Holloway University of London, and Sue Killam Professor Emeritus in the Foundations of Economics at the University of Texas at Austin. His A.B. is from the University of Chicago (1965), his Ph.D. from Yale (1969). He taught from 1969–73 at Princeton, from 1973–93 at Michigan State, from 2009–12 at Maastricht University, and has held visiting professorships in the United States, Europe, Australia and Asia. He is a Fellow of the Econometric Society, a research associate of the National Bureau of Economic Research, and was President of the Society of Labor Economists in 2001.

He authored *Labor Demand, The Economics of Work and Pay, Economics Is Everywhere, Beauty Pays*, and a wide array of articles in labor economics in the leading general and specialized economics journals.

His research concentrates on time use, labor demand, discrimination, social insurance programs (particularly unemployment insurance), and unusual applications of labor economics (to suicide, sleep and beauty).

He joined IZA as a Research Fellow in July 1998. From December 2001 until July 2008, he was IZA Program Director for the institute's research program "The Future of Labor." He served as IZA Director of Research from August 2008 until January 2009.

Since 2016 he has been acting as Chief Coordinator of the IZA Network and Editor-in-Chief of IZA World of Labor.

Daniel S. Hamermesh received the 2013 IZA Prize in Labor Economics.

...and the Editors

Corrado Giulietti has been Associate Professor in Economics at the University of Southampton since February 2016. He received his PhD from the University of Southampton in January 2010. He joined IZA as a Research Associate in March 2010. At the institute he served as Deputy Program Director for the Migration Research Area (2010–2013), Deputy Director of Research (2011–2013), and Director of Research (2013 until February 2016). His research interests are labor economics, development economics, and applied econometrics, with a focus on the determinants of migration, the labor market and welfare effects of migration, the assimilation of immigrants, and the estimation of migration flows.

Klaus F. Zimmermann has been Full Professor of Economics at the University of Bonn since 1998 (currently on leave), and Visiting Professor at Princeton University since 2016. He serves as Co-Director of the Center for Population, Development and Labour Economics at UNU-MERIT, Maastricht (since 2016). From 1998 until February 2016 he was Director of the Institute for the Study of Labor (IZA). He also acted as President of the German Institute for Economic Research (DIW Berlin, 2000–2011). Zimmermann is Honorary Professor of Economics at the Free University of Berlin and the Renmin University of China, Editor-in-Chief of the Journal of Population Economics, Chair of the Economics Section and a Council member of the Academia Europaea, and is a member of the German Academy of Sciences Leopoldina.

The manufacturer's authorised representative in the EU for product safety is Oxford University Press España S.A. of El Parque Empresarial San Fernando de Henares, Avenida de Castilla, 2 - 28830 Madrid (www.oup.es/en or product.safety@oup.com). OUP España S.A. also acts as importer into Spain of products made by the manufacturer.

Printed and bound by CPI Group (UK) Ltd, Croydon, CR0 4YY

12/09/2026

02215930-0001